TOTAL
PROPAGANDA

From Mass Culture to Popular Culture

Alex S. Edelstein
University of Washington

LEA   LAWRENCE ERLBAUM ASSOCIATES, PUBLISHERS
1997   Mahwah, New Jersey   London

Abigail Fein, Foundation
1715 East Olive Way
Seattle, WA 98102

Copyright © 1997 by Lawrence Erlbaum Associates, Inc.

Lawrence Erlbaum Associates, Inc., Publishers
10 Industrial Avenue
Mahwah, New Jersey 07430

Cover design by Abigail Fein, Foundation

LIBRARY OF CONGRESS CATALOGING-IN-PUBLICATION DATA

Edelstein, Alex S.
  Total propaganda : from mass culture to popular culture / Alex S. Edelstein.
    p.   cm.
  Includes bibliographical references and index.
  ISBN 0–8058–0891–4 (cloth : alk. paper). — ISBN 0–8058–0892–2 (pbk. : alk. paper)
    1. Mass media and culture. 2. Popular culture. 3. Propaganda. I. Title.
  P94.6.E34   1997
  302.23—DC21   96–49160
                                                                                      CIP

Books published by Lawrence Erlbaum Associates are printed on acid-free paper,
and their bindings are chosen for strength and durability.

Printed in the United States of America
10   9   8   7   6   5   4   3   2   1

TOTAL PROPAGANDA
From Mass Culture to Popular Culture

CONTENTS

From Many With Love

This is the best and the worst part of any book. The best part is acknowledging so much help; the worst is knowing that it is practically over; now what to do?

First to thank my friend and literary critic, Jean Godden, who made suggestions writers hate to hear but profit from exceedingly; her influence is clearly present in her own writings and in mine, as well.

My first editor, Hollis Heimbouch, at that pleasant restaurant in Montreal and again, in New York, gave me the freedom to think and write. Amy Olener kept me going until Kathleen O'Malley arrived to lend the constant good cheer and pithy counsel that brought me through; thanks also to Teresa Horton for her fine production work. Then there were behind-the-scenes operators: Dr. Jeff Godden rescued me from bouts of computer madness, and Dr. Harry Hecht was my designated book-namer.

I worried about my adoption of the term *popular culture*, but a confident Dr. Katharine E. Heintz-Knowles assured me that there was an inclusiveness to the term as I used it. I asked trusted colleagues such as Barry Mitzman, the public affairs director of KCTS-9, if the terms *old* and *new propaganda* and *total propaganda* were useful parameters and fit within their conceptual boundaries. Yes, they agreed, but they urged me to assert more strongly the many threats to survival that were faced by a popular culture.

Many helped with chapters. Pop music critics Gene Stout of the *Seattle Times* and Bud McDonald of the *Seattle Post-Intelligencer* spoke eloquently about the Seattle alternative rock scene, and Jon Pareles, *New York Times* music critic, talked about the national picture. Allison Pember, publisher of *The*

Flavor rap magazine, and colleagues Sarah Honda and Rachel Crick, gave me insider perspectives. Brian Kabatznik of Ticketmaster put me back in touch with The Stones. Virtually a focus group of one, Leslie Boba offered insights into 30-somethings and their symbioses with their sitcoms.

Scarecrow Videos owner George Latsios, and his crew, Chris Schneider, store manager, and Tom Hyland, assistant manager, are genuine film buffs; I could not have made my selections without them. Kit Boss, formerly of the *Seattle Times*, strengthened a view about "sitlifes" that seemed at first to be a tough sell.

David Horsey, political cartoonist and author of the comic strip *The Boomer's Song*, spoke passionately for the baby boomer generation. Political reporter Joel Connelly reflected on the nirvanas of the journalist, and he invested weekends of talk on a level with that he was to enjoy with "Elvis, we know who." Richard Kielbowicz and Doug Underwood chatted with me about the new journalism; I was fortified by a longtime mutual mentor, political scientist Lance Bennett. Cathy Allen, director of The Campaign Connection, who by 1996 had elected 80 women to public office, cooked up a storm and squared me away on gender issues. Leonard Rifas encouraged me to discuss *humorprop*. Ric Dube talked and walked as we surfed the Web.

My older son, David, a creative advertising executive, was full of ideas, good counsel, and pertinent examples. My younger son, Douglas, a reader and a teacher, kept putting challenging material in my hands and offering equally imaginative ideas. Steve Goldsmith, a *Seattle Post-Intelligencer* writer and fellow San Franciscan, put his intellectual mark on the book at my Lummi Island retreat, planting a California redwood to commemorate our tall thinking. Tom Corddry of Microsoft showed me what an industrial "campus" looked like, and he spun off intriguing ideas about the technological revolution. Peter Rinearson, Pulitzer Prize winner, software entrepreneur, and one of Bill Gates' writers de plume, encouraged my thinking on a new journalism for the new media. Dr. Stuart Elway, an insightful pollster, shared his thinking and means of getting closer to real public opinion.

There were chatty walks around Green Lake with my daughter Susan on whom I "tried" the book, and similar discussions with Dr. Clay Vollan, East–West Center collaborator and creative administrator at City University; he did some of his best (and most distracting) talking in Teddy's bike-rider tavern as I tried to make a corner shot. I watched my daughter Jane, a prize-winning teacher of students and teachers in the Seattle Public Schools, explain math on television, and that was a valuable lesson. David Clees reviewed my media psychology, to say nothing of my personal psychology, and he thought both to be plausible. Never out of my thoughts was my grandson, Alex, who was taken away on May 22, 1993, in an accident that should not have been.

When I needed a keen librarian I called on Karen Hedelund in the Department of Political Science, now performing her magic in the Charles Odegaard Undergraduate Library. She knows everything and helps everyone, particularly wayward authors such as myself. And Susan Colowick, an MA in Librarianship, earned her degree checking my footnotes. Dr. John Bowes, my coauthor of *Information Societies*, posed issues about the superbyways.

My old friend megamillionaire Dr. Kenneth Flynn insisted I devote a chapter to *sportsprop*, so what to do but recognize it as *businessballprop*. For insider views on *sportsprop* I turned to a brother and sister act, Nancy and Rick Welts, of the Seattle Sonics and the NBA, and I prevailed upon KIRO top reporter Patti Payne to allow me to hassle President John Ellis of the Seattle Mariners at her awesome parties. When I wanted a global perspective on sports, Dr. Nancy Rivenburgh assured me that "Dream Team," the first U.S. professional basketball Olympic champion, was the most often used expression in global sports in the 1990s and a new global vehicle for propaganda.

A longtime colleague in the field of international communication and propaganda, Dr. Jim Richstad of the University of Oklahoma, the East–West Center, and the National University of Singapore, hopes his colleagues will be stimulated by this book to shift from an exclusive attention to the old propaganda of war and political hegemony to the more inclusive rhetoric of international trade, a combination of diplomacy, intelligence, and propaganda. As the book entered the final editing process, journalist and freelance writer Frank Chesley lent energies and ideas for the future.

The book evolved from a class I taught for Director Ed Bassett, which was intended to deal with international propaganda, but it occurred to me that it might prove to be more challenging to exploit the students' personal interests and experiences. That led to our concepts of the popular culture, of *total propaganda*, the *old propaganda*, and the *new*. As one of our respected reviewers observed, the old propaganda and the new do not represent formal theory, but it is possible to think with those concepts, and theory lies ahead. Indeed, I must thank the reviewers who gave up their commitments to the *old propaganda* to consider the *new*. Please join them, my students, and me in the excitement and challenge of that same commitment.

—*(aedel@u.washington.edu)*

Popular Culture and the New Propaganda

Katharine E. Heintz-Knowles
University of Washington

One of my favorite advertising campaigns of recent memory is that for Sprite, a soft drink vying for some of the market dominated by Coca-Cola and Pepsi. The radio version of the ad, which I heard on the local "alternative" music station in Seattle, features a young male's voice telling us that he knows that the advertising claims made by other manufacturers are untrue—drinking a certain beverage will not get him a date or a better grade in school, and he knows that we, the listeners, know that, too. Therefore, he is not going to try to "sell" us anything, but remind us to ignore advertising and "obey our thirst," which, of course, means quenching it with Sprite. This ad attempts to flatter listeners by recognizing that they are media savvy, that they see through advertising and will not believe any contrived claims. The ad is, of course, not above selling us something—as long as we do not define it as selling.

This particular ad and its related campaign is a perfect exemplar of the *new propaganda* examined in this book. It targets a younger, more media-savvy (if not necessarily media-literate) generation who are more likely to be participants in the messages than members of any previous generation. It is similar to the Van Halen music video "Right Now," which encourages viewers to turn off the TV and go outside, played on a television channel that requires viewers to be inside the tube to receive ad messages. Or the video game ads that celebrate the active nature of game-playing versus the more reactive activities of nonmediated life.

The students I teach like these types of messages as well. They are tired of hearing about media power and control—after all, it is *they* who control the video games and the TV remote control devices, right? They can create their media experiences through manipulating existing forms, and many participate in the creation of new forms through video production or computerized music composition.

One of the biggest difficulties I have in teaching students about the concept of power in media is that they expect power and politics to be explicit in media messages—much as they are in what the author calls the *old propaganda*. It is not difficult to identify the ideology in the *Why We Fight* films, for example, but what about *Geraldo's* discussion of polygamy or Nintendo's "Street Fighter?"

Critical and cultural theories are often prohibitive for undergraduate students, but the author's formulation offers an accessible way to discuss power and ideology in media texts. Without using the critical discourse, the author provides compelling arguments that power and ideology are created and maintained through the active participation of audience members. Without identifying them as such, the author illustrates concepts like hegemony at work.

It is widely recognized that the mass media provide us with ample information that we then use to construct some sense of the world around us. It is not as widely recognized that consumers of media messages are *active* in this constructive process, making meanings that are sensible to them in their particular life circumstances. The Aboriginal children of Australia identified more with the villain than the victor in a popular children's program because he better expressed the experience of this oppressed, excluded group.

One of the key concepts of the study of popular culture is that producers create texts with certain ideological meanings, but consumers actively interpret the text to create their own meanings. The amount of "work" involved in attaching a relevant meaning to the text depends on the fit between the ideology of the producer and the consumer.

The news reports of the coming of the Information Superhighway promise us access to the arts, literature, movies, news, and each other. Anyone with an Internet link can not only e-mail the President with ideas for policy, but can join any number of "virtual communities"—groups of people with a common interest but not a common geography. The Information Superhighway is just the latest extension in a decadelong trend of electronic media segmentation. Satellites and cables made possible the expansion of the television dial well beyond VHF capacities and brought with it opportunities for specialized channels that targeted children (Nickelodeon), sports fans (ESPN), or old movie buffs (American Movie Classics). The role of the mass media as the providers of the common experience, or the glue that holds society together is being challenged by this trend of specialization and segmentation.

With rare exceptions (Super Bowls, Olympics, Academy Awards broadcasts), the model of a single source providing information to a mass audience is no longer applicable, hence the need to redefine and reconceptualize propaganda. As our media landscape continues to diversify, the messages audience members consume will be more specialized and participatory. Consumers are able to download only those stories they want from their electronic newspapers, skip to the desired track on their programmable CD players, zap or zip through commercials on videocassettes, and engage in electronic chats about *Melrose Place*.

Is this diversification a crisis of some kind? For those who desire a powerful, centralized media system, yes. However, in a postmodern society, one in which generations are defined by their cultural artifacts more than by age, the answer is no. As the author argues, the crisis in control can be redefined as a shifting of power from the few to the many, and keeping it so. Popular culture theorists have for years recognized that consumers make their own meanings from texts presented in the mass media, regardless of the intent of the producer. So the audience has always had the power of resistance, in some sense. But with the new media, the audience participates not only in the decoding of messages, but in the encoding as well—in the creation of the texts. As the author notes, the new audiences produce the new propaganda for their own use.

The participatory aspect of new media is central to the author's language and definition of the *new propaganda*. Whereas the *oldprop* was characterized by the attempt of a few to impose a picture of reality on the many, *newprop* underlined a process of negotiation among many participants. As our media allow us to interact globally with others in a community of interest, we need a new way to think about reality construction. And as economic and political interests require global cooperation, we see political communication taking on the visage of cooperation more than conflict; we see international cooperation in trade as well as conflict resolution.

This cooperation, the author suggests, is evident in news media accounts of trade agreements and treaties, but also in entertainment media, where the United States provides a major portion of the entertainment media (*diet*) of some foreign countries, or where global "town meetings" allow U.S. and Soviet citizens the opportunity to "get to know each other." Through his examination of popular culture, the author shows how cooperation and participation can meaningfully illustrate political ideology—it does not reside solely in the realm of conflict.

Nowhere has the proliferation of consumer participation been so evident as in the explosion of talk media. Oprah Winfrey reigns as one of the richest entertainers in the world; an empire built on (self) disclosure and participation. It is in this realm that the real discussion of politics takes place; how do people negotiate their lives in this complex society? What principles guide their activities, and are they the same principles as mine? In this type of forum, there is no pretense of "objectivity": Neither the medium nor the respondent is unbiased. Oprah cries and Phil Donahue chastises, while camera operators search the audience for emotional close-ups. But is this propaganda? Not according to traditional definitions of the *old propaganda*. However, using the author's formulation, we can see how the openness of the exchange and its participatory elements work together to create the *new propaganda*.

The conceptualization of the old and the new propagandas helps move the study of propaganda out of the realm of world politics into the study of popular culture; in fact, the author views all of the participatory functioning of the society as aspects of membership in a more embracing popular culture.

This approach helps us to get through the thickets of political discourse. There are many examples, but one will suffice. Professor Edelstein takes on the furor over negative campaigning and attack advertising by simply invoking his new paradigm: If negativeness promotes a more stimulating discourse, if it adds relevant information, if it seeks to refute a stated position, if it contributes to a balanced picture, then it is as much the new propaganda as the old. We need not confuse substance with form. It was easy then for him to characterize the challengers in the Republican primaries in his lexicon as slightly oldprop (Tennessee governor Lamar Alexander); leaning newprop (Senator Robert Dole); awkwardly newprop (publisher Steve Forbes) and crudely oldprop (Patrick J. Buchanan).

The author's point of view recognizes that the mass media are extremely important forces in the consumer's construction of reality, and that they are no longer exclusive channels for disseminating the messages of the powerful elites. Instead, the media—particularly the new media—are accessible to and used frequently by the less powerful members of society (i.e., children, ethnic minorities, and marginal members of society) to create realities that more satisfactorily fulfill their needs.

As examples, KidStar radio, a soon-to-be network currently based in Seattle, empowers children through their interactive "phone zone." Young listeners call and suggest topics for features, leave messages for their U.S. Senators (who, incidentally, answer their voice mail in a feature played on the air), or listen to comments other kids have voiced about selected topics. Although the radio programming is ultimately created by adults, the children's input informs their decision making.

In the same way, members of each generation—20-somethings, Boomers, and Aarpies, to use the author's definitions—create and sustain media texts that define and redefine their experiences. The sheer size of the generations makes them important to politicians and advertisers, and so their ideology figures prominently in many media texts. And, although many in these generations did not grow up as active participants in their media experience, they have learned to use the media for the expression of their interests—they have become participants.

The key actors in the author's formulations are the generations; the contrasts and similarities in participation in mass and popular culture that they afford, mirrored in their use of the old and the new propagandas, offer opportunities to illustrate the workings of the political in popular culture, not just entertainment—in arenas ranging from film, music, radio, television, and humor, to public opinion, social issues, journalism, governing, and trade. The formulation is accessible to students at all ages, and it provides a discussion of propaganda that is far more comprehensive and relevant to our lives today than is any formulation of the old propaganda.

Framing Totalprop

THE OLD PROPAGANDA AND THE NEW

There comes a time in every paradigm when new perspectives are required to supplant the old. That time has come in the field of propaganda, which for more than a half century has been tied to war and conflict, but now is an integral part of the emerging popular culture.

Part I of this book frames propagandas in their cultural and meaning contexts and answers these questions:

* *What is total propaganda, and how does it come about?*

The answer: It represents the synergies of propagandas and the energies that these produce. In effect, the whole of total propaganda is greater than the sum of its parts.

* *How do we define and distinguish between the old propagandas and the new?*

The answer: If the propaganda enhances the functioning of the popular culture it is new propaganda; if it inhibits it, it is the old propaganda.

* *How do we think and speak of the propagandas?*

The answer: A language of propaganda abbreviates and fuses related concepts and transforms them into *uninyms*. The uninyms help us to "think and speak" propaganda.

* *Who produces and consumes these propagandas?*

The answer: Generations and social classes are more or less able and willing to create and utilize the old propaganda and the new.

* *What will be the means of communication of total propaganda, the old propaganda, and the new?*

The answer: Cybercommunication will be both the agent and the vessel of total propaganda; it will create new voices, new media, and new audiences for both the old propaganda and the new.

TOTALPROP

From Mass Culture to Popular Culture, The Old Propaganda and the New

To those of us who were weaned on *mass propaganda*, this book asks a great deal. Those who remember World War II know that because of ignorance and passivity we almost succumbed to the mass propagandas of hate and totalitarianism. Although we are in a new era, homegrown varieties of these *old propagandas* continue to be exploited by radical social and political movements, making more difficult the transition from a mass to a popular culture.

The most radical of these old propagandas is willing to shut down the federal government, put an end to federal protections of the rights and welfare of the individual, impose religious beliefs and teachings on public education, desert the environment, ban abortion, assert Aryan supremacy, and permit the autonomy of armed militias. Marked by incidents such as the shoot-out at Ruby Ridge, Idaho, the firestorm at Waco, Texas, the bombing of Oklahoma City, and the armed resistance of "Freemen" in Montana, these old propagandas of the deed flow from a self-indulgent sense of anger and alienation. Foremost among the beliefs of the militia groups is that Blacks and Jews should be excluded from the popular culture, an old propaganda of exclusion once practiced by totalitarian governments.[1]

There are an estimated 12,000 members of these militant groups. The danger has grown to the point where it has infected the armed forces, bringing an investigation as to its extent and meaning. Research by private organizations such as the Southern Poverty Law Center in Montgomery, Alabama, and the Simon Wiesenthal Center in Los Angeles forced 1996 Republican presidential hopeful Patrick J. Buchanan to drop two members of his campaign team because of their associations with militia groups.[2]

The Southern Poverty Law Center has urged the U.S. Attorney General to establish a task force to address domestic terrorism. Referring to "false patriots" and "false propaganda," its report identifies more than 800 groups, including 441 self-proclaimed militia units, that are linked by their paranoid hatred of the federal government and express it through a virulent old propaganda. Members of these groups are generally White, male, Christian and at odds with the popular culture. And in mid-June 1996, President Bill Clinton and the governors of states were required to address the spate of arsons that burned down many Black churches in the South.[3]

A great deal of the angry old propaganda fueled the midterm elections of 1994 and the Republican primaries of 1996. Beyond this, the popular culture must respond to the daunting structural changes that are being brought about as the affluent become rich, the moral become pervasive, the techies become remote, and political subsets become radical. Obviously, we need new tools to deal with these challenges. That is what concepts such as the popular culture, total propaganda, and the old and the new propagandas seek to provide.

A NEW PROPAGANDA PARADIGM

The propaganda paradigm presented in this book is directed at the problems of a dynamic society. For one, it distinguishes *popular culture* from *mass culture*, and it points to the emergence of new genres of propaganda; generically, there is the old propaganda and the new.

The modern origins of the old propaganda are linked to the control and manipulation of mass cultures in the early and mid-20th century, culminating in World War II and the Cold War. Charismatic leaders directed propaganda to mass publics and mass media amplified those messages. From this we gained the impression of an irresistible propaganda created by omnipotent leaders. In some respects, we have not put this experience behind us.

The new propaganda is a product of the more egalitarian, participant forces that emerged in the post-World War II period. Unlike members of mass cultures, who were almost wholly dependent on their leaders for propaganda, members of the popular culture have gained the ability to initiate messages as well as respond to them. No one knows this better than the students who will be reading this book. Through music, writing, and performance, they have been creating means to permit their participation in the popular culture. This is the key to our cultural nirvana, and our definitions of the old and the new propaganda express those values:

• If the rhetoric or actions limit the functioning of individuals in a popular culture, it is an old propaganda.

• If the rhetoric sustains or enhances participation in the popular culture, it is a new propaganda.

Restated in philosophical terms, a broadly participant popular culture with its bedrock of First Amendment rights, knowledge, egalitarianism, and access to communication is the bedrock of a democracy and the breeding grounds of the new propaganda, whereas a narrowly participant, uninformed, and hierarchical mass culture, in which only a few speak to many, recreates the context for the old propaganda. This is an ethical question that all members of a popular culture should consider and address.

As readers will observe, neither propaganda entirely excludes the other, and conditions under which either or both are more effective vary. The two propagandas are vying for hegemony in the debates about abortion, the environment, gender, global trade, race, sexual liberation, and—as a growing force—in the debates about social class and economic well-being. Unlike our experiences with propaganda in a mass culture, the producers and consumers of propaganda in a popular culture perceive their propagandas to be moral rather than immoral, they are indigenous rather than alien in their genesis and diffusion, and they defend them as truthful rather than exaggerated or falsified. This is completely at odds with definitions of the old propaganda, which asserted that all propaganda was alien, immoral, and lying. Those who have been schooled in the old propaganda may find it difficult to call something that is considered to be moral and truthful propaganda, but that is what this book asks of the reader in many places.

We incorporate in these formulations the *propaganda of the deed*. When Congress loosens regulations that will lead to the despoiling of the environment, and the actions are met by a disapproving public opinion, the actions as well as the words are propagandas: old propagandas if they diminish a vital resource and any sense of reason to which the individual can relate, and new propagandas if they enhance that resource and create a sense of its use.

Acknowledging a lack of participation in the popular culture, or an alienation from it, old propagandas in many situations may be more effective than the new. Given also the diversities and ideologies that continue to confront us, we face continuing challenges in substituting the new propaganda for the old. Our premise, however, and its *nirvana*, express the hope that a more participant popular culture will accommodate emerging diversities, and that as a part of the process much of the old propaganda will give way to the new.

THE TESTING GROUNDS

In the political discussions in the spring of 1995 that followed demands for the reassessment of affirmative action, both old and new propagandas poured forth; indeed, a University of Washington legal scholar defined affirmative action much as popular culture is defined in this book—an affirmative process that has as its goal equal access to higher forms of participation:

> The principle of "diversity" has its origin in the landmark case of the University of California Regents vs. Bakke (1978). The Supreme Court ruled that . . . taking race into account to create a diverse student body as a means of promoting the general educational experience is justifiable.[4]

At the time of the writing of this book, the nation was deeply involved in its national elections. The widespread concern during the Republican primary campaigns about "attack advertising" and negative campaigning brought the author to ask if our new paradigm provided us with keener insights into what was occurring than the old paradigms could afford. Were we confusing competition with conflict? And is conflict that addresses issues necessarily demeaning or dehumanizing and hence reflective of the old propaganda rather than the new?

It all depends. The old paradigm suggests that attack or negative advertising and campaigning are by definition bad and positive campaigning is good, but our new paradigm asks if the attack advertising or the negative campaigning helps us to think about a problem or if it constrains us from engaging in that process. If conflict enhances our abilities to function knowledgeably and politically, it takes on the character of new propaganda, but if it constrains the individual or demonizes the opposition, it is old propaganda.

Another distinction was articulated in a theatrical performance that addressed the perverse genius of the late political "spin doctor," Lee Atwater, the Republican national chairman who set a modern campaign standard for negativism. Just before he died, Atwater regretted his transmogrification of rapist and murderer Willie Horton into a euphemism for Democratic candidate Michael S. Dukakis in the 1988 presidential campaign. More than being simply negative—which the old paradigm would have condemned—Atwater had used the old propaganda to demonize an individual and cast him beyond the pale of the popular culture.[5]

Our paradigm also will lead us to evaluate as old and new propaganda the tendencies by press, polls, and publics to adopt catch phrases and treat the rhetoric as reality. From the point of view of this book, terms such as *gridlock* and *credibility* substituted the hegemony of insider power for outsider diversity; that is, each articulated a leader-centered old propaganda rather than a participant-focused new propaganda. What was more, gridlock was a misplaced metaphor: In gridlock, nothing moves, whereas diversity often is proactive whether it solves a problem or not.

Perhaps the most important application of our new paradigm occurred in the 1996 elections and may reoccur in those that follow it—in 1998, 2000, and beyond. If one believes in the efficacy of the new propaganda, one would reason that despite the inevitability of the old propaganda, whichever candidate and party better articulates the new propaganda would gain an edge.

Early in the 1996 campaign, the polls suggested that Republican candidate Bob Dole was victimized by propaganda tactics of his party's Contract with America, particularly as they affected women, the elderly, and the poor. However, Dole distanced himself from these actions. For his part, President Clinton portrayed himself as a surrogate for the popular culture who sought to protect it from those who asserted exclusivity and political hegemony. Even this book is propaganda—new propaganda, in our terms. But it doesn't pursue a political bias. It tries to hew strictly to the definition of new propaganda and not indulge in the old.

TEACHING "OUT OF"

The swirl of events in a popular culture makes it necessary that this book be taught "out of" rather than "with." By the time the book is in your hands, many of its examples will have been superceded by events. Thus it becomes a book that is impossible to complete but continues to be relevant. It is important to say, as well, that although this relevance is not couched in formal theory, it lends itself to that effort. Both empirical and critical theorists will find it possible to formalize the major concepts and test them.

The author acknowledges a regional flavor that pervades some chapters, notably that on the alternative rock culture, but this was inevitable: At the time this book was begun, the Pacific Northwest was the apex of the new rock culture, Asian trade (notably in U.S. relations with China and Japan), computer software, biotechnology, the wireless telephone, citizen activism (notably environmental movements), street-corner espresso coffee, the production of fashion (the Northwest look and the less stylish "grunge"), and "businessball"— the last-ditch efforts that took place to save professional baseball and football franchises. As for regional politics, writer Walt Crowley, a rebellious member of the 1960s Seattle Seven, tells how the Pacific Northwest became the center of a protest movement that led to the opening of the society to many who had been excluded from it—the apotheosis of a popular culture.[6] And although it is difficult to decide if Seattle has just become notorious or is actually worthwhile, the May 20, 1996, issue of *Newsweek* heralded Seattle with the headline "Swimming to Seattle: Everybody else is moving there. Should You?" Pictured on the cover was the new Microsoft "cybereditor" Michael Kinsley, former resident liberal on CNN's *Crossfire.* Not to be outdone, *Rolling Stone* magazine described Seattle as the dope as well as the grunge capital of the country. That was a lot of notice in a single week.[7]

REDEFINING MASS AND POPULAR CULTURE

The author recognizes that from World War II, the term *mass culture* was used to describe the introduction of culture to the masses. Mass culture incorporated media, advertising, comics, and selected aspects of politics and public opinion. The effect was to emphasize the access of the masses to an essentially pop culture. But this book takes the view that the limited conception of a passive membership in a mass culture has yielded to more active participation in a popular culture. The question asked a half century ago about the mass culture can be posed more meaningfully to members of our popular culture:

> Can such a society, under the most favorable material conditions ever experienced, rise to the occasion and prove itself worthy? Can it provide for the continuous free play of opposing systems of values and tastes, within the framework of democratic forms? Can it make room for an expansion of those spiritual, creative impulses in man which meaner conditions of life do not allow to come to the surface?[8]

Without question, the popular culture has become the vessel of our participatory democracy—in politics, race, religion, the environment, trade, and almost every other concern—and the new propaganda as well as the old has played a dramatic role in the emergence of each of these concerns. The annual Iowa Republican straw poll, the political clout of the radical Christian Coalition, the lobbying of the National Rifle Association, the bickering in professional sports between owners and players and movement of franchises out of loyal communities, the memory of "sucking sounds" of U.S. jobs going south to Mexico (remember NAFTA?), and political and trade conflicts with China and Japan all have become democratized in the popular culture.

The corporate sector has recently acknowledged its errors in framing its "downsizing" as a business politics of exclusion, and hence an old propaganda, and has adopted a new tone of inclusion and the new propaganda. Where press releases once spoke of "reductions," "closings," "exiting," and "significantly reconfiguring," they now are talking the new talk. Cutting too many people leads to "corporate anorexia," people are needed "to grow the revenue line," and "too few employees is not going to help anyone."[9]

As the author of *The Unreality Industry* put it, the phenomenon of unreality as represented by the new presence of all of these events cannot be understood by examining any single facet or level of society. They are so multifaceted and intertwined that they defy examination through any single lens. Like watersheds, the onset of one unreality after another is an inevitable byproduct of diversity in a popular culture, and this synergy and the resultant energy give rise to the consciousness of a total propaganda.

All media have taken new forms in the popular culture: Television news often crosses the line from an information to an entertainment medium in which it employs glitz, high-tech studio sets, newly created celebrities, and artificial pleasantries. The "evening news" is a subtle transmogrification of the "evening meal" into a family melodrama in which the anchorpersons play the roles of father and mother and the erudite young weatherperson and sports anchor are their children reciting their accomplishments. This interspersing of the bizarre and the meaningful has made the task of differentiating information and entertainment as difficult as drawing distinctions between information and propaganda, a task that the old and the new propaganda will make more possible to address.[10]

Talk radio presents its own fictions. Described as "hot air" and "hot radio," it has leaped light years from a medium that transmitted light news and shades of contemporary music to angry talk that is the apotheosis of the old propaganda. Even the information highway, with its transporters, sites, and interactive capabilities, has supplanted its wealth of knowledge with a marginal playground of entertainment and involvement.

Certainly, there will be resistance to the freer use of the term *propaganda*. Journalists, particularly, will be reluctant to think of themselves as propagandists, whether the old or the new. Yet columnist Jeff Cohen noted on his Web site on the Internet (August 29, 1996) that all shades of journalism carry propagandistic overtones, not just the journalistic ideological left and right. Centrism just as fervently expresses its own core of values, beliefs, and opinions, challenging the journalistic credo of objectivity.

A CONSCIOUSNESS OF TOTAL PROPAGANDA

Members of the popular culture are aware that they are experiencing an increasing consciousness of *total propaganda*, each of them aroused and involved in the old and the new. This presence can be identified and defined

- As an empirical proposition, total propaganda represents the totality of the old and the new propagandas plus the energies they generate by their synergies and interaction.
- At the subjective level, much like indicators of "environmental warming" of our physical habitat, total propaganda measures the "propaganda warming" of our popular culture.

As one of many recent examples, the old propaganda of the Christian Coalition movement has been introduced into the fiction potboiler. Frightened victims turn to prayer and the teachings of conservative theology to solve life-threatening problems and provide prospects of redemption and happiness. This contributes to a totality of religious propaganda as it supplements training classes, the religious shopping mall, T-shirts that carry evangelical slogans, and children's videos with cartoon Bible stories. Sports palaces have become malls, as well, sublimating the action on the field by the overriding purpose of selling amenities.[11]

It was difficult to exclude treatments of many of the most obvious propagandas. Perhaps the most notable omission is public relations, except as it is discussed in relation to lobbying. Add to that political campaign management, most recently described autobiographically by controversial Republican operative Ed Rollins and James Carville, the equally ebullient Clinton operative, both of whom became almost as famous as the politicians they helped to elect. Dick Morris, President Clinton's notorious spin merchant, made a meteoric ascent to power and plunge to disgrace.

Developments such as these have taken on the character of "watersheds" in our cultural communicating. The challenge—and the danger—is that where watersheds once occurred once or twice in a century, total propaganda has contributed to their emergence in almost every recent generation: The 1990s are not entirely gone but we already have seen the emergence of the cybergeneration and new classes of elites emerging as "overclasses" who communicate via cybermedia. Bill Gates, president of Microsoft, the world's dominant producer of software for home computers, tells us that in the decade of the 1990s we watched events that were so historic that they will affect the world to the same extent as the scientific method, the invention of printing, and the industrial age.[12]

THE ROLE OF GENERATIONS

Opening a symposium organized by the author of this book on information societies, a University of Washington sociologist observed generational distinctions in access to technologies:

> I am optimistic about high communication technology and its impact on our society. I have reached that stage of life where I stand between two generations on either side. I have a son and a grandson, and I have a father and a grandfather. That is five generations with respect to telecommunications.
>
> My grandson, who was born in 1970, hasn't lived in a world without satellites or computer facilities in communication. My son cannot remember a world without television, but I can. My father remembers a world without radio. He was born in 1885 and can't remember a world without motion pictures or the telegraph, both of which came about that time.
>
> My grandfather, his father, was born in 1845; he remembered before all of those things, but he couldn't remember a time without photography and the mass daily press. Each of those generations had a very special input from mass media. It was enriching for each. Sociology makes me look at it in that way.
>
> /s/ Otto N. Larsen, University of Washington.[13]

PROSPECTS AND DIRECTIONS

Over the next 27 chapters, this book assesses trends and locations of the old propaganda and the new. Are we moving in the direction of the new propaganda or are we regressing in the direction of the old? What loci of our popular culture are more controlled by the old propaganda and which have most seen the advent of the new? How do we stand at the crossroads of the old and the new propaganda about the environment, gender, gun control, homosexuality, international trade and peacekeeping, race, and changing structures that are creating gaps between the rich and the poor, the religious moralists and the secular, the technologically gifted and the unskilled? And which of the generations—the 20- and 30-somethings, the Boomers, or the elderly—or the overclasses and the underclasses—will exploit more effectively the new propaganda and the old? Will we reach our nirvana of the new propaganda, or are we condemned in the next century to the old?

฿ ฿ ฿

The reader is asked to consider two genres of propaganda that have emerged in the popular culture, the old and the new.

The old propaganda grew out of mass and totalitarian cultures; by contrast, the new propaganda expresses the imperatives of participation in a popular culture. The old propaganda has persisted in the popular culture, however, expressing the ideologies of substantial segments of a diverse population and providing a forum for the anger and alienation of a militant minority.

Bottom-up political tactics in the political culture were established as a popular culture genre in 1996. Based on conservative estimates, government would have to act on at least half of the more than 90 citizen initiatives that were being waged in 20 states, more than double the number of a decade earlier. Many of these, such as the banning of affirmative action, legalization of marijuana for medical purposes, and school financing drew participation in states through the nation, creating a surrogate for a national initiative. Although many of the proposals represented old values, the processes were quintessentially new.

Our purpose in this book is to examine the myriad of events and actors who are using the old and the new propaganda—in many cases producing synergies that have produced a consciousness of total propagandas—to advance their material, social, psychological, and political goals. Ultimately, the author of this book asks if a popular culture, with its commitment to diversity, nevertheless can generate a transition from a predominantly old propaganda to the new.

NOTES

1. Creed of hate called Christian identity is the heart of the Freemen's beliefs. (1996, April 12). Niebuhr, G., *New York Times*, Sec. A, p. 8.
2. Private groups lead challenge in war on Far Right. (1996, April 14). Janofsky, M., *New York Times*, Sec. E, p. 3.

3. Keeping a closer watch on paramilitary groups is urged. (1996, April 11). Janofsky, M., *New York Times*, Sec. A., p. 9.

4. On a path toward cultural diversity. (1995, March 12). *Seattle Times*, Sec. B, p. 5.

5. A spirit from Presidential campaigns past returns with a timely lesson. (1995, November 1). Clines, F. X., *New York Times*, p. 1.

6. Crowley, W. (1995). *Rites of Passage: A Memoir of the Sixties in Seattle*. Seattle: University of Washington Press. 351 pp.

7. Seattle Reigns. (1996, May 20). *Newsweek*, Adler, J., pp. 48–58. See also: Annals of communications: The reeducation of Michael Kinsley. Auletta, K. (1996, May 13). *The New Yorker*, pp. 58–73. See also, Heroin. (1996, May 30). *Rolling Stone*, pp. 35–39.

8. Tumin, M. (1956). Popular Culture and the Open Society, In (Eds.) B. Rosenberg & D. M. White, *Mass Culture: The Popular Arts in America*, pp. 550. Toronto: The Macmillan Co.

9. Layoffs are out; hiring is back; Consultants are all abuzz; growth is route to success. (1996, June 18). Uchitelle, L., *New York Times*, Sec. C, p. 1.

10. Mitroff, I. I., & Bennis, W. (1989). *The Unreality Industry*. Oxford, UK: Oxford University Press.

11. The newest Christian fiction injects a thrill into theology. (1995, October 30). Niebuhr, G., *New York Times*, Sec. A., p. 1.

12. Gates says info superhighway could displace many workers. (1995, November 20). Associated Press, in *Seattle Post-Intelligencer*, Sec. A, p. 4. See also, Gates, B. (1995). (With Myhrvold, N., & Rinearson, P.) *The Road Ahead*. New York: Viking.

13. Edelstein, A. S., Bowes, J. E., & Harsel, H. (1978). (Eds.). *Information Societies: Comparing the Japanese and American Experiences*. Seattle, WA. University of Washington Press, p. 93.

2

DEFINITIONPROP
Distinguishing the Old Propaganda
From the New

Propaganda never has been easy to define. There are, indeed, as many definitions of propaganda as there are definers, and they express every interest, activity, and area of knowledge.

It is no different in this case; traditional definitions that were conceived in
mass cultures and in academic cloisters are less applicable to popular cultures
and in diverse settings. To achieve functional definitions of the old and the
new propagandas we must review the nature of all propagandas and their
functioning in a popular culture.

THE NEW AND THE OLD PROPAGANDIST

The Ross Perot political movement in 1992 offers that opportunity. Many
who joined the Perot movement did so in considered ways. They gave up
their long-held attachments to political parties to seek more open and direct
communication, a sense of community, and a propaganda of self-actualization
that promised fuller participation in the political process. This proactivity
and sense of inclusion is the essence of the new propaganda.

Members of the movement had a voice and could communicate with
Perot. That was portrayed on the *Larry King Live* television show when Perot
said he would not run unless his followers placed him in nomination, thus
empowering each member of the movement. But the new propaganda was
transformed into the old propaganda when Perot took on the role of one per-

son speaking to many. Add to this the quirky rhetoric that became his trademark and gave him more of a unique than an accessible quality as a communicator. Although Perot insisted he was the follower, and the members of his movement were the leaders, the agenda was largely his. Thus the movement became characterized as much by the old propaganda as by the new.

THE PROCESS OF DEFINITION

It is common to provide defining attributes of a concept, and Table 2.1 assigns some defining attributes to the old and the new propagandas. But providing these attributes represents only the first step toward the process of definition. Our definition fuses process with the attributional approach.

1. *The Process Approach:* If the communication enhances the abilities of individuals and groups to participate in the popular culture, it is a new propaganda, but if it limits such functioning, it is the old propaganda. This clearly is a value orientation, and we justify it on the basis of democratic traditions and theory.

2. *The Attributional Approach:* We have listed a number of representative attributes of the old and the new propaganda, but these are not exclusive or exhaustive. In fact, the author assumes that other attributes for both the old and the new propaganda will emerge as we discuss a variety of situations and foci of social and political action. Of those that we have listed in Table 2.1, we discuss at this point only a few:

Technology

One of the most clearly defining attributes of propaganda is the technology that conveys it—its scope, its speed, its intimacy, and the diversity of its users. Computers have offered opportunities for citizens to contact the President through electronic mail (e-mail and other means). The President, himself dependent on legal-sized yellow pads of writing paper, surrounded himself with a new generation of aides who were steeped in technologies.

The President's messages—a new propaganda because of the accessibility and intimacy of the technologies that convey them—are penetrating households and offices in nontraditional ways. Indeed, the author has contacted the President via these networks. But many of the messages that are being trafficked on the superhighways are imposing themselves on unwilling participants and threatening their values; these factors of exclusion and domination introduce elements of the old propaganda.[1]

Let us consider a sample of attributes of the old and the new propaganda, putting off for a moment their context and functioning.

TABLE 2.1
Comparing Newprop With Oldprop

	Newprop Is Essentially	*Oldprop Is Essentially*
Actor Values	Democratic	Totalitarian
	Knowledge	Claims
	Many to many	Few to many
	Membership	Marginalization
	Outsider initiatives	Insider decisions
	Participant concerns	Control concerns
	Personal enhancement	Demonization
	Self-actualization	Minimization
Media Values	Broad access	Limited access
	Diversity	Homogeneity
	Facilitated by high-tech	Manipulated by high-tech
	Global output	Constrained output
	High density of output	Attenuated output
	High speed of output	Variable speed in output
	Freedom	Control and censorship
Contextual Values	Communication rules	Controller rules
	Contemporary	Historical
	Convergent	Divergent
	Diversity of audiences	Homogeneity of audiences
	Enhances choices	Limits choices
	Innovation	Redundancy
	Interactive	One way
	Global cooperation	International conflict
	Nonideological	Ideological
	Inclusive	Exclusive
	Intimacy	Anonymity
	Openness	Closedness
	Proactive	Reactive
	Accessibility to knowledge	Exclusivity of knowledge
	Complexity of messages	Simplicity of messages
	New language forms	Protection of forms
Attitudinal Values	Consumption values	Production values
	Defined by consensus	Defined by leaders
	Defined by generations	Manipulates generations
	Ethical concerns	Moral concerns
	Equity concerns	Protective concerns
	Governed by situations	Governed by rules
	Cognitive attitudinally	Affective attitudinally

◆ *Self-actualization and personal enhancement.* The new propaganda works to create new opportunities for self-actualization and personal enhancement. By contrast, the old propaganda limits those processes.

◆ *Marginalizing.* If the propaganda marginalizes the individual, as with Generation X, it is the old propaganda; if the individual is free to enter and participate in a normative environment, it is the new propaganda.

◆ *Limiting alternatives and choices.* The old propaganda limited alternatives and choices either by outlawing their consideration or by rejecting them on specious grounds; the new propaganda embraces alternatives and encourages choices.

◆ *Homogeneity and multiversity.* The old propaganda imprinted itself on a homogenized mass culture, whereas the new propaganda embraces multiversity in a popular culture.

◆ *Singularity and multiplicity of sources.* In mass cultures, a few powerful people spoke to many, and the direction was downward rather than upward or even across. In the popular culture, many speak to many and the directions are upward as well as downward and across.

◆ *Access and control.* Where the old propaganda often was combined with censorship, the new propaganda permits broad access to information. Ordinary citizens may petition for information about matters of interest to them. Government's demand that it be given a "key" to compucommunication was rejected by the electronics industry.

◆ *Production and consumption.* Those who create the new propaganda are also its greatest consumers. The late French philosopher Jacques Ellul wrote that every generation needs propaganda and that—contrary to popular conception—the most involved, most informed, and most knowledgeable now most require it.[2] Ellul observed that modern elites use propaganda to defend their own values, and having produced this propaganda, they are the first to consume it. This is a radical departure from the teachings of the old propaganda that said that only the least involved, the least informed, and the least knowledgeable are the readiest consumers of propaganda.

◆ *Social distance and intimacy.* The element of intimacy infuses the new propaganda more than the old. A variety of new news programs reveal our most intimate selves to others. George Orwell told us that Big Brother was *watching,* but in the new news everyone is *participating.*

◆ *Proactive and reactive.* The new propaganda exploits opportunities in the popular culture for the individual to initiate as well as to respond. In mass culture, activity is more normative than creative.

◆ *Audience diversity.* Audience diversity is integral to the popular culture and the production and consumption of the new propaganda. The new online information services permit access by children, the middle-aged, the elderly, women and men, and even the poor.

♦ *The new propaganda is the message.* To borrow from the philosopher-theorist Marshall McLuhan, the new propaganda is the massage. It satisfies the needs of those who create it.[7]

♦ *A profusion of media forms.* Although the old propaganda diffused art, film, and music to the masses, all expressions of culture were controlled. Now art, theater, ballet, and music are diffused by television, video, video discs, and other media forms from which audiences can make selections.

♦ *Bases for social analysis.* Scientific studies of the old propaganda grew largely out of the study of diary entries made by Dr. Joseph Goebbels, the minister of propaganda and culture (so-called "people's enlightenment") in Adolph Hitler's Third Reich. First offered as operating principles of effective propaganda in a totalitarian society, these evolved into empirical studies of the processes and effects of communication. Today, studies of popular culture look at propaganda "critically" and theoretically as well as empirically.

♦ *Accommodation versus conflict.* The new propaganda seeks to achieve accommodation and minimize conflict; means of accommodation range from informing and discussion to compromise and conciliation. This does not rule out culturally defined areas of competition and conflict such as politics, but how their purposes are defined.

♦ *Inclusion versus exclusion.* The new propaganda is inclusive of diverse members of a popular culture; "we *and* they" contrasts with the "we *versus* they" that characterizes the old propaganda.

♦ *Functional knowledge.* Knowledge is useful only if it may be validated by facts or human experience. It is dysfunctional if it is shrouded in an exclusive ideology or an idiosyncratic point of view.

Although Table 2.1 appears to dichotomize the old and the new propaganda, it is necessary to examine combinants, as well. Both the old propaganda and the new propaganda must be judged ultimately by the extent to which they contribute to the functioning of a popular culture.

Definitions of the Old Propaganda

The old propaganda was grounded in the needs of totalitarian societies to create and exploit mass cultures. Propaganda flowed from a leader to the led, from a few to many, not from many to a few.

This formulation of the old propaganda gave rise to many of the principles of effective propaganda that are prevalent today in advertising, public relations, politics, and various means of public communication and persuasion.

Historically, each of our academic disciplines defined the old propaganda as a precedent to studying it systematically. A cornucopia of definitions emerged, each reflecting the unique interests of the definers. Political scientists defined propaganda as an instrument of power, sociologists pointed to group processes, psychologists looked at learning and motivation, and communication scholars explored the prevalence of propaganda in the mass media and society.

AVERSION TO PROPAGANDA

There always has been a cultural aversion to the use of the word *propaganda*. No U.S. international propaganda agency ever used the word *propaganda*; it was always *information* or *communication*. Our World War I propaganda was conducted under the umbrella of the Committee on Public Information. In World War II, it was the Office of War Information; today it is the U.S. Information Agency (USIA) at home and the United States Information Service (USIS) abroad. The Jimmy Carter administration changed the name of the USIA to the International Communication Agency (ICA), but the name was too suggestive of the Central Intelligence Agency (CIA), so USIA was restored.

TRUTH THROUGH SCIENCE

In the period before World War II, the United States was startled to discover the extent to which the totalitarian nations had advanced the study of propaganda. As a consequence, several institutes were established at American universities to undertake studies of propaganda and counterpropaganda.

An Institute for Propaganda Analysis translated propaganda to the public. The institute was committed to teaching children as well as adults, so it constructed a detailed system for analyzing propaganda on the assumption that if one could analyze propaganda, one could cope with it.

Approximately 14 techniques for identifying the old propaganda were defined and symbols were created to illustrate them. These included such familiar techniques as *cardstacking*, where the propagandist "stacked the cards" in one direction or another, and the symbol was the face of a playing card. Several other major techniques and their symbols included:

- *The testimonial.* Someone of high prestige endorsed the point of view or the policy. The symbol was the Good Housekeeping Seal of Approval.
- *The glittering generality.* An unsupported generalization that was somehow appealing. The symbol was the Rising Sun.
- *The hot potato.* The use of emotional appeals to confuse the opposition. The symbol was a steaming potato.

This work was interrupted by World War II, when more empirical and reliable approaches were taken to propaganda analysis.[4]

NO "TRUTH" IN DEFINITIONS

After World War II, little agreement came about as to which definitions of propaganda were the most relevant and useful. Rather, attributes of propaganda ruled, as seen in Table 2.2. These assumed the existence of a mass culture rather than a popular culture.

• *Truth and lies.* Early definers said propaganda conveyed lies, whereas nonpropaganda reflected truth. However, much early propaganda was framed as truthful to permit greater lies to be served, and that is true in politics and society today.

• *Bad vs. good.* Similarly, early propaganda definitions said propaganda was bad, whereas nonpropaganda was good. However, in every culture, propaganda campaigns are carried out to raise money for such praiseworthy causes as health, education, and welfare.

• *Appeal to the masses.* Totalitarian propaganda was simplistic and was designed to appeal to members of a mass culture; (i.e., undifferentiated members of the society who lacked communication skills and access to others); now we appeal to demographic and value-oriented publics. Yet talk radio has emulated mass appeals and has found resonance among those who would find comfort in a mass culture.

TABLE 2.2
Sampling of Attributes of the Old Propaganda

It Is Propaganda If It Is	It Is Not Propaganda If It Is
Controlled	Accessible
Controversial	Consensual
Emotional	Rational
Bad	Good
Intentional	Unintentional
Involves masses	Involves publics
Maintains power	Diffuses power
Nonscientific	Scientific
Not truthful	Truthful
Opinionated	Informational
One-sided	Two-sided (or more)
One way	Interactional
Systematic	Random

Note. These attributes were abstracted from definitions of propaganda that are common referents in social science.

◆ *Purposeful or not.* The perceived purposefulness of a message was seen as determining its character as propaganda, but purposiveness occurs in many communication situations, especially when there are competing perspectives.

◆ *One-sided and two-sided.* One-sidedness was considered to be propagandistic; a two-sided message was not. Skilled propagandists know, however, that two-sided messages often are persuasive as propaganda and appeal to members of a popular culture.

◆ *Appeals to emotions.* Mass propaganda emphasized emotional appeals rather than rational assertions; in a popular culture more knowledge-based propaganda is projected.

◆ *Concealing the source.* If sources were concealed, information traditionally was perceived as propaganda, but if the sources were open it was not. The U.S. Foreign Agents Registration Act, which was adopted in the mid-1930s in fear of Nazi propaganda, required operatives from other nations to register so their identities would be known. They nevertheless produced propaganda that was believed.

◆ *Scientific versus nonscientific.* It was said that propaganda could be studied scientifically only in an open society. Hence, the United States committed itself culturally to empirical studies. Yet propaganda was also being studied scientifically in totalitarian nations.

Terminological concerns. Were advertising, publicity, and public relations propaganda? Each was purposive and one-sided, and hence propaganda. But their defenders pointed to them as commercial rather than political and said that because of this they were not propaganda. In his most recent political dictionary, William Safire concluded that *propaganda* is an "attack word" and continues to be viewed as a pejorative:

> Your side disseminates information, deals with the issues, communicates the facts, publicizes the truth, gets the message to the people; the other side engages in pseudo events, puffery, deliberate distortion, the big lie, smoke screens, media hype, and propaganda.[5]

LOOKING TO THE FUTURE

As one observes the emergence of the old and the new propaganda, one becomes reminded that although the old propaganda lacks much of the power and acceptance that it enjoyed in a mass culture, many individuals remain uncritical audiences for it today. The essential question is whether our culture has become more or less able to cope with the old propaganda or the new.

In the filmed documentary, *Manufacturing Consent,* and in the book that heralded it, linguist Noam Chomsky spoke about the seeming anomaly of thought control in a democratic society. Chomsky likened the prevalence of total propaganda in a democracy to violence in a dictatorship. But Chomsky adopted a top-down model of the old propaganda, the antithesis of the functioning of a popular culture.[6]

೮   ೮   ೮

At a conference at the University of Washington School of Communications hosted by the author, Japanese participants expressed fears about the overproduction of information. As the ratio of output to consumption increased and decreased, they asked what the effects might be.

Dr. Gerald Kline, then Dean of the School of Journalism and Mass Communications, University of Minnesota, said there could not be too much information, just too few choices. Dr. Kline said we should not fear more information, but we must be increasingly aware of it.[7]

On that note, good reading and good thinking!

NOTES

1. "Hey Prez!": Computers offer new line to Clinton. (1993, April 5). Berke, R. L., *New York Times*, Sec. A, p. 1.
2. Ellul, J. (1965). *Propaganda: The Formation of Men's Attitudes.* New York: Knopf.
3. McLuhan, M., & Fiore, Q. (1989). *The Medium is the Message.* New York: Simon & Schuster.
4. Lee, A. M., & Briant, E. (1939). *The Fine Art of Propaganda.* New York: Harcourt Brace. Also, Lee, A. M. (1965). *How to Understand Propaganda.* New York: Rinehart.
5. Safire, W. (1993). *Safire's New Political Dictionary.* New York: Random House, pp. 618–619.
6. Chomsky, N. (with E. S. Herman). (1988). *Manufacturing Consent: The Political Economy of the Mass Media.* New York: Pantheon Books.
7. Discussion with Ito, Y. In (Eds.) A. Edelstein et al., *Information Societies, Comparing the Japanese and American Experiences.* Seattle: University of Washington Press. pp. 253–258.

3

LANGUAGEPROP
Inventing the Uninym

If we were to address only the old propaganda, an old language might suffice. However, if we take into account a new propaganda, a new language is essential. That is why I created a new word—the *uninym*—to charactererize the phenomena with which we deal.

In his breathtaking novel *1984*, George Orwell fused the words *new* and *speak* into *NewSpeak* to articulate the cognitive and verbal functioning of his new society in a new millennium. Fortunately for us, Orwell's millennium did not arrive, but he forecast that many forms of group life would be affected by the improvisation of new language. Once OldSpeak had been forgotten, and NewSpeak had been introduced, any heretical thought should be unthinkable to the extent that thought was dependent on words: "Our new vocabulary is constructed so as to give exact and often subtle expression to every meaning that propaganda may express—while excluding other meanings."[1]

Orwell was writing fiction, of course, and he qualified his bet on language being the core of all thinking; that is, he did not say that all thought must be dependent on words, but that some thought was dependent on words. However, in politics and social issues, there are constant efforts to bring about correct thinking by producing "correct" language.[2]

INVENTING THE UNINYM

The author sees himself as inventing a new word that describes what already has been practiced. That word is the uninym:

Uninym: A product of the fusing of two or more words (related meanings) into a single, contextualized word or meaning that rests on a synergy between the two words that have been fused.

This excludes, of course, the fusing of words at random. Although the fusing of many words occurs—cognitions and constructions have been prevalent for a long time—*uninym* gives the process a distinctive name and may even cause some thinking about it.

Uninyms are everywhere. Book titles such as *DoubleSpeak* and *MediaSpeak* are exemplars. As awkward, or even as belabored, as this wordsmithing may seem, it is consistent with the speeding up of all language in the age of Pentium microchips and television sound bites.[3] It has worked itself into the vernacular: Bill and Melinda Gates' baby is a *microtot,* children of the cyberrevolution are *cybertots,* and those of us who have not gotten aboard are *cyberduds.*

Need for the Uninym

Past efforts to cope with propaganda have been vague and oftentimes confusing because we have isolated terms that are synergistic; as an example, we insist on distinguishing between information and propaganda when the realities are that propaganda contains information, and information contains propaganda. Why, then, not utilize the uninym *infoprop* to describe the synergy that exists between the two concepts? Because the media inevitably contain propaganda and propaganda exploits the media, we may call this synergy *mediaprop,* and we need not debate whether advertising is propaganda. Call it *adprop!*

Television and radio talk programs may be described as TV and radio *talkprop.* The same goes for music, as in *rockprop* and *rapprop.* Again, the purpose is not to be cute but to reflect reality: Rock and rap music incorporate a great deal of propaganda, some old and some new. So do films, and that is *filmprop.*

The uninym has had a long play in the history of propaganda, most notably in communist theory. The Soviet Union maintained a Department of Agitation and Propaganda, which it described as *Agitprop.* The wordsmithing should not put the reader off but, rather, link concepts in ways that will encourage new thinking.

Someone's Listening: Enter Oldtalk and Newtalk

Someone must be listening to us out there. We recently encountered a discussion of *oldtalk and newtalk* with some startling similarities in the treatment of concepts: *Oldtalk* was "tough talk," as in our oldprop, including threats, warnings, and conflicts. One example of oldtalk was the shouting among jurors in the admired film *12 Angry Men.*

Contrast this with the *newtalk* of personal enhancement by Mia Farrow in the film *Miami Rhapsody,* or John Travolta in his delight about being able to buy a glass of beer in a movie theater in Amsterdam (in the film *Pulp Fiction*), or comic Paul Reiser distinguishing between *nuance* and *gesture* as good and bad words: "With gesture," he says, "you know where you stand. With nuance, (you) don't."

Newtalk also has its roots in the discussion of marginalia, the bull sessions on television's *All in the Family*, and the banter in Woody Allen films. Newtalk may sound like a conversation between a psychiatrist and a patient. One writer, Paul Iorio, says he has not completely defined the differences between oldtalk and newtalk but he knows them when he sees them. Readers may experience similar success with oldprop and newprop.[4]

A CORNUCOPIA OF UNINYMS

The proliferation of uninyms has been increasing: Communicating by computer is *compucommunication*, public television offers a course on *technopolitics*, *Rolling Stone* magazine has a section devoted to *Technopop*, Nintendo's *edutainment* fuses education and entertainment with electronic technologies, and *ecosystem* and *infotainment* made it into *Roget's Thesaurus* in 1992.

Uninyms contribute to wry forms of humor: The newly rich do not get the flu, they contract *affluenza*, and in this status they do not just chat, they become members of the *schmooseoisie*.[5]

Paris once had *intellocrats* who directed the thoughts of citizens toward political correctness. Now we have spin-doctor *consultocrats* who earn their livings dreaming up ideas that others use. Electronic communication gave us *cyberprop* and a cornucopia of related concepts, such as *cyberbrats*, *cyberspaces*, and *cyberstreets*. A political movement calls itself *Communitarianism*—located between civil liberties and conservatism. *Infomercials* that combine informing and sales have become commonplace.[6]

Syn-sizing and Nym-sizing

Uninyms reflect what is occurring broadly in the language reductionism that has become so prevalent in business and industry: Businesses have *downsized* (the newest cliché is *rightsized*) and electronics has been *miniaturized*. We calculate communication in bits and megabits. Because long quotes and citations slow down communication, the length of "bites" in broadcasting was reduced threefold in the 1990s, and the length of quotes in print was cut more than half.

The mentor of American abbreviators of language is none other than John Horne Tooke, the radical English politician and cleric of the 18th century, who wrote a book from his jail cell on language known as *The Diversions of Purley:*

> Words have been called *winged*, and well they deserve that name, but compared with the rapidity of thought, they have not the smallest claim to that title. (While we have) . . . calculated the difference of velocity between sound and light, . . . who will . . . calculate the difference between speech and thought! What wonder then . . . they stretch to add such wings to their conversation as might enable it . . . to keep pace in some measures with their minds.[7]

Today's need for quick talk has made us dependent on "nyms" of all kinds: *acronyms, antonyms, aptronyms,* and *eponyms.* As one example, I recently asked two persons, one a newspaper columnist and the other a learning specialist, for a precise translation of AIDS. Although each gave various combinations of words that stood for AIDS, neither stated precisely Acquired Immune Deficiency Syndrome. The acronym, as a *lingua franca,* prevailed.

The modern use of acronyms to conduct public discussion began during the New Deal era when Democratic former President Franklin D. Roosevelt, fittingly known by the acronym FDR, imposed on our present-day Aarpie generation an "alphabet soup" of acronyms so extensive that everyone was forced to communicate in *NymSpeak.*

The Federal Communications Commission became the FCC, the Works Progress Administration became the WPA, the Federal Trade Commission became the FTC, the Federal Housing Agency became FHA (now known as Freddie Mae), and so on. With the onset of World War II, the propaganda and intelligence agencies became known almost exclusively by their acronyms: the Office of Facts and Figures (OFF), the Office of Government Reports (OGR), and the Office of War Information (OWI). The Bureau of Intelligence (BI) became the Office of Strategic Services (OSS) and on to the Central Intelligence Agency (CIA). The grandparent of all propaganda agency acronyms was OCCRBAR, the Office of Commercial and Cultural Relations Between the American Republics.

In an amusing description of the language of abbreviation that exists within The White House and federal agencies of government, a former George Bush staffer described "conversations in a hurry" between insiders: POTUS is President of the United States, and FLOTUS is the First Lady. Each of the federal agencies was referred to by its initials, or else it would mean using terms like the Old Executive Office Building rather than OEOB.[8]

The Internet has its own abbreviated language: Just a few examples include BTW (by the way), IMHO (in my humble opinion), and FAQ (frequently asked question). Columnist Jean Godden of the *Seattle Times* told us that her city has its own language of acronyms, including ABL (another Boeing layoff), AMM (another Microsoft millionaire), LLL (looks like lutefisk), MBFC (must be from California), RLNJW (real locals never jaywalk), TMOT (the mountain's out today), and WONE (was on *Northern Exposure*, the short-lived regional TV icon).[9]

PARC Your Acronyms Here

Compucommunication has spawned a large dictionary of acronyms: PARC, as an example, stands for the Palo Alto Research Center. It is PARC that gave us the graphic user interface (GUI), which Macintosh adopted as cheese for its mouse. And our new compucommunication language is full of acronyms. However, *compuprop* is not going unchallenged. The newest acronym is BOOK, standing for Built-in Orderly Organized Knowledge. This new aid might replace electronic learning.

Physicists are debating as to whether the universe's missing mass is in WIMP (weakly interacting massive particles) or MACHO (massive compact halo objects). Heart surgery patients learn that their bypass has been operationalized as CABG, and pronounced like *cabbage.*

Many acronyms are overtly propagandistic. AIDS implies the need for assistance; NOW, the National Organization for Women, communicates the urgency of the women's cause; MADD represents Mothers Against Drunk Driving; DARE describes the initiative and courage of those who work in Drug Abuse Resistance Education; and DAWN is a new force in gender relations, describing the Domestic Abuse Women's Network.

In the wave of oldprop and newprop that is accompanying the debate over the new welfare laws being debated by Congress and the President, *acronymspeak* says it all. Utah has redesignated its Department of Public Welfare as SPED, the Single Parent Employment Demonstration project, and Virginia calls it VIP, the Virginia Independence Program.

On the local level, people who have resisted construction projects or the placing of public facilities (such as jails or halfway houses) in their neighborhoods have adopted the acronym NIMBY (Not in My Back Yard), exceeded only by BANANA (Build Absolutely Nothing Anywhere Near Anyone!).

One cannot master *globalspeak* without utilizing NATO (the North Atlantic Treaty Organization), or cope with *liberalspeak* without considering the ACLU (the American Civil Liberties Union). In recent international trade negotiations, we have been inundated with references to GATT (General Agreement on Tariffs and Trade), NAFTA (North American Free Trade Agreement), and APEC (Asian Pacific Economic Cooperation). Acronyms beget acronyms: The World Trade Organization (WTO) was created to administer GATT.

The language curmudgeon of the *New York Times*, William Safire, got off on *Spookspeak*, the language of the CIA. We now have FUSS (Fleet Underwater Surveillance System), FORMICA (Foreign Military Intelligence Collection Activity), and the NIOs (National Intelligence Officers) must keep in touch with members of SIB (Strategic Intelligence Board), who as "brothers under the skin" must be known as SIBlings.[10] As I sit here I am wearing my newest T-shirt, appropriately named CLEAN, but it is an acronym that means Citizens for Leaders with Ethics and Accountability Now.

LANGUAGE, OLDPROP, AND NEWPROP

The creation of socially and politically correct (PC) language has produced conditions of oldprop and newprop. Intended to rid us of old associations and introduce the new, they are a reminder of the need to revise our thinking about the newly designated object and to learn new words to describe it. Where the use of the old words constrain the object, it is oldprop; for example, *retarded youngsters* can't do things, but *challenged youngsters* can. However, critics have asked if PC language is not counterproductive in sacrificing the richness in meanings that original words once conveyed.[11]

On the other hand, it is clearly necessary to modify language to reflect changing functions. The word *zoo* has become too limited a concept because zoos now conserve wildlife—they do not only exhibit it—and they conduct research. Because it runs 158 conservation and research projects, the former New York Zoological Society is now The Wildlife Conservation Society.[12]

A GENERATIONAL PERSPECTIVE

Every generation invents its own rhetoric and language. Gen X actually rebelled against boomer demands for better language manners. The *Generation X Reader* defends their "ranting" as the defining of a new dialectic. The "rant" transcends the telephone, computer bulletin board, and other mediated technology to achieve a new oral and literary form:

> Rants mix fiery passion with ironic distance, bold assertions with smirky nuance, and (afford) intellectual complexity by disarming simplicity. . . . The rant is to Gen-X what the blues was to African America. No matter how angry, cynical, forlorn or hopeless a rant gets, the underlying energy is a pure joy of expression, inventiveness, and a deeply felt urge to entertain those around us.[13]

One of the most appreciated uninyms of Generation X was *McJobs*, a wordplay that fused McDonald's and its wage structure for young employees. *Fuhranoia* was a profound distrust of charisma, *manotune* was a brief zap to MTV during a televised political debate, *microallegiance* was voting for the last candidate whose TV commercial you saw, and *elderoids* were elder citizens who felt disconnected from modern culture. When boomers lost their jobs, it was described as *dejobbing*.[14]

Watergate became the impulse for reducing public misdeeds to uninyms that incorporated the word *gate*. Even in France the dilution of Bordeaux wines was called *winegate*. Criticisms of Congressman Daniel Flood emerged aptly as *Floodgate*, errors in expense accounts were dubbed *double-billingsgate*, and kiting of checks by congressmen became *rubbergate*. Former New York Governor Mario Cuomo denounced a report on New York ("The Big Apple") finances as *Applegate*. There were *Irangate* and *Iraqgate*, and President Clinton's $200 haircut on the presidential plane became *scalpgate*. When four major dictionaries updated in 1994, among the dozens of uninyms of special interest to our thesis were *cyberpunk*, *dockominium*, and *splatterpunk*.[15]

Creating Buzzwords

Although he did not employ uninyms, Marshall McLuhan redefined commonly used words into *buzzwords* that became a part of his challenging constructions of reality. As examples, the words *hot* and *cold* described media processes and effects. Television was hot (personal or intimate), but print was cold (impersonal and detached). Print was linear and hard; in constrast, television was curvilinear and soft. One needed to speak McLuhanesque to get around in his global village, much as the reader is asked to speak oldprop and newprop to get around in our popular culture.[16]

꜡   ꜡   ꜡

Your journey through this book should be speeded by the use of uninyms, and they should help you focus your thoughts on propaganda in a popular culture. As you move through the book, you will have an opportunity to assess the premises that govern the definitions and utilities of the oldprop and the new.

NOTES

1. Orwell, G. (1983). *1984* (paperback edition). New York: The New American Library, p. 246, Appendix.
2. Senate OKs a "radical" budget bill. (1995, October 28). *Seattle Post-Intelligencer,* Sec A., p. 1.
3. Lutz, W. (1989). *DoubleSpeak.* New York: Harper & Row; Cross, D. W. (1983). *MediaSpeak.* New York: The Putnam Publishing Group.
4. Talk, talk, talk, talk, talk, talk: OK, next scene. (1995, April 9). Iorio, P., *New York Times,* Sec. H, p. 20.
5. Soukhanov, A. H. (1994). *The Stories Behind the Words of Our Lives.* New York: Henry Holt & Co., 419 pp.
6. Past Imperfect: French Intellectuals, 1944–1956. (1993, January 10). Sturrock, J., *New York Times Book Review,* Sec. Y, p. 1.
7. Lingual Lips. (1994, February 20). Safire, W., *New York Times Magazine,* pp. 16–18.

8. Podhoretz, J. (1994). *Hell of a Ride: Backstage at the White House Follies 1989–1993*. New York: Simon & Schuster, pp. 22–33.

9. Seattle gets an e-mail shorthand. (1994, August 28). Godden, J., *The Seattle Times*, Sec. B, p. 1.

10. Spookspeak in Deutschland. (1995, November 19). Safire, W., *New York Times Magazine*, pp. 40–42.

11. Beard, H. (1992). *The Official Politically Correct Dictionary Handbook*. New York: Villard Books.

12. Pinker, S. (1994). *The Language Instinct: How the Mind Creates Language*. New York: Harper Perennial, pp. 55–60.

13. Rushkoff, D. (1994). *The Generation X Reader*. New York: Ballantine Books, p. 206.

14. Coupland, D. (1991). *Generation X: Tales for an Accelerated Culture*. New York: St. Martin's Press, Inc.

15. Starting Gate. (1992, June 7). Safire, W., *New York Times Magazine*, p. 12.

16. McLuhan, M. (1967). *The Medium is the Massage*. New York: Random House.

4

MULTIPROP
Generation and Class

The reader may or may not consider himself or herself to be a member of a specific generation or any of the newly emerging "overclasses," but if you identify with any of them, you have gained special avenues to communicate in the popular culture.

- If you're a contemporary 20-something, you share a special appreciation of cyberprop and the cybersociety.
- If you're 50 or a few years more, you are a baby boomer who enjoyed unparalleled musicprop and economic opportunities.
- If you're an Aarpie, you were privy to watershed international propaganda and the reaping of extraordinary educational opportunities.
- If you identify with any of the emerging political, moral, technological, or affluent "overclasses" you are an *inprop* party to social restructuring.

Each of these generations and classes has adopted a multifaceted approach to their rhetoric, or the absence of one, as they have faced the demands of the new propaganda and the old:

Older generations first were exposed to the oldprop of war and conflict, and then became newprop participants in a political and economic New Deal that was to fashion a safety net around them for a lifetime. Boomers became profoundly interested in the oldprop of material progress and the newprop of music and the arts. Many 20-somethings rejected the oldprop of material culture but responded to the newprop challenges of cyberspace and technology.[1] An older subset, the 30-somethings, became the new achievers and the foci of *communicationprop* in a rapidly changing culture, whereas a younger subset, Generation X, was shortchanged by events and less able and willing to communicate with it, adopting an oldprop of irony. However, most 20-somethings were born into privilege and education and became achievers in the popular culture.

MULTI-IDENTITIES AND MULTIPROP

Not everyone actively seeks identification with a generation or an overclass but because of their heightened consciousness of *multiversity* and their roles within it, they may acknowledge the perceptions that others hold of them. Illustrative is a graduate student at Princeton University, Daniel Strong, who decried being thought of as a Gen-Xer although he conceded that he fit most of the demographics—he was 28, a child of divorce, hirsute, he wore Gap T-shirts and lived at home, but he resented being stuck with a membership that diminished his diversity and created oldprop stereotypes.[2]

THE 20-SOMETHINGS: A NEWPROP GENERATION

The 20-somethings were essentially a newprop generation, but that, too, masked a great deal of diversity. Mark Saltveit, a Harvard graduate, put his manifesto on a computer bulletin board although it did not spell membership:

> We worked hard at low-paying jobs (some arty, some just bad), lived in shared houses; drove old American muscle cars; and shopped at thrift stores. Our hang-outs were brew pubs and bars with cheap, strong drinks and funky, dated furnishings. Or we went to rock clubs where good live bands played alternative rock for a three dollar cover or less.[3]

Although their tendencies were strongly newprop, it became easy to understand why Gen-Xers were characterized as the generation most in need of a public relations agent. They needed to communicate the complex message that they were more than angry, anomic wearers of unpretty fashions, pierced noses, ear adornments, and tattoos—children of "latchkey" parents who had MTV as a baby-sitter. There was a much more positive story to tell. Most 20-somethings grew up free of the prejudices of other generations, particularly the Gen-Xers among them. As perhaps their greatest contribution to the inclusiveness of newprop, they made equal and close friends of the opposite sex and actively engaged all racial groups. They would not become protesters—that had been done in the 1960s—but would help others with their hands and hearts. Too many myths characterized the Xers:

- *As slackers?* Only a "sliver" of this group, not the majority, were slackers as popularized by Linklater.
- *Whiners?* Although they had inherited a declining economy and an enormous national debt, they were not whiners. A Roper poll showed no differences in mood among the 20-somethings, the Boomers, and the Aarpies. Perhaps we were a nation of whiners.
- *Caucasians?* It is the most racially diverse of the generations, 70% white and 30% non-white.
- *Isolates?* More are products of divorce, and fewer are married than was true of prior age groups.
- *Druggies?* Kurt Cobain was not an Xer, although he dressed grunge, and his drug addiction was not a standard.
- *Consumerists?* Xers were a tough sell. An ad writer asked: "How can I appeal to their apathy?"[4]

Many 20- and 30-somethings were new communicators. A VIX (Very important Xers) list was dominated by artists, authors, CEOs, dancers, designers, editors, film stars, government figures, journalists, musicians, news anchors, singers, songwriters, and film and television stars. A diverse generation, their milieu was newprop.

An army of 20-somethings was drawn to Washington, DC, by the Clinton campaign, and they became known as "Stephanopouli," friends and acolytes of George Stephanopoulos, the handsome, young "Greek political God" who helped Clinton to gain his improbable triumph and who placed the stamp of youth on his administration. When Joshua L. Steiner, 28-year-old assistant to the (soon-to-be-deposed) Deputy Secretary Roger C. Altman, was forced to appear before the Senate panel investigating Whitewater, he was initiated into the ways of Capitol Hill oldprop:

> It was a remarkable moment, rich with the cultural tension of the old and the new, the young and the old, on a day when the numbing Whitewater hearings came vividly to life. Mr. Steiner, who had shot to the top of the Clinton Administration's Gen-X meritocracy, now found himself in the excruciating position of holding a "smoking" diary pointed in the direction of his boss.
>
> Six months ago, he was just another anonymous, hard-working, smart, ordering pizza-at-midnight Clinton kid on the rise. Now he was under oath on national television, as all of his colleagues . . . were glued to their sets, watching these nasty, tough old men . . . making him say things he doesn't want to say.[5]

Oldprop, it could be said, had introduced a naive newpropster into the mysteries of the old political order.

The Lively Arts, Invitations to Newprop

Each of the lively arts became an invitation to newprop and in their diversity an expression of the popular culture. As I sit at my word processor, I am wearing a T-shirt on which is inscribed, "Lamestain," freely translated as "an uncool person." It is based on a misadventure in assessing grunge that was experienced by a *New York Times* reporter in Seattle. The other side of the T-shirt notes the extent to which grunge created its own language: *wack slacks* means old ripped jeans, *fuzz* means heavy wool sweaters, and so forth. The Xers advanced not only a "postindustrial thrift-shop look," or grunge—flannel shirts, baggy or ripped jeans, Doc Marten boots, Teva sandals, reversed baseball caps, wool caps, pierced noses, and tattoos—but a language to give it vitality.

Grunge became more than a look or a sound; it was a spin-off of a subculture, at its oldprop outset a slovenly, asexual, "antifashion fashion," but it soon evolved into an antioldprop "chic," where waiflike models sported long, lank hair, faded flannel shirts, clunky workboots, ripped sweaters, old jeans, corduroys, long flowing skirts, pierced noses, and a bleak look.

Style traveled quickly across the generations. The 20-something alternative rock star Kurt Cobain dressed in grunge fashion, as did other Seattle groups such as Pearl Jam, Soundgarden, Mudhoney, and Screaming Trees. The grunge look and feel invaded Los Angeles, and in New York rappers such as Ice-T and the hip-hop artists and women's rock groups adopted similar looks. Where once we were judged by our birth, then by our deeds, now we were being judged by our appearance. This transformation produced synergies of "look," language, music, and self-concept that created a consciousness of totalprop.[6]

Creating Generational Consciousness

Hollywood was generation and even class-conscious, but it tended more to make films "for" 20-somethings than by them or about them. Major studios shied away from young directors and 20-something searches for personal effectiveness. Youth was served by independent film companies who would produce Linklater's *Slacker*, Hal Hartley's *Simple Men* and *Trust*, and Gus Van Sant's *My Own Private Idaho*. These films subscribed to an ambivalent newprop of hope and desperation.[7]

Perhaps the best example of the tendency for Hollywood to make films about marginal youth is *Generation X*, adapted from a Marvel comic book, *The X-Men*. The plot line: Teen-aged mutants are spurned by society. Because society misunderstands them and fears them, they become outcasts. But the mutants are trying to save the society from itself by making it more inclusive, hence newprop prevails.[8]

It was the same with television; it also told us much less about the 20-somethings than the 30-somethings and little about the Xers. Shows such as *A Different World* and *Out All Night* were canceled, and *Melrose Place* was deserted even though it won acclaim. The *Class of '96* finished lowest in the prime-time ratings and was quickly axed. Yet *The Simpsons, Wayne's World, Beavis and Butt-Head,* and sitcoms such as *Seinfeld* became immensely popular.

Only when they placed 20-somethings in key management roles was NBC able to turn things around. Most sitcoms described lovable and/or achingly vulnerable young urban professionals who laughed, cried, lived, loved, and had not seen a 34th birthday. *Seinfeld, Friends, Mad About You,* and *Hope and Gloria* gave NBC a stranglehold on the 18- to 34-year-old audience. They learned that they had to hire 30-somethings to reach 30-somethings.[9]

The novel *Generation X* won attention as a newprop allegory and was described as the 20-somethings' *Catcher in the Rye.* Coupland's novel speaks for the Xers through a persona—Andy (Andrew Palmer, a Portland bartender) —and his friends Claire and Dag, each in their 20s, who have quit "pointless" jobs and lifted themselves from the "detritus of mass culture." This oldprop of alienation and irony was to pervade that subset of generational thought through the early 1990s.

THE PROLIFIC BOOMERS

The Boomers are the most prolific and self-conscious generation, and they span almost four decades since World War II. In contrast to the 20-somethings, few Boomers deny their identity and most assert it. They share an extended sense of age and identity as early (born soon after World War II) and late Boomers (born in the 1960s) and insist that they helped to create as well as to consume the benefits of society. More than a personal statement of success, it is an assertion of identity, the essence of *generationprop* and class-consciousness.

But not all Boomers ascended the peak of success. One prominent subset evolved into a blue-collar and predominantly white-collar class. As a generation of mixed interests and classes they became both avid consumers of newprop and willing parties to oldprop. Most Boomers felt indebted to President Ronald Reagan's deregulated society that had nurtured and permitted them to indulge their appetites as consumers. The "fatal attraction" of the most ambitious Boomers to the artifacts of popular culture allowed them to have it both ways: They could become affluent; indulge their tastes in art, fashion, films, glitzy cars, music, theater, and gourmet cuisines; afford a home in the suburbs; smoke pot; and feel that they were participating in a cultural revolution. Those synergies made the Boomer generation an apotheosis of totalprop.

Mediaprop and Totalprop

Eager to exploit a new market, *mediaprop* focused attention on the Boomers and their capacity for totalprop. Their cultural vanguard—the creative Hippies and Beatniks—had instituted ceremonials such as Woodstock and endowed them with a lifestyle, dress, music, and drugs that the Boomers avidly enjoyed. Through the comic strip *The Boomers' Song* cartoonist David Horsey projected Boomer ascendancy, continuity, and change.

Jack Boomer is a young father, musician, muse, liberal, and prototypical producer and consumer of Boomer generationprop. He strums his guitar and sings:

"Now, here's a song I wrote just for you;
"Raised by Captain Kangaroo as the TV generation;
"We began as Mickey's Mouseketeers and became the Woodstock nation;
"Through Vietnam and Watergate we struggled and we grew;
"And when the 'Me Decade' arrived, we all said, 'Me, too!'
"Now with babies, second mortgages and BMWs,
"We sit back in Swedish saunas reading *Esquire* for the news;
"Some of us are Yuppies and some of us are slobs;
"Most are just New Collar folks;
"Taking DRUG tests at our jobs!
"We've compact discs inside our cars and Walkmen (and now cellular phones)
    in our ears;
"We dance through life to music that details our loves and fears;
"No matter where we go to next the music comes along;
"To the beat of different drummers it's the Baby Boomers' Song!"

Thus Boomer culture was founded in childhood, family, hope, fear, love, marriage, music, and career. Yet it was not an entirely lovable generation. Although its newprop expressed the "we-ness" of its generation and its place in a popular culture, when its prerogatives were challenged it listened to the sirens of oldprop. It is said that the Boomers profited more from culture than they invested in it. One of their critics saw the Boomers as moral, preachy, and full of false values. Pat Robertson and Jesse Jackson did better in the 1988 primaries among Boomers than other groups, and such bearers of offbeat and dark messages as Jerry Brown and Pat Buchanan were more embraced by Boomers than by the public as a whole. They promised they would get things done, a core value for the Boomers and a part of their self-fulfilling generationprop. When Clinton, himself a baby Boomer (he turned 50 in 1996) promised he would get things done, some Boomers shifted to him, and then away from him in 1994 because he had not done enough well enough.

A Cartoon Generation

Horsey is one of a generation of Boomer cartoonists that includes Tim Menees, Linda Barry, Mike Lukovich (who began cartooning on the *University of Washington Daily* and won the Pulitzer Prize for political cartooning in 1995), and Gary Larson, the comic cartoonist who attended Washington State University. Horsey is self-conscious about Boomer culture:

I guess I'm a bit of a Yuppie. I've been to Europe six times, I'm not rich but I'm comfortable, I drive a sports car, I eat ethnic and think global. But being a Yuppie hasn't prevented me from thinking like a boomer.[10]

Certainly, the Boomers were emancipated by a revolution in music, rock 'n' roll, a music that freed them from dependency on the music of their parents' generation. They responded to the "Summer of Love" that uplifted the drug culture. The *musicprop* was Janis Joplin, Jimi Hendrix, Joe Cocker, Bob Dylan, and the Jefferson Airplane, among others. Dr. Timothy Leary advised them to tune in, turn on, and drop out. Make love, not war. Its freshness of voice made it newprop, but in its appeal to hedonism, it was oldprop.

From 1996 to 2014, almost 70 million Boomers will enter into their 50s. That means changes in lifestyle and in communicating and suggests that there will be more of a desire to retain stable institutions and less of a tendency to respond to radical oldprop.[11]

The media tend to be optimistic as well as forgiving: *Time* describes late Boomers as "real points of light" in the efforts of the nation to reinvent itself.[12]

THE AARPIES: "MIDDLE AGED FOREVER"

The oldest generation has experienced the worst of the oldprop as an alien concept and is eager to respond to the best of the new. For them, an improved diet, exercise, and medical care have forced chronological time to yield to real time. At the turn of the century, 4% of the population was 65. Now it is 13% and it is increasing: Within several decades, the over-65 population will make up one fifth of the population. The Republican nominee for president in 1996 was Bob Dole, age 72, and Democrats were warned that they would not get away easily with age-bashing even though the political strategists were coding it the "A" word and the late-night comics were having field days with it.[13]

Musical icons express that young agedness: In music, one may quickly name Tony Bennett, Pete Townshend, Eric Clapton, Aerosmith, Led Zeppelin, The Rolling Stones, Paul McCartney, Aretha Franklin, Bob Dylan, Frank Zappa, Paul Simon, and Art Garfunkel, among others. All are getting younger as they are getting older.[14]

The new Aarpies fought the war in Korea and on their return became labeled a "silent generation." Dubbed the "lonely crowd," they were inner-directed in finding rules of conduct within themselves, but they were other-directed in looking outward for cues as to values and conduct. They contributed far more to the popular culture than they received, and despite their unrewarded sacrifices they were predisposed more to newprop than to the old.[15]

Alvin Toffler feared that *future shock* and *ecospasms* brought about by technological and social change would break down the fabric of Aarpie and post-Korean War society and their families, produce social chaos rather than community, and generate the oldprops of fear and disorientation.[16] However, although it was, indeed, the children of the Aarpies that would engage in protest and rebellion, introduce new clothes, music, drugs, ways of thought, and liberated lifestyles, that spirit of improvisation, invention, and hope would create a popular culture and send messages of newprop to us all.

The oldest of the Aarpies experienced the great depression of the 1930s, made up the 13 million military personnel who rescued Western civilization from Hitler and Stalin, defeated the Japanese Navy, dropped atom bombs on Nagasaki and Hiroshima, and survived the Cold War. They had experienced directly the oldprop of World War II and its aftermath, but after the war almost 8 million entered prestigious universities through the G.I. training bill, making up almost half of the students in colleges and universities. President Clinton told a D-Day assemblage that this produced 450,000 engineers, 360,0000 teachers, 240,000 accountants, 180,000 physicians and nurses, and 150,000 scientists who were to become the core of the popular culture.[17]

Now it is said that members of the Aarpie generation are becoming an overclass, largely because they are enjoying the fruits of the investment they made in the economic maturation of the popular culture.

CREATING NEW CLASSES

Although the generations remain identifiable, they are fragmenting visibly under the impact of economic and social change into a number of highly diversified overclasses. These common-interest groupings cut across generations and are identifiable by their remarkable success in their professions. Boomers and many 20- and 30-somethings have become members of overclasses in politics, technology, the professions, and along such value dimensions as Christian faith and morals. In many ways they are similar in their demographics:

* Many are graduates of leading universities.
* Despite the increase in the number of the elderly, the new overclasses span the age groups of the 30-somethings to the 50-somethings.
* The economic and technological overclasses favor competitive achievement.
* All transcend the one-time Yuppies by combining their material success with social consciousness.

Newsweek published a list of 100 of these success stories. In the arts and the media they included writers and producers of the top sitcoms (*Roseanne, Home*

Improvement, The Cosby Show, and others), newspaper editors, managers of rock bands (Nirvana, Hole, and The Breeders), network presidents (of MTV), writers of controversial tomes (such as *The Bell Curve*), talk show hosts, television correspondents and anchors, and others too numerous to mention. They were committed largely to the popular culture and to newprop rather than the old.[18]

The new overclasses varied, however, in their tendencies to adopt the new propaganda or the old.

The Technological Overclass

As beneficiaries of dramatic economic growth, invention, and the mastery of new skills, the technological overclass has exploited every modality of *communicationprop.* Quantitatively, more have addresses on the Internet than on Fifth Avenue in New York, and qualitatively, by virtue of education, knowledge, and skills, they are disposed to newprop. As bystanders, however, they may be more disposed to be witnesses than participants in the conflicts that have emerged in the popular culture.

Newsweek magazine, which prided itself on having identified the Yuppies of the 1960s and 1970s, identified the most affluent of the new technological overclass as graduates of the best schools, holding the best jobs, driving the best cars, and most capable of exploiting cyberspace, but they feel no need to share their status with the less gifted or, for that matter, with those who might be equally gifted but who have not "made it."[19]

The technological overclass works flexibly and individually and feels less loyalty to corporations (although there are many exceptions), and finds its work to be highly satisfying. Because of a command of technology, they can imagine the extended community that was visualized by software guru Bill Gates, president of Microsoft. The technological overclass has invested itself in inventing languages of universal and global communication that have become their own form of propaganda.

The Wealthy Overclass

An overclass of 650,000 millionaires and numerous billionaires—most of whom are engaged in finance, computers, entertainment, and media—have upset the social and economic equilibrium of the popular culture without making a statement about either the new propaganda or the old.[20]

The growth of affluence and the deprivation of the lower classes have been dramatic. As average earnings over the past two decades fell 11%, top earnings rose 29%. The share of wealth held by the top 1% (40%) doubled to the point where it approached that of a quarter century earlier, when there was no progressive income tax. While wages have gone down, gross national product has risen, the differences accruing to the rich.

The erosion of dreams about achieving economic equality was vitiating a social contract of long standing; that is, that workers and managers would share in the prosperity of their companies. Instead, layoffs and takebacks were extracted from workers in the face of record profits and bonuses to management, and the affluent continued to work prodigiously to add to their fortunes, neither engaged in nor attracted to propaganda, either the old or the new.[21]

The Moral Overclass

The moral overclass has eschewed newprop for the old. By late 1995, Republican *politicalpropsters* had counseled candidates that the 1996 campaign should eschew newprop debates over issues to exploit oldprop "morality" themes. The obvious targets of demonization would be a still vulnerable President Clinton and the remnants of liberal political ideology. Moral overtones were present in the action of Dole's primary staff in returning funds to the Log Cabin Republicans, when it had solicited the funds in the first place. Thus the Dole campaign abandoned an elite, insider group whose right to advance an agenda within the party should have been sacrosanct.[22]

Dole also had demonized the music and film industries for diminishing American "family values," even though he had accepted funds from producers of violence and pornography and had not himself (until after he had engaged in the criticisms) seen the performances he had condemned. He even broadened his attack to blanket "elitist liberals" who were undermining American values in schools and other cultural institutions. He insisted on English as a single language (as an act of inclusion) and the act of taking pride in our true history and traditional American values.

All this could be presumed to be newprop in its appeal for a greater community, but it was oldprop in its demand for conformity and its potential denial of membership. This suggested class warfare in which a moral overclass exploited a less powerful underclass.

> Criminals, the addicted, alcoholics, the homeless, the mentally ill, the welfare recipients, the school dropouts, and the residents of publicly supported housing projects are victims of their own behavior. They are the illegal immigrants and the teenage gang members—all poor. The men . . . are lazy and unwilling and unable to work; their women are immoral and slothful, dependent upon welfare, and they are engaged in antisocial acts.[23]

The "moral war on poverty," a newprop that was designed to uplift a class, had become transformed into a class war of oldprop on those who were suffering from poverty. Class warfare inevitably would rationalize support for the radical oldprop advanced by Louis Farrakhan, leader of the Nation of Islam, in his Million Man March:

Class has been the dirty secret of American history, denied by promises of individual freedom, by dreams of upward mobility and by memories of solid communities and coherent families. (In reality) America has plunged into a new round of class warfare.[24]

The Political Overclass

A new subset of the political overclass is emerging whose métier is propaganda. The young Republican counterculture that took form in the late 1980s and early 1990s created a constellation of think tanks and opinion media that was intended to create a propaganda that would articulate their goals. However, because the rhetoric was not inventive, it took on more of the character of oldprop than the new. Its stylizing satisfied only those who already held the language codes. As an expression of exclusivity, it denigrated competing views rather than engaging in creative exchanges. Writer James Atlas said the stylizers remained too close to their beginnings as oldprop liberal haters to articulate a newprop.[25]

When young Republican intellectual Bill Kristol was asked what he was going to say about Newt Gingrich's Contract With America, he replied off-handedly, "We're pretending to like it."[26] Kristol acknowledged that most of what he does in politics is to oppose bad ideas, particularly the conservative oldprop that has demeaned feminism, homosexuality, race, and the performing arts. Yet he must live with other young Republicans such as David Brock, the 30ish journalist who authored a devastating biography of Anita Hill in which he described her as "a little bit nutty and a little bit slutty," a stylized oldprop.[27]

Kristol and John Podhoretz have achieved the status of a uninym; each is called a *minicon*, because Kristol's father is Irving Kristol, a prominent academic who was a founder of the neoconservative movement; Podhoretz, a Bush staffer and at one time a television columnist for *The New York Post*, is the son of Norman Podhoretz, a prominent conservative original.[28]

Caught between Republican forces, self-isolated from the Contract With America and the radical religious right, the new young Republican political overclass sought to build a critical mass. Restrained about "the uncouth fire-and-brimstone Protestant evangelicals, who have big problems with Jews, women, homosexuals, and most anyone who isn't one of them," and forced into bashing liberals with whom they share social backgrounds and principles, they doggedly sought a new identity.[29]

They found it in a new magazine edited by Kristol, *The Weekly Standard*, avowedly conservative but committed to irony and a diversity of Republican thought. Thus it ridiculed Bob Dole's efforts to "woo female voters," comparing him to a "tired roué" whose pick-up lines keep falling flat; described Pat Buchanan's views as "anti-American," and subscribed, unabashedly, on its cover, to a second term for Bill Clinton, at the same time questioning the implacable views of conservatives on abortion. This created a newprop with an edge and earned them a reputation for being iconoclastically conservative where the *New Republic* once had beem iconoclastically liberal.[30]

☙ ☙ ☙

The generations are different enough to be talked about and to talk about themselves, but they are giving way in part to the fragmentation that evolves in a popular culture, in this case the taking on by generations of additional identities as members of emerging overclasses.

Each produces and consumes both the oldprop and the new; the Boomers, as an example, are more tilted toward oldprop than the young or the Aarpies, yet they also are responsive to newprop as situations define themselves. The moral overclass predominantly leans toward oldprop, whereas the technological overclass distances itself as much as possible from the old and the new; yet, captive to their knowledge and experience they are more committed to newprop than the old.

Because of its education and eliteness, the political overclass finds that its political tastes and requirements force it to engage in both the oldprop and the new, whereas the economic overclass finds itself more remote. As each generation finds itself fragmented into increasingly complex roles, we will be limited to generalizing about them.

NOTES

1. Coupland, D. (1991). *Generation X.* New York: Saint Martin's Press, Inc.
2. Generation Hex. (1994, October 1). *New York Times.* Sec. Y, p. 15.
3. *The Generation X Reader* (1994). New York: Ballantine.
4. Generation X: The images boomers have of 20-somethings mostly are unfair and untrue. (1994, June 6). Giles, J., *Newsweek,* p. 62.
5. Bentsen's aides' lessons, penned in diaries, emerge painfully in public. (1994, August 3). Dowd, M., *New York Times,* Sec. A, p. 9.
6. Grunge, success for the great unwashed. (1992, November 16). *New York Times,* Sec, B, p. 1.
7. Twenty-nothing: Many films are made to appeal to those in their twenties, but few are willing to deal with their issues. (1993, August 8). Rauzi, R., *Seattle Times,* Sec. C, p. 1.
8. Uh-oh. They're superhuman and teen-agers, too. (1996, February 20). O'Connor, J. J., *New York Times,* Sec. B, p. 1.
9. To Reach Generation X, Hire Generation X'ers. (1995, September 25). *New York Times,* Sec. C, p. 7.
10. Discussion with author, May 16, 1993.
11. No free rides: Generational push has not come to shove. (1995, December 31). *New York Times,* Sec 4, p. 1. See also, Middle age catches up with the Me Generation. (1996, January 2). Elliott, S., *New York Times,* Sec. C, p. 4.
12. The Real Points of Light. (1994, December 5). Morrow, L., *Time,* pp. 52–78.

13. The birth of a revolutionary class. (1996, May 19). Thurow, L. C., *New York Times Magazine*, pp. 46–47.

14. Facing the age issue. (1995, July 31). Duffy, M., & Gibbs, N., *Time*, pp. 23–26.

15. Reisman, D. (1969). *The Lonely Crowd: A Study of the Changing American Character.* New Haven: Yale University Press.

16. Toffler, A. (1970). *Future Shock.* New York: Random House.

17. G.I. Bill turns 50, having built a knowledge society. (1994, June 22). *Seattle Times*, Sec. A, p. 3.

18. The rise of the overclass. (1995, July 31). Adler, J., *Newsweek*, pp. 32–49.

19. The rich: Who are they? (1995, November 19). Lewis, M., *New York Times Magazine*, pp. 65–68.

20. Why their world might crumble. (1995, November 19). Thurow, L., *New York Times Magazine*, p. 78.

21. Back to class warfare. (1994, December 27). Sennett, R., *New York Times*, Sec. A, p. 15.

22. Dole, in shift, says refund of gay gift was staff mistake. (1995, October 18). Berke, R., *New York Times*, Sec A., p. 1.

23. What the poor deserve. (1995, October 22). Frankel, M., *New York Times Magazine*, p. 46.

24. Extremist fringes are on the move. (1995, October 16). *International Herald Tribune*, Sec. A, p. 8.

25. The counter culture. (1995, February 12). Atlas, J. New *York Times Magazine*, pp. 32–38, 54, 61–63.

26. *NYTM*, Ibid., p. 54

27. *Newsweek*, Ibid., p. 34.

28. *Newsweek*, Ibid., p. 37.

29. *NYTM*, Ibid., p. 37.

30. *NYTM*, Ibid., p. 39.

5

CYBERPROP
The Path to Totalprop

It was August 24, 1995, and a bewitchingly cloudy day in Redmond, Washington, the "campus" of Microsoft, the world's leading computer software designer and maker. It was the kickoff of Windows 95, the latest and greatest operating system in the Microsoft line. Inside a great tent sat 2,600 journalists, dignitaries, and high-tech executives. Outside were 1,500 young employees whose stock options would make many of them millionaires and who had taken a rare few hours off to celebrate the event.

I sat with Tom Corddry of Microsoft, a one-time multimedia publishing group leader, and gazed at a gigantic screen whose skyscape, filmed the day before, was indistinguishable from the scene about us. Warm, blue skies were broken only by rhapsodically formed clouds. All were imbued with enthusiasm: Bill Gates and the project team had done it!

They were 20-and 30-somethings and their dress was casual; formality meant tucking in your T-shirt. However, all were top graduates of the top schools, far more gifted than the "nerds" that once typified computer geniuses. They admired "Bill" and they shared his enthusiasm for putting personal computers in every home that would operate faster, more reliably, and advance the pace and flow of communication in a popular culture. "At least 50% of what we do is communication," Bill said. The workforce cheered because they knew they would increase that ratio and move toward the ultimate in newprop.

The theme song was "Start Me Up," a Rolling Stones melody that had "turned on" an earlier Boomer generation. Because the "start" button was so much a feature of Windows 95, Microsoft paid Mick Jagger and his band millions for its use. It was the only song The Stones had sold in this way, but they joined Bob Dylan with "The Times They are A Changin'" and Janis Joplin, whose Mercedes Benz tune was used in an auto advertisement, among others. The cost of marketing Windows 95 was estimated at about $150 million, with sales expected to exceed $8 billion. Retail outlets would spend another $350 million. The TV advertisements, print ads, and 30-minute segments aired in the top 70 TV markets as prime-time infomercials, making it *total communicating and marketingprop.*[1]

NBC *Tonight Show* host Jay Leno, who had prepped for 6 weeks with Windows 95 so he could become a convincing salesman, quipped that NBC stood for "Now Bill Compatible." Program excerpts were broadcast via satellite to 43 cities in 30 countries and were posted on the World Wide Web through Microsoft's home page. Microsoft purchased a full day's run of the *London Times*, the Empire State Building in New York was lit up, and a barge was floated carrying a four-story high Windows 95 logo in Sydney harbor in Australia. A cartoonist pictured the rural Microsoft "campus" against a backdrop of mountains out of which came the cry:

> "All 100 million copies have been bought and installed, O omnipotent one! Is it time to activate the hidden mind-control program?" The answer: "I don't think we need to bother."[2]

BEYOND THE VISION

Even as Windows 95 was being celebrated, work on Windows 97 and Windows NT was proceeding. The vision incorporated communication functions such as multimedia, greater integration with the Internet and the Microsoft Network (MSN) online service—later to merge with NBC News—and responsiveness to voice commands. Cyberprop would become the ultimate newprop. The technology would move vast amounts of digital information globally as well as nationally. Videoconferencing and electronic collaboration in the workplace, on-demand entertainment services, and electronic commerce would flourish.

Gates said we were in the midst of an industrial revolution that rivaled the watersheds that had preceded it. Where once the railroad and the automobile had signaled a change of life, the popular culture had adopted electronic means of transportation—radio, television, and now the PC—that carried our imaginations and invited the individual to follow. Once the PC was in every home, it would diffuse power to the people. Cyberprop was the apotheosis of newprop; it promised that everyone who had access could participate meaningfully.

Even among these visionaries, no one realized at that moment that the idea of a global cybersociety would so quickly take form and that the process would be played out in so many ways. Some actions would be driven by competition among communication titans and others would be affected by considerations of content and control.

• There was little question that communication systems were being constructed that would make functions easier and connections more accessible and affordable for everyone.

• Threatening as it might seem, major communication entities would engage in successive rounds of megamergers and redefine their infrastructures to meet competition. Some companies would be forced to reinvent themselves to ensure their place in the global system.

• Consumers would be given an increasing number of choices among technologies, paths, and destinations; indeed, the consumption of communicationprop would become the badge of membership in the popular culture, diminishing the significance of birth and occupation as hallmarks of membership. Being a consumer of communicationprop was becoming as much of a self-identity—as in exchanging information about one's ownership and use of technology—as any other psychographic.

• The very ownership of new means of communicating would create new appetites for communication, taking the form of a positive feedback loop, a synergy that generated new communication energies as each fueled the other. And the more communicationprop that was generated, the more inventive the high-tech communication industry would be in meeting and exploiting those needs. This would be a dynamic process with the promise of including everyone at some point and at some level. Despite the gaps and disparities, this held the greatest promise of ensuring access to the popular culture for everyone. Cyberprop would become the ultimate newprop.

Competition in Designing the Future

Gates' view was that where the desktop computer once had been used primarily for accounting and word processing, new systems would be designed for communicating, allowing the computer to take over functions of the telephone and fax machines. As everyone became even more connected, computers would be used primarily for communicating and accessing information. On other fronts, Microsoft was looking to the acquisition of content and alliances with distributors of information and entertainment. According to the dream, the computer would perform so many functions it would never be turned off.[3]

That was a vision that others, in addition to Microsoft, sought to carry out, and the design of new systems and the inevitable marketingprop was not long in getting underway. Sun Microsystems, another titan, and Oracle announced that they would produce a new generation of "information machines," a so-called Internet Computer that would sell for $500 and dedicate its functions only to communicating; that is, services on the network and the World Wide Web. Although it would have no storage or processing capabilities, and thus operate only in "real time," it would be adequate for the functions it would serve. Of course, Sun would use its own software, challenging Microsoft on its own turf.

As had every actor affected by the proposal, Microsoft had studied the market for and functions of a $500 communication center and appeared to have taken themselves out of it. Was this the best way for individuals to communicate and preserve a history of it, Gates wondered? At the marketing level it was a question as to whether the $500—some said $300—price was real or if it was an effort to squeeze out the competition on the premise that entering it might prove to be unprofitable? Or was it a bigger battle whose paradigm was to be adopted and whose vision of the future was to be seen? Would nirvana be achieved by a terminal or by a modified PC or, as part of a paradigm shift, could PCs go the route of mainframe computers?

Microsoft bet that most consumers wished to store and manage their knowledge, not rely on others to do it for them. Gates decided to speed development of an all-information appliance that would cost more than $500 but less than a full-featured PC. Called the simply interactive personal computer (SIPC), it would become a center for communications and entertainment in the home or at the office. Projected onto a large screen, it would provide stereo sound, recording, and television services; engage in high-speed Internet surfing; and play new multimedia videodiscs, called DVDs. Given the functions and the standards set by Microsoft, manufacturers would compete to build it. Gates bet that the public would prefer a smart PC with Microsoft software to a dumb video without it.

Pathways and Destinations

The operating systems were one thing, and transportation to content was another. The online services were the libraries of content, and the Web was the repository for thousands of individual and group sites, but browsers were required to surf the Web.

Netscape's Navigator became the most effective system of browsing, quickly attracting 70% of potential users. In a brief time, the company saw its stock value multiply more than fourfold. The prices bore no relationship to earnings but to the promise that Netscape, along with its partner Sun Microsystems, Inc., would dominate the field with a superior entry language, JavaScript.

However, Microsoft licensed JavaScript to give it time to perfect its own product, and it announced it would ensure compatibility of its technology to facilitate everyone's entry to the Internet.[4] The Internet as highway and the Web as destination would spur the competition between Netscape's Navigator and Microsoft's Internet Explorer to take the user to the content—hopefully, their own. Microsoft quickly rewrote the rules by promising that Windows 95 would take users to the Net for free. Once there, the user could decide what was compelling, and the Explorer (as well as the Navigator) could lead the user to it. In early 1996, both Microsoft and Netscape signed deals with America Online (AOL) to promote their browsers, but the Explorer would be the recommended tool. In turn, AOL acquired an icon on Windows 95, making it easier to bring up than the competition.

In a similar move, American Telephone and Telegraph (AT&T) announced that its telephone lines now would take users directly to the Internet. A broad-scale competition was at hand that would improve services, drive down prices, and promise greater access to everyone. Users could apply the money they saved on access to choices among content. As technology and competition worked to the benefit of the user, the popular culture would benefit and newprop would thrive.

CYBERSPACE AND SOCIALPROP

Indeed, if the competition in functions, price, and service continued at that pace—and the likelihood of that was high—cyberspace ultimately would become accessible to everyone who wished to enter it, and that was the apotheosis of newprop. Certainly a variety of services had evolved that would attract potential users.

As I surfed the World Wide Web via Netscape's Navigator, I was overwhelmed by the choices before me. There were home pages maintained by graduate students: one on propaganda analysis by Aaron Delwiche, another hosted by Jeanette James as Sistah Space, who invited users to discover the mysteries of Sistah Power through controlling their self-expression. It was astonishing that at the University of Washington, with a population of almost 36,000 students, 38,000 sites had been established. Some students had two or more, but the penetration was almost total. Certainly, the new technology had opened new lines of communication to those with the opportunities and skills that were required to use them.

There was a flyer about *ONE*, a magazine devoted to Life, Art & Culture for a New State of Mind. It told how it was first published as a bimonthly oversized tabloid that was distributed in the Washington, DC, area. It was created as a generational response to traditional African American oriented newspapers that had failed to meet the needs of a younger generation.

A 17-year-old gay male cannot come to grips with himself until he ventures a message to a teenage youth bulletin board. He receives more than 100 supportive letters and winds up putting his message together with a book, some flowers, and a tell-all letter to his mother. Thousands learned about themselves and others and felt closer to them in cyberspace than they did at school and at home. This was a newprop that was the essence of a popular culture.[5]

Becoming a Host(ess)

It was not long before I got the bug. Why not get a site and become a host? I wouldn't put all of *Total Propaganda* on a site because anyone's $20 fee to a provider would get them the complete text; that's no way to merchandise a more costly publication. But why not create an index of oldprop and newprop and cover national elections just like the public opinion polls and predict the results of the races based on measures of the campaign ratio of oldprop to newprop. Perhaps I could sell adprop!

When Michael Bolanos set up an online service on Compuserve that permitted subscribers to dial in for information, conversation, and entertainment, it ballooned into demands that required a staff of 30 people to field a half million calls a month.

Lynne Bundesen, author and former war correspondent, hosted a news bulletin board on Prodigy, on which she posted questions on topics of her choice that generated discussion and debate. As a forum leader, she became wealthy, but she commanded the skills of a radio talkprop hostess.

Elin Silveous, who hosts a health and medical forum, created her audience when she was looking for electronic support groups for her illness of multiple sclerosis. She and many of her callers found that the dialog on the health forum was better than medicine or medical advice.

Georgia Griffith, a 63-year-old forum leader for Compuserve, runs six forums from her home, composes hundreds of online messages, and is known as a "Net Queen," writing faster than most people can talk. She has a distinctive voice, and is witty, forceful, and at times self-deprecating. What makes her so remarkable is that she is deaf and blind and worked as a Braille music proofreader for the Library of Congress. She commented wittily, "I was born blind; a few years later they said I was visually handicapped; then I became visually impaired; now I'm visually challenged, and I can't see a bit better. I just feel blind and politically incorrect."[6]

They and many others had created "virtual communities" online, and that is the essence of newprop in a popular culture.

Visiting the CNN Site

As I visited CNN on its Web site on the first day of Spring, 1996, I saw the newest of journalism, and like its print counterpart, advertising was supporting it. There were signature ads from AT&T promoting its business network;

SWATCH, the watch company, promoting its "cool" watches and interactive games; and Intel signifying its services. It would not be long before there would be more adprop designed to appeal to the psychographics of Internet users.

That day's menu was extensive—world and national news, financial news, politics, sports, technology, show business, technology, the weather, food, health, and style. There were literally dozens of stories, each written for the Web rather than for the printed page. There were invitations to interaction: "Please send me your comments." And apropos the current dispute over censorship of cyberspace, "Should indecent material be banned on the Internet?" The answers were not as important as the interaction.

PoliticsNow became the major Web politicalprop site of 1996; it was sponsored jointly by the *Washington Post, Newsweek*, ABC News, the *Los Angeles Times*, and the *National Journal*. Its content on any day would satisfy any politicalprop junkie. On one day it headlined the anniversary of the Contract with America; argued in a feature, "Medium Cool," that journalists and pollsters had rushed to judgment on the outcome of the election; invited audiences to enter The War Room and advise Dole on how to close the gender gap; explained ways of "living in Spin"; invited participation in the political trivia game, Inaugural Bowl; and encouraged listening to Dan Quayle's dramatic reading of Al Gore's new book in *Doonesbury Flashbacks*.

I found myself testing my own positions on issues against those held by my two senators and my district congressperson, and I was surprised to see whom I agreed with on two of the five issues. What made *PoliticsNow* involving was both its cyberprose and its presentation. I could read and be informed, just as in the old media, but I stood a better chance of being entertained, as well.

From *Slate* to *Stale*

The Microsoft magazine *Slate*—edited by Michael Kinsley, intellectual and former "liberal" voice on CNN's *Crossfire*—promised to be a success, and it quickly drew a humorous accolade in the immediate creation of *Stale*. *Slate* offered entry to other magazines, as well, such as *Time, Newsweek, U.S. News & World Report, The New Yorker*, and *The Weekly Standard*. Its features were glitzy, the commentary pointed. One feature was headlined, "The Democrats Deserve to Suffer." The writer noted that the pundits analyzed the elections, but he analyzed the pundits.

It was quintessentially cyberprose. "Therapeutic laws" were designed to make you feel good, not to do anything. Democrats weren't ready to retake Congress because they hadn't suffered enough. Interactive? Butt into *Slate's* reader forum, send e-mail to the editors, mull over *Boilerslate* comments, and browse in the compost of articles.

The *Stale* wit was a testimonial to *Slate's* success. Otherwise, why bother?

There was "Readme," the Spin, and The Gist (a form of indi-Gist-ion). It asked, "Is Microsoft Evil?" and *Slate*'s Compost feature was described to "netizens" as a pile o' shite!

By mid-1996, up to a dozen major content providers provided knowledge, news, entertainment, and opportunities through postings to talk and chat. That competition spurred lower prices, better interfaces, and easier access. Many afforded the luxury of *weaving*, where data was linked by code into organized increments of knowledge. By the mid-1996, 40 million users were projected to be linked to the major services. Still in the future, however, was the point at which the PC or its equivalent would become so essential to the ordinary person that—reverting to the social and economic model of the adoption of television—the 90% who once decided they must buy a television set, even if they could not really afford it, also would find it imperative to get on the information highway. This addressed the question of access, the lack of which was the most serious criticism of cyberprop as newprop.

COMPETITION AND ACCESS

All providers would be required to reinvent themselves in order to survive. Compuserve, AOL, and Prodigy, preeminent among the early providers, now faced competition from many sides. Each realized it could not continue to exist as only a path to the Internet and the Web. They would have to ensure that users would spend time attending to their holdings, and adprop would be attracted to them. The new owner of Prodigy had a vision of the future that saw it transformed into a panoply of programming and services.

Microsoft had set that pace, acquiring an impressive collection of art, photography, and literature and an unrivaled dictionary, and signing up famous chefs, theater buffs, filmmakers, and myriad other talent. In 1 week Microsoft signed 43 content servers, bringing its total to more than 220 with hundreds more to come. These included such prominent agents as the Home Shopping Network, Starwave, Ziff-Davis Interactive, C-Span, QVC, the *New York Times Magazine*, *Hollywood Online*, *Women's Wire*, and *Jazz Central Station*, among others. Attaching those services to Windows 95 brought federal threats of a suit to prevent monopolistic practices.[7]

Microsoft technologies also challenged other servers by offering more effective interaction and effects. Better graphics were easier to use and afforded more versatility. One could click on part of a picture and jump to a new content area while the rest of the picture remained the same. This lent itself to interactive computing, advertising, and electronic commerce and would allow people to use their TVs much as they used computers. Programs could be ordered at any time; someone watching *Seinfeld* could order a past episode or even purchase the kind of jacket Seinfeld was wearing. Whether entertainment, purchasing, or banking, users would pay a percentage of the transaction, more remunerative to Microsoft than payment for time.[8]

Then came the alliance with NBC, which provided news content, and would permit users to watch television news on their computers and run computer functions on their TV sets. This and a proposed all-news network, patterned on CNN, would add a competitive news production resource and a renewable source of entertainment. A consortium called Dreamworks, SKG, enlisted such talents as director Steven Spielberg, former Disney Studios chairman Jeffrey Katzenberg, and recording executive David Geffen. They would feed futuristic features and films into Microsoft services.[9]

In October 1996, Microsoft announced a dramatically revised MSN that took a television rather than a computer personality and emphasized multimedia applications that gave its users a sense of involvement. Some of its new shows included:

- A travel-adventure game show that takes place partly online and partly in the real world. Players work together to solve puzzles, riddles, and historical/geographical mysteries to win prizes.
- An interactive comedy-drama about a small private school struggling through hard times.
- A virtual music studio where visitors interact with big-name recording artists.
- An interactive Web serial about high school students searching for their identity.

APPROACHING TOTALPROP: THE MEGAMERGERS

A number of industrial giants had engaged in megamergers that positioned them to respond to the demands of the global information and entertainment marketplace. In each case, the major components of the communications empires-in-building rested on turf where they had been preeminent. However, acquisitions would give them much more: they would prepare them to become actors in the production of totalprop. AT&T began with telephone lines and acquired content providers; John Malone, the king of cable, sought to acquire content providers; ABC–Capital Cities began with content and acquired connections. Now each of them not only had the means to communicate but could provide the substance for it; this meant total communication, and in each case carried the potential for total propaganda.

AT&T Restages

Once AT&T was again permitted to buy into local telephone and cable companies, to sell connection services, to send electronic mail, create sophisticated paging systems, and promote data communication to link far-flung computer networks, it could restage for its already prominent role in *global-prop*. In late 1995, it split itself into three companies—its telephone services, which included wireless communications and connections for online companies; manufacturing; and global information systems.[10]

Nonetheless, AT&T faced problems. E-mail was making international calls local and, for many, free. The fact was that with the new technologies in place it would cost AT&T little more to carry a message internationally than nationally or locally. To charge substantially higher rates was exclusionary and an arbitrarily imposed rate structure that carried implications for oldprop.

What was more, its telephone services faced competition from the cable companies, most of whom were better positioned to offer wideband services. It had to increase its carrying capacity and offer consumer packages that would provide more lines at lesser cost. One home office with a fax, PC, and voice phone would require three lines; most tried to get by with one or two. New information and entertainment products would demand even more. The result was that consumer applications were being slowed down when they should have been speeding up. The challenge was to build up volume and structure rates in ways that would meet needs and forestall competition from other sources.

AT&T moved quickly to make its connections more attractive. In April 1996 it announced its second alliance with a server, this time with Compuserve, by which consumers would receive a discount on information services if they entered via an AT&T line. This followed on a similar agreement with AOL, meaning that 10 million users of the two major content providers would be tempted to use their existing or new or supplementary AT&T lines to access their services. Whether this would preclude cable, MCI, Sprint, or other telephone services (such as the newly emerging Baby Bells) from enjoying those benefits had not been resolved.[11]

Through its Worldnet services, AT&T now promised its 90 million long-distance customers that they could gain Internet access at a nominal fee, comparable to what they would pay through other services, but with the added convenience of having it at their fingertips at the sound of the dial tone. However, that would require the company to engage in a massive creation of new lines and expansions of bandwidth, a capability that it had lacked. AT&T would compete as aggressively with itself as with the competition.

The merger of McCaw Cellular with AT&T coupled the country's largest provider of cellular telephone service with its largest long-distance carrier. It was the largest telecommunications merger that had yet occurred and the fifth largest corporate merger in U.S. history, taking AT&T a step further toward *worldprop*. McCaw Cellular, already possessing a customer base of more than 3 million, forecast 20 million users by 2000 who could talk to one another or exchange data from virtually any location in the world. The *Wall Street Journal* headlined:

> Look! No Wires!
> The cord has been cut and communications may never be the same. Brace your-
> self for a new world. It's a world in which invisible communications networks
> gird every major metropolitan area, link workers inside office buildings and
> warehouses, and surround the earth via flotillas of satellites. It's a world in
> which wireless devices combine the functions of telephone and computers,
> sending and receiving voice, text, and graphics, and sifting through reams of in-
> formation on behalf of their human masters. It's a world in which we are all
> reachable—anytime, anyplace. And it's a world about which the main question
> isn't if, but when.[12]

AT&T was expanding the communications capabilities of the popular culture on a scale that had not been forecast and in a remarkably short period of
time. But within months, the two largest East Coast "Baby Bells" merged and
NYNEX was linked to another Baby Bell. Other mergers would follow, each
gathering diverse capabilities so that they could compete on a total and a
global basis.

Creating Media Empires

The alliance of MCI and Rupert Murdoch's News Corp. created another
model for totalprop in that it plotted the directions in which media empires,
rather than transportation systems, could expand. This would make them active not only in the creation of printed news distributed in conventional ways,
but in the creation of new news for new media. In late November 1994, MCI
brought the "Father of the Internet," Dr. Vinton Cerf, out of academic retirement to create the InternetMCI Service, making them the biggest firm to
sell access to the global network.[13]

In purchasing MCI, Murdoch acquired a total communications empire: an
electronic shopping mall, simple software for consumers, programming tools,
and consulting services for businesses. This would permit MCI to touch almost every individual, a model of totalprop:

> Until today no one has put together the right building blocks—programming,
> network intelligence, distribution and merchandising—to offer new media ser-
> vices on a global scale. MCI's strengths are terrifically synergistic with News
> Corporation's.[14]

MCI's version of Internet service, InfoMCI, customized news reports and
offered a new shopping network. It created a 24-hour news channel to compete with CNN and the new NBC–Microsoft networks and set up a news-on-
demand site on the Internet. It was said that Murdoch had "joined the rush"
to join in the all-news television field, but he had actually staked out ground
that all major media networks would have to reach.[15]

With each of these mergers and others to come—such as the marriage of
the enormous cable holdings of Time Warner and Turner Broadcasting, and
Westinghouse and Infinity Broadcasting, which dominated radio—the pros-

pect arose of the dangers of monopoly as an exclusionary oldprop. (Time Warner regained its status as the world's largest media and entertainment company, adding CNN and Turner to a formidable stable that includes HBO, *Time* magazine, and many others.)

The economics of consolidation and management would force one-time diversified holdings to adopt similar formulae to compete in the marketplace. A problem arose: How to weigh this emerging oldprop of consolidation and positioning for global competition against the need to preserve singularity?

Expanding Entertainment Empires

The megamerger of Disney with ABC–Capital Cities communication created yet another model, this the wedding of enormous entertainment resources to newspaper, magazine, radio, and television holdings to produce the world's largest entertainment complex. Disney already included Touchstone, Hollywood, and Caravan studios, animation capacities, and Buena Vista and Miramax distribution, plus an interest in Dreamworks.

ABC provided Disney with new connections as well as content, the essential components of any venture into totalprop: a television network, a news and sports division, entertainment programs, studios, and syndication capacities. Its ll television stations, radio networks, and 21 AM and FM stations provided outlets for Disney's content; thus, another synergy. These, in turn, would join with the cable and satellite TV capacities of the Disney Channel, ESPN, Arts and Entertainment, and Lifetime not only in the United States, but in Europe and Japan also. And it would own *Larry King Live* and ABC's *Nightline*.[16]

There was another side to this. Already enriched by the productions of *Aladdin* and *Pocahontas,* Disney could collect its outtakes and produce them for television. It would not wish to produce an *Aladdin 2*—the pattern adopted by film producers—because Disney was as much selling books, videos, CDs, costumes, stuffed dolls, toys, T-shirts, and other by-products of its animated hits as selling the film itself. Disney did not want children keeping its stuffed Aladdin dolls, which would occur if they produced *Aladdins 2* and *3;* it wanted them to adopt Pocahontas dolls in their stead. New productions sold products, echoes did not. This was the exploitative oldprop character of the synergy that Disney was building into its vast, point-of-sale media empire: first the thrill of the film experience, then the trips to the book, video, and toy stores to buy the images.

These synergies dramatized the upsides and downsides to the megacommunication environment and the new conception of totalprop. In some cases and at some stages they were costly, exclusive, and in their power and exclusiveness evocative of oldprop; at another stage they would be marked by lower thresholds for access and utilization.

EUPHORIAPROP: ANOTHER VISION

Another vision is that of a virulent *technoprop* that may promise more than it delivers:

> A new technology is opening up new vistas for democracy, education, and personal enrichment. . . . The government will be a living thing to its citizens instead of an abstract and unseen force. . . . Elected representatives will not be able to evade their responsibility to those who put them in office.
>
> The new medium will be like a gigantic school and have a greater student body than all of our universities put together. The year was 1922, and radio was the new technology.[17]

The lesson of history is that each time new media come along, euphoriaprop reigns, but although every new medium provides benefits, it also creates opportunities for abuse. Antitechnologists have sought to stir up a backlash against cyberprop, notably members of the Luddite Congress who, like their namesakes, wish to reject technology if not smash it. They insist that people do not have to live in a virtual Disneyland of technology but can choose to reject it.

Luddites deplore the Unabomber's use of violence, but they note that his manifesto contained numerous references to the threat of technology that were essentially valid:

> These are scary times. How much are computers going to take over our lives? We're moving toward this uniformity of commerce, this homogenization of culture . . . a lot of us want to slow things down, touch the earth again . . . create a counterculture that provides an alternative to "virtual reality."[18]

What is more, the problem of addiction among users in the home is growing; after one becomes familiar with the Net one can invest hours per day on it, much as a couch potato ingests television, although somewhat more proactive. Browsing can become a way of life, nearly as addictive as a drug, and it becomes questionable whether the individual enhances his or her experience or sublimates it by this experience.

Perhaps technoprop has taken on the character of oldprop most through its singling out the secretary as an occupational class for exploitation and potential elimination, substituting for their human services avenues for addiction as much as efficacy. As more and more middle managers use e-mail and voice mail to replace the secretary as a clerical worker, they lose their ability to filter messages. Although communication is quicker, it becomes less precise, more extensive, and less manageable.

Many people are so busy wading through overloads of e-mail—very often as many as 50 to 100 per day and in some cases up to 500 a day—that they do not have time for other work. Some even brag about their e-mail volume, an attitude described as *technomachismo*. In many cases, the excesses of communicating produce *overprop*. One executive returned from a week of vacation to find 2,000 e-mail messages awaiting him, some of them primary addressee, but most intended to inform him of an exchange between others. As a result, some companies have shut down their e-mail system for up to 4 hours per day in an effort to restore productivity.[19]

DOWNSIDES: PORNPROP AND VIOLENCE

There are downsides to entertainment and access to the network—the presence of *pornprop* and *hateprop*. In 1994 and 1995, the most visited forums were "alt.sex" versions of bondage, pictures, and spanking. AOL forums included "Women4Women," "Men4Men," "Intelligent Intimacy," and "Le Chateau." *Penthouse* publisher Bob Guccione conceded that although there was a great deal of emphasis on sex in cyberspace, all new technologies invariably were driven by publishers' interest in sex: Witness film, the movie camera, the Polaroid, and of course, the VCR. Sex and erotica were among the top four or five most attended features on the Internet, appearing as hot chat, erotica, pictures, and X-rated film clips.[20]

This brought a swift response by parents' groups and the federal government. By early 1996, Congress produced a Decency Act that held content providers and many others liable for indecencies that exceeded vaguely defined limits of content, particularly if they were accessible to, and exploited, children. Some programming relief already existed, notably New-View's iscreen software designed for parents and schools that wanted to filter and rate Web site content, Microsystem's Cyber Patrol, and Trove Investment's Net Nanny, all which recognize specific terms or phrases that are objectionable and immediately log off any chat line or service that uses those words.[21]

Certainly, child pornprop is the most abject form of oldprop, and defining permissible limits is an essential newprop. However, Sherry Turkle, an MIT professor who authored *Life on the Screen*, said this should not constrain efforts by children to gain a sexual identity, and that "no one had gotten pregnant in cyberspace."[22]

The Communication Decency Act requires installation by 1998 of a V-chip on every television set. Although the act itself was rejected on constitutional grounds, the television industry committed itself to developing its own rating system by 1997. The dispute over pornography reached international proportions when the German government—whose major cities are hotbeds of pornography—insisted that Compuserve exclude from its menu objectionable programs. Unable to do so, Compuserve shut down its European service temporarily.

Protestprop on the Net

The Internet continues through other forums to create a human-rights communication system. Where in China the freedom movement was articulated through fax machines, which were relatively slow and uncertain, the Internet afforded speed and scope. About 60 countries and territories have connections capable of tapping directly into "Gopher" sites, and e-mail is employed by 40 million users worldwide.[23]

At home, campus activism has entered cyberspace. Students have turned to the Internet on a nationwide basis to protest social policies. One result was a day of protests against the Contract With America, the campaign manifesto on which House Republicans built their legislative agenda for 1995. The demonstrations were carried out at more than 100 colleges and universities and neighboring communities.

A march in Ann Arbor, Michigan, a sit-in in Duluth, Minnesota, a fast-in Ithaca, New York, leafletting in Cedar Rapids, Iowa, and rallies in New York City, including a mock funeral procession organized by students at Columbia University, were all publicized and promoted on the Internet. At Wellesley College, students designed an "Unpetition" of the Contract With America that opposed proposals on social services, education, and the environment. Transmitted by Internet, it was printed and distributed across the country.[24]

Coping With Hateprop

A white racist group that named itself *Rahowa* (an acronym that stands for "racial holy war") has been exploiting the Internet. Resistance, Inc., marketed White separatism on its record label, produced video documentaries, promoted its bands and publications on its Internet site, and published *Resistance* magazine.

By the spring of 1995, Rahowa's membership increased from 1,000 to 4,000 and the magazine's circulation reached 13,000. White supremacists established four areas on the Internet and created seven bulletin boards to exchange messages and receive news items, documents, broadcast schedules, order sheets for racist publications, and addresses for other supremacy groups.[25]

In Germany, banned rightists found safety and anonymity online. Subsequent to a wave of neo-Nazi and skinhead violence that hit Germany in the early 1990s, federal authorities had banned at least 10 extreme rightist groups, placed hundreds of neo-Nazis under surveillance, put others on trial, and sought to penetrate their ranks.

The Thule Network is a string of electronic mailboxes that authorities say is being carried out with professional skills and whose oldprop seeks to encourage a neo-Nazi resurgence. The 90 bulletin boards offer a forum for rightist intellectuals to propagate the ideology of a New Right that embraces exclusivist, radical thinking without invoking the stridency of Nazism. The network is named for the mystical northern place that rightists view as the cradle of European civilization. However, the Thule Network is not connected to the Internet.[26]

HOW BIG, HOW COMMERCIAL?

In the final analyis, the pertinent question is not merely how the Internet and the Web will achieve a critical mass of users but how much advertising they will attract to sustain them. They will not be profitable only by selling services. Some adpropsters are experimenting with the Web despite the fact that the numbers are questionable and the demographics are concentrated. A challenge will be to get more women on the Net; another is to increase the median usage rate, as only half of all users are on the Net regularly.

For anyone who has surfed the Net, there is also the realization that time and resources are significant barriers to its use. Not everyone is willing to become addicted, and few users have the resources to buy every offering. It is likely, therefore, that other ways must be found to pay for the site products. One, of course, is to make more of them free; that is, loss leaders in the grocery store sense. Another is to depend on adprop rather than subscriptions to fuel visitations at Web sites.

By 1996, more than 250 advertisers were using them, producing a forecast that by the year 2000, $1 billion will be budgeted. This would be only .5% of the annual expenditures for advertising, but this should escalate, producing a replication of other adprop patterns.[27]

Servers must also adopt a variety of products. As one example, marketing surveys and public opinion polling are being tested. One experiment used a sample of self-selected respondents who subscribed to Prodigy. The experiment indicated that online polls can be reliable. Comparing results of a telephone and the online poll, President Clinton's popularity rating varied only a few points.[28]

ß   ß   ß

The cyberspace revolution has expanded the access, availability, and utility of information and entertainment to all generations, but most notably to the young and affluent. As a technology, however, it permits an intimacy where many communicate with many, proactivity supplants passivity, and facility replaces tedium.

Although the technology has neglected the poor and must cope with problems as diverse as ennui, addiction, violence, and pornography, steps (some technical) are being taken to address the worst problems, thus reducing its use as a conduit for oldprop.

There are structural effects, as well. Ever larger communication empires have been created to cope with innovation and marketing on a global scale. They have opened doors to a variety of services. The industrial revolution in communications carries vast implications for totalprop in the popular culture.

In a burst of political newprop, President Clinton culminated his 1996 campaigning by promising to spend $100 million to create a second Internet, and he expanded those promises in his State of the Union address in January, 1997.

> *The day is coming when every home will be connected to it, and it will be just as normal a part of our life as a telephone and a television. It's becoming our new town square, changing the way we relate to one another, the way we send mail, the way we hear news, the way we play.*
>
> *The number of people on the Web has been doubling every eight months. The Internet will be the most profoundly revolutionary tool for educating our children in generations. I want to see the day when computers are as much a part of a classroom as blackboards, and we put the future at the fingertips of every American child.*

Clinton projects himself as the cyberprop President of the techno future. At the 1997 inaugural one of the seven pavilions featured a technology playground for children and "a virtual bridge to the 21st Century." The ultimate in totalprop was President Clinton's promise that by the year 2000 every student, classroom, and library would be hooked to the Internet. That would contribute to a critical mass of 100 million people interacting on the most facile technology that ever had been devised. Clinton waxed humorous and enthusiastic. Four years ago no one but scientists had heard of the Internet; now even his cat, Socks, had a Web site. That was a level of participation in the popular culture that even the scientists had overlooked.

NOTES

1. Launch Time. (1995, August 20). Holmes, S., *Seattle Times*, Sec. F, p. 2.
2. Windows 95 Greets World Today. (1995, August 24). *Seattle Post-Intelligencer*, pp. 1/8. See Mike Smith, *Las Vegas Sun*, (1995, August 28), in *New York Times*, Sec. C. p. 3.
3. Microsoft party is just a pause. (1995, August 25). Erickson, J., *Seattle Post-Intelligencer*, pp. 1/11.
4. Gates: Internet battle just starting; Microsoft presents confident strategy; Java will be incorporated into Microsoft's Explorer browser software for Internet. (1995, December 7). Flores, M. M., *Seattle Times*, Sec. D, pp. 1/4. See also Microsoft raising the online stakes. (1995, May 10). Matassa, F. M., *Seattle Times*, Sec. D, pp. 1/4.
5. Some online discoveries give gay youth a path to themselves. (1995, July 3). Gabriel, T., *New York Times*, Sec. A, p. 1.
6. They let their fingers do the talking. (1994, December 27). Lohr, S., *New York Times*, Sec. C, p. 1.

6. An early flood of users is seen for Microsoft's online service. (1995, June 28). Lohr, S., *New York Times*, Sec. C, p. 1.

8. From calculator to communications tool; as the role of the computer changes, companies try to keep pace. (1995, June 7). Lohr, S., *New York Times*, Sec. C, p. 1/7. See also Microsoft at 20; Bill Gates at 40: A look ahead. (1995, August 13). Matassa, M. F., *Seattle Times*, Sec. A, p. 14.

9. Microsoft, NBC form media alliance. (1995, May 16). Matassa, M. F., *Seattle Times*, pp. 1/12.

10. AT&T, Reversing Strategy, Announces a Plan to Split into 3 Separate Companies. (1995, September 21). *New York Times*, p. 1.

11. AT&T Net Service to include Compuserve access. (1996, April 4). Lewis, P. H., *New York Times*, Sec. C, p. 4.

12. What a time to be online. (1995, April 23). Taylor, C., *Seattle Times*, Sec. C, p. 1.

13. For "Father of the Internet," new goals, same energy. (1995, September 25). Hafner, K., *New York Times*, Sec. F, p. 4.

14. MCI and Murdoch to join in venture for global media. (1995, May 11). Andrews, E. E., & Fabricant, G., *New York Times*, Sec. A, p. 1. See also Huge cable merger. (1994, February 24). Fabricant, G., *New York Times*, p. 1.

15. Murdoch is joining the rush into the all-news TV field. (1996, January 31). Carter, B. *New York Times*, Sec. A, p. 11/Sec. C, p. 5.

16. That's entertainment. (1994, July 10). Corr, C., *Seattle Times*, Sec. F, p. 1.

17. The great, unplugged masses confront the future. (1996, April 21). Lohr, S., *New York Times*, Sec. 4, pp. 4/6.

18. A celebration of the urge to unplug: Technology is unwelcome at gathering of modern-day Luddites. (1996, April 15). Johnson, D., *New York Times*, Sec. A, p. 8.

19. @ wit's end: Coping with e-mail overload. (1996, April 28). Dobryzynski, J. H., *New York Times*, Sec. E, p. 2.

20. Battle of the soul for the Internet. (1994, July 25). Elmer-Dewitt, P., *Time*, p. 54.

21. The Gift of Gag. (1996, March). *MultiMediaWorld*, p. 22.

22. No place for kids? A parents guide to sex on the net. (1995, July 3). *Newsweek*, pp. 46–51.

23. On the Internet, dissidents' shots heard 'round the world. (1994, June 5). Lewis, P. H., *New York Times*, Sec. E, p. 18.

24. Students turn to Internet for nationwide protest planning. (1995, March 29). Herszenhorn, D. M., *New York Times*, Sec. B, p. 8.

25. Hate groups use tools of the electronic trade. (1995, March 13). Schneider, K., *New York Times*, Sec. A, p. 8.

26. Neo-Nazis penetrate cyberspace. (1995, October 22). Cowell, A., *New York Times*, in *Seattle Times*, Sec. A., p. 17.

27. Here's the pitch: Advertisers betting Internet browsers will soon be buyers. (1995, December 18). Wilson, W., *Seattle-Post Intelligencer*, Sec. B, pp. 1/4.

28. The Prodigy Experiment: Creating a benchmark using online polls. (1995, February/March). Maisel, R., Robinson, K., & Werner, J., *The Public Perspective*, pp. 27–29.

PART II

Entertainmentprop

SURPRISINGLY NEWPROP

Because entertainmentprop often is at the margins of culture, there is a tendency on the part of politicians and social critics to condemn it. Yet it remains our greatest hope for newprop and the enhancement of the popular culture.

Filmprop, as one example, spoke in the early 1990s for the generations, but in the mid-1990s, it absorbed itself with new techniques and fantasies, each a part of a passion for profits and creativity. In the early 1990s, filmprop was mostly newprop; in the mid-1990s it became ambiguously oldprop.

Adprop has exploited the popular culture with an oldprop that is remorseless in its search for sales and profits, yet its creative energies have enhanced many desires for membership in the popular culture. The key concept is "cool," and that is newprop.

The sitcoms only flirt with reality, yet in humorous fashion they communicate the creative tensions that are experienced by younger generations. Sitcoms thus become sitlifes.

Humorprop itself has always been the opiate of the people; now its essential newprop is expressed ever more widely in television, magazines, books, theater, and in an infinite variety of literary forms—irony, parody, wit, and exaggeration.

MTVprop has been inventively newprop in its outreach to the 20-somethings and those who identify with them. Rockprop and rapprop have found their apotheosis of newprop in *Unplugged* and other programming. They have risen above their oldprop of violence and smut to become newprop voices of their generations.

By contrast, sportsprop has transformed itself into an extraordinary commercialism, often more businessballprop than a mecca for sports heroes. The 1996 Olympics created a young American heroine who was transcended by the frequency and intrusiveness of commercial messages. Dream Team III became known as "The Millionaires."

One must concede that in entertainmentprop, the newprop has far exceeded the old, but the distinctions have become blurred.

6

FILMPROP
Picturing the Generations

Filmprop does more than picture the generations; it speaks to them and for them. Sometimes exploitative of generations, filmprop in the 1990s was more newprop than oldprop, more boomerish than young or old, and more fictional than real. More importantly, it idealized the diversity and creativity of its audiences and stimulated their imaginations. However, as an art form that depended on ticket sales for its success, its descents into profit taking made Hollywood vulnerable to attack for debasing the popular culture.

The social concerns in the 1990s were broad—ambition, anger, apocalypse, conflict, death, diversity, the environment, gender, generosity, humanism, idealism, morality, politics, racism—and others too numerous to mention. Much of the filmprop of the early 1990s pictured the problems and accomplishments of generations with sensitivity and concern. However, some generations were portrayed less frequently and as less able to function within the popular culture. In some cases this responded to marketing considerations and in its exclusiveness expressed oldprop rather than the new.

SPANNING THE GENERATIONS

In some films, Hollywood spanned the generations rather than focusing on one or another of them; of these, the author chose four that were most inclusive: *Do the Right Thing, When Harry Met Sally, Schindler's List,* and *The Terminator.* Because filmprop is a dramatic form, each of these films spoke both in the oldprop and the new, but of the three generations the youngest experienced the most struggle, accomplished the least, and offered the least hope to themselves and others. The result was a sense of oldprop, the idea that an entire generation could not function in the popular culture.

Do the Right Thing: And They Did

Producer Spike Lee put it up to the three generations—the Aarpies, the Boomers, and the 20-somethings—to "Do the Right Thing!" In a vivid documentation of the tensions that arise among the generations and the races, and the conflict of poverty with the idealized values of entrepreneurship, Lee exploited both the oldprop of conflict and the newprop of self-actualization.

Two Aarpies play critical roles, one the self-appointed "mayor" of the neighborhood, a stereotype of an affable and sage old drunk (Ossie Davis) who hopes to regain the esteem of his judgmental "sister" (Ruby Dee). He spends most of his time philosophizing with three elderly Black cohorts who see failure as a race because they have been surpassed in entrepreneurship by Italians and Koreans. "Why can't Blacks do it?" they ponder.

The other prominent Aarpie is Sal (Danny Aiello), the Italian owner of Sal's Pizzeria, which is a social center for teenaged Blacks. Sal and his two sons—ineffective Boomers—are doing business in a Black neighborhood in the Bedford-Stuyvesant area of Brooklyn. There is too much competition from Italians in their own neighborhood, and their lack of a choice of locations is the source of their frustrations.

One of Sal's boomer sons (John Turturro) vents his feelings on their Black 20-something delivery boy, Mookie, who feels himself to be exploited and a failure—he is only a part-time father to his infant child and an inadequate husband to his serious-minded wife. Mookie also resents the elder Sal's flirtations with his immature young sister. All this reflects an oldprop of despair and lack of self-actualization, but it is underlined by a determination on Mookie's part to change things.

Finally, violence erupts. A Black teenager comes into the pizzeria with his boom box blasting away, angering Sal. This is Sal's territory, as he has often told the teenager; in this instance he loses control and bashes the radio with a baseball bat. That sets off a melee and brings on the police. The young man is then killed by a forearm grip fastened on him by an overzealous cop.

The film is prescient: The neighborhood becomes a mirror image of East Los Angeles as Mookie makes his statement by heaving a garbage can through the window of the pizzeria. An angered mob trashes and torches it, then moves to trash all other racial intruders and exploiters, notably the Korean grocers up the block. However, in a surprising turn of sentiment, the Koreans shout that they are "Blacks, too"; they are outsiders in that neighborhood just as the Blacks are the outsiders in the larger society. They, too, have been excluded and now want to be included.

What follows is a newprop epilogue that pleads for avoiding violence. The oldprop is demeaning and solves no problems. There must be Black entrepreneurship through a sharing and pooling of all talents—White, Black, and Korean. A new pizzeria shall rise with Mookie as a part owner; the mayor who demonstrated his heroics shall be respected by his sister ever after. Finally, each of the generations is "doing the right thing."

When Harry Met Sally: They Finally Got It

When Sally (Meg Ryan) first met Harry (Billy Crystal), they were 20-something college graduates bound for New York and success. But they were to travel the complete generational cycle into Boomerhood and Aarpieism. Wisdom, the moral tells us, is cumulative in a popular culture.

According to the special rules of 20-somethings in their small-college milieu, Harry can not become interested in Sally because he has a girlfriend and she has a boyfriend. So although they are attracted to each other, they go on to New York and career success in a prescriptive friendship that excludes commitment. To assure this outcome, they hone up on word games that guard against openness.

This struggle with their identities continues into yuppyism and Boomerism, lightened finally by the unforgettable scene in which Sally fakes an orgasm in a diner. This elicits the comment from an Aarpie woman sitting across from her when she is asked to place her order, "I'll have whatever she had!" Obviously, the Aarpie lady is into the newprop of openness, whereas Sally has just ventured into it.

Over the years, Harry and Sally earn their way into a world beyond Boomerism. In an expression of their self-actualization, they are one of several loving Aarpie couples who recall how they met, proposed, got married, and remained so. Undergirded by maturity, it is the ultimate newprop.

The Terminator: Spanning Eternity

The Terminator does not merely span the generations, he spans eternity. Arnold Schwarzenegger rides a high-tech vehicle to portray the sense of nonbelongingness and anonymity presumably felt by everyone from the Generation Xers to the jaded Boomers and the querulous Aarpies. After all, everyone is interested in Armageddon, even if its first name is Arnold and it speaks with an accent.

Our compelling character is part computer, part machine, and part flesh and blood. The flesh and blood conceal his real nature, that of a *cyborg*, a handy uninym. Arnold just happened as the result of a permutation in programming engendered by smart computers that turned out to be dumber than dumb.

The technoprop permits a parable: Teen gangs are out of control because of a senseless society that denies them economic and educational opportunities but lavishes guns on them. The Terminator, denied humanity, will destroy all of the generations so that a society that has the capacity to create and control can supercede them. But there is still hope; a woman exists who can give birth to the man who can destroy Arnold and give the popular culture another chance.

Technoprop makes the Armageddon utterly absorbing: acres of skulls, space machines, glaring lights, tortured metal, and heavy metal rock. Bare skinned (and thus immaculate in his own conception), our hero passes through time barriers (his time, Los Angeles, 2028).

His mission is to find and destroy the woman who might give birth to the man who can break this awesome cycle of oldprop conflict and lead a newprop revolution of humanism.

Schindler's List: Requiem to a Generation

For the Aarpies, this film is commemorative; for Boomers it affords a glimpse of their parents' ethical and moral experiences; and for the 20-somethings, it is a moralistic credo that documents the aberrations of modern society.

Schindler's List is addressed to all generations as a lesson in the sacrifice of humaneness. The totalitarian society was schooled by the oldprop of demonization to exterminate a race. Filmprop permits us to participate in an exalting adventure of hope while experiencing deep remorse.

The "final solution" for 1,100 fortunate prisoners is defined in pragmatic terms; Schindler (Liam Neeson), their hedonistic defender, persuades his Nazi superiors that the prisoners are trained to make critically required implements to aid the Nazi war effort. Why kill the Jewish geese who are laying the Nazis' golden eggs? Schindler will make a little money for himself, and there will be good times for good Nazis. Good deeds come from unlikely places.

The downside of *Schindler's List* continues to play for all of the generations in the Holocaust Museum in Washington, DC, where the message, again, is one of oldprop and newprop; the oldprop is reflected in the evil that mastered the minds of a generation, whereas the newprop is the construction of edifices that tell us of the tragic fruits of the old propaganda.

THE YOUNG SUBSET: GENERATION X

Let us shift context from the filmprop that encompassed all of the generations to that which addressed a single generation or a subset of it. The reader might ask, "What has filmprop taught us about these generations?"

If you felt yourself to be a member of Generation X, you were portrayed as slackers and singles, subsisting on McJobs or having no meaningful means of support. That wasn't any different from the books that were devoted to this subset of the 20-somethings, but the result was an oldprop that asserted the poverty of youth values and rationalized their exclusion from the popular culture.

Slacker: Satirizing a Generation

This film by Richard Linklater satirizes the aimlessness of Generation X, expressed largely by characters who lack purposefulness and productivity and dislike themselves for it. There are no alternatives but the present, and there are no pursuits other than the colonization of outer space and making aimlessness relevant.

Thus the book *Rush to Judgment* about John F. Kennedy is satirized by an imagined book title: *Profiles in Cowardice*. All that was, isn't, and everything that wasn't, is. That gets you mileage without the need to purchase fuel; it gets you an idea without having to reach for it; it provides a laugh without having to work for it. That's the stuff slackers are made of. *Slacker* tells us about young people who have never been there and won't get there, haven't done it, and won't do it! To do something would be premeditated; to help others is an escape from helping oneself.

Singles: An Ode to Alternative Rock

Singles gives the 20-somethings a bit of a break. At least they've got things to talk about and think about. *Singles* also turns out to be an ode to the alternative rock scene in Seattle as well as a reminder of *The Big Chill*. Contrasted with the angst of Boomers who already had made it, *Singles* tells us about the confusion of 20-somethings trying to make it and barely succeeding.

Matt Dillon plays the romantically aloof rocker, and Bridget Fonda is the lovestruck neighbor who pursues him. He hopes to make it, and even pretends that he has; Bridget does not know that she ultimately will succeed; a young professional in city planning will toss over his job out of creative frustration; a laid-back restaurant maitre d' will become an environmental professional. This is a confusing melange of failure and success, oldprop and newprop.

Singles captures the Pacific Northwest alternative rock scene. The music was provided by Alice in Chains, Soundgarden (winners of two 1995 Grammys), and members of Pearl Jam in cameos, as well as Screaming Trees, Mudhoney, Mother Love Bone, the Love Mongers, and glimpses of the late Jimi Hendrix, Seattle's long-lost rock love. This was a generation that lost and found itself in music.

THE MANY LIVES OF THE BOOMER GENERATIONS

If a cat has nine lives, the Boomer generations—early and late—have experienced at least a dozen: to transcend youth to maturity; to free themselves from the constraints of race, gender, and sexuality; to carve out careers; and to cultivate tastes for material things and the arts.

Some critics of the Boomers—even Boomers themselves—have acknowledged that they are members of "get" more than "give" generations where it was more difficult to fail than to succeed. This was the case for the ultimate Boomer, Forrest Gump, who on the basis of his shortcomings should have achieved much less.

Forrest Gump: Ultimate Boomer

Gump "spoke to" every Boomer, even to the Yuppies. Most of his success was dropped in his lap, as Boomers expected theirs to be. He did not have much in the way of an IQ, but he did not let that stand in his way. Even the story of the unlikely triumphs of an idiot savant won the film and Tom Hanks Oscars.

It has been said that *Gump* is the most successful film to equate low IQ with inner goodness, although other films have played on that theme. This was not to say that Boomers were only slightly better than dumb; far from it, but the prosperous 1980s permitted Boomers like Gump to walk into most of their opportunities.[1]

Gump didn't impress on first sight, but although crippled at birth he learned to run faster than anyone else; he couldn't carry a tune, but he could wail with a harmonica; he couldn't add 2 + 2, but he mastered intricate physics formulas, and he also philosophized, picking his way through boxes of chocolates as if he were selecting tarot cards.

Through morphing techniques, Forrest was pictured teaching Elvis Presley how to shimmy, and he inspired John Lennon to write "Imagine." Thus the film telescoped the four decades of the Boomer miracle into an anthology of rock hits. Vietnam was underscored with Creedence Clearwater Revival, Jimi Hendrix, and the Doors; Hippies streamed westward to the strains of "California Dreamin'" and "San Francisco, Flowers in your Hair." As Gump ran across America, the soundtrack blared out "Running on Empty," "On the Road Again," "Against the Wind," and "Go Your Own Way." All this honored the mythic place of rock 'n' roll in Baby-Boomer consciousness.[2]

Forrest related well to the Aarpies: He talked to them, mostly women, on park benches, and when he was old and rich, he gave his money away. Although a Boomer through and through, he never dressed for success. What does IQ measure, anyhow?

Philadelphia: A Problem With AIDS

Tom Hanks plays the Oscar-winning role of a once brilliant young Philadelphia lawyer, Andrew Beckett, who seemed, like all Boomers, to inherit the earth: first in his class at Harvard, first to be recruited by a prestigious law firm, and first in the strength of his libido.

His senior colleagues allow him to compose briefs for important cases, and they appreciate his willingness to produce compelling billing hours to match. But then things inexplicably go awry. It starts at Beckett's apartment and it somehow gets to the office.

Beckett is a homosexual, and he and his lover have known for some time that he is a victim of AIDS. He keeps doing his work, but things are going wrong at the office. Suddenly, he is asked to resign. He is told that the quality of his work has declined, but he is suspicious about the real basis for the firm's decision, and he decides to face them with his complaints and sue them for the loss of status and income that he thinks that he has suffered.

Beckett's family and lover close ranks, and we applaud when he wins the case. Law, we learn, is what he loves best, and the outcome of the trial vindicates his love. He leaves us with a powerful thought: "Law doesn't always bring justice, but when it does, it's beautiful." That is newprop.[3]

Thelma and Louise: Boomers On a Roll

Not all women who were born into the Boomer generation enjoyed the good life. One problem was male dominance: In Thelma's case it was a thoughtless sports jock of a husband and for Louise it was a male friend who was well intentioned but did not know enough about love.

They decide to stake out some freedom on a fishing trip, but it doesn't happen that way. They stop along the road to have a drink, and perhaps a dance, in what proves to be a redneck tavern. Unfortunately, they encounter a man who is used to imposing himself on women. He doesn't accept that Thelma and Louise only want to drink tough and perhaps dance tough, they don't want to love tough. When he tries to rape Thelma (Geena Davis) in the parking lot, Louise (Susan Sarandon) puts a stop to that, and when he gets uppity, it reminds her that she once had been raped by a guy like him. Still full of anger, she blows him away.

Thelma and Louise weren't men haters. They just wanted respect. They weren't teasers, they were romantics. They were as surprised as anyone when they found themselves in a classic case of role reversal. Think of it: Attractive woman shoots handsome although crude man; woman holds up a grocery store; woman stuffs a police officer in the trunk of a car after blasting air holes into it with the officer's own gun—these are newprop parodies of male violence.

Unlike more fortunate Boomers, though, Thelma and Louise run out of choices. Pursued hotly by angry male sheriffs, they drive off a cliff rather than surrender. But in seeming defeat, they self-actualize; they do what they want to do. Hard to think of this as newprop, but it is. Remember Butch Cassidy and the Sundance Kid?

Disclosure: More Role Reversal

Disclosure shows us that role reversal is the order of the Boomer day, in this case reverse sexual harrassment.

Meredith Johnson, an oversexed woman executive in a high-tech firm (Demi Moore), wants to do to male subordinates what male bosses long had been doing to her—and she does. Unfortunately, she picks Tom Sanders (Michael Douglas) as her sex slave. Somehow, Sanders manages to resist, but perhaps he resists too much.

The plot line: Meredith got the high-tech job Tom had sought for so long. ("Ugh," he had said to himself, "Not passed over, again!") But Meredith does not feel secure, so she uses the high-tech lore she has mastered to set up Tom for a fatal management error. If it succeeds he will be shipped off to Cyberia Southwest.

But Tom hires a tough woman lawyer, and he wins his case. Still, to expose fully Meredith's lack of high-tech credentials, he needs to invade a closely guarded Cyberian world of virtual reality. When he succeeds, Meredith is undone, but she is as indomitable in defeat as she was insufferable in victory. She vows she will be back from Cyberia Southwest—and Tom better believe her! Oldprop lives!

THE AARPIES HAVE THEIR DAY

Filmprop for the Aarpies has tended to be more biographical than fictional and more oldprop than newprop. *Chaplin* and *JFK* were biographical downers, and *Nobody's Fool* and *Quiz Show* illustrated the failures of a generation. However, there was redemption in *Nobody's Fool*, realization in *Quiz Show*, and sadness and joy in *Wrestling with Hemingway* and *Cocoon*, all more newprop than oldprop in their consequences.

Chaplin: More Than a Memory

How could *Chaplin*, the film, be such a downer? Charles Chaplin was a comic of the soul, and he spoke for all generations. Although he portrayed his characters as woeful and pathetic, his audiences experienced joy in the renaissence of their spirit. Chaplin was newprop to his audiences, oldprop only to the detractors of his personal life and whims.

Speaking to generations of industrial workers, *Modern Times* mimed the factory culture that dehumanized the working class, and *The Dictator* warned against the dangers posed by Adolf Hitler and the Nazi state. This was a humanist newprop in which Chaplin sought to hold open the doors of society to a downtrodden class. Those films won him respect from the Aarpies.

But *Chaplin*, the film, seemed more to censor the comic genius than to articulate his will. Only Robert Downey, Jr., who played Chaplin, saved it at all. At 22, steeped in Chaplin lore, Downey bought a house in the Hollywood Hills in which Chaplin had lived. At the Museum of the Moving Image in London, he persuaded someone to open a glass case so he could try on a pair of Chaplin's shoes, and they fit perfectly.

Chaplin lived in self-imposed exile from his political critics in Switzerland. There one of Chaplin's former maids gave Downey one of the real Tramp wing collars, and he keeps it in a safe—a reminder of Chaplin's humanism— a symbol of newprop to Aarpies everywhere.[4]

JFK: Icon for the Generations

When Oliver Stone adopted the plot line for *JFK*, he turned off a saddened generation of Aarpies, a dubious generation of Boomers, and the morbid curiosity of the 20-somethings. What was absent was what was required: JFK, icon for the generations.

Instead of bringing together the reflections of his contemporaries, Kevin Costner (as New Orleans District Attorney James Garrison) gathered a collection of political voyeurs; instead of flashing JFK's humor and style, Costner imposed the dour countenances of a legion of investigators and humorless intellectuals; even comedian Mort Sahl subordinated his sense of humor to an avocation of investigation. And Mark Lane, who had written *Rush to Judgment* and who had prospered as a lecturer on the JFK death circuit, lurked in the background.

What the Aarpie generation wanted out of *JFK* was a solution, not another problem; they wanted an icon, not an exhumed corpse.

Nobody's Fool: But We Knew That

What Aarpie has not made mistakes in life? Unfortunately, not all of us got a chance to correct many of them.

Don Sullivan (Paul Newman) has pretty much wasted his life, and at this point he doesn't have many choices. He's 60 years old (70 in real life) and about to go to jail for punching out a cop. He has turned over his halting little drayage business to his son, whom he deserted as a child.

He finds himself acquiring a taste for being grandfatherly, which, with its complications, leads him to make overtures to his son. But this impetuous act alienates his misfit best friend, who thought the business, such as it was, also was his. Finally, Sullivan acquires the sense to tell his friend that he *is* his best friend, which makes everyone happier.

This interweaving of the oldprop of irresponsibility with the newprop of awareness tells us that no matter how much we Aarpies may have failed, we still may look to the newprop of hope and redemption. As Spike Lee said, "doing the right thing" works for everyone.

Quiz Show: Destroying a Myth

I am an Aarpie, and *Quiz Show* was made for people like me. I sat on the floor every week and watched *Twenty-One* and *The $64,000 Question,* the two reigning quiz shows; however, I was more into the latter than the former because my friend, Hal March, was the MC.

The myth that the networks sold was that a person's knowledge could be infinite (i.e., the oldprop of perfectability), and my generation bought it. Professor Charles Van Doren was the son of a distinguished professor, wasn't he? But the oldprop that anyone could be perfect was demythified. Goodbye, innocence; hello, cynicism.

Wrestling With Ernest Hemingway

Francis (Richard Harris) said he had wrestled with Ernest Hemingway in Puerto Rico in 1958, but he was a braggart and a drunk. On the other hand, he might have been the kind of guy Hemingway would wrestle with, and, at his age (which varied with his recollections), no one was going to argue with Francis. After all, he had charm to go with his rascality.

Walt (Robert Duvall) never lied about his age or anything else. He was once a barber and always a Cuban and a gentleman. Lonely people, the two men became friends, but they tried to maintain their own illusions. Occasionally, they shouted at each other because friends sometimes disappoint one another, and shouting is what they sometimes do.

Francis makes passes at the equally lonely Georgia (Piper Laurie) in the coolness and virtual isolation of the noon picture show, but on a crucial Saturday date he is late and stands her up, so she puts him down. He also drinks, cusses, and courts Helen (Shirley MacLaine), but when she yields, he confesses at the critical moment that he no longer is able to oblige. She understands, and there is a beauty in it, because now Francis doesn't have to play games with her anymore.

It seems that for an alcoholic at his age, there's not much else to do but go with the flow. One could call that oldprop because it portrays all the warts. However, it is newprop because it portrays struggle, hope, and the quiet passions of Aarpies.

Cocoon: Let's Fantasize

Should Aarpies seek a better world or play the hand they are dealt? Put together a seniors cast of Don Ameche, Hume Cronyn, Jessica Tandy, Gwen Verdon, and Maureen Stapleton, and whatever imaginings they contrive almost seem to be attainable; that is, if wishing would make it so.

Rejuvenation is the first step, found in a swimming pool full of cocoons of long lost peoples from outer space. The population of the old people's residence at St. Petersburg, Florida, believes it's the water. Don Ameche's character certainly dances like it does, and when three elderly couples all get it on the night that the boys have been swimming, it becomes downright convincing. So what's wrong with wanting to get a life where one can go swimming in rejuvenating waters all the time?

But there's a holdout, a conscience, who would rather succumb as an earthling, as did his beloved wife, and stay with his roots rather than live forever in the beautiful beyond. Is this a metaphor for the Aarpies that there are no solutions, only problems, or that real problems are solutions in the higher order of things? It is oldprop that one can escape all one's problems for fantasized solutions and death can only be a problem and not a solution. Is it only Aarpies who face metaphors like this, or are they just slower to deal with them?

A PERSPECTIVE ON VIOLENCE: METAPHORS AND PARODIES

For all of their violence, *Natural Born Killers* and *Pulp Fiction* were parodies that held violence up to ridicule. Contrast such filmprop with *Rambo*, an oldprop version of retribution that has gone unchallenged as American myth. When Republican presidential aspirant Bob Dole condemned *Natural Born Killers* and ignored *Rambo*, it was self-serving oldprop.

Natural Born Killers: A Parody of Violence

"What's wrong with murder? Violence is natural," asks Mickey (Woody Harrelson). "The birds and the bees do it."

"I'm just naturally born bad. If I don't kill you," he tells television producer Wayne (Robert Downey, Jr.), "what's there to talk about?" Wayne had dreamed that he would produce a television special on "Maniacs in America" and insisted that "key-lime pie was an acquired taste." But Mickey blew him away. Under the circumstances it seemed more in the public interest—removing a self-serving exploiter of the creative process—than a remorseless act of violence.

Mickey did not care much for Wayne or television; as would be the case for many of us, he was not crazy about appearing on *Hard Copy* and *America's Most Wanted*. He thought media culture should stick to its sitcoms and its family values and stop exploiting violence. How otherwise might one react to Diane Sawyer interviewing Charles Manson and Stone Phillips chatting with Jeffrey Dahmer? But Mickey says with refreshing candor and vintage newprop, "I know what's right and wrong, but I don't give a damn."

Mallory, Mickey's young lover (Juliette Lewis), also was "born bad," and Rodney Dangerfield, Mallory's foul-mouthed father, is a parody of Archie Bunker. But there is a happy ending. After a more than successful career of wreaking mayhem, Mickey, Mallory, and their brood of kids drive off into the desert sunset in their pop phaeton to "get a life." Mallory is pregnant (again) with one of the next generation of natural born killers. If that is not the newprop of hope, what is?

Oliver Stone came to Seattle, Washington, to test *Natural Born Killers* with a young audience at the Neptune Theater in the University district. The audience members in their late teens and early 20s loved the pseudoviolence, the Tasmanian Devil, the animated cartoons, and the electronic and artistic bells and whistles, including the random switches from black and white to color and back again. And despite oldprop to the contrary, there were no reports of violence in Seattle after the film made its run.

Pulp Fiction: Looking for Redemption

Pulp Fiction simulates oldprop in its violence but it is an apocryphal tale of redemption, a brilliant newprop satire that tells how a paid killer (Samuel L. Jackson) gains a vision of his moral nirvana, holsters his piece, and sets out to find a new comfort zone.

Before he seeks his redemption, he has been an accomplice in numerous acts of mayhem with partner Vincent Vega (John Travolta), but even the gang-style excutions they carry out are surreal, and most of the principals live, die, let live, and return to review their lives. Most unreal is the interior of a VW Beetle splattered by blood and brains. The viewer realizes that it is only commentary; no mortal, however brainy, could provide that much grisly decor. And the viewer is struck by how profoundly a professional killer (Vega) actually mourned the accidental shooting. In its brilliant and curious fashion, *Pulp Fiction* is essentially newprop as it invades the distant corners of the mind.[5]

Rambo: An Ode to Vietnam

An observer of popular culture links NRA oldprop to the Rambo film culture and the Vietnam generation. This tie was first fictionalized in the 1976 film *Taxi Driver,* an oldprop novel about a veteran who is out to cleanse America of the "scum"—liberals, feminists, minorities, homosexuals, Jews, and the government itself—"who cost America the war."

This same cultural nightmare is portrayed in several books, some of them almost apocryphal.[6] *The Turner Diaries* is an eerie forecast that features the fertilizer bombing of a government building, a book that is known to have been a favorite of Timothy McVeigh, the primary suspect in the Oklahoma City bombing of 1995.[7]

COMPLEXITY ENFOLDS MORALITY

Hollywood filmprop returned in 1996 to themes that described the complex lives of diverse members of the popular culture. Most notably, they required audiences to make moral decisions rather than depend on film directors and producers for answers. All this is a quintessential newprop that tests audiences where they live.

As only one example, Susan Sarandon plays a nun, and Sean Penn is the death row inmate in *Dead Man Walking*. The audience is required to weigh the brutality of capital punishment against the consequences of a heinous crime. One oldprop is weighed against the other.

What audiences witnessed was an amoral convicted killer working his way painfully to the point of self-admission as to the pathology of his crimes. This leads him to an apotheosis of guilt and shame, but at this very moment he is led off to be executed. The audience sees a "new" human being paying the price for the old simply because both reside in the same body. Should audiences change their views of capital punishment? The film does not answer that question; the decision is left to each conscience.

In *A Time to Kill*, Samuel L. Jackson plays the Black father of a 10-year-old girl who is raped, sullied, and left for dead by two young White men. One confesses, the other is implicated clearly, and they are taken off to jail. But Jackson remembers that in a previous case like this Whites had escaped punishment for their crime, so he shoots them down on the courthouse steps.

Jackson's attorney, played by Matthew McConaughey, frees him on a plea of temporary insanity, but it promises to be a pyrrhic victory, if one at all. The Ku Klux Klan torments the young attorney, his wife takes their child and deserts him, his attractive volunteer assistant attempts to seduce him, and his community turns against him. One may be convinced that murder is never anything but oldprop, but in *A Time to Kill* the audience is forced to consider another solution.

Similarly, the filming of the book *Primary Colors* leaves the viewer to decide if he or she can accept an era of politics in which the principals, who are clearly flawed, nonetheless make vital contributions.

Thinly disguised as a fictionalized biography of President Clinton, the film asks the audience to decide what personal acts should be held truly account-able in the public eye. Mike Nichols is director, and multiple-Oscar-winner Tom Hanks and Elaine May play the major roles of President and woman po-litical guru, respectively. This powerful array of talent challenges the audi-ences to place their oldprop values of character on hold.

In another dilemma, a young Black woman reporter on *The Washington Post* tries to please her editors, confront readers, and inveigh against drug use by children in her journalistic account about an 8-year-old heroin user. But it turned out to be scarcely journalistic; she had made up the story. She could only plead in her own defense that she did not know that it would win her a Pulitzer prize, nor did she suspect that her deception would be revealed and she would embarrass her newspaper, lose the Pulitzer, and be fired from her job. One could say that the story was true, just the details were contrived.

Sixteen years later, her friend wrote the story of this woman journalist's life after journalism, and film studios vied to produce it. When filmprop actually takes up her case, audiences will be asked to pronounce her guilty or inno-cent. Did she knowingly sin against her newspaper and society, or was she se-duced by her own troubled childhood? What answer should be given to her plea for redemption?

DESCENDING INTO OLDPROP

George Lucas's film *Star Wars* brought young Americans to explore the galax-ies with Luke Skywalker, and they were captivated by the special effects and stirred by the haunting figures. Then came its equally absorbing sequels, *The Empire Strikes Back*, and *The Return of the Jedi*, each newprop for their time.

But reissued in 1997 as an even more advanced wizardry, *Star Wars* de-scended as much into the service of the marketplace as it once soared power-fully into the heavens. Now a study in nostalgia for sale, it has become an all too candid interplay of the newprop and the old—art in the service of marketing.

By early 1997 there were sales of more than $500 million in videos, $300 million in CD-Roms and video games, $1.2 billion in toys and playing cards, $300 million in clothes and ornaments, and $300 million in books and comics. Bantam Books alone published more than 25 *Star Wars* books. The sheer weight of these products turned many users into passive consumers rather than imaginative participants. And that is more of the oldprop than the new.[8]

ꓮ   ꓮ   ꓮ

Despite its tendencies to treat the generations differently, more out of commercial considerations than as artistic truths, and despite criticisms of its penchant for vi-

olence and sexuality, filmprop remains one of our most powerful forces for providing access to the popular culture.

In any balance struck between newprop and oldprop, the popular culture is overwhelmingly indebted to the newprop that underlies most of what filmprop presents. It has made passionate appeals to higher reason and equity. It has stirred imaginations. Granted its thematic exploitation, its digressions, and its profit taking, to force it to bear a constant burden of political and critical caveats would not only limit its contribution to the popular culture, but it would, in the words of its own critics, debase the culture. It is not the newprop of film but the oldprop of conformity and conventionality that will condemn us to the prisons of our minds.

Nowhere is this dilemma more explicitly defined as in The People vs. Larry Flynt, in which a publisher who first printed porn for profit discovered to his surprise that he was protected by the First Amendment to the Constitution. Intending only oldprop, he was blessed by newprop. The fortuitiveness of the situation was embraced fully by Flynt (played by Woody Harrelson) and his wife, Althea (Courtney Love).

NOTES

1. At the Cineplex, it's dumb, dumber, dumbest. (1995, January 8). James, C., *New York Times*, Sec. H, p. 1.
2. Why two soundtracks are music to boomers' ears. (1994, September 4). Holden, S., *New York Times*, Sec. H, p. 22.
3. Is Philadelphia on target in its portrait of gay life? Reactions to the film have been personal and volatile. (1994, January 10). De Nicolo, D., *New York Times*, Sec. H, p. 3.
4. Robert Downey, Jr., is Chaplin (on screen) and a child (off). (1992, December 20). *New York Times*, Sec. H, p. 9.
5. Pulp Fiction. (1994, October 10). Lane, A., *New Yorker*, p. 95.
6. Gibson, J. W. (1994). *Warrior Dreams: Paramilitary Culture in Post-Vietnam America*. New York: Hill & Wang.
7. The "Rambo" Culture. (1995, May 11). Rich, F., *New York Times*, Sec. A, p. 19.
8. The return of the merchandiser. (1997, January 30). Sterngold, J. *New York Times*, Sec. C, p. 1.

ADPROP
Appropriately Cool!

For at least half a century, a debate has raged over whether advertising is or is not propaganda. Advertising was considered to be propaganda because of its tendencies toward mass deception and exploitation, yet it also provided information on behalf of socially important causes and helped satisfy personal needs, which deemed it not to be propaganda. This book argues, of course, that we are observing propaganda in both instances, but in some cases we are addressing oldprop and in other cases the new.

In the 1990s we no longer have a mass society with a uniform state of vulnerability to mass advertising. Instead, the popular culture is characterized by diversities of generations, of tastes, of interests, and of statuses. Adprop is the child of those diverse needs. It is no longer necessary to judge if adprop exists, or if it is good or bad, only how functional or dysfunctional it is for individuals.

The bases for judging the welfare and opportunities of an individual have shifted dramatically in the 1990s. At one time, birth and family were the primary bases on which individuals were judged, and although those criteria still exist today, they are rivaled in importance by achievement and diversity. Adprop has provided members of the popular culture with a choice of images they can adopt to certify their achievements and enhance their reputations.

This is not an easy obligation for adprop to fulfill. Where in a mass society there were dichotomies between young and old, rich and poor, urban and rural, these differences are now suffused. Mass adprop, as we once knew it, has much less of a place. Instead, there has emerged a need for the segmentation of audiences into ever smaller and finite psychographic units. This has called for creative strategies on the part of adpropsters to exploit new media and production techniques.

Each of the generations has been identified and targeted. MTV devised techniques of visual presentation that became central to the psyches of the teenagers and 20-somethings—synergies with beauty, music, and fashion—and these were deemed to be "cool." Swift-paced visual and audio images were linked to products and appeals, all of which sought to create angst and allay these fears at almost the same moment in time. Adprop said it was cool to look good, even sexy, and what is wrong with being perfect?

COMBINANTS AND SYNERGIES

By a profusion of content and techniques, adprop and marketingprop have achieved one of the most dynamic synergies in our popular culture, each energizing the other. Adprop makes social judgments and sets social standards and marketing defines and segments the audiences to be messaged. Techniques speed up, the cuts come faster and faster, and everything is more symbol laden. The techniques are newprop, but the effects can be oldprop, because adprop's promises are for *you* to keep.

Adprop needs to be noticed, either by increasing the frequency of images, slowing them down, or speeding them up. No subject escapes attention; adprop and marketingprop embrace beauty, entertainment, fashion, food, personalities, politics, sexuality, sports, and hopes and dreams for the future. The frequency, the combinants, and the energies they produce contribute to a raw consciousness of total adprop.

Nothing more defines the synergies of advertising and marketing than the contrasts that can be drawn between Woodstock and Woodstock II. If Woodstock was the newprop of a generation with a sense of reckless participation, Woodstock II was an oldprop packaged for sale to a market-defined generation. The top rock groups literally counted their blessings. They came to play and be paid.[1]

The Boomers at Woodstock gathered as a tribe or generation, but they left as a market; Woodstock II began as a market and stayed that way. Every jeans manufacturer and record company was there. There would never be another Woodstock '69 because it instantly would become a part of the industrial-entertainment complex, as it did in 1994.[2]

A MATURE ADPROP FOR AARPIES

Because of the new adprop, even the Aarpies could look and feel young and beautiful. A *Newsday* correspondent described how a Manhattan poster campaign said, in a black-and-white motif: "Beauty isn't about looking young," and in a later version, "but looking good."[3] That's newprop!

The 50-Plus Expo in New York drew more than 8,000 older consumers and 100 businesses to its product exhibition in April 1994. The event included the announcement of a new discount and service program by American Express. Its marketing director noted that a tremendous group of Baby Boomers were getting into their post-50s, and they would join an already healthy, wealthy, and trendy class. The right product and the right adprop responded to upscale Aarpie needs.

The Aarpies no longer were a stereotype. That is why Geritol, which sponsored the quiz show *Twenty-One*, did not want its old brand to be shown in the film *Quiz Show*. It is customary to pay a fee for exposure in a film, but Geritol refused to do so. It insisted it had changed its product from a geriatric pick-me-up to an ordinary vitamin aimed at middle-aged women that promised to say goodbye to middle age. Did that make it oldprop or newprop, or did it depend?[4]

YOUTH MOVES IN

The cover of *BusinessWeek* foretold the shift from an emphasis on Boomers becoming a young middle-aged generation to the recognition of new and younger generations: "MOVE OVER, BOOMERS: The next generation of Americans—46 million people between 18 and 29 (the 20-somethings)—is coming on strong. Call it Generation X. It's about to change our lives."[5]

Up to that time the marketing potential of 20-somethings had been neglected. The 18-to-29 market had been considered to be lacking in affluence as well as purpose. But the realization of a huge demographic and an increased market share of cars, mountain bikes, personal computers, in-line skates, eating out, beer, fast food, and cosmetics encouraged the marketeers and merchandisers to rethink their adprop and marketprop presentations and appeals. As sales increased in response to this shift a new respect grew for 20-somethings as a generation that was based on factors other than purchasing power; it became based, as well, on their values and the necessity for being cool.

Marketpropsters were zeroing in on a segment that boasted an income of $125 billion per year. Their cohorts and their lifestyles were more diverse than those of the general population. They were more diverse racially, they differed in their needs for excitement, and they imagined themselves doing new things. Many were well educated and held a sense of optimism about the nation and their future. They were the embodiment of the popular culture, they saw adprop as newprop, and they embraced it.[6]

Many were children of television but did not see it as disabling. Sensitive to media artifices, they set high standards for commercials. Intelligent, sharp, and cool ads collected loyal followings. A Gen-Xer told writer Karen Cooperman that a friend actually had taped Levis For Women commercials so she could replay them and see all the images blinking across the screen; ads for Nike's women's line became pinups on dorm walls. Just because Gen-Xers laughed at Beavis, Butt-Head, and Bart Simpson did not mean they were imbeciles.[7]

The adprop that was devised to reach these groups was unlike the 1980s-style yuppie ads that treated luxury cars and expensive cosmetics reverentially. The new imagery was designed to appeal visually to those who had grown up on nonlinear structure and blizzards of images on MTV. The 20-somethings had been trained to receive images at a swift and multidimensional rate. But they were more complex than that; in print and in film it was necessary that the story lines—not the techniques—be slowed down so that viewers could consider the problems more cautiously; that is, be laid back and cool. This reluctance to commit was exemplifed in their preferences for T-shirts, where the favorite themes were industrial products such as drain opener and toothpaste!

IT'S CULTURE, STUPID!

As an expression of this culture, adprop in the 1990s became more subjective than literal, tongue-in-cheek rather than open, entertaining, hip, cool, and in the know. It addressed the culture in the context of its problems and their solutions. There might be reasons for consumers to feel bad, but adprop would make them feel good. Newprop addressed heightened senses of consciousness. Adprop became a license to produce coolprop:

♦ In a television advertisement, Maybelline model Christy Turlington looks cooly glamorous against a moonlit sky. A voice-over asks, "Was (it) . . . a strange celestial event . . . that gave her such bewitching eyes?" Turlington, magically transported to her living room sofa, laughs and says: "Get over it!" In effect, she says, "Don't worry about it." She's aloof, yet cozy, and perhaps even sexy, the ultimate in coolprop.

♦ Revlon has Cindy Crawford playing basketball with a racially mixed group of young men; is the newprop of diversity a problem? Certainly not for the more open 20-somethings!

♦ Rockabilly music and MTV-style musicians play in the desert. Why there? To reassure the consumer that the American West (and Taco Bell) are alive and well.

♦ 20-somethings in-line skate down a volcano and kayak over a waterfall. The context is "doing it" in the beauty and boundlessness of nature. Diet Mountain Dew became a part of that adprop of play signifying success.

♦ Women wore little footwear or apparel as they ran, walked, or carried out aerobics. These were fitness consciousness messages. Nike was only a plaything of the real thing; the adprop of a beautiful body and remaining youthful was the cool thing.

♦ A teacher urges a child to color only between the lines, but in the next shot the child is a 20-something who has abandoned traffic lanes and roared off the highway onto a dirt road in his Isuzu Rodeo off-road vehicle. That is a metaphor for "having a life," and it acts out a generation's sense of rebellion.

Beauty More Than Sex

Just as the natural beauty of the American outdoors was the physical location where every individual wanted to be, so beauty and naturalness became the psychological place where every individual wanted to be, and that was coolprop.

Kate Moss looks at you, eyes widened, full lips slightly parted, in Calvin Klein underwear, the simplest of bikinilike underpants and bra. (A fashion advertising guru told me that she is 30 pounds over her usual modeling weight for this shot, meant to give women who do not have a model's slimness permission to be beautiful at their own weight.) It is not just the usual Calvin Klein sexiness; it is beautifulness. The new adprop told you that you did not need to be perfect to be beautiful!

The cover of the March 1995 issue of *Raygun* pictured Mudhoney, a top-selling Pacific Northwest alternative rock and grunge band. They were interviewed by Eddie Vedder, lead singer of Pearl Jam, another top Northwest grunge rock band, all colleagues of the late Nirvana rock lead singer and lyricist Kurt Cobain. Inside, an ad for the magazine *Bikini* features lips and eyes, some wide open, some covered, all inviting the reader into a cryptic table of contents that tells you that everything is mysterious and beautiful, not necessarily perfect or sexy. That is coolprop.

When one thinks ordinarily of shoes, it is Nike, Reebok, Adidas, and only a few others. They have segmented the lion's share of the market by walling in the sports scene. So music and fashion have become the new means of segmentation. Interviews with rock stars and roving muses enfold a double-truck, cover-opening photo of 20-somethings, one tilting a foot over an axe, the other curled inside a shopping cart. Both are wearing Airwalk shoes, one for casual and fashionable walking, and the other with the laces untied. The men are handsome, the women are beautiful; it is relaxed and casual, a *sexprop* that is coolprop.

IN THE BEGINNING

It all began with profit-driven shifts in gender autonomy, but the consequence was that women were given full license to join the popular culture.
The profit-driven aspect was that if one could manufacture clothing that both
sexes could wear—as in the case of health and fitness apparel—it would be
that much cheaper to produce and market. Thus adprop and marketprop subtly shifted design and manufacture from sex to unisex—addressed to beautiful men and women.

Fashion guru Hal Rubenstein is credited with recognizing that the process
toward unisex began a half century ago as the first major steps were taken toward the emancipation of women. The emancipation that was being docu-
mented in adprop embraced the new *genderprop* in four unforgettable appeals:

- The Revlon "question" is embodied in allure and the reddest of cherries:
  "Who knows the black-lace thoughts you think . . . the secret, siren side of
  you that's female as a silken cat?"
- Cutting through modesty to *lèse majesté,* "Modess . . . because."
- "I dreamed . . . in a Maidenform bra."
- A couture that said, "Only your hairdresser knows for sure!"

Each model spoke for many and to many. Each was a harbinger of the new
adprop that introduced a more refined beauty and sexuality that was accessible to men and women. The understated tensions between the sexes were appropriately coolprop.

Adprop in such upscale magazines as *W* underlined the energy of youth,
their beauty, and their sexuality. The issue of April 4, 1995, ranges over crowds
in Paris, "Brits" in Los Angeles, New York's night-crawler glitterati, health,
global beauty, film stars, and Tommy Hilfiger's campaign to sell the fragrance
of a man. In that same issue is a Calvin Klein array of 20-somethings, dressed
casually chic, looking casually natural, three of them handsome African
American males and females, some talking animatedly to one another, others
looking quizzically at the reader. The message is that Calvin Klein's CK One
is a fragrance for a man or a woman. As an acknowledgment of the parity of
the sexes, it is newprop and even coolprop. As an effort to create needs, it's a
familiar oldprop.

Success, Sexuality, and Security

A noted fashion group in the Pacific Northwest who helped to innovate a
look for men and women that swept the country sees the fashion field creating niches that incorporate needs for success, sexuality, and security. Sexu-

ality is defined as a beauty and elegance that appeals to both sexes and to all generations.

Ralph Lauren's Polo label sells wealth, breeding, and success: Wear a Polo shirt and step into a mansion in Connecticut. It sells elegance, as well. The Fall 1995 issue of *W* portrays a strikingly attired, beautiful, 30-something businesswoman. She is seated opposite the reader speaking into a cellular phone. The only text on that page is "Ralph Lauren," but on a full adjoining page there is a message that says, "Work to make things better. Work because your ideas need a place to go. Work because it's part of being good to yourself. Work for all your own reasons." It is newprop in its work ethics and in its intimacy, yet because it takes the role of the other it is also cool.

Adprop in *Vanity Fair* represents Lauren elegance for the "new romantics." The couple dances ballroom style; they are young, beautiful, handsome, quietly confident, and appealing. An African American looks handsome and steadfast in a pin-striped blue suit, white shirt with wide collar, and nearly matching striped cravat.

Lauren sells elegance to the body-conscious new-rich youth. "Tyson," an extraordinarily well-formed and muscled African American, holds a mountain bike aloft; he has conquered the peak, and he is experiencing a moment of triumph and beauty. Three pages later we see a beautiful model gently filling out a white halter with "USA" printed boldly across the front; "Ralph Lauren" and an American flag are shown as binding on her biking pants. Her traveling bag says simply "Polo Sport." There is surpassing beauty, if not perfection, but as unattainable it stretches the limits of newprop.[8]

Lauren as Verticalprop

Verticalprop will come about when one designer can produce a line that facilitates the entire life experience for a generation. As one example, the "New Age in Home" has become become almost entirely *Laurenticated.*

A dramatic multipage, multicolor, modern lifestyle ad in *W* and other national magazines offers a panorama of art, furniture, bedding, lamps, clocks, and living necessities that encourage you to adopt "A (Ralph) new age, in home design, in clean lines, bold colors, that inspire a new way of looking at your home." Ralph dresses you, perfumes you, puts you into Polo stainless steel eyewear, tells you where to live, and advises you how to decorate your home.

The principle leaps out at you: Once a label is established it can take its shot at becoming total adprop. The work is done by the label, not by the products. Soon Lauren will be taking you out and getting you home, and teaching you to enjoy your wealth. All work, living, leisure, and identity will be fused by the label.

In late 1995, Calvin Klein made the commitment to vertical merchandising that would place him in a position to compete with Lauren, Yves St. Laurent, and Giorgio Armani for international prominence and control of a vast market segment. He opened a 20,000-square-foot flagship store on New York's Madison Avenue, unwrapped Calvin Klein Home, and pushed his CK One perfume worldwide.[9]

It's a Niche

These vertical and horizontal structures of adprop nonetheless produce gaps. Some of these are not large enough to yield a segment, but many are small enough to permit a niche. Thus although Lauren's Polo label sells to the affluent Boomers and Aarpies, a very sizable segment, he has left a gap for the affluent 20-somethings, and Tommy Hilfiger is one of those who has identified it as a niche.

Hilfiger's adprop invariably pictures the young, hip, affluent, and satisfied. They are beautiful, WASP, and patriotic. They go to the best places and to the best universities. They are from America's heartland of sophistication, the Eastern Seaboard. They are a slice of American cultural life, and culture is what they have to share with other young and wealthy. Sharing is newprop.

Four of Hilfiger's young male models crowd together to lean on the back bumper of a vintage car; the touch is that it has a scar or two and has been prepared in that way. It all heightens the casual, Eastern, preppie look. All are wearing bulky, loose-fitting walking shorts and casual knit shirts; they are crowded together, Tommy's boys. It is enhancement and newprop. *W* gives us a half-dozen of Hilfiger's handsome, young male models as they sit and lean against a pasture fence with a backdrop of an American flag. The red-and-white rectangular logo and text say, "Tommy, the new American fragrance." It is enhancement; it is newprop.

- The Levis brand sells safety and middle-of-the roadness; wear Levis and you will be safe, warm, and comfortable. The Levis message is a benign old-prop because it promises to take care of you and may not do so. However, there is no anxiety arousal, no problem to solve, no need to fulfil; there is a sense of comfort and a good feeling. And once this adprop has been seen, it is almost forgotten, not because the message is ineffective but because it *is* effective. It was not intended to be memorable. It simply provided assurances that with Levis you were fitting in, not acting up; nothing was demanded of you other than that you be comfortable.

- Guess jeans sell sex. The message is framed graphically in black and white, the women look like Marilyn Monroe, and the men are suave, older country-club types or they can be suave young Latinos.

In mid-1995 the look was casual and windblown, surprisingly cool. Two tousled blondes, natural looking, looking at you and perhaps talking to you, in halters with midriffs bared, full-bosomed, full-lipped, and open-eyed. They fill a page of *W*. Surprisingly, it seems, Guess jeans are not pictured in the first of several full-page shots; although the jeans are there in another shot, the labels hardly can be seen; finally in the sequence of photos, there is a young, bare-chested man with the looks of a Kennedy. He stands brazenly by a Guess jeans logo and smiles with satisfaction at us all. Everybody is happy, and as a generational value, everyone is cool. But this makes promises that it cannot keep, and that is deceptively oldprop.

Sex Isn't Out; It's New

As Guess jeans and similar products have demonstrated, sex has always been a part of advertising and has never been "out," only its approach is new. Thus adprop embraced the emergence of the "himbo," the successful, sexy, and safe hunk whose predecessor was its antithesis—the "bimbo"—an oldprop caricature who was long on uncouthness, short on brains and manners, and exuded male dominance. In the new adprop the "himbo" is a muscular, suave, and attractive male who is counterposed against female allure and allowed to radiate the same aura of sexuality. This borders on a second sexual revolution, comparable to the exploitation of female sexuality.[10]

The popular culture has become receptive to a changing image of men; muscular, bare-chested late Boomers are permitted to clasp their infants in their arms as if to extol the virtues of parenthood; sleek hairless men with bodies like Greek gods appeal to gay consumers; and "power women" are placed in business and romantic settings. This enhancement and sharing of a changing image is a new adprop, but its exploitativeness makes it oldprop.

By fusing images with a depth charge of desire adprop sells fantasy. The images promise happier, more successful, romantic, and more lustrous existences—if youth would welcome style and beauty into their lives. Why not? They had welcomed other innovations in culture. So adprop and marketprop shifted fashion appeals from content to context, to attitude and atmosphere, and to the promise of an endless future. To the extent that they delivered on their promises, it was newprop; to the extent that they were exploitative, it was oldprop.[11]

THE YOUNG, BUT NOT AFFLUENT

The young but not affluent presented a different array of challenges. On the one hand, adprop and marketingprop were responding to Gen-X innovations; on the other hand, soft drinks had become the venue for campaigns that accented the concept of coolprop. But both the Xers and the teens shared one characteristic—an aversion to anything that hinted at imposing oldprop values on them. Aging rock star Pete Townshend saw the Xers as worrying about what people were trying to do to them and reacting to it.

The Xers were committed to their own values and creative designs. Their modes of expression were music and dress. The musical expression was alternative rock, and the fashion look prescribed flannel shirts, baggy or ripped jeans, Doc Marten boots, Teva sandals, backward baseball caps, wool caps, pierced noses, and tattoos. It was not surprising that the style became known as *grunge*, a term borrowed from a corruption of "garage" as it had been applied to alternative rock music. Garage music was transformed into grunge dress. Enhancement meant dressing down, not dressing up; functionally, it was a new adprop.

Columnist Jean Godden of the *Seattle Times*, who often speaks for Seattle, asked, "Is grunge so cool that only the British could have invented it?"[12]

Whoever discovered it, a new industry emerged whose sole function was to search for used and tattered jeans—preferably torn at the knees—and for jewelry that could be worn in one's ears, eyebrows, nose, and navel. The new adprop suggested minimization as a signet of membership; to claim to be more was oldprop.

THE PEPSI–COKE WARS

Having seen the Pepsi Generation elevate youth to public consciousness, Coke sought its own specific, hip, cool, homogeneous group. But the campaign turned out to be more oldprop than newprop; somehow it was too explicit in its appeal to age rather than to youth. April 1995 was the 10th anniversary of the original Classic Coke campaign. For Coke that celebration became the commemoration of a research, marketing, and advertising fiasco rather than a successful search for a niche.[13]

But 10 years later, with both a New Coke and a renamed Classic Coke occupying comfortable consumer positions, Coke's marketpropsters were again ready to contest Pepsi's claims to the young generation. This time they were closer to the mark. The messages presumed that the teens had honed higher sensibilities and would be responsive to antidotes to the currently gloomy outlooks on the future. The creative concept was that a new Coke soft drink, to be called "OK," would address those anxieties. It assured teens that "No matter what, things are going to be OK. And this drink is OK for you!" It was appropriate that the commercial would play on MTV.[14]

The adprop would not promote the drink itself but would be expressive of the youth culture and the concept of "OKness," so-called nonadvertising advertising. According to marketing analyst Richard Yaich, the drink had so mild, fruity, and bubbly a taste, it might have qualified as a placebo. Youth were more into what they were up against than their achievements, and they would be more into what they opposed than what they supported: "They don't want to be captured. They rebel against grouping them together and then comparing them with someone else." [15]

So Coke invented a generic teenager who was assured that the true nature of OKness embraced mistakes and contradictions, optimism and irony. Guaranteed—like the adprop—not to offend but only to crawl into their consciousness, the drink was packaged in gray cans that bore inconclusive scribbled messages such as, "What's the point of OK? What's the point of anything?"

"OK" was interaction. That was newprop, but its goal, like the subtlety of the appeal, was oldprop. It was OK to talk back to "OK" through a national 800-number hotline—I-FEEL-OK—and one even could sit for a true–false "OK Soda Personality Inventory." In deep, ironic tones, a male voice said, "Sometimes people who feel OK don't deserve it," and "Groovy is just one of the ways weather can be."

Several images appear on the can. One of them is a blank-looking teenager with dark circles under his eyes. In a second image, a bar code obscures a teen's face. Yet another is the back of the head of a teenager of indeterminate age and sex, with black hair and wearing a black T-shirt. It is counterposed against the black imprint of "OK" on a white background outlined in red. The can itself is a shiny metallic gray seen by some teenagers as "cool" because it is so nondescript. And because Gen-Xers, particularly, sensed a hook in any advertising message, the adprop message said, "We're told that we're losing everyone with our advertising. It's just too hip! So now we'll do a commercial for everyone who wants to play. All you need is a little mirror. We'll play it backward, and only you can see it." [16]

The message came on the screen with letters that were reversed so that if you stood in front of a mirror and tried to read your T-shirt you could. For a generation of game players, that was cool. OK Cola was cool, so they should buy it. This was a heady combination of the oldprop of persuasion and the newprop of cultural acknowledgment.

The larger question raised by adprop is its role in the popular culture. On the one hand, adprop identifies needs and, admittedly, seeks to create them. One might argue that in identifying needs, it is functionally newprop, whereas in creating needs or diminishing standards, it utilizes oldprop. When Calvin Klein was pilloried in September 1995 for exploiting children and pornography, he pulled the offending advertising; however, to many viewers it was fresh and exciting. Klein insisted that he was "taken aback" by the reaction; the intended message was that young people had real strength of character and independence. [17]

An Answering Shot

But a cadre of trendy, Canadian, counterculture guerrillas in Vancouver, British Columbia, is launching an attack on American adprop because it has created a "shop 'til you drop" mentality in their country as well as the United States. They have adopted American techniques to fight the scourge—the 30-second spot—which it labels as an "uncommercial":

> Through the dim light of semi-consciousness, a young man stares at a television screen, transfixed by flickering images and global slogans. His head is shaved, his skin sickly pale, and like a can of corn he bears a Universal Product Code. Your room is a factory, the product is you.[18]

Is excessive consumption depleting souls and devastating the planet? Are primal instincts being supplanted by consumer urges and is our freedom being replaced by shackles of debt? Yes, say critics, and that is a consequence of oldprop. No, say their critics; the consumer and fellow consumers decided—about themselves and others—and that is newprop.

Adprop Begets Adprop

As if adprop in the 1990s was not invasive enough, the television broadcast networks launched an adprop war in which they spent so much time extolling their own programming that they overshadowed sponsor adprop. One major advertiser said it was becoming difficult to compete with the self-promotion of the networks.

The goal on the part of the networks was to achieve totalprop, an intensity of images that would lead viewers to think in terms of networks rather than programs. Just as sponsored products sought to sell their brands, so networks sought to brand their own programming so that viewers would have expectations for total network programming as well as individual shows that expressed the image. The purpose was to overcome a slippage of viewing from network television to cable programs where selection was by program rather than by cable carrier.

The goal of each network was to match the interests of a target public to genres of programming. Thus viewers would know what to expect from each network. NBC stressed its sitcoms as appealing to urbanites and singles, ABC put on comedies that appealed to the youngest suburbanites and their families, and CBS sought the return of its older viewers with the new Cosby show. Two fledgling networks, UPN and WB, appealed to Blacks and young, hip audiences in big cities.[19]

Déjà Vu: It's Coke Again

Whether adprop is oldprop or newprop is posed by the commitment of Coca-Cola to a half-billion-dollar budget in support of its involvement in the 1996 Summer Olympic Games held in Atlanta, Georgia, birthplace of Coca-Cola as an entrepreneur and a global purveyor of totalprop. The road has been both long and alluring from the standpoint of Coke, as it has sought to create its label in the image of world consciousness and achievement. That would be, on the face of it, newprop, because it represents actions that meet challenges in the search for self-realization.

However, critics of this intended newprop contend that it is essentially oldprop: a search for economic dominance, insistence on hegemony, the denial of access to others, and what seems most bizarre, an intent to associate a "junk drink" with the purity and commitment to diet that is made by every world-class athlete to his or her profession. There is no question that it is propaganda; instead the question is if it is propaganda that advances the goals of the Olympics or impedes them. To the extent that the latter is the case, it is essentially oldprop; to the extent that it has a hallowing effect, it can be newprop, even if some of those effects are to the advantage of Coca-Cola.[19]

▷   ▷   ▷

Taking into account the validity of the arguments of its critics, most adprop can be said to enhance the human experience and spur the imagination, and in these terms it is essentially newprop. Even when adprop seeks to raise our consciousness only for the purpose of exploiting it, it still contains elements of newprop that permit us degrees of choice. Adprop is not unlike music, theater, and art, in that all invite our attention, although some repel our sensitivities. In that same respect, adprop is similar to politicalprop and opinionprop, both of which seek consensus, at the same time permitting a choice that they openly and predeterminedly seek to influence.

NOTES

1. Woodstock '94, Back to the garden. (1994, August 8). Schoener, K., *Newsweek*, p. 44.
2. Yuppies to Yuppies, Seeking the soul of Woodstock, '94. (1994, August 9). Gabriel, T., *New York Times*, Sec. B, p. 1.
3. Headline surfacing. (1994, October 9). Muha, L., *New York Times*, Sec. E, p. 1.
4. Geritol does film as a pick-me-up. (1994, September 21). Elliott, S., *New York Times*, Sec. C, p. 1.
5. Move over, boomers. (1994, December 14). *Business Week*, p. 14.
6. Marketing to Generation X: reality bites, but group learns to cope. (1995, February 6). Cooperman, K., *Advertising Age*, p. 27.
7. Cooperman, K., *Advertising Age*, p. 27.
8. (1995, March 23). *Rolling Stone*, p. 2.
9. Calvin's world. (1995, September 11). Ingrassia, M., *Newsweek*, pp.60–65.
10. Beefcake on parade. (1993, October 8). Gaines, J., *Boston Globe*, in *Seattle Times*, Sec. D, p. 1.
11. How they stole the story. (1993, October 24). Rubenstein, H., *New York Times Magazine*, pp. 129–135.
12. Fashion Shade. (1995, November 10). Godden, J., *Seattle Times*, Sec. B, p. 1.
13. *Diet Coke:* has taste for old tag. (1994, September 12). *Advertising Age*, p. 1.

14. Ten years later, Coca Cola laughs at "New Coke." (1995, April 11). Collins, G., *New York Times*, Sec. C, p. 4.
15. Coke hopes the teen soft drink market finds its new product 'OK'. (1994, June 9). Huyuh, D., *Seattle Post-Intelligencer*, Sec. C, p. 1.
16. Huyuh, D., *Seattle Post-Intelligencer*, p. 1.
17. *Newsweek*, p. 63. See also Will Calvin Klein's retreat redraw the lines of taste? (1995, August 29). Elliott, S., *New York Times*, Sec.C, p. 1/6.
18. "Uncommercials" battle have-it-all world of TV ads. (1995, July 1). Williams, M., *Seattle Times*, Sec. A, p. 1.
19. A TV season when image is everything. (1996, September 20). Elliott, S., *New York Times*, Sec. C, pp. 1/5.
20. It's an Olympics homestand: Big blitz by Coke comes on its own turf this time. (1996, March 28). Collins, G., *New York Times*, Sec. C, pp. 1/6.

8

SITLIFEPROP
Flirting With Realities

Everyone calls them *sitcoms*, short for situation comedies. But many sitcoms aim for more than a laugh; they flirt with reality. They wrap the social, political, and moral lessons in humor so that each episode, each cameo, becomes a reminder of something useful to us all. Many sitcoms are innocuous, but other sitcoms address almost-real problems with almost-real people, and because they rely as much on drama as on humor, they take on the character of sitlifeprop, which, because of its messages of enhancement and hope, is essentially newprop.

Sitlifeprop has become a vital ingredient in the popular culture because it often transforms conflictual and indeterminate situations into scenes of ultimate triumph. Many of the scenarios are reflections of and catalysts for social experimentation and change. What is more, rather than expressing the loss of confidence and self-esteem that are the targets and milieux of oldprop, they lend themselves to the newprop of hope and self-enhancement. A pollster friend told me recently that the socially conscious sitcoms are "surrogate focus groups" that make judgments about problems in thoughtful and amusing ways.

THE ESSENCE OF POPULAR CULTURE

If a popular culture were to be defined by its ability to reflect diversity, the sitlife would become popular culture itself. It has given license to unbridled diversity—eccentrics, youth, the elderly, minorities, women, children, liberals, conservatives, and bigots. Admittedly, its formulaic approach to humor indulges the most repetitious of farces—which create the aura of oldprop—yet the content often is challenging, and the acting approaches high comedy. Defenders of sitcoms contend that, in any case, all comedy is formulaic.

Sitlifes and sitcoms tell it all to 30 million people who tune into them each half-hour almost every weeknight. Seven of the top 10 rated shows in the 1990s were sitcoms, appearing during prime time on the networks, on local channels, on Turner Broadcasting, Christian Broadcasting, the Family Channel, and Nick At Nite. Their profusion and their synergies of humor and moralizing make them popular reflections of ourselves. If we were to judge their contribution to our environment of totalprop it would be considerable, if only because of their number and rerun potential. There is nothing more likely to be discussed the morning after than what was on a sitcom the night before.

Today's sitlife is no longer an idealized *Leave it to Beaver*, in which a startlingly conventional family raised Beaver to be an all-American boy. Although some boomers still identify with the idealized roles of father, mother, son, and dog, most sitlifes and sitcoms have gone on to more sophisticated families and beyond them to more extended "friendship families" that exist outside the home. In fact, members of families from one show visit families on another show, thus creating a global village of sitcoms populated by sitcom characters. This broadens and even heightens the relevance of problems that they may consider.

In This Corner: "Boo" to Sitcoms

Decades ago, I sat in a New York ABC studio, where former FCC commissioner Newton Minow had condemned television in a memorable phrase as a "vast wasteland"—one, presumably, in which formulaic comedies developed plots about totally unbelievable families. More recently, the creative genius Stephen Spielberg called *Cheers, Roseanne,* and *The Cosby Show* part of a wasteland of homogenized milk, a conclusion I do not share. Minow made his reputation by describing television as a vast wasteland and opined later that he had seen a few green shoots springing up in that wasteland. Minow has not given sitlifeprop its due.

Critics persist in their contempt for the sitcoms, alleging that they lack redeeming qualities in form, content, and function; they are superficial, unrepresentative, repetitious, and maudlin, all expressive of an unredeeming, nonenhancing oldprop. To the response, "They must have some value; everyone is watching," the critics reply, "What do they get?"

The critics perceive the profusion and increasing transference of sitcom themes and characters to animation, films, and other comedic arts as the bad taking away from the good and oldprop taking from the new. They say "boo" to *The Addams Family, The Beverly Hillbillies, Dennis the Menace, The Flintstones,* and *The Brady Bunch* for reducing us to pathetic figures such as Chance, the gardener hero of the book *Being There,* a virtual moron who learned everything from gardening and television. But this comparison is tenable only in part; in its original form the irony of the book (by Jerzy Kosinski, which became a film, as well) ran far deeper than did the book and film *Forrest Gump,* the story of an idiot savant who himself succeeded only by chance.

In many respects, sitlifeprop is becoming as large and even larger than life. President Clinton hired sitcom writers and producers Harry Thomason and Linda Bloodworth-Thomason, creators of *Designing Women* and *Evening Shade,* to reshape his media image, although it can scarcely be said that what was intended came to pass. And former Vice President Quayle's effort to direct the oldprop of demonization at Murphy Brown for having a child out of wedlock boomeranged. Candice Bergen (Murphy Brown) was more able to deliver a baby—and a put-down—than was Quayle.

Ironically, the programs that contain the most frequent references to casual sex have the highest audience ratings. What is more, the humorprop in which the sexual allusions are couched permit the audiences of urban 30-somethings to find insightful, although perhaps exaggerated, reflections of their own behaviors, and this is newprop. Yet critics point to a neglect of some of the consequences of casual sex, such as AIDS. Nor do the sitcoms give much attention to sexual abstinence, safe sex, planned parenthood, social commitment, or responsibility. This is an oldprop of omission.

Perhaps the most serious criticism of sitlifeprop is that it blurs the differences between the invention of characters and real life. Much as journalists refer to other journalists for validation of journalistic reality, sitlifeprop writers and producers play off one another in cameo appearances on each other's shows to validate reality. However, major sitlifeprop characters have gained credibility in their own right: Bill Cosby, Mary Tyler Moore, Jerry Seinfeld, and Roseanne play themselves and contribute to an environment in which everyone enhances their opportunities. This is the essence of newprop, and sitlifeprop has conveyed it.

In Defense of the Sitcom

In a loving defense of the sitcom, writer Tad Friend mooned over Mary Tyler Moore's goodness. Friend had never met—on television, or off—anyone as cute as MTM, as insouciant, as loyal, and as loved by everyone. He had met different people who boasted some of these qualities, but MTM put them together into an irresistible whole. And MTM was able to deal with everyone's problems in less than 30 minutes. Friend found MTM to be exalting:

For me, now, even hearing the Mary Tyler show theme song on Nick at Nite is fiercely exalting. It's partly because the shows were weekly time capsules and conjured up those family Saturday nights . . . when I was freshly bathed, in my flannel pj's, not to be sent to bed . . . because I had a crush on Mary.

But it's mostly because MTM was so well written, well acted, and funny that it subconsciously schooled me through seep (seeping into my head and body because it enfolded it). I knew those people better than I knew anyone outside my family, and I understood them better than I understood most people in my family. So I believed that my friends, too, would get married and give birth in my apartment.[1]

Friend believed that MTM also taught him such profound lessons as how to cope effectively with loneliness, separation, and divorce; he learned that death can be borne and that life is a hard journey eased by love. All this was enhancement, a signal newprop. It didn't matter that the stories were fairy-tale truths, that fairy tales simplify things, as in Mary's version: A young woman sets out in her car toward Minneapolis alone and uncertain and finds a TV family of Murray, Ted, Sue Ann, Georgette, and Mr. Grant. In her final episode, MTM made explicit the message that was encoded in sitlifeprop: "What is a family? I think I know. A family is people who make you feel less alone and really loved. Thank you for being my family."[2]

THE FRIENDSHIP FAMILIES

Each sitlife family maintains a hearth that nurtures its identity. In *Happy Days* the creator, Garry Marshall, spoke of the difficulty of working Arthur Fonzarelli into the family. The audience liked him but he was perceived as a loner, a sex object, and someone who was somehow adrift. So Marshall made The Fonz move in over the Cunninghams' garage and got him into the kitchen, and he quickly became perceived as "family," at which point the show went to the top of the ratings.[3]

An almost infinite number of familylike groupings convene and communicate in workplaces, houses, apartments, living rooms, kitchens, taverns, and tents, as in *M*A*S*H*, spreading the newprop that openness and nurturing bring about problem solving. The myth of membership is sustained, and no one is neglected. That also is newprop; everyone gets their minute of self-actualization. No matter that most of the apartments cost more than their sitlifeprop characters could possibly afford in their roles, but this stretching of reality is justified by its ends.

The central characters of sitlifeprop span the social imagination—from the outrageous Archie Bunker in *All in the Family* to his equally redneck and talented female star of a more recent era, Roseanne. Cosby affects urbaneness, Seinfeld has a gift for procrastination (remindful in a sense of Jack

Benny), Bergen conveys astuteness, and MTM offers essential goodness. All are enhancing values.

It also is possible to experience the bizarre. *Twin Peaks* was faddish, and *Northern Exposure* was escapist, but those programs introduced viewers to the green and wet ecosystems of the Pacific Northwest and Alaska. In those *lifesitprops*, the audiences learned about "damn fine coffee" and puzzled over the inexplicable personality of Dr. Joel Fleischman. Locals were introduced to provide a suggestion of reality, and almost everyone had a "real" message to deliver that was intended to illuminate problems, if not to solve them.

I attended an auction of the sets and properties of *Northern Exposure* in Redmond, Washington, where Cicely, Alaska, population 623—cross that out, make it 607—elevation 6,572 feet, was staged. Thousands of fans, most of them 30-somethings with a goodly sprinkling of early Boomers and Aarpies, were bidding on the contents of several warehouses the size of gymnasiums. Maurice's 1967 Lincoln Continental sold for $13,500, and Chris' Harley-Davidson went for $13,000. Over a 3-day period, fans cheered each other's purchases of furniture, clothes, and oddities. They were clearing out the wardrobes and effects of friends who had just died. Sitlifeprop resembled life.

An extraordinary degree of reality pervades such sitlifes as *All in the Family, Roseanne, The Simpsons,* and *Beavis and Butt-Head.* In these cases, the consciousness is achieved by an exaggerated representation of real problems of class values. These are softened by humor, lifted by challenges, and clarified by exaggeration. *Beavis and Butt-Head,* among other animated series, illustrates how reality can be accepted in the nonthreatening atmosphere achieved by animation techniques.

The Attractions of Roseanne

The suggestion is often made that it is only because Roseanne looks and acts lower class that she manages to get away with what she says and does. But despite being named annually to Blackwell's list of "worst dressed women," she is far from unattractive. The better explanation of her success is her déclassé selection of social problems and her pragmatic solutions to them. That goodness of fit transforms her and the problems into realities with which her audiences can identify, and this is the epiphany of newprop. Forget about her conduct offstage; her audiences believe she is real.[4]

Roseanne takes on controversial issues much as does Oprah Winfrey, and she does so at a far less forgiving hour in prime time: Adolescent sexuality, parent–teenager personal space, physiological quirks, spousal abuse, female autonomy, parenting responsibilities, and economic failures and successes are her métier. She, like her audience members, often works at nonfulfilling, near-minimum-wage jobs, but she manages to buy Hamburger Helper, and this modicum of success spells a newprop of personal achievement and growth. A one-time feminist who worked as a waitress for $1.50 per hour, Roseanne exudes more than a touch of reality. Angry about her childhood, her family, her upbringing, her multiple personality disorder, and her critics, she told Jay Leno and his audience defiantly, "I think what they're really mad about is that I'm a woman calling the shots; and that I was a waitress, and that I was a maid, and I never went past the ninth grade, and I *still* do a better show than any of them."[5]

The quality of her supporting cast adds to the meaningfulness of the dialogues. Her sister, played by Laurie Metcalf, a winner of accolades for theatrical portrayals, offers no apologies for her TV role, asserting that she is proud of *Roseanne*, the writing of it, the quality of it, and what she does with it. And like Metcalf, John Goodman, who plays Roseanne's husband, is an accomplished actor in films and theater. A cast of that quality ensures that messages will be delivered with feeling, and that is newprop.[6]

All (or None?) in the Family

All in the Family was the first sitcom to wrap newprop around hard realities. One of its lessons was that even if some members of families were dysfunctional, others could pick up the slack, and they were expected to do so. An unsophisticated viewer could conclude that "all in the family would be well advised to move out," but newprop tells us that even the most dysfunctional family can find ways to work through their problems.

Ironically, the bigotry that Archie (Carroll O'Connor) mouthed was in some cases so realistic that it persuaded bigots to agree with him rather than recognize the joke. Horrendously, Bunker referred to his African American neighbors as "you people," and he mouthed freely such ethnic slurs as "coons," "Hebes," and "spicks," making the utterances seem almost natural. He described his son-in-law, Mike Stivic (Rob Reiner) as "Polack" and "Meathead," and he berated his daughter Gloria (Sally Struthers) for having married him. Yet from each vignette, viewers could gain a sense of the prevalence of a problem and the need to deal with it. The goal of the humor, risky as it turned out to be in practice, was to satirize the threat of diversity. It was tongue-in-cheek oldprop, seeking to leverage the new.

Despite Archie's crudeness, the viewer often is comforted. Bunker's emotionally impoverished wife, Edith (Maureen Stapleton), learns to guard her identity and insist on her relevance. Sometimes she protests, at other times she accommodates. Meathead and Gloria are better placed to coerce Archie, and they do. Finding bases for accommodation that would permit her to move on was not always easy for Edith, but in real life, how easy is any accommodation?[7] Yet Edith accomplished it, embodying an integral newprop.

The Simpsons: When Unreal is Real

The father is not Archie, he is Homer, the dad of *The Simpsons*. He's not as smart as Archie, but just as real. His wife, Marge, is a bit like Edith, a little less flighty, perhaps. But Lisa, the precocious, saxophone-tooting 8-year-old, and Bart, her sometimes obnoxious older brother, are something else. They can't be compared to Gloria and Meathead, who after all are married adults. However, if one takes the entire family into account, there is a resemblance. Like the Bunkers, the Simpsons are into the newprop of candor and problem solving.

The Simpsons and the Bunkers are different in that all of the Bunkers are equally responsible for the inanities, but in *The Simpsons*, the kids—Bart, and notably Lisa—do the observing. They contrast with Dad, who is a mild-mannered but undependable sort, and Mom, who does her best to cope with uncertainty. She notes that the family is forced to pinch pennies, while Homer pinches Bart's piggy bank for a down payment on a beer. The creator of *The Simpsons*, Matt Groening, also does the comic strip *Life in Hell*, and that is how Bart and Lisa characterize working-class life. The intent is to dispel the myths that being poor is its own reward and that the rich are condemned to an unhappy wealth.[8]

Thus in *The Simpsons*, poor Homer gets fired, Marge gets drunk at the company picnic, and although Bart isn't quite into rebellion, he's sometimes insubordinate, often irreverent, and even sassy to his parents. The more precocious Lisa intellectualizes and toots (on her irrepressible saxophone) everyone into defenselessness. One wonders why the Bunkers didn't assault one another. By contrast, the Simpsons actually like each other and show each other affection. Where the Bunkers by reverse strategies exaggerated ethnic diversity, the Simpsons embraced multiversity openly, from African Americans to Hispanics and South Asians, accents and all.

Bart and Lisa become our eyes, and their mischievous words express our unspoken thoughts. That is as close to reality as most of us wish to get. They speak for us when they take aim at the endless hypocrisies and deceits of the adults around them—the town's leading industrialist, the family minister, and their elementary school principal. The animation gets us in close, helping sit-lifeprop to articulate an engaging newprop.[9]

Three Cheers for *Cheers*

Cheers was a friendship family that gathered every evening in a neighborhood tavern where they could tell each other about their days at the office—although few of them had one. Surrogates for parents and professional colleagues were everywhere, but members of their nuclear families were mentioned only in passing. That wasn't reality, but it was a slice of life.

Bartender Sam (Ted Danson, who played the lead role of Lemuel in NBC's impressive 1996 production of *Gulliver's Travels*), the surrogate big brother of *Cheers*, doled out drinks and advice. Carla (Rhea Perlman), the aging and worn bar mistress, served the extended family and sometimes disciplined them in ways practiced by surrogate mothers. In the final episode, Sam set the record straight when he told his barfly friends, "I'm not your mother, and this is not your home."[10]

Cheers clings to reality by defying political correctness. It created a bar setting when bars were going out of fashion; it was sexually promiscuous (particularly Sam) at a time when AIDS was burrowing deeply into the national consciousness; it permitted excessive drinking when everyone was trying to control it; and Sam's sexuality was chauvinistic at a time when feminists were making significant gains. It was an in-your-face oldprop that had the effect of newprop because it sought to keep the social group intact against any dysfunctional intrusions of the outside world.[11]

The show enjoyed top performances not only from Danson, but from Shelly Long, George Wendt, Woody Harrelson, Kirstie Alley, John Ratzenberger, and Kelsey Grammer, among others. The governor of Massachusetts, William Weld, summed up *Cheers'* contributions as a sitlife: "*Cheers* has brought Massachusetts more fame than Paul Revere's ride, as much hometown pride as the Red Sox, and more pseudo-intellectualism, if you can believe it, than a Harvard Square Cafe."[12] One critic said *Cheers* proved that a 23-minute sitcom could be a valid art form, a creative environment that addresses the essence of a popular culture.[13]

Cheers and Jeers for the Huxtables

The Huxtables of *The Cosby Show* were an upper middle-class, African American family with a strong father, Cliff (Bill Cosby), a younger, attractive, supportive, and sometimes independent mother (a trophy wife for the older husband?), and a host of bright but oftentimes yielding children. The rationalization of this family would bring about a positioning of the oldprop in relation to the new. As one familiar oldprop, the family permitted Cliff, a doctor, to prescribe for whatever problems beset them, and he dispensed his advice with a boyish humor, overlaying the controlling oldprop with the new.

The family "lived" in a townhouse in Manhattan that boasted a lavishly decorated living room and an expansive kitchen full of electronic conveniences. Their hearth was a luxurious sofa on which Cliff constructed his oldprop moralisms, and around it his children acted out their roles as clones of idealized White upper middle-class families. In the hands of a deft comedian such as Cosby, this formula worked. As a newprop directed at the understanding of diversity, it promised its millions of viewers that there were no racial problems, just family problems: Put a Huxtable family in every White upper middle-class living room and kitchen, and your racial problems are solved.

Intermixed with this daring newprop of upscale egalitarianism, Dr. Huxtable was practicing the oldprop of hierarchical family relationships, and he promised that with love and understanding it could work. Critics contended, however, that although he loved his family, he intimidated them more than he led them. There is an episode in which Dr. Huxtable ridicules his daughter's verses for the school choir. When she rewrites them, this time including an ode to her parents, he sends her off to bed with a forgiving kiss.[14]

Indeed, one of Cosby's writers agreed that Cosby relied principally on oldprop: He dominated the children verbally rather than discussing things with them openly, he lied to them rather than pursuing common truths that were accessible to them, and he hid things from them, presumably in their best interests. This dominating and prescriptive posture of oldprop was idealized as a loving and protective father's role, but it brought the tongue-in-cheek observation that if the Huxtable family were for real, the children would require psychotherapy.[15]

Cosby obviously used sitlifeprop as a platform for projecting a threatening as well as an idealized reality. Viewing the television entertainment world about him, he saw that minorities had to be lifted above comedic to dramatic roles, and that these roles must invoke traditional as well as emancipatory values, or else Blacks would not be taken seriously in drama or in real life. Thus an oldprop of espousal of traditional family values could become the stepping stone to the enhancement of the Black professional community in the arts and in life itself. Cosby lamented that in the 1950s all Blacks had to be off the streets at an early hour and that nothing had changed; now Black performers had to be off the TV screen by 9 at night. Prime-time casting has, however, become more diverse. Nine of 10 prime-time episodes include a Black actor and more than half feature an African American in a continuing role. As a result, negative minority stereotypes have been reduced; ironically, negative majority stereotypes are substituting for them.[16]

EXTENDING MARKETINGPROP

Sitcoms and sitlifes were required to entertain if they were to attract audiences and advertising. Marketing the successes began in the early 1980s and escalated in the 1990s. Then an early Thursday evening NBC lineup (consisting at that time of *The Cosby Show* and *Family Ties*) led into later prime-time programming for even larger audiences:

> The format of these series, with their discrete themes for teen-agers, small children, and adults, as well as for the family unit as a whole, suggests a new "demographics," in which several markets are laced together to create a new kind of

mass audience . . . and moves smoothly into adult markets with the work-families of *Cheers, Night Court,* and *Hill Street Blues,* now bounced in favor of the glossier *L.A. Law;* in short, an advertiser's paradise.[17]

This has become even more the story in the 1990s. The newest of a market-segment sequence of Thursday night sitlifes includes frenetic action by an ensemble of 20-something *Friends,* cool and laid-back Jerry Seinfeld performances for 30-somethings, and an outreach to all the generations with an emergency-room hospital show, *E.R.* It has evolved into an adprop and marketingprop dream, an almost total sitlifeprop.

Friends was designed for the 20-somethings. Its story line describes the efforts of six neurotic lead characters trying to "get a life." That is in contrast to the 30-somethings, who have a life and are seeking to enjoy it. One member of the cast said it differs substantially from the 30-something plot line about people who already have made their choices in life and are trying to figure out how to live with them; for the 20-somethings this is the time when they are at the beginning of everything and are about to make those choices. This spirit of challenge is strictly newprop.[18]

One critic said that in this constant search for solutions, the "friends" interact so much they never seem to spend time by themselves. They are like the high school clique that once hung around the mall together and is just becoming grown up enough to meet in a coffee bar or someone's apartment. Although *Friends* copies *Seinfeld's* multiple story lines, quick scenes, and the density of its comedy, in affecting its "snappy" air, it falls short of *Seinfeld's* urbanity. Fortunately, that is all right with the 20-somethings, for whom urbanity is not everything. This is a value that sitcom critics do not acknowledge.

NOTHING + NOTHING = SOMETHING

It has been said that the secret of *Seinfeld* is nothing, and that is what his laid-back audience enjoys. But making almost something out of almost nothing is Jerry Seinfeld's true bête noir, and his 30-something followers identify with it. They know it is the little things that count, and they appreciate the ways in which *Seinfeld* makes sense of their lives. That enormous degree of trust and identification conveys the newprop that makes Seinfeld so easy to know.

Seinfeld once was asked about a report that he was writing a book. He hesitated slightly, then answered, "This book is not just my idea. Some editor called and asked would I be interested in doing a book about nothing based on my stand-up monologues. Why not? The stuff is already written down; all I need to do is add page numbers."[19]

Cast member Jason Alexander (George) intervenes: "A book needs a title."

"I got it," Jerry replies, "Sein-Language."[20]

On a crosstown bus to Lincoln Center, a man and woman who had just met one another rambled through a disjointed account of their jobs, families, and former spouses. Overhearing them, two friends whispered to one another, "Seinfeld." It was of minutiae such as this that the show was made: tiny problems discussed by ordinary people. In Seinfeld's hands, a hoot![21]

Triviaprop is Newprop

Fate seems at times to govern most of us, so when George notices a suspicious spot on his lip, he fears it is cancer and explodes: "God will never let me be successful. He'd kill me first." And there are endless trivial matters for the 30-somethings to identify with, like when Elaine (played by Julia Louis-Dreyfus) notices that there is a new hint of lemon in the tuna salad at the diner. Call this *triviaprop*, but the 30-somethings dig it. Trivia is reality for 30-somethings, and that makes it newprop. Seinfeld's genius is that he exploited it as something in an age of nothing:

> He (Seinfeld) spoke out fervently about not much of anything, about the implications of socks and cereal and pens and pockets—about Nothing, really. Eventually, he was given a television show on which to not do a lot. . . . Nothing gloriously transpired as characters waited in lines, looked for a parking space, smelled things or tried not to abuse themselves. "Even nothing is something," Seinfeld himself (said). Soon thereafter, people began to invest new pride in how little they did. All of a sudden, you realized you couldn't even really know another person until you saw him or her do Nothing."[22]

And Kramer (Michael Richards), his sidekick, is of the same bent. When moving men were carrying his daughter's things into a truck to be taken to her new apartment, he stopped to say, "I want to watch them." Perhaps a truck would roll down the hill unattended or the moving men would fall over a hedge. If anything at all happened, Kramer would take note of it.[23]

PROGRAMMING TO GENERATIONS

Broadcasters like successful shows, of course, but they love even more successful programming, and they love audiences who will go home with the person that brought them; that is, they will stick through a sequence of programs. It is the sitlifes that are most amenable to this phenomenon, and it is the generations at which the programming is aimed. Achieving the loyalty of one generation spells success; maintaining the attention of several generations is a smash. Each network has earned its reputation with the generations, and critic Bill Carter said that they have to meet these expectations or they will lose their audiences.[24] The following are some examples.

• ABC had a reputation for appealing both to children and to adults. *Full House* was a smash hit and a signature show for the network until it was canceled in spring 1995; it featured five children, from infants to teenagers. ABC still has *Home Improvement*. In fact, ABC shows that feature children, such as *Roseanne* and *Grace Under Fire*, are thus considered to be adult in content. In fall 1995 ABC moved *Roseanne* and *Ellen* up to 8 p.m. to try to pull adult viewers from NBC.

• Fox came onto the scene in 1986 and in 10 years established itself as a viable network choice; for its first 7 or 8 years, it relied on viewers under 25 and experienced success with *The Simpsons* and *Beverly Hills 90210*. It hired the writer of *Friends* to produce *Partners*, but it had too much of the exclusively generational sound and character that *Friends* exudes.

• CBS turned to a glitzy new identity with *Central Park West*, a prime-time soap opera. The writer had succeeded with *Melrose Place*, but with an exclusively younger audience. Trying to be slick and hip with shows like *Can't Hurry Love*, *If Not For You*, and *Almost Perfect* that were comedies, CBS failed to capture a generation, seemingly turning their backs on an older generation.

An increasing absorption with sex has posed a brooding challenge to sitlifeprop, giving it a patina of exploitation. Three of every four shows during the "family hour" contain sexually related talk or behavior. Producers protest that it's all in the eyes of the beholders; sitcom sex is not steamy, and it seldom goes beyond flirting and talk. But the verbal frankness is extraordinary, and it attracts ratings—a familiar oldprop strategy.

       ℙ   ℙ   ℙ

The reader doubtless will wish to add his or her own favorite programs and lessons from sitlifes to this sampling of pseudoreality. But whatever programs are chosen, by and large sitlifeprop works as newprop, an art form that uses comedy and drama to create approaches to problems and their solutions. It has established intimate ties with its audiences and perceives their needs for validation, itself a quintessential newprop. It has has become a genre in its own right that embraces diversity and all of the generations.

NOTES

1. Friend, T., Fleming, M., & Armitage, M. (1993, March). The stupid guy, the fat guy, the bratty White kid, the cute Black kid, the saucy wench, the bitch, the fop, the big furry dog, and the quite dead Chuckles the Clown: Sitcoms, seriously. *Esquire*, pp. 112–124.
2. *Esquire*, Friend, p. 115.
3. *Esquire*, Friend, p. 119.
4. Sitcom Reality. (1993). Berkman, D., *TV Quarterly*, *114*, pp. 63–69.

5. Dealing with Roseanne. (1995, July 17). Lahr, J., *New Yorker*, p. 42.
6. So what if she wants to stay on Roseanne? (1994, September 4). Diliberto, G., *New York Times*, Sec. H, p. 28.
7. Taylor, E. (1987). TV Families: Three Generations of Packaged Dreams, in *The Boston Review*, October, p. 5.
8. Butsch, R. (1990). *For fun and profit: The transformation of leisure into consumption.* Philadelphia: Temple University Press, p. 19.
9. *Sitcom Reality*, Berkman, p. 68.
10. The warmth of Cheers will outlive the hype. (1993, May 21). O'Connor, J. J., *New York Times*, Sec. B, p. 1.
11. O'Connor, *New York Times*, p. 8.
12. "Cheers," super sitcom, bows out with class, emotions. (1993, May 21). *Seattle Times*, Sec. C, p. 1.
13. After a fun run, curtain comes down tonight on Cheers. (1993, May 20). Voorhees, J., *Seattle Post-Intelligencer*, Sec. E, p. 8.
14. *Esquire*, Friend, pp. 119/122.
15. *Esquire*, Friend, p. 122.
16. Must Blacks be buffoons? Bill Cosby and others blast how sitcoms depict African American life. (1992, October 26). *Newsweek*, pp. 70–71. See also (1996, April 15). TV's frisky family values. *U.S. News & World Report*, pp. 58–62.
17. Taylor (1987). p. 27.
18. The joy of six. (1995, April 17). *People*, pp. 80–86.
19. It's really nothing. (1993, April 16). Boss, K., *Seattle Times*, Sec. E, p. 1.
20. Boss, *Seattle Times*, Sec. E, p. 1.
21. Boss, *Seattle Times*, Sec. E, p. 1.
22. A few qualms from a fan of Seinfeld. (1993, April 30). O'Connor, J. J., *New York Times*, Sec. H, p. 27.
23. Jerry and George and Kramer and Elaine: exposing the secrets of Seinfeld's success. (1993, July 8). *Rolling Stone*, p. 40.
24. Identity Crisis: Networks get picture: Stick to your own kind, TV viewers say. (1996, January 29). *Seattle Post-Intelligencer*, Sec. C, pp. 1/6.

9

MTVPROP
Inventively Newprop

The music was rock 'n' roll, and the channel was MTV. The programming would cater to the tastes of an audience that was young, seeking an identity, and holding unexploited purchasing power. As part of its search for identity, this generation would create a symbiosis with MTV; it would provide the audience, and *MTVprop* would provide an oasis of musical entertainment and things to buy. At its best, MTVprop would be inventively newprop; at its worst it would become a self-boosting network and a televised shopping mall.

Its inventiveness was not to be minimized, although its commercial intent was not to be ignored. From listening to music on the radio while watching television a young audience would graduate to a broadcast product that fused radio and television into a new artistic form and synergy. By setting pictures to music, MTV would win the attention and loyalty of its new audience more quickly than anyone had imagined, but it could lose them almost as quickly. Although critics said MTVprop had turned its "latchkey kids" into couch potatoes, those kids saw MTVprop as their haven in the popular culture.

The young audience responded passionately to the magic of video and multiple overlaid sights and sounds. One fleeting impression imposed itself on the other, one message compounded the other, cacophonies of bursting sounds succeeded one another, and one vision was created a microsecond after the other. Quick-cut editing and MTV became synonymous.

All these techniques were criticized as a demeaning oldprop. Had MTV techniques shortened the attention span of its youthful audiences? Perhaps, but short could be beautiful. It was faster and more efficient, rewarding the practiced eye by requiring a minimum investment of time. Where records had 33 revolutions per minute (rpm) compact discs have 360; MTV operated at 1,000 rpm. The purpose was to keep the audience's attention, create movement, keep the rhythm, eliminate visual slack, and create ideas per minute (IPMs). If the viewers kept up their IPMs, they would do all right.

Thus MTV became a product of its creators, its technologies, and the opportunities that it quickly seized. The beauty of it from a ratings standpoint was that it became necessary, not merely expedient, to repeat the high-speed visuals again and again so that all of their content could be absorbed; the speed and overlay of impressions left a great deal of connecting to be done. Viewers who wanted to tune into all of the messages had to come back to watch the same performances. Even the same viewers count in the ratings.[1]

MUSIC TO LOOK AT

As an innovation, music became something to look at, not just to listen to. The glitzy, fast-paced imagery and montage became recognizable as a style that told stories quickly. MTVprop became not merely an acronym but a uninym—it truncated and fused messages in ways that multiplied their meanings and effects.

Far from producing couch potatoes, music as pictures made the young viewer work. Where there was a gap, the viewer filled it. It became a fast-paced and expansive vehicle for the expression of problems and solutions and the creation and satisfaction of commercial needs. MTV projected messages from many to a few, substituted new forms for old, and provided new sights and sounds—primarily rock 'n' roll and rap. Its style invaded traditional media forms: Commercials became shorter and livelier, news produced smaller and smaller bites, magazines and newspapers copied television, and MTV copied life. This was an inventive newprop for a media-engaged popular culture.

Growing With Its Audiences

But MTV recognized that it could not rest on the status quo, however recently that had been staked out. It became increasingly necessary to gain a better appreciation of its audiences and to search for new ones. A Baby Boomer executive, Robert Pittman, who had grown up on rock 'n' roll, saw potential for a continuous all-music channel—not just music programming —for a young audience just as there were to be all-sports and all-news channels for jocks and news junkies.

There was evidence to support his thinking, notably the sales slump in U.S. albums and cassettes. Pittman saw this as a weakness of appeal of audio records in the face of the promise of new technologies. MTV would take on this challenge. On the day of its inception on August 1, 1981, MTV took out a full-page ad in *Billboard Magazine* that heralded "music television" (MTV) as merging the power of stereophonic sound with the visual impact of TV. Cable's first all-music channel would be beamed by satellite in stereo 24 hours a day and would show highly stylized video performances of contemporary artists.

Introducing Gender

This required a special breed of performers, those who were glamorous enough and bright enough to capture the essence of the new medium. That led to the effort to present MTV as a woman's as well as a man's world. MTV became the newest and brightest stage for such stars as Tina Turner, Pat Benatar, Cyndi Lauper, and Madonna, each of whom shifted their venues from club and concert stages to tell their stories as a newprop of self-revelation.

* Turner sang of her marital problems and her sense of slavery in her first rock solo album, *Private Dancer.* MTV heavily promoted the album's most successful single, "What's Love Got To Do With It?"
* Benatar's 1983 video, "Love is a Battlefield," achieved a multidimensional visual quality for which MTV was a perfect vehicle.
* Lauper learned to create songs by rewriting stories. As she interpolated meanings and attached them to visual properties, she became a natural on video and MTV.
* Madonna transferred her talent for flirting and daring from music and pictures to video. *Rolling Stone's* first cover story in 1984 described her success with the title, "Madonna Goes All the Way." That ability to convey her messages by images brought her fame on MTV.[2]

A Baby Boomer's Delight

This star-studded programming would appeal not only to the teenagers and 20-somethings, but to the Boomers who were attracted to musical innovations. MTV would become a launching platform for a virtual host of familiar programs such as *Night Tracks* and *Video Soul* (on the Black Entertainment channel). The networks quickly picked up on that theme, creating NBC's *Miami Vice* in the image of MTV; its working title actually had been *MTV Cops.* This was followed by *Fresh Prince of Bel-Air, In Living Color, Baywatch, Hull High,* and *21 Jump Street,* and films such as *Flashdance.* More powerful soundtracks were featured in a film genre that included *Ghostbusters* and *Eddie and the Cruisers.*[3]

PLUGGED BY *UNPLUGGED*

MTV continued to innovate with a new music program, *Unplugged*, that "pulled the plug" on electronics and turned attention back to acoustic instruments. The use of computer sequencers or prerecorded vocals would be eliminated or minimized. The music would be live, and although the resultant video clips would not be perfect, only the most patent of false starts and bad takes would be edited out. MTV again was into musical newprop.

Unplugged was a response to the flood of "virtual reality" of computer-generated, computer-manipulated sounds that was overwhelming the warmer but less flashy sounds of vibrating strings and reeds. *Unplugged* soon evolved into a controlled miniconcert that showcased old-fashioned rockers and their softer melodies. Ron Wood and Rod Stewart had not done "Reason to Believe" since they had recorded it 22 years earlier. Now they were doing it on MTV. And Eric Clapton and his cohorts could be reborn on the same stage.[4]

The disk that recorded Stewart's performance, *Unplugged . . . and Seated*, became the second best-selling album in the country. Almost three decades after The Who sang, "My Generation," the Billboard charts again were full of older rock stars. MTV had resurrected them, and even the deceased were being remembered. In 1993 The Doors, Jimi Hendrix, and Elvis Presley sold a million or more discs. Marvin Gaye, Janis Joplin, Bob Marley, Roy Orbison, and Stevie Ray Vaughn approached or exceeded a half million; the reason was MTV.[5]

When Tony Bennett was featured in an *Unplugged* segment, he jumped to the top of Billboard's Top Jazz Albums chart and remained there for 9 weeks. Bennett had come across to the 18- to 35-year-olds as sincere and even cool; he, in turn, viewed them as an audience with expanding horizons. Bennett was the ultimate in hip; his black-and-white "Steppin' Out with My Baby" video played on MTV; he appeared on the MTV Music Video Awards show with Seattle alternative band the Red Hot Chili Peppers; he did *Unplugged* with The Lemonheads and other rock artists; he did voice roles with *The Simpsons,* and he appeared on MTV's Jon Stewart talk show. He became an acquired taste for the new youth culture as an exemplar of the best of the old music.[6]

The very term *unplugged* entered the language, connoting that something or someone had stripped off the gaudy trappings of the disinformation age. When in 1995 Courtney Love and her punk-rock group Hole taped a performance for *Unplugged*, the band's ragged sound seemed to be enhanced by the format. She played an unreleased Kurt Cobain tune, "You've Got No Right," ironic in the face of Cobain's earlier refusal to sing his greatest songs on MTV. Thus oldprop became transformed into newprop.[7]

Confirming Nirvana and Pearl Jam

The miniconcerts would not only revive old talent such as Bennett, but confirm the successes of contemporary talent and put its imprimatur on promising new talent, as well. The confirmations would exploit the success of the stars whose sales already were enormous. MTV could play their edited video performances around the clock, creating a new cycle of fame and wealth.

Two of the many successes that lent themselves to confirmation were the alternative grunge rock groups of the Pacific Northwest, Cobain's Nirvana and Eddie Vedder's Pearl Jam. Both already had sold millions of records and appealed to audiences who fit the MTV specifications—the young and the Baby Boomers. They were to air on New Year's Eve, December 31, 1993, in a "Live and Loud" MTV concert special to be staged in a gigantic warehouse on Pier 47 on Seattle's Elliott Bay, the site of the shooting of the film *Singles*. MTV acknowledged that doing the concert where the alternative rock craze was born was a plus for the network.

But Vedder pleaded illness, and *Unplugged* was left with Nirvana as the headliner. Cobain took advantage of Vedder's absence to engage in vintage shrieking and caterwauling, bouncing his guitars off the stage, and helping stage divers to launch themselves into the mosh pit. Cobain even dressed conventionally, in contrast to his attire of dresses on other MTV appearances.[8] However, Vedder would be back for his confirmation, for MTV filming would give his songs exposure and the network would have Pearl Jam songs to fill out its programming, including that band's best-selling album *Vs.*

Imprimaturing the New

When MTV scouts decided to host Liz Phair and her three-man band, it was a prelude to a struggle as to who would imprimatur whom. Phair's band reluctantly agreed to perform on acoustic instruments in exchange for the MTV imprimatur as a coming talent.

Phair is one of a wave of female rockers who drew the attention of critics because of their musicianship, their politics, and their skills as image manipulators. This wave had grown up with MTV, aping Madonna in flaunting their sexuality. A critic characterized them as crafty, primal, enigmatic, and candid, but none was a prude or purely a sex kitten. All sought to expand boundaries with a social and psychological newprop. As an example, in "Divorce Song" from the album *Exile in Guyville*, Phair sang:

> It's true that I stole your lighter, and it's also true
> that I lost the map
> But when you said I wasn't worth talking to
> I had to take your word on that.[9]

But the horizons of the MTV audiences needed to be pushed out in other directions, as well. To retain its maturing audience, MTV would explore politics and such cultural interests as gender, literature, and poetry; the programming would be in the image of its audiences—from virtual reality to the bizarre.

POLITICS AS POP CULTURE

An obvious tactic in MTV's determination to become involved in politics was to invite the 1992 presidential candidates to present themselves to their youthful audiences. Predictably, Democrats Clinton and Gore accepted, but Bush postponed his appearance and Perot declined outright. Without realizing it, they had turned their backs on an MTV generation and its introduction to MTV politics. It began typically. The television screen exploded with a flash of light and a blast of hard rock from the fabled rock group Aerosmith. This signaled the enunciation of their generation's political bill of rights. The lead guitarist, Joe Perry, invoked startling sexual imagery, then intoned, "Freedom is the right to use handcuffs for friendly purposes." Steven Tyler, the lead singer, yelled: "Hey! Protect your freedoms. Vote!" "Even for the wrong person," added Tom Hamilton, the bass player.

The presentation was part of MTV's Choose or Lose and Rock the Vote campaigns, whose goal was to get out the youth vote. A free concert by Pearl Jam registered 2,400 grunge rock fans. Polls taken in late October 1992 found that 75% of the 18-to-29 age group said they would vote, compared with a 40% turnout in 1988, and they would vote heavily for Clinton (more than 60% to 40%).[10]

CEO Thomas Preston said MTV had known all along that their youthful audience was concerned and politically independent. He expanded public affairs programming to biweekly features, quick-paced news, and even hourlong minidocumentaries. *Rolling Stone* critic Jon Katz contrasted the network old news with MTV's dynamic new news: "Forty years ago, when television was born, the news consisted of middle-aged white men reading for 22 minutes into a camera. Today network news consists of middle-aged white men reading 22 minutes into a camera."[11]

Katz argued that the old news perpetuated the myth of a homogeneous national culture—an America of Ozzies and Harriets. By contrast, the new news conveyed through MTV, daytime talk shows, and other pop media reflected a country that had grown ethnically, culturally, and economically diverse; that is, it had transcended a mass culture to a popular culture. In terms of diversity, the audiences for MTV were more likely than others to differ with their parents about sex, jobs, the environment, and racism.

MTV Comes to the Conventions

MTV rocked the political conventions in 1996. On camera and in speeches and interviews the MTV-like newprops of flash, speed, and brevity substituted for the oldprops of repetition and boredom. Where once conventions were televised because they were held, now they were held to be televised.

The Republican convention was punctuated by swinging music, Hollywood sets, video and satellite transmissions, cameo appearances by Olympic heroes, a former Miss America, a paraplegic policeman injured in the line of duty, a bevy of infants in the arms of beautiful mothers and handsome fathers, survivor Captain Scott O'Grady from the hell of Bosnia, cold warrior Jeane Kirkpatrick, and ordinary citizens, great and small. Elizabeth Dole wooed the delegates with an Oprah Winfrey-type performance.

The scripting was so precise, the content modules so scheduled and interdependent, that the networks experienced difficulties in evaluating them for news content. High-tech programming had been fused with network news, infomercials, and infotainment to produce a fast-paced *varietyprop*.[12]

The "New News"

Certainly, the format of the 10-minute evening news on MTV afforded a contrast with Walter Cronkite. The program was called *The Day in Rock*, or *The Week in Rock* on weekends. The anchor, former *Rolling Stone* magazine writer Kurt Loder, dressed in black and rarely smiled, a caricature of the Reverend Dimmesdale of rock.

A typical program began with news about rock stars, for example, the controversy surrounding Madonna's new book, *Sex*. Then there was information about tours of prominent rock bands, and an interview with a rock or rap star, such as Nirvana's Cobain. There was a personal note, then a report on Michael Jackson's new multimillion-dollar contract to stage concerts for his children's foundation, sponsored by Pepsi.

MTV feature reporter Tabitha Soren took over for a 3-minute segment in which she noted that the Bush campaign had "squirmed out of another debate" with Clinton and the Senate had failed to override President Bush's veto of a motor-voter bill. Ultimately, Soren was to have President Bush and his entourage in an 8×12-foot holding room behind Bush's private car on the campaign train. Those present included Brent Scowcroft, National Security Council chief; campaign director James Baker; and presidential aides Mary Matalin and Tory Clark. However, it was 3 days before Election Day and there was only slim hope for a Bush victory. Until that day, the Bush campaign had refused MTV any access. "I'm not going to be a teeny-bopper at sixty-eight," Bush quipped.

The distractions of noise, activity, and Bush's lack of interest in the interview were telling. Soren was someone like his daughter, and he could not take her seriously. It was not until after the interview that the President's attitude changed from someone who did not want to be there to a nice guy. All of a sudden he became full of life. Oddly, it was Newt Gingrich who told MTV that he had watched the pieces they had done on the President and thought they were very professional.[13]

By contrast, Clinton's first MTV forum showcased his flair for spontaneous give-and-take with a studio audience, and it proved to be a turning point in his campaign. The demographics had become appealing: a Boomer-expanded audience that was mainly White, suburban, economically conservative, and socially liberal. And the audience numbers were formidable: 2 million a week, with as many as 8 million watching a single MTV political special. In postelection polls of 18- to 29-year-olds, 12% said MTV coverage influenced their vote. Of that age group, 22 million voted, and Clinton surpassed Bush by 5.5 million votes.[14]

With those successes, MTV news soon was to be expanded. It covered the breakdown of the Berlin Wall, the plight of dissident Chinese students, the Los Angeles riots, and Operation Desert Storm. Soren's interview with Michael Stipe, lead singer of R.E.M., an alternative rock band, rested on the assumption that that band would become the successor to Nirvana. Stipe and Cobain both were prone to ambiguous messages about sexuality and AIDS as ways of raising consciousness to honest, affirmative levels.

Tom Preston, one of the founders of the network, assessed the presence of a "sensibility gap" as a reason for MTV's special treatment of news:

> This generation, the baby busters, is totally different from us. We baby boomers felt that we had inherited the world, that we could make it anything we wanted it to be. They feel that they inherited . . . a recycled popular culture, AIDS, debt, college, and job worries, a planet on the brink of ecological suicide.
>
> So sure they're disconnected, alienated; sure they have low self-esteem. But they're not passive. They don't sit around at political protests or in front of the television. On an average, these kids watch less television than we do. They have jobs after school. They're working their (expletive deleted) . . . off. They're very conservative and hate giveaways. They don't have a lot of time for counter-culture.[15]

BOOSTERING WITH THE BEST

MTVprop took to the oldprop of self-promotion with its exclusive MTV awards program, and it has continued "in house" ever since. Beneficiaries such as the Rolling Stones, Bruce Springsteen, Aerosmith, and Snoop Doggy

Dogg have their performances filmed as videos and played repeatedly on MTV. Pearl Jam won in 1993 for "Jeremy," but it was edited five times so it could meet MTV policy standards. The nominees for 1994 included Aerosmith, Nirvana, R.E.M., and the Beastie Boys, all of which were reedited.[16]

Of an Ethical Mind

MTV audiences are sincere and ethical in their personal outlooks, but they despair of the public ethic. Thus MTVprop has focused on such issues as censorship and free speech in broadcasting. One story condemned a concert organizer's decision to drop the band Body Count, led by rapper Ice-T, from a Guns 'n' Roses concert. Their lead singer, Axl Rose, told program director John Loder, "Freedom of speech is O.K. as long as it doesn't (expletive deleted) . . . some public official." Weeks before the networks had heard of Body Count's song "Cop Killer," Loder excised the passage that suggested L.A. police officers might be killed.

In late May 1994, MTV decided to do a documentary on gangsta rap, which was coming in for its usual criticisms of obscenity, pornography, violence, and sexist attitudes toward women. MTVprop noted that although generated by a street culture that was peopled by Blacks and criminals, most purchases of gangsta rap were made by White, middle-class youth. MTVprop conceded that gangsta rap was smut, but as a social chronicle it would play itself out.[17]

RETAINING AUDIENCES

Not able to rely on an aging audience, MTV is seeking to retain one generation while courting others. Health care specials mirror the problems of youth; a 15-year-old's drug problem and easy access to handguns ensnares him in tragedy. AIDS invades John and Mary—the solution: No glove, no love. Parents abuse a young couple, but now they have joined the cycle.[18]

In June 1994, MTV broadcast its first action/adventure show. Communication was carried out through video rather than in person, and the climactic chase sequence took place in a video superstore. The soundtrack was powered by songs from a bevy of rock bands, including Nirvana, Alice in Chains, House of Pain, Stone Temple Pilots, Helmet, Anthrax, Radiohead, and Digable Planets.

MTVprop also invaded literature. In one adaptation, a performer read a bit of Kafka's *Metamorphosis*, and concluded by peering through a keyhole at a giant beetle. The program *Spoken Word* pictures writers in their milieu of cafe settings where poetry clubs sprang up in the 1990s. However trivial their subject matter, the poems spoke bluntly to their youthful generation. Rap was street poetry, a vocal, visceral expression of contemporary life:

> My Air Jordans cost a hundred with tax
> My suede starters jacket says Raiders on the back
> I'm stylin', smilin', lookin' real mean cuz
> It ain't about bein' heard, just bein' seen.[18]

In the film *Poetic Justice*, Janet Jackson played a young woman from South Central Los Angeles whose poetry expressed her emotional isolation and response to the death of those she loved. The poem, "On the Pulse of Morning," was written by Maya Angelou, the Clinton Inaugural poet. The intimacy of this content gives it an essential element of newprop.

To attract this younger audience, for whom music is acceptable content but not its only interest, MTV has accentuated its style. Clever promotional clips, smirky hosts, and quick edits exploit the short attention span and avid consumption patterns of the young audiences. MTV must provide them with information, education, merchandise, and even friends; MTV is on the computer network America Online, where its family of viewers can meet one another and exchange ideas.

Not only MTV, but sister stations Nickelodeon and VH1 moved into direct sales, so direct that by use of an 800-number the viewer could order what a performer was wearing, or the car he or she was driving. In the offing is a 24-hour home shopping channel for the MTV audience. That audience targeting proved itself when a single Rolling Stones appearance produced sales of almost $2 million, higher than the average for TV shopping malls. Shopping cameos could be shown between performances of programs such as MTV's dramas *Dead at 21* and *The Real World*. Sadly, MTV's newprop of inventiveness was subdued by the oldprop of commerce.

MTV's ascent into *total merchandisingprop* was no better orchestrated than during its Fall 1996 Video Music Awards, where everyone vied to sell their own products as well as one another. Tim Robbins ran the soundtrack of his own film, *Dead Man Walking*, before he presented the award for best alternative video. The late rapper Tupac Shakur walked around surrounded by a coterie of men in matching T-shirts advertising the controversial label Death Row Records and in the surrounding stage areas everyone was selling something, most of it having little to do with award-winning music videos.

MTV still strokes the libido of its Gen X audience. Beavis and Butt-Head are two irrepressible dunderheads who are so dumb that they are smart, so ugly that they are cute, and so inarticulate that they are profound. They are surrogates for society and serve to parody the larger culture. The show even has its own line of marketing paraphernalia, including T-shirts and underwear. David Letterman saw them as the voice of a generation and quoted them liberally. Their first book is coming out, and a movie is inevitable. *Rolling Stone's Beavis and Butt-Head* cover was the best-selling issue of 1994.[20]

THREE HEROINES GO TOTALPROP

Three heroines of MTV, Madonna, Courtney Love, and Whitney Houston have gone totalprop, diffusing their talents to film from photo spreads in fashion magazines, concerts, and CDs. Both possible Academy Award nominees, Madonna as the lead in *Evita* and Love (Aretha) as the wife of pornographer Larry Flynt (Woody Harrelson) in *The People vs. Larry Flynt*, they have pushed exhibitionism and MTV-style fare to the limits.

Houston plays the role of a gospel singer in the film, *The Preacher's Wife*, a remake of Cary Grant's *The Bishop's Wife*. She also starred in *The Bodyguard*. Janet Jackson appears opposite (the late) rapper Tupac Shakur in *Poetic Justice*, and Michael Stipe has become a production mogul.

Film stars also are going totalprop, moving into music and dance. Johnny Depp plays in a band named P., Keanu Reeves plays bass for Dogstar, and Kevin Bacon has started a band called the Bacon Brothers. Even Bruce Willis, Brad Pitt, and the late River Phoenix got into rock 'n' roll. Although they are not MTV creatures, they articulate MTV's influence in linking rock to movies and fashion.[21]

⅌   ⅌   ⅌

MTV established itself as the youth and music network and as a source of inventiveness, but it has shifted attention from the psyches of its audiences to their cerebral functions and physical needs. Past musical innovations have been extraordinary, and the creations of genres, stars, and myriad performers have been staggering.

More recently, however, MTV has gone overboard in self-promotion and award giving—neither of which has the freshness of new music—and it has headed toward becoming the shopping mall of television broadcasting, becoming as much merchandise mart as music impresario.

NOTES

1. As MTV turns 10, pop goes the world. (1991, July 7). Pareles, J., *New York Times*, Sec. H, p. 1.
2. Lewis, L. A. (1990). *Gender Politics and MTV: Voicing the Difference*. Philadelphia: Temple University Press, pp. 73–108.

3. Goodwin, A. (1986). *Dancing in the Distraction Factory: Musical Television and Popular Culture.* Minneapolis: University of Minnesota Press, pp. 24–27.
4. Unplugged in the age of electronics. (1993, May 30). Pareles, J., *New York Times*, Sec. H, p. 22.
5. Jurassic rock: do we still want to be like a Rolling Stone now that Grandpa Mick Jagger is older than the President? (1993, July 5). *Newsweek*, p. 42.
6. Tony Bennett: Mr. Cool to young and old. (1994, September 9). MacDonald, P., *Seattle Times*, Sec. M, p. 6.
7. Low voltage, high power. (1995, March 27). Farley, C. J., *Time*, pp. 70–72.
8. Nirvana's night. (1993, December 14). MacDonald, P., *Seattle Times*, Sec. E, p. 3.
9. Liz Phair; blunk rock. (1994, October 2). Pareles, J., *New York Times Magazine*, pp. 38–41.
10. But can you dance to it? MTV turns to news. (1992, October ll). *New York Times Magazine*, p. 31.
11. Katz, J. (1992, August 6). White men can't rule: A melting pot revolt. *Rolling Stone*, pp. 33–36.
12. G.O.P. readies a made-for-tv convention. (1996, August 14). Bennet, J., *New York Times*, Sec. A, pp. 1/10.
13. Cunningham, L. (1995). *Talking Politics: Choosing the President in the Television Age.* Westport, CT: Praeger, pp. 66–67.
14. Cunningham (1995), p. 67.
15. MTV meets R.E.M., a star of a different Stipe. (1995, January 13). Soren, T., *Rolling Stone*, pp. 4–6.
16. MTV awards are here. Who will be listening? (1994, September 8). Strauss, N., *New York Times*, Sec. B, p. 3.
17. Gangsta rap. (1994, May 25). O'Connor, J. J. *New York Times*, Sec. B, p. 3.
18. Out of order. Rock the Vote targets health care. (1995, May 16). O'Connor, J. J. *New York Times*, Sec. B, p. 3.
19. O'Connor, ibid.
20. Keeping Beavis and Butt-Head just stupid enough. (1993, October 17). Kolbert, E., *New York Times*, Sec. H, p. 33.
21. Music, Wlm stars overlapping in multimedia era of entertainment. (1996, November 21). Gilbert, M., *Seattle Post-Intelligencer,* Sec. D, p. 1.

10

ROCKPROP
Alienation, Fame, and Liberation

On April 8, 1994, famed alternative rock singer and leader of the band Nirvana Kurt Cobain was found dead of a self-inflicted gunshot wound in his Seattle home. As a moralist and individualist, he had expressed the complex sources of alienation of all of the generations in songs about life, but he found liberation from fame only in death.

Cobain followed the same path to eternity that was taken by another Seattle rock star, Jimi Hendrix, also a victim of fame, drugs, and alcohol. Hendrix left a legacy of unschooled genius and affability, but Cobain entangled a complex oldprop of anger and exclusion with a troubling newprop of disclosure and intimacy. Long after his death, Hendrix was to be memorialized as a favorite son by Microsoft cofounder Paul Allen with the construction of a museum to harbor his memorabilia. By contrast, Cobain's widow, Courtney Love of Hole, painfully sought a resting place for her more controversial husband.

Cobain no less than Hendrix was a rock leader of enormous stature, and he possessed an unassailable integrity. Right after his death, three Seattle bands performing in New York spoke of him as the leader of their alternative rock culture: The Melvins, who had mentored Cobain in his birthplace of Aberdeen, Washington, the heralded Pearl Jam led by Eddie Vedder, and Mudhoney. Two other limelight Seattle bands, Alice in Chains and Soundgarden, were touring elsewhere but also eulogized Cobain.

Their selections reflected the complex contributions that Cobain and the alternative rock movement had made to a generation. It was not just the musicianship; far more vital was the struggle against cynicism and profit, and the offering of hope, visceral honesty, and creativity. Just as the *rockprop* of the 1960s flowed throughout the culture to produce new forms of expression and combinants of energies, the new rockprop produced synergies among music, art, fashion, film, ideas, and even behavior. Once again, a youth culture had achieved a consciousness of totalprop.

The new music rivaled its predecessors in its energy, integrity, and creativity. Its vitality, its staggering sales, its national touring, and the constant playing of videos on MTV transformed the sound into a national phenomenon. By 1995, no one questioned where the sound actually was, but what city might be "the next Seattle." In the late 1960s it had been San Francisco, in the 1970s it had been New York's East Village, and in the 1980s it popped up in several regions. Almost every garage had spawned a grunge band. Regionalism in rock had become as trendy as microbreweries and narrowcasting cable channels, for all the same reasons.[1]

In heralding Cobain, Pearl Jam quoted Neil Young's sentiment that "It's better to burn out / Than to fade away." Mudhoney played songs like "No End in Sight," which culminates with "No one's safe until they're deep in the ground." The Melvins started their set with Alice Cooper's "Ballad of Dwight Frye" about "someone who could feel his lonely mind explode."

An analysis of Cobain's childhood revealed the agony he had suffered and the genius it shrouded. Neglected and abused as a child, he was deeply hurt and vengeful. Now that things were so different, it produced an uncomfortable and self-destructive alchemy: He wasn't happy with success, but it was a perquisite to failure; honesty was essential, but it only made lies more unbearable.[2]

One might ask, "Why Seattle?" Was it its seaport, its beauty, its diversity, its affiliation with the arts, its blend of cosmopolitanism and localism, its universities, its intellectuals, and its entrepeneurs? Or did the stimulus come from the perpetual rain in the Pacific Northwest, the rebellious subculture in which Cobain often lost himself, or the easy access to drugs? In any case, it appeared to outsiders that Cobain had fashioned his grunge music into "an elegy with an edge."[3]

Cobain's widow, Courtney Love, eulogized Cobain from his song, "In Bloom": "When I heard the song, I felt his voice . . . that presence . . . that sadness. You know the idea that someone once wrote that every abused child in America bought Nirvana's album? It's so right. I felt a comfort and soul in his voice . . . a solace that I needed."[4]

At a wake attended by thousands of followers, Love read from Cobain's suicide note that "he had lost the thrill of the crowd and did not want to fake it." He and his milieu had ridden the success and wealth of the alternative rock sound farther than any of them had dreamed. It became, in Madonna's terms, "a material sound."

On our last three tours I had a much better appreciation of all the people I've known personally as fans of our music . . but I still can't get out the frustration, the guilt or the empathy I have for everybody. There's good in all of us and I simply love people too much, so much that it makes me feel too . . . sad. So remember . . . it is better to burn out than to fade away." The note ended, "Peace. Love. Empathy—Kurt Cobain."[5]

Perhaps Cobain's greatest tributes came from the host of magazine covers in the wake of his death and a collection of writings from the editors of *Rolling Stone*, which that same year had devoted much of an issue to his achievements and foibles. The title said it all: "Our Man in Nirvana rages on about stardom, fatherhood, his feud with Pearl Jam, the death of grunge, and why he's never been happier in his life." But happiness was highly transient.[6]

Like two pioneers of rock, Pete Townshend and Neil Young, Cobain feared that the most popular sound and themes could be the most damaging messages. Rockprop must condemn societal failures and uplift the alienated and oppressed. If one could not speak from the heart, one should not sing happily. This meant that Cobain could produce a rockprop that was too raw and demanding for his audiences, but finding him was up to them; it was not up to him. Many 20-somethings, in turn, loved Cobain for his music, not for his angst; he agonized too much about the dark side of life.

Cobain performed only on his own terms; he wrote what he wrote, and he sang what he sang. The rest was a matter of interpretation. His was a dark voice, a poetic voice, or a creative voice. As he screamed his rage and confusion, his sense of ambivalence and loneliness, and his torment beyond grief, his voice shifted from drawl to howl and his guitar jumped from riff to stubborn single notes and squeals of feedback. Not every message was for everyone.

But Cobain's rockprop was show business, as well. It reechoed old sounds and exploited old approaches—smashing guitars to culminate concerts in cacophonies of expression; innovations in images, dress, and style, combining the grunge look with Madonna-like sensuality; generating anger, cynicism, and giving expression to youthful disappointment. Cobain combined this with poetic qualities, a lyrical sensitivity, and a willingness to reveal himself and his innermost thoughts to those who could identify with them, an epiphany of newprop.

Making Statements

Cobain could not resist making statements, as he called them. At a benefit for Bosnian rape survivors he performed his single, "Rape Me!," which caused widespread consternation; later, he was denied permission to play it at the MTV Music Awards. But Cobain was plaintive: "It's a life-affirmative rape song. It's like she's saying. 'Rape me, go ahead, rape me, beat me. You'll never kill me. I'll survive this and I'm gonna _____ rape you one of these days and you won't even know it.'" Cobain insisted to a *Rolling Stone* reporter that "Rape Me" was a song of retribution; the rapist was sowing the seeds of his demise.[7]

Cobain once greeted a reporter in a grungy black thigh-length thrift store dress over his flannel longjohns. He told him that wearing a dress showed that he could be as feminine as he wished. This was a plea for diversity, for although he was a heterosexual, that was no big deal; if he was a homosexual, it wouldn't matter, either. Cobain told a gay and lesbian magazine that he was definitely gay in spirit and probably could be bisexual; he angered a television producer when he kissed one of his band members, bassist Krist Noveselic, on the lips. His theme was inclusiveness, but it was an angry newprop, and it played out sometimes as an abusive, exclusionary oldprop.

Cobain's turmoil was constantly expressed in public—his use of drugs, his awesome stomach pains, marital woes, sexual ambiguities, self-doubts, and skepticism over stardom. But his troubles were a key to his popularity with a subset of Xers for whom his music expressed their own confusion. "Smells Like Teen Spirit" played on those themes. Some themes of the *In Utero* album were so ugly that vendors such as Wal-Mart and K-Mart refused to sell it. Yet *In Utero* jumped quickly to the top of the charts.[8]

His staccato style was alternatively gentle, then harsh, and it whipped his young fans into virtual frenzies. The mosh pit soon became transformed into a ritualized intimacy. It was the album *Nevermind* that led critics to hail Cobain as a voice of the new generation. To Cobain's discomfort, it largely served to make him a millionaire. The album sold 10 million copies. In "Lithium," it mixed studied self-absorption with reaching out:

> I'm so happy because today
> I've found my friends
> They're in my head
> I'm so ugly, but that's OK, 'cause so are you
>
> We've broken our mirrors.
> Sunday morning is everyday for all I care
> And I'm not scared
> Light my candles in a daze—
> Cause I've found God—hey, hey, hey.

In the second verse, Cobain welcomes his audiences in one breath and discards them with another. That is the pattern of "Radio Friendly Unit Shifter," from *In Utero*:

> This had nothing to do with what you think
> If you think at all
> Bi-polar opposites attract
> All of a sudden my water broke

> Hate, hate your enemies
> Save, save your friends
> Find, find your place
> Speak, speak the truth.

"Serve the Servants" in *In Utero* says plaintively but forgivingly:

> Teenage angst has paid off well
> Now I'm bored and old
> Self-apppointed judges judge
> More than they have sold.
>
> I tried hard to have a father
> But instead I had a Dad
>
> I just want you to know that I
> Don't hate you any more
> There is nothing I could say
> That I haven't thought before.

Although many of his young audiences took his openness as an invitation, Cobain didn't want to be the leader of a generation. On *In Utero* he shouted in desperation, "Go Away, get away, get away." That wasn't what his fans wanted to hear, so *In Utero* dropped in the charts. Ironically, after his death it climbed, but among the thousands of letters that were written by youths to newspapers, there was a consensus that Cobain had aroused them and had the courage to express their thoughts. One letter read:

> The national rock scene was yawning along. . . . Then came a compelling young musician with a dynamic, throaty voice, and a wellspring of talent that seemed endless. Kurt Cobain had a social conscience, and the courage to write about it—a cherished quality, rare in the industry today. It was, in the estimation of the countless who adored Nirvana, the best marriage of lyric and music to set us dancing and wondering, to challenge and charm us for a very long while. It was a voice for the age, and a very important one for our times. *Katie Hess.*[9]

Pearl Jam: More Instant Fame and Terror

Often a protagonist of Cobain as well as his successor in the instant riches of the alternative rock movement, Eddie Vedder became another Northwest victim of instant fame. Virtuoso in sound although less dynamic in lyrics, from his first hit song, "Alive," to the hard-hitting album *Vs.*, Vedder reached out more deliberately to pursue a newprop of inclusion for those Xers who had suffered more of what is bad and less of what is good, who had endured confusion, despair, and abandonment. Drummer Dave Abbruzzese said he was happy that Pearl Jam "finally is in a position to make a difference. A lot of the time you feel pretty powerless as a single person."[10]

Although their childhood experiences were somewhat similar, Vedder seemed to be looking for new friends whereas Cobain avoided them. Unpleasant as they were, and however limited his friendships, Cobain knew his roots. On *Nevermind* Cobain sang satirically, "Our little group always was and always will until the end . . . a mulatto, an albino, a mosquito, my libido." But Vedder sang ruefully of his mother's cruelty in withholding his identity:

> "Son," she says, "I've got a little story for you . . .
> What you thought was your daddy was nothin' but a . . .
> While you were sitting home alone at age 13,
> your real daddy was dyin'
> Sorry you didn't see him but I'm glad we talked."

Vs. struck a chord with its pleading lyrics of despair, asking "don't go on me now," bemoaning "a daughter, painted room, can't deny there's something wrong," noting "a dissident is here, she couldn't hold, she folded," and addressing racial bias in "W.M.A," "who won the lottery when he was born," among other haunting themes. This was a complex newprop of compassion and despair, and it quickly became the top rock album in the country, selling more than 1 million copies in its first week and 2 million copies in its first month. Pearl Jam's debut disc, *Ten*, had sold more than 5 million. The band landed on the covers of *Rolling Stone, Musician, Spin,* and *Time* magazines.

Himself part Cherokee, Vedder sang of the need to resist the loss of native Indian ceremonial grounds atop Mt. Graham near Mesa, Arizona. Known as *dzil n'chnaa si'an* to the San Carlos Apache people, the community included descendants of Geronimo and Cochise and was regarded by the tribes as a spiritual pathway that carried their prayers to their creators. Urging concertgoers to get involved in the saving of a culture, Vedder draped a University of Arizona sweatshirt over his microphone and set it afire.[11]

In its enthusiasm for inclusiveness, Pearl Jam picked a quarrel with Ticketmaster, the corporation that services ticket sales for most major rock performances. Vedder insisted that the agency join in cutting prices to permit lower cost concerts for young people. The result was to block appearances in major tour cities, but Pearl Jam was willing to pay for its principles. In an awkward fashion, Vedder's newprop sought to open the doors of the popular culture to the poor, the misunderstood, and the abused, to assess relationships, urban violence and decay, racism, overpopulation, and adolescents' fears for the future.

Pearl Jam continued to fight Ticketmaster and espouse family values. Opening a concert swing in September 1996 that would take him across the United States, to Europe, and Australia, Eddie Vedder sang passionately in "Habit" against drug abuse, and he pledged that he would be there at the turn of the century to lead that crusade. His emphasis was on exploration and meditation and that, coupled with his passion, sounded the tocsin for a newprop of engagement and commitment.

RETURN OF THE MESSIAHS

A revived generation including Neil Young, Pete Townshend, and Eric Clapton returned in the 1990s with a newfound appeal and financial success. They sang a sentimental newprop of love, loss, and rebirth.[12]

Townshend won five Emmys with The Who's production of *Tommy*. He wrote *Psychoderelict* as his own disturbing history, the saga of an aging rocker who overcame drugs and failure to achieve his hopes for "creative rebirth." The album failed, but as I watched the Broadway production, and listened to the plaintive songs, I could see why *Tommy* had succeeded as a stage play. But as Cobain and Vedder expressed it, the unseemly financial success was what the aging rocker feared.

Clapton had fallen into eclipse because of his grief over the loss of his 4-year-old son. At one time a victim of alcohol and drug addiction, Clapton returned to tell his story. Although he swept the 1993 Grammy Awards in the pop and rock categories, he feared that his albums were not worth releasing. There were better songs than "Tears of Heaven," the ballad he wrote and sang for his son, yet that was named the record of the year, best pop vocal performance, and song of the year.

Clapton believed that for the Boomers the distant horizon of mortality no longer appeared infinite. Because of AIDS, large numbers of talented and decent people were not going to get their three score and 10. The mysterious ways of God had become an immediate concern, and death had come to be disproportionately final, overwhelming, and arbitrary. Disturbing as this was, the profundity of sharing it with the popular culture made it the essence of newprop.

A Family of Deadheads

Concertgoers of the Grateful Dead were not just fans, they were family, and they enjoyed a sense of community. Jerry Garcia was a pied piper for the generation of the 1960s, leading his "deadheads" to the next divide. His music was everything and everywhere—rock, jazz, and blues. It was gentle and kind. If a sense of inclusion defined newprop in the popular culture, the Grateful Dead was its apotheosis.[13]

When Garcia died in August 1995, he left a legacy of musical adventure. Steve Goldsmith, a reporter who had followed Garcia during his beginnings in San Francisco's Haight-Ashbury district in the 1960s was at his Seattle concert in May 1995. Incredible bursts of energy shot through the crowd. When a flock of Canadian geese winged its way in formation it drew spontaneous cheers, and the Dead had a song for it; and when the moon was rising they broke into "Standing on the Moon."

The deadheads represented every generation and every station in life: the great and the powerful, from senators to artists, and even the President of the United States, Bill Clinton, who collected Jerry Garcia ties and gave them to his friends. The Dead reveled in American myth; they loved the country and its diversity; they were musically diverse, creative, and inspiring. They loved America by loving their music without anger or anarchy. Aptly named, Jerry Garcia was a soul of newprop and the inimitable psychedelic Uncle Sam.[14]

CALL IT BUSINESSROCK

The voices of the popular culture would soon defer to a *businessrock* that was produced by pioneers who had become transformed into purveyors of entertainment. It was driven by the purest of profit motives, the motives that the idealists had resisted.

Mammoth bandstands, monster gates, and prolonged tours, both national and global, became the norm for the once great rock bands—The Grateful Dead, Led Zeppelin, The Who, Aerosmith, and The Rolling Stones. The showmanship was powerful, but the visceral feelings were subdued.

The date was December 15, 1994. I was sitting in the Kingdome in Seattle where fans were moshing near the stage awaiting the start of the concert. It was a typically well run Ticketmaster event, and the more than 50,000 people and the energy that they produced gave one a sense of "being there." But the Stones, noted once for their darkness, irreverence, bravura, and romanticism (and no less for their musicianship—Keith Richards, Charlie Watts, Ronnie Wood, and Mick Jagger), had shifted their concerns from the newprop of values and mortality to the *nonprop* of financial immortality. Just as sports had become businessball, rockprop was transformed into businessrock.

The Stones used their *Voodoo Lounge* tour to place their tongue-and-lips logo on 65 products from removable tattoos to motorcycle jackets. One could pay with Visa cards offered by the Chevy Chase Bank of Maryland, which offered merchandising discounts. A critic noted, tongue-in-cheek, that Jagger, the Stones' icon, had become a "graduate" of the London School of Economics, as they sang in "Street Fighting Man": "What can a poor boy do but sing for a rock 'n' roll band?"[15]

In earlier times, the Stones had set themselves apart from the Beatles, the acknowledged balladeers. They sang the dark songs. When they sang on *Beggar's Banquet* of the paroxyms of the 1960s, and in "Shattered" of the successes of the 1980s, they forecast poverty and social disorder. Their early songs about sex were explicit and raw, and those about gender demeaned both sexes. They sang only occasionally about the newprop of love, ballads like "Wild Horses" and "No Expectations," and the always comforting "Satisfaction." But in their time they had displayed musical integrity and invited everyone to join up. Now they mythologized America as a land where the present mattered more than the past and you always got what you wanted. Less often did they acknowledge the gaps between dreams and realities: "Love also has gone away, and there's not much that can be done about it."

The Stones played a 20-minute concert on the Internet, they were the first major rock band to exploit the Multicast Backbone or M-Bone on that channel, and they promoted pay-per-view on the cable channel Showtime. They were even accessible for live chat sessions. The Stones' financial fast forward projected a 1994–1995 tour that would net $120 million, and 1996 would outdo it.[16]

Now the balladeering Beatles would return to participate in their own special version of businessrock, reviving memories of the *Ed Sullivan Show.* Certainly, the Boomers welcomed them back, but they got more than the familiar music and lyrics. The Beatles had captured the new mood: Musicprop had merged with adprop.

Let a Boomer speak for his generation:

> I sensed there was something wrong right after the opening when the announcer's voice boomed that the evening was being brought to us by something called Pepcid A.C. (acid controller) . . . and a credit card designed by Ringo.
>
> The next two hours contained 47-odd commercials, one ad for every 2.5 minutes of nostalgia, a hard night's work, indeed. There was Taurus wagon, Ikea, Hanes, Tostitos Chips, Tylenol Flu, Kodak, Volvo, Mercedes, Xerox, Pizza Hut, Arizona Jeans, Motorola Pagers, etc.
>
> Twenty-five years ago, when the Beatles broke up, the only acid that concerned my boomer generation came in windowpane, blotter, or little orange pills called California Sunshine.
>
> Finally, the great moment had arrived . . . there they were, George, Ringo, Paul. And Paul said: "We didn't see how to do a reunion without John, but we figured out a way." He winked, and "Free as a Bird" began to play. It was good to hear John's voice again. And the CD was available on December 11. Elaborate business musicprop.[17]

Even Vedder and Pearl Jam yielded to the need to survive in the marketplace. They would be piped through to the new Hard Rock Casino in Las Vegas, Nevada, where the synergies of exciting music, messages, and glitz made a special breed of jeweled-ear patrons feel at home. Recognizable outside by an 82-foot guitar, inside it had been transformed into a gambling nirvana and merchandising mecca.

The $25 souvenir gambling chips were decorated with the likenesses of Jimi Hendrix. The patrons considered the music, the merchandising, the guitar-shaped slot-machine handles, the Harley-Davidson motorcycles hanging above the tables, and photos of The Beatles to be "awesome, man; simply awesome." Rock had found an ultimate synergy with the crassest of merchandising.[18]

WAL-MART ROCKS POP

What now is rocking rockprop and rapprop to their lyrics is the oldprop of censorship. Wal-Mart, K-Mart, Blockbuster, and other large distributors are forcing the reediting of CDs, videos, and tapes so that they meet their self-imposed criteria of family values. Major bands and filmmakers must design acceptable covers and booklets, omit songs from albums, electronically mask objectionable words, and modify lyrics. Film studios are forced to recut movies to delete scenes, sometimes without advising the film directors.

At the same time that other market forces are squeezing independent distributors out of business,the censorship is increasing, and the major distributors are dominating the market. The title of the Nirvana song "Rape Me" was changed to "Waif Me." The number one albums by the late Tupac Shakur and Snoop Doggy Dogg do not appear on shelves because they carry "parental advisories" denoting explicit sexual content.

Unlike the content of films and videos on television and in movie houses, the choice is neither personal nor made by parents for children, it is made before it reaches screen or video. It is a pervasive censorship of a few governing many, rather than individuals making their own choices, the apotheosis of oldprop.

GENDER ROCKPROP: A GRRL AND A SMILE

Women's rockprop made statements of its own in the 1990s, varying in "grrling" by Cobain's widow, Courtney Love of Hole, to instrumentalists such as Kim Gordon and Donita Sparks. All symbolized emotional oldprop demands that women be admitted to the rock culture; why should they be excluded?

One could travel back in time and see Gordon crouched in a miniskirt, her words balancing rage and desire above the nervous sounds of shrieking guitars. Headlining a concert for reproductive rights, Sparks of the all-female group L7 curled her lip, carved out a guitar riff, and snarled: "Get out of my way or I might shove." The reproductive rights movement was spearheaded by L7 and the organization Rock for Choice and it took on national proportions.[19]

More women were challenging the virgin–vixen–bimbo stereotypes. L7's grunge stood out from the male-dominated Nirvana style in its sexual expressions and refusal to be treated as objects. Hole offered a woman's view of sexual violence and abuse with vocal howls and raw guitar, the musical equivalents of gore. This was oldprop in its anger, but it was newprop in its demands for an end to exploitation.

Women's rockprop became as sensual and frank as men's. They invented their own beauty, from thrift store funkiness to gothic vampirism, to punk's black-leather tomboy cool. They defined their bare waists as erogenous zones. L7 rapped a feminist oldprop view of sex in "Fuel My Fire":

> I've got a word of thanks
> Thanks that I'd like to say for the rage that I feel, the rage that I feel today
> Gotta stack, gotta stack . . . of chips on my shoulder in everything I do
> 'Cause I made . . . the mistake the mistake of trusting you
> * * *
> Gotta grudge . . . that I'm holding for as long as I live
> 'Cause you lied to my face and that's something I can't forgive.

It was no surprise when the coed Cranberries and Smashing Pumpkins sold more than a million albums. Of the 10 groups named in *Rolling Stone* magazine as the hot bands to watch in 1994, three were coed, including *Arrested Development*, which headlined at Woodstock 1994; the group led by Rapper Speech (the Afro-Centric hip-hop band); and the Australian mixed gender rock group, Frentell's Marvin the Album.[20]

As acceptance grew, more subdued forms emerged. Kathi Wilson of Bikini Kill stopped belting it out to more quietly spell it out. Christina Kelly, former editor of *Sassy*, a magazine for teenage girls, said women players did not want to be thought of as sex objects. Nevertheless, "lipstick feminists" transformed "I wanna *be* with a Rock-and-Roll girl" to "I wanna *beat up* a Rock 'n' Roll girl." *Rolling Stone* characterized this as "Grrrls at War," "fox corps," and "chick rock."[21]

In "Pretty on the Inside," Love gathered the clan to express frustration and shame as well as rage:

> Slutkiss girl, won't you promise her smack
> Is she pretty on the inside, is she pretty from the back
> Dead moon girl won't you rot
> Black strap
> Is she rotten on the inside, ugly from the back?
> There's no power like my pretty power. There's no power like ugly . . .
> Not sorry, not ever, forever my power . . . forgive my power.

After diving into the mosh pit and being mauled by the fans, tattered dress hiked to her waist, Love shouted her signature phrase, "You guys pick up every stitch / Must be the season of the witch." Wreaking revenge and falsely prophesying, it was a heavy load of oldprop.[22]

ρ   ρ   ρ

Many of the youth in the popular culture recognized that for all of its rage, plaintiveness, crudeness, cacophony, and commercial exploitation, rockprop was a voice of conscience in the 1990s. It promised integrity, truths, creativity, and member-

ship, each the essence of newprop. The new rockprop reached across the genera-tions, contributing to a sense of membership in the culture.

Despite the turn to commercialism by popular rock bands, there is dedication, as well. Bruce Springsteen has always voiced the struggles of ordinary people and now is speaking for those who are fearful and displaced. It's not enough to be "born in the U.S.A.," he sings. America is the promised land but it must keep its promises. "No surrender."

NOTES

1. Striving to be rock's next Seattle. (1994, July 17). Pareles, J., *New York Times*, Sec. H, p. 1.
2. The big no. (1994, July). Wright, S., *Esquire*, pp. 55–63.
3. Conversation with Jon Pareles, *New York Times* music critic, New York, April 2, 1995.
4. Wife shared concerns days before death. (1995, April 9). Hilburn, R., *Seattle Times*, Sec. A, p. 10.
5. I haven't felt the excitement. (1994, April 11). *Seattle Post-Intelligencer*, Jamieson, R., Sec. B, pp. 1/2.
6. Kurt Cobain: The *Rolling Stone* Interview. (1994, January 24). Fricke, D., *Rolling Stone*, pp. 34–38/56.
7. Fricke, *Rolling Stone*, p. 38.
8. Nirvana, the band that hates to be loved. (1993, November 14). *New York Times*, Sec. H, p. 44.
9. Letter. Suicide of Kurt Cobain. (1994, April 17). *Seattle Times*, Sec. B, p. 11.
10. The most popular band in the world. (1993, December 5). MacDonald, P., *Seattle Times*, p. 1.
11. The highs and lows of being Eddie. (1993, November 18). Stout, G., *Seattle Post-Intelligencer*, Sec. C, pp. 1/3. See also *Rolling Stone*, cover, November 1993.
12. Troubadours of fickle time and its passing. (1994, September 4). Kakutani, M., *New York Times*, Sec. H, p. 26.
13. Requiem for the dead. (1995, August 21). *Newsweek*, pp. 46–52.)
14. A death in the family. (1995, August 10). Goldsmith, S., *Seattle Post-Intelligencer*, Sec. C, pp. 1/7.
15. Ladies and gentlemen: The Rolling Stones Visa. (1994, September 24). Bloomberg Business News, Pickering, J., *Seattle Times*, Sec. D, p. 1.
16. Rolling Stones live on Internet; both a big deal and a little deal. (1995, January 23). Strauss, N., *New York Times*, Sec. B, p. 1.
17. The Pepcid generation remembers the Beatles. (1995, November 21). Buckley, C., *The Washington Post* via Internet.
18. Turning rockers into high rollers. (1995, November 1). Sterngold, J., *New York Times*, Sec. C, p. 1.
19. No longer rock's playthings. (1993, February 14). Powers, A., *New York Times*, Sec. H, pp. 1/34.
20. Rock goes coed. (1994, August 8). Farley, C. J., *Time*, p. 62.
21. Climbing rock's walls. (1994, August 16). Griest, S., *Seattle Post-Intelligencer*, Sec. C, pp. 1/4.
22. Hole: Roseland, New York, N.Y. (1995, February 18). Strauss, N., *New York Times*, Sec. Y, p. 11.

■

RAPPROP
Telling It Like It Is

A more angry music than rockprop is seeking its apotheosis in our popular culture; its tone sometimes violent and obscene, rapprop carries the deep imprint of oldprop. Although it has not yet led its racial, ethnic, and youthful segment of a generation to the promised land, its vernacular will continue to tell it like it is. Its tone, form, content, and instrumentation nonetheless have expanded the dialogue between the races as a newprop of inclusion.

As an art form, rapprop has hallowed traditions. It traces its musical heritage to West Indies celebratory reggae and a hip-hop in rhythm. But in late 1968, a trio of Black poets established a precedent for The Last Poets to weld revolutionary politics, incendiary street language, and jazzy musical accompaniment into a polyrhythmic genre of rap music. Mainstream rap retains that exuberance, but it protests the infliction of pain on generations who have been excluded from the popular culture. Where it describes exclusion from the popular culture and proposes steps toward inclusion it aspires to newprop, and with its success, it is not simply "talkin' and talkin,' it's talkin' and walkin.'"

A quarter of a century after The Last Poets, Dr. Dre commanded worldwide attention as one of hip-hop's angriest young men, a one-time member of the N.W.A., the California group that put gangsta rap on the charts with imagery of an urban landscape bristling with blood and bullets, profanity, misogyny, and potent beats.[1]

Despite the smutty lyrics of Snoop Doggy Dogg, mentored by Dr. Dre, and Ice-T, oldprop became somewhat subdued by the mid-1990s. Even Ice-

T's "Home Invasion," which topped the charts, had a newprop edge to its oldprop explicitness.

Submerged in its defensiveness was an imagined ideal of racial harmony in which people were judged not by their color but by their willingness to treat others with respect. At the same time, L. L. Cool J. and other gangsta rappers found outlets for their talents on television and in films. However, the more extreme gangsta rap continued to express its anger and its marginal culture in trenchant language. Aggressive, abusive of gender and police, and sexually explicit, gangsta rap became commercially exploitable. However, as booming sales—largely to young Whites—rewarded the most outrageous, they became targets for politicalprop.[2]

THE OLD POLITICS

In early June 1995, Time Warner, Inc., a major producer and distributor of gangsta rap, was forced to the wall when Senate Republican Majority Leader Bob Dole made gangsta rap a centerpiece (together with film violence) of his campaign to capture "family values" and the Christian coalition for his 1996 run for the presidency. He was joined by William J. Bennett, former Secretary of Education in the Reagan administration, who demanded that Time Warner stop distributing music with lyrics that depicted violence against the police or that were sexually degrading to women. The results of the assault were devastating: The Time Warner music executives who were defiant were fired. Time Warner then divested itself of its profitable operation.[3]

The artists who were criticized included groups such as Cannibal Corpse, Geto Boys, and 2 Live Crew, but Time Warner also controlled top-selling gangsta rappers Dr. Dre, Tupac Shakur, and Snoop Doggy Dogg. Dole had touched a "hot button" in the parlance of politicalprop, and the response came from the entire political spectrum. Even liberal political cartoonist David Horsey was guided by family values, not First Amendment values, when he asked, "Who is to help us protect our families from a radio spectrum that is replete with sex and violence?" Normative culture, under supposed siege by a marginal culture, could be mobilized to fight back. Dole railed at Time Warner executives: "I would like to ask the executives . . . a question: is this what you intended to accomplish with your careers? You have sold your souls, but must you debase our nation and threaten our children as well?"[4]

A Defense of Rapprop

A group of women entertainment executives termed the Dole speech "unbelievable hypocrisy," and Norman Lear, creator of *All in the Family*, likened Dole's attack to the efforts of the music industry to sell records; politicians, similarly, try to get elected. The head of the Warner Music Group, Michael

Fuchs, said Dole had made no effort to have a dialogue or try to look at the situation in anything less than an expedient political manner. Fuchs asked, "Did gun ownership, which Dole supported—or gangsta rap lyrics—more rip the fabric of society?"[5]

On the one hand, Dole presented himself as engaging in newprop—he wished to protect innocents from the ravaging language and ideas of gangsta rap—but his motives were self-serving and calculating, and that was oldprop. A media critic pointed out that Dole actually had contact with gangsta rappers 4 years earlier, in 1991, when he and fellow Republican Phil Gramm welcomed Eazy-E (Eric Wright), a member of the most notorious gangsta rap group, N.W.A. (Niggaz wit' Attitude), which had been banned from MTV. Dole and Gramm accepted campaign contributions from Wright, who at the time was a confessed woman-beater and drug dealer. He gave $1,000 to the Republican campaign and attended their Salute to the Commander-in-Chief political function. Dole and his wife extended the invitation and warmly acknowledged the gift.[6]

Taking Steps

Although acknowledging exclusion by the popular culture, as early as December 1992, Black ministers, educators, and other community leaders had formed an alliance to challenge the gangsta rappers. The National Association for the Advancement of Colored People (NAACP) insisted that rap music that encouraged sterotypical and inappropriate behavior should be rejected. A number of churches crusaded against hard-core gangsta rap, and others asked for more constructive rap.[7]

A California professor, Dr. Maulana Karenga, accused rappers of selling a distorted view of Black life and culture through White recording companies: "The reality is that we are a working-class people and have held things together with religion, self-respect, creativity, and a remarkable adaptive vitality and durability under some of the worst conditions of oppression in human history."[8]

The National Council of Negro Women created a series of annual celebrations of the Black family for seven major cities from New York to Los Angeles and attracted more than 6 million participants over the first 6 years of the program. The purpose was to show the strength of Black family values, to stress that Blacks are not a problem people but instead people with problems. The foci were expressive of newprop, people convening to deal with their problems. Spunky D., a female member of the rap trio To Be Continued, accused hard-core rap of losing its way:

> At first they were telling the truth. It told of the drug dealer, the gang banger, the prostitute; they said everything that was going on in the Black community.

But now they're tripping over it. So people do what they're hearing *now;* shooting up people and having big money and stuff.[9]

But rapper MC Lyte says this is too facile a claim; the critics are believing their own oldprop of ignorance:

People don't really go along with the words, they go with the hook and the beat. Parents, not rappers, have to take more responsibility for how their children choose to behave.

Whatever the youth is doing today you can't blame it all on rap music because they kill in movies, they rape in movies, they do the exact same thing that may or may not go on in a rap song.[10]

Angry rappers confronted journalists from CNN and described themselves as the CNN for their own constituencies. They were just telling it like it is, they insisted, and that made it newprop. Perhaps they were sociologically correct, but their output could not be judged entirely as motivated by social consciousness,

Neil Young: Give Rap a Break

On the occasion of his 1994 Grammy for the song "Heart of Gold," aging artist Neil Young expressed fears about the lack of attention that was being paid to rap artistry. He did not distinguish between rap and gangsta rap but he said he loved rapprop because it was a new way of communicating that permitted people to say exactly what was on their minds; what extenuated the words was the clever way in which they were expressed. We could not only listen but move our body to the rhythm. Young said that Bob Dylan could be thought of as early rap. An artistic genre should not be closed off simply because we do not fully understand it.

That many of the themes reflected reality could not be denied. There were deep-rooted problems, many turbulent, some deadly, others vengeful, but none of which Dole sought to address. In the neighborhood cultures of the South Central Los Angeles gangs, the Crips (named after their crippled leader) and the Bloods (a reference to the deaths of Black soldiers in Vietnam) were typical of other names, all sending a gangsta message: the Eight Tray Gangsters, the Playboy Gangsters, the Venice Shore Line Gangsters, and the Budlong Gangsters. The Bloods nurtured the Miller Gangsters, the Mid-City Gangsters, and the Van Ness Gangsters.[11]

Their dress was adopted everywhere—baggy pants, baseball caps, and Starter jackets—by stars such as Ice-T, Too Short, and The Geto Boys. Their anger was apparent, their language crude and offensively repetitive, and their style abrasive, but it was little different from what dominated Hippie culture in the 1960s. But they were Black, not White; urban poor, not suburban middle class. Ice-T's hard-core song, "Body Count," which first appeared on the album *Original Gangster,* defines this sense of exclusion:

You know sometimes I sit at home, you know,
and I watch TV, and I wonder what it would be like
to live somewhere like the Cosby show
Ozzie and Harriet, you know

Where the cops come and get your cat outta the tree
and all your friends died of old age.
But you see, I live in South Central, and
unfortunately . . . S—- ain't like that!
It's all f——- up!

Goddamn what a brotha gotta do
to get a message through
to the red, white and blue?

Tell us what to do . . . F—- you!
(Repeated 4 times)

I hear it every night
another gunfight
then tension mounts
on with the Body Count.

ACTING IT OUT?

Gangsta rap became alarming because some stars seemed to be acting out their own lyrics:

1. Tupac Shakur won critical acclaim for his acting in *Juice* and *Poetic Justice*, but he was first convicted, then cleared in the shooting of two policemen. Some of his best known lyrics in the 1991 *2pacalypse Now* album discuss gang members shooting police. He also was convicted of a felony sex-abuse charge, and he suffered gunshot wounds in what police said was a robbery. In September 1996 he was shot again and died.

2. Gangsta rapper Snoop Doggy Dogg, protege of Dr. Dre, was indicted as the driver of a getaway car in which a passenger shot and killed another person.

3. Flavor Flav of the group Public Enemy was charged with attempted murder for shooting at a neighbor during an argument.

However, Ice-T claimed that his songs were only pseudodocumentaries and flights of fantasy designed to titillate a White suburban audience. "How can an album hit the silvers and golds with only a ghetto clientele?" he asked rhetorically. It could be argued that Ice-T merely produced body count movies for the ear rather than for the eye, satisfying the same tastes for tough talk, violence, and sex that films provided. Ice-T in "Body Count" rationalizes violence on moral grounds, hence laying claim to a measure of newprop.

In "Smoked Pork," Ice-T sings about killing a cop, but the cop had refused to help him fix a flat tire, a degrading situation for a Black:

> Now radio stations probably won't play,
> this record because of the things I say
> They'll say I'm glamorizing the hustlin' hood
> and a record like this can do no good!
> But I'm not here to tell ya right or wrong
> I don't know which side of the law you belong.[12]

Dr. Dre boasted that his criminal rap sheet was longer than his musical credits, but along with protege Snoop Doggy Dogg, he shifted to the commercial race for platinum after he discovered that rapping was more profitable than crime. He caught the moment with "Niggaz4life," and although it shocked many listeners with its oldprop of self-deprecation and hate, it hit the top of the pop charts. *The Chronic* and the notorious *Doggystyle* sold more than 7 million copies. So many rappers had written about killing policemen that the subject had become a genre, much like hedonism:

> On Dre tracks from "Boyz-n-the Hood" to "Let me Ride," life is a house party where male bonding is the rule, women are attractive nuisances, and enemies are something to wave guns at from a safe distance.
>   "Now . . . I feel like I'm one of the power speakers, like a Malcolm X . . . a lot of times white kids come up to me, and it makes me feel damn good . . . because it's the feeling of a straight ghetto man finally proving his stuff to the whole society. Sometimes I ask them if they really listen to the tape, and they know every word. I'm not prejudiced in my rap. I just kick the rhymes."[13]

South Central Is the Place

The rapper Ice Cube's album, *The Predator*, shows him to be almost prescient—he warned that the lid was going to blow off the precarious subculture in South Central Los Angeles before it happened. His album *Death Certificate*, released on Halloween in 1991, not only articulated the rage but showed where the flashpoint would be. The song "Black Korea" described the resentment between Korean shopkeepers ("chop-suey eatin'") and Blacks, who felt that the Koreans treated them contemptuously. It was a scene of warring gangs with deep-seated prejudices who could never share turf, but despite the vengeful and derisive tone it shot to number one on the *Billboard* charts. Ice Cube rapped that the Rodney King riots were necessary for Blacks "to get some respect."

> It wasn't just the Blacks
> Everybody was lootin' and had each other's backs
> We all had a hand in the cookie jar
> And we took it far enough to make a statement.

A social critic believes that rap is an older and more common propaganda than we suspect, traceable to gunslingers in the West who single-handedly cleaned up a town, and seen in contemporary form in the Rambo character who wins the Vietnam War. Certainly, rappers are not the only ones who long for actions backed by guns:

> A rapper can identify with the community and merely shock listeners to paying attention to real problems, but at the same time realize that sensationalism will sell recordings. Meanwhile, the gunslingers and guerrillas can be portrayed as only as hard and tough as the competition.[14]

Dissing the Rappers

When in the 1992 election campaign candidate Bill Clinton "dissed" Sister Souljah, a Black woman rapper who he said condoned Blacks murdering Whites, he was accused of political cynicism, which (as in the case of Dole) became justified by the facts; then Clinton took oldprop a step further by criticizing the Reverend Jesse Jackson for inviting Sister Souljah to a Rainbow Coalition forum.

Sister Souljah had not, herself, advocated the phrase, "If Black people kill Black people every day, why not have a week and kill White people?" It was true only that she preached Black self-improvement alongside an open hatred for Whites. "The White man's the weasel," Sister Souljah sang. "White women want to steal Black men while . . . White feminists are lesbians." She called for revenge on the policeman who murdered her child. "They say two wrongs don't make it right, but it damn sure makes it even."[15]

RAP IS BECOMING LOCAL

Rap has exploded on local scenes where diversity exists. A city known for alternative rock, Seattle became a haven for "forgiving rap" that was less baleful about society. Its most noted star, Sir Mix-A-Lot, struck platinum twice. A magazine, *The Flavor,* now covers the local and regional hip-hop scene. An album, *Seattle, The Dark Side,* promoted Mix-A-Lot and other Seattle talent. Mix-A-Lot's *Mack Daddy* won a 1993 Grammy for "Baby Got Back" and sold more than 3 million copies. When I visited the offices of *The Flavor,* the rapper Supreme spoke of an increasing impact on the West Coast scene, with E. Dawg, a disciple of Mix-A-Lot and Six in the Clip.[16]

GETTING RELIGION

Recovering from alcohol abuse and a police encounter, Run D.M.C., known as "The Grand Old Men of Rap," experienced a spiritual reawakening. They assumed the image of monks in Japanese designer clothes, shaved their heads, donned baggy black shirts and pants, and hung big crosses around their necks. They accompanied this with a strict personal code of no profanity, drinking, or smoking.[17]

Arrested Development fused religious revival with rap production techniques. In "Tennessee," lead singer Speech (Todd Thomas) asked God to help him rise above racial hatred:

> Lord, I've really been stressed
> Down and out, losin' ground
> Although I'm Black and proud
> Problems got me pessimistic.

Rolling Stone named Arrested Development the band of the year, and *Musician* magazine and the *Village Voice* both selected their *Three Years* as album of the year. "Tennessee" won the Soul Train Award for best rap single. Speech sang:

> Take me to another place
> Take me to another land
> Make me forget all that hurts me
> Let me understand your plan.[18]

Along with those awards came several Grammys. By retaining the technical techniques of rap, Speech was able to venture into lyrics that in constructive ways permitted Blacks to channel their anger. This newprop "life music" was intended both to recognize problems and solve them.

IT'S AN ART FORM

In *Flyboys in the Buttermilk*, a collection of essays about Black culture, playwright and screenwriter Greg Tate conceded that the promotion of anarchism, agitation, and criminal behavior was a staple for performers such as Ice Cube, Public Enemy, and KRS-One, but he observed wryly that the "hardly subtle difference" between real violence and violence in recordings seems lost on pundits and politicians as well as on self-appointed Black spokespersons.[19]

It was art that responded to life. The failure to address the sources of Black America's economic, political, and psychological problems caused Blacks to turn to those who were in tune with the source of their woes. These included Dr. Dre and (his protege) Snoop Doggy Dogg, as well as Ice-T and others. Denied status as a newprop art form, hip-hop was demonized by oldprop and devolved into an object of culture wars.

The refining of digital audio technology and the creating of rhythmic games affirmed a sense of African American culture rather than denied it.

Metaphorically, it provided a database, an electroencephalogram, and a psychic hotline with walloping volume to back it up. Rapping itself was a rhythmized Black speech that aspired to music and theater in which performers were required to present a forceful delivery, a facility with the spoken word, and a convincing portrayal of character. Hip voices talked, testified, bragged, and roasted and toasted one another, offering personal insights and enriching experiences, all the essence of newprop.[20]

Rapprop As Comedyprop

Mediaprop depictions of Flava Flav, Tupac Shakur, and Snoop as hard-core gangsta rappers—with rap sheets to match—overlooked that prior to becoming rappers they were known for their sense of comedy.

- In Public Enemy, Flava plays the fool to Chuck D's Hamlet.
- Tupac made his debut with Digital Underground by doing the bump and grind with a rubber doll. In his breakthrough video, "I Get Around," he portrayed the clown prince of gigolos.
- Snoop's portrayals of unabashed bashfulness won him more loyalty than his often bashed lyrics.

Ice Cube's "Nigga You Love to Hate" says, in part, "They asked me, how did I like Arsenio? / I said about as much as the Bicentennial." Brand Nubian's "All For One" rhymes:

> Some rappers think l like Engelbert Humperdink
> or better yet, Dick Cavett
> I got a bad habit
> similar to the girl from "She's Gotta Have It"
>
> I think with the brain and not with what's behind the zipper
> I'm living kind of good similar to Jack Tripper
> A landlord named Roper did a show at the Copa
> When I'm finished with this, I'll be paid like Oprah.

One of the groups criticized by Bob Dole, 2 Live Crew won a Supreme Court ruling in defense of its parody of "Oh, Pretty Woman," a Roy Orbison song that was the theme of the motion picture of the same name. In the film a man falls in love with a pretty woman walking on the street. The rappers saw in this a parody of reality; in Black street culture, pretty women were not treated with grace on the street or even off it.

So "pretty woman" became "big hairy woman," "bald-headed woman," and "two-timin' woman," more consistent with the oldprop image of women portrayed in rap music. Lawyer Alan Dershowitz, who was part of the successful O. J. Simpson legal defense team, defended 2 Live Crew from legal harrassment in Florida, pointing out that the language of rap was certainly no dirtier than that heard nightly by millions of Americans on cable comedy shows and clubs around the country. "As with comedy," he said, "rap is both entertainment and politics."[21]

Supreme Court Justice David Souter ruled that the lyrics represented a fair use and criticism of a point of view, and the rap song legitimately cast the original song into another, equally relevant cultural perspective. The court received supporting "friend of the court" briefs from *Mad Magazine*, the *Harvard Lampoon*, and the political satirist Mark Russell. In addition, The Capitol Steps, a musical group that performs topical political parodies, sent the Justices a tape on which the group performed a musical history of parody in America dating back to the revolution. Even the highly controversial album *Body Count* contains a song called, "There goes the Neighborhood / We're movin' right next door to you!"

Rapprop in theaters also tends to humor. The stage production *Fear of a Black Hat* features the notorious N.W.A. rap group as the N.W.H. (Niggaz Wit' Hats) as contrasted to Niggaz Wit' Attitudes. Its characters parody Ice-T as Ice Cold, Ice Tray, Ice Coffee, Ice Water, Ice Berg, and Ice Box. However, the lyrics are unprintable.[22]

EAST AND WEST COASTERS

New voices and rhythms are making rapprop more aesthetic, although they have not exploded on the charts. New Yorkers are deemed to be more clever, stylistic, and poetic; they have more things to say and say them more euphoniously than in rhyming with cacophonous sound effects. In that sense, they are into the newprop of achievement and pride.[23]

Los Angeles rappers dominate the charts with albums by Ice Cube, Cypress Hill, Snoop Doggy Dogg, and Dr. Dre, whose album, *The Chronic* (1992) was the year's rap equivalent to the film *Jurassic Park*. Only one New York rapper made it into the top 10 in album sales. Whereas the Los Angeles style wallowed in violence and drugs, the New York style sought to escape those obsessions. As an example, in "One Love" by Whodini:

> So I be ghost from my projects
> I take my pen and pad for the weekend
> A two-day stay you may say
> I needed time alone to relax my dome
> No phone. Left mine at home.

The defining New York aesthetic is that great hip-hop is less a matter of what rappers say than how they say it. Style is the thing: the inventiveness of rhyme schemes, the compelling nature of voices and tone, and an ability to create rhythm with words—what is called *flow*.

The New York concern with aesthetics began under street lamps and in the corners of nightclubs where young rappers stood in circles and took turns leaping into the center and improvising rhymes. The idea was to create rhythm with words to produce a sense of flow. A textbook example is the 1986 single, "Eric B. Is the President" performed by Eric B. & Rakim:

> I came in the door
> I said it before
> I'll never let the mic magnetize me no more
> But it's bitin' me
> Fightin' me
> Invitin' me to rhyme
> I can't hold it back
> I'm looking for the line
> Takin' off my coat
> Clearin' my throat
> The rhyme will be kickin' it
> 'Til I hit my last note.

By contrast, the Los Angeles' Ice Cube of N.W.A. rhymed:

> Since I was a youth
> I smoked weed out
> Now I'm that . . .
> That you read about
> Taking a life or two
> That's what the hell I do.

And Wu Tang, in "Protect Ya Neck," rapped:

> The Wu is too slammin' for these Cold Killin' labels
> Who ain't had hits since I seen Aunt Mable
> Be doin' artists in like Cain did Abel.

Touré concluded that whereas L.A. rappers used their rhymes to describe their reality, New York rappers sought to escape that reality.

Rapprop is expressing newprop in its return to its origins as street poetry and, with it, the adoption of the "spoken word" movement. This has turned from the violent imagery of the old rapprop to the more sophisticated meditations that examine issues of passion, pain, and poverty and whose heroes are literary figures rather than the present generation of rappers. Their purpose is to end the ranting and raise the thresholds of self-help and personal enhancement.[24]

Chuck D of Public Enemy described rap as the means by which teenagers in Los Angeles neighborhoods learn about the struggles of their peers in New York or Houston. and this is achieved with an air of intimacy. It is one thing to discuss single parenthood in detached, clinical terms; it is another to rhyme a powerful, personal portrait of a mother struggling to raise her daughters on a tight budget, which Yo-Yo does in "Mama Don't Take No Mess." Run-D.M.C.'s hit record "Ooh, Whatcha Gonna Do" was filled with optimism and hip-hop upmanship. Life, again, was a game that everyone could play:

> I'm a feasible fellow, teasable mellow
> Easily diesel, 'cause it's ego from the ghetto
> Perhaps you said, the brothers were dead
> But we smother all others, and under covers we spread.

Rapprop is also moving toward making itself more real, reaching beyond the oldprop stereotypes that created a gangsta-rap cult while maintaining emphasis on its swagger and bluntness. The death by shooting of Tupac Shakur in September 1996 seemed to punctuate *Gangstaprop's* own reappraisal. When a confrere of Tupac's, the heralded Dr. Dre, portrayed a high-rolling life, a fellow rapper chided: "You tried keeping it real, but you should try keeping it right."[25]

THE CONGLOMERATE EFFECT

As rap stars such as Dr. Dre and LL Cool J have carved out careers in television and film, they have gone totalprop with the marketing of themselves and their products. The most prominent of the deal-making and marketing rap groups, the Wu-Tang Clan, already is a conglomerate. Each of its members markets its own labels, and develops its own lines, but the conglomerate promotes the Wu-Tang label, its clothing lines, and other products.

℞   ℞   ℞

Despite its oldprop of anger and confrontation, rapprop has made the leap from MTV to network television and is attracting millions to its concerts both at home and abroad. Its rhythms, its affording of cultural identity, its humor, and its energies make it an essential element of diversity in a popular culture.

Some rappers tell it like it is, others tell it like they imagine it is, and still others tell it as their audiences want it to be. The problems that gave rise to the music of protest continue, as do those who attack its symptoms rather than its causes. As long as hate and anger remain, rap will convey oldprop, and many will exploit it.

NOTES

1. Day of the Dre: Dr. Dre and his protegé, Snoop Doggy Dogg, take hardcore rap from SouthCentral L.A. to your house. (1993, September 30). Gold, J., *Rolling Stone*, p. 38.

2. Words from the "Home" front. (1993, May 27). Light, A., *Rolling Stone*, p. 20.

3. Dole scores entertainment industry, Time Warner, for "debasing" America. (1995, June 1). *Washington Post*, Sec. A, p. 6.

4. Dole lashes out at Hollywood for undermining social values. (1995, June 1). *New York Times*, Sec A, p. 1.

5. Time Warner Inc., criticized by Dole for sex, violence. (1995, June 1). Seib, G. F., *Wall Street Journal*, Sec. B, p. 8.

6. G.O.P. Gangsta rap; Bob Dole and Easy-E. (1995, June 11). Rich, F., *New York Times*, p. 15.

7. NAACP raps 2 Live Crew, reflecting division among blacks over the music. (1995). Wynter, L. E., *Wall Street Journal*, Sec. B, p. 6.

8. Harsh rap lyrics provoke black backlash. (1993, August 15). Marriott, M., *New York Times*, Sec. H. pp. 1/16.

9. Marriott, *New York Times*, Sec. H, p. 16.

10. Marriott, *New York Times*, Sec. H, p. 1.

11. Bing, L. (1992). *Do or Die*. New York: Harper Perennial.

12. How real is "realness" in rap? (1994, December 11). Pareles, J., *New York Times*, Sec. H, p. 34.

13. Day of the Dre . . . (1993, September 30). Gold, J., *Rolling Stone*, pp. 33–43.

14. Pareles, *New York Times*, Sec. H, p. 34.

15. Clinton stuns Rainbow Coalition. (1992, June 14). Edsall, T. B., *Washington Post*, Sec. A, p. 1.

16. Underground, overshadowed. (1993, August 1). Benjamin, J., *Seattle Times*, Sec. F, p. 1.

17. The grand old men of rap strike back. (1993, June 20). Linden, A., *New York Times*, Sec. H, p. 33.

18. Arrested Development travels its own road. (1993, March 28). Poulson-Bryant, S., *New York Times*, Sec. H, p. 29.

19. They go where few rappers dare to follow. (1993, October 17). Tate, G., *New York Times*, Sec. H, p. 34.

20. Tate, *New York Times*, p. 34.

21. Dershowitz, A. M. (1994). *Contrary to Popular Opinion*, New York: Berkeley Books, p. 77.

22. Fear of a black hat. (1994, June 3). Maslin, J., *New York Times*, Sec. B, p. 7.

23. Only one star in the two schools of rap. (1994, August 14), Touré, *New York Times*, Sec. H, p. 26.

24. From rap's rhythms, a retooling of poetry. (1996, September 29). Marriott, M., *New York Times*, Sec. A, pp. 1/16.

25. Can rap move beyond gangstas? (1996, July 28). Pareles, J., *New York Times*, Sec. H, p. 30.

SPORTSPROP
Businessball and Heroes Great and Small

What once was an intimate sportsprop was transformed in the early 1990s into a psychologically distant businessballprop in which sports became less a mecca for heroes than a meeting place for negotiators. The sports cathedrals gave way to luxury hotel suites where wealthy players, agents, and owners convened to disagree.

Advertising, fashion, marketing, and music joined in a synergy with sports as a multifaceted business in which the fan was more object than subject. Fans clad themselves in Nike or Reebok shoes, hats, sports fashions, and T-shirts; drank the right beer; were seen with the right sex symbols; and drove the right cars. These symbols pervaded television, promoted pay TV; filled magazines, newspapers, and CD-ROMS; and were being consumed by the interactive generation. Businessballprop promoted a consciousness of totalprop.

A TOTAL EXPERIENCE

In Portland, Oregon, Seattle, Washington, and in other cities, shopping at Nike is a total experience. Lifelike sports figures loom overhead, films roll, and music envelops the customer. Beyond shopping, the broader purpose is to bring about brand and image conversion. Only the windows and walls limit the boundaries of the presentation: It is total business sportsprop.[1]

Chicago's Nike Town houses a high-tech sports museum, fitness theme park, basketball court, and video theater. Visitors are asked to carry away images of the brand even more than a pair of shoes. Reebok has three similar flagship stores. OshKosh is known for its children's pajamas, and historically, for making overalls for trainmen. A huge wooden train station evokes brand consciousness. Mannequins seem to dive from the swimming-pool-tiled ceilings of The Authentic Fitness Corp.'s Speedo store.

Stores of this kind do not make sensational profits, but Nike's chief executive, Linda J. Wachner, says it is the best advertising the brand can buy. In a coup that startled filmgoers, Nike outfitted Forrest Gump, main character of the Oscar-winning film, in their Cortez shoes and a bold Nike T-shirt for his monumental run across country. This was oldprop in new clothing.[2]

SUPER ADPROP

Whether it is the Olympic Games, the World Series, or the NBA or NFL championships, adprop commands super prices. That is what businessball-prop is all about. During a third-quarter break in the 1984 Super Bowl, Apple Computer announced the introduction of a new product: the Macintosh. It depicted a huge projected image of Big Brother. A shapely young woman dressed in shorts and halter ran toward it and flung a sledgehammer at the screen, exploding its Orwellian visage into a million shards.

Then the final shot: "On January 24th, 1984, Apple Computer will introduce Macintosh. And you'll see why 1984 won't be like 1984." Newscasts that evening carried more about the adprop than the game. The 60-second spot cost $400,000 to produce and $5,000,000 to broadcast and was directed by *Blade Runner*'s Ridley Scott. It aired only once but it did the job. The 1996 Super Bowl pulled in more viewers, but 1984 was the apotheosis of total business sportsprop.

REMEMBER THEN?

The game of baseball was once played in the afternoon when salesmen and children could sneak out to the ballpark. The leagues once wrote their schedules on the back of a program; home-and-home arrangements and dates for travel and play were evened up from year to year. Everyone felt they were in the loop. However, in businessball, the computer calculates what games should be televised in what markets to maximize viewership. Travel is shoehorned into the gaps. In businessball, it is better for everyone to be rich than for the players to be rested. When teams play back to back in different cities it is said to be a test of their fortitude; in fact, it is an oldprop that exploits both the exhausted players and the gullible fandom.

The new businessballprop can be seen not merely in the synergy of the retailing and licensing systems but in the drives to build new sports arenas that are devoted to the retailing of the corporate sports imagination. Every market is demanding the construction of a lavish new stadium to permit the ultimate in sports promotion and sales. As a consequence, communities are building businessball profit centers, not just playing fields.

In Seattle, the baseball Mariners demanded a $275-million stadium with a retractable roof and intractable luxury suites. Only because of an unbelievable late season that gave the Mariners the American League Western Division championship—described as a "miracle"—did the stadium come close to gaining approval, losing by fewer than 1,500 votes. This set off a search for a formula that would overcome the vote and keep baseball in Seattle. However, failure was ever close. As player union chief Donald Fehr commented, "If a city can't afford a team, they shouldn't have one." This was businessballprop in the raw, but Fehr was seldom mild.

In early November 1995, the mayor of Baltimore announced that the Cleveland Browns were moving to his city, leaving their football stadium behind them because it was unsatisfactory in generating revenue; Browns fans wept. This was one of five NFL teams seeking to relocate in 1995, with two leaving Los Angeles (one for St. Louis and another to return to Oakland). In Seattle, the football Seahawks demanded $150 million in updates to the Kingdome. "Renovate or we vacate!" was the theme, and on February 1, 1996, vacate is exactly what they did, waving an earthquake hazard study as the ultimate oldprop imperative for breaking a 10-year lease and retreating to Los Angeles, mother of all faultlines! Even the most seasoned franchise jumper of them all, Al Davis of the Oakland Raiders, gasped in disbelief. The owners intimated that they would not let the Seahawks set up camp in Los Angeles. The King County, Washington, executive, Gary Locke, lamented to President Clinton and told the owners he would see them in court, the latter move calculated to force the sale of the Seahawks to a local owner.[3]

DIFFERENT FOLKS FOR DIFFERENT STROKES

Many players today are different folks, and it does not demonize them to say that some of them regard businessball as an occupation that is fitting and proper. Sports myths at an earlier time embodied the ideals of masculinity, guts, loyalty, and stiff upper lips, but many athletes today look at their vast fortunes and do not see themselves as inappropriately macho, arrogant, selfish, or spoiled. The popular culture has been introduced to an era of trash talk, show-off, dope-off, and put-off. Where once the halfback who scored a touchdown trotted off to the cheers of the crowd, he now dances, ducks, and spikes the ball to celebrate his achievement. Defeated opponents no longer are told, "nice try," but instead, "in your face!" The sportsprop of humility has been transformed into an oldprop of humiliation.[4]

We still have heroes and humility, but it is more extraordinary than everyday. When Magic Johnson, one of the heroes of the NBA, decided to return to play in January 1996, he and fellow players agreed tacitly to put his HIV infection behind him; there had been earlier times when the players received the news with less evident delight. In his first game, having faked his defender out, Johnson calmly laid the ball into the basket and jogged unceremoniously back to the defensive end of the court. The defender was aware that if he had taken that same fake from a younger player, the player would have jammed the ball home, pointed a finger at him, and screamed.[5]

We now know too much about the seamy side of sportsprop. Our diet includes too little of the Bill Russells, the Joe DiMaggios, the Jackie Robinsons, and the Muhammad Alis. We are learning to cope with the trial of O. J. Simpson; the forlornness of Pete Rose; and the plights of those hooked on drugs, alcohol, gambling, and other temptations. When Mickey Mantle died of cancer in August 1995, he left a legacy of greatness but he told youth, "Don't be like me!" He had worn the mantle of hero, but he had wasted his body with alcohol.

When Michael Jordan, the acknowledged basketball genius, returned from his brief retirement, he brought back incredible skills and his boyish smile. Soon afterward, he scored 55 points against the New York Knicks on an assortment of swishers, razzle-dazzle leaps over the hoop, and ricochet moves toward the basket. However, Jordan's return was far more businessballprop than the overcoming of adversity. Scalpers never had it so good. Jordan was counterposed against endorsement personality Shaquille O'Neal of the Orlando Magic.[6]

O'Neal's endorsements totaled $12 million a year and included Reebok, Pepsi, a Shaq Fu computer game, Shaq action figures, sports memorabilia, and Spalding sporting goods. Jordan's major endorsers, totaling $30 million, included Quaker Oats, Nike, Gatorade, Sara Lee, Hanes, Ballpark Franks, General Mills (Wheaties), McDonald's, Upper Deck trading cards, and Rayovac batteries. It was the Nike empire versus Planet Reebok, Gatorade versus Pepsi.[7]

In the first Gatorade commercial after Jordan's return, he was shown hiking through the Himalayas, heeding the voice of a mysterious guru from whom he could learn the secret of life. The answer: "Life is a sport. Drink it up," Gatorade's new slogan. Lipsyte observed:

> It's harder (now) to find inspiration in Michael Jordan's shuttles between basketball and baseball, especially when we know that the same team owner and the same shoe company are behind him in both sports (baseball and basketball) and that the politics of capital and labor may have more to do with his decisions

than the love of challenge and competition. Just by taking a new basketball jersey number (the old one was retired), he created a sporting goods bonanza.[8]

Lipsyte mourned what he saw as the loss of emotional investment by fans in the stars. He opined that Jordan, quarterback Troy Aikman of the Dallas Cowboys, and home run hitter and Seattle Mariner star outfielder Ken Griffey, Jr. offer athletic grace on a rare scale, but it does not extend beyond the sensation of the moment. The reason is that the fan must be cautious about making emotional investments because the stars and the franchises may be gone before long. That is businessball, an oldprop of transient excitement as contrasted with the newprop of permanence and commitment. The Mariners sought to ease that anxiety by extending Griffey's contract 5 years, and they did it the hard financial way, making him the highest paid player in baseball — $8.5 million per year. But the community celebrated it, for "Junior" was gentle and warm, his smile radiating that old-time newprop.

We Knew It in 1964

Gussie Busch, the beer magnate owner of the St. Louis Cardinals, was outraged by the salary demands being made on him by his stars. He saw this as insensitivity to his position, so he entered the dressing room and berated them: It was he who built a new stadium for them to play in, it was he who financed it, and it was he who guaranteed their salaries and gave them a stage on which they could achieve fame. And what were they required to do? Only to play the game of baseball—to be boys of summer, so to speak—and leave financial matters to him.[8]

The amazing Dizzy Dean bargained directly, and often fruitlessly, with owner Branch Rickey of the St. Louis Cardinals about his contract—as well as his brother Paul's. There was no question that they would play; that was baseball. But in businessball, Dizzy and Paul each would have agents, they would belong to a players' union, and they would go out on strike if their demands were not met.

Halberstam recounted that the whole new thrust of baseball—a more aggressive union, higher salaries, and greater player freeedom—was as alien to Busch then as it is common today. He saw the Cardinals as his success, not as the success of his players. But as a businessman, Halberstam observed, Busch made a fatal mistake. In his pique, he traded his stars away and the Cardinals fell from a team of championship caliber to basement dweller.

If Busch in his time thought that baseball was being transformed into businessball, he was not only prescient but he understated the case. When Cardinal star Curt Flood sued for his freedom from control of Busch and other owners, he took the first step in opening the floodgates of collective bargaining on owners who were determined not to let the players take control; for his time, Flood had introduced the newprop of emancipation.

Branch Rickey was also a notoriously sharp businessman, but like Busch he was as closely associated with the game as with the desire for profits. The shift of the Brooklyn Dodgers to Los Angeles was a searing act of businessball, and that scarred the era, but that move was more of an exception than the rule. In businessball today, owners buy and sell franchises as commodities off the shelf.

WHERE HAVE ALL THE PLAYERS (AND FANS) GONE?

On the verge of the walkout in 1994, canceling half the season and the World Series, Major League Baseball was enjoying its heroes great and small. Frank Thomas of the Detroit Tigers was chasing New York Yankee Roger Maris' home run record, and the super-talented Griffey was close behind; he not only hit like Joe DiMaggio but he fielded like Willie Mays. They gave all that up, they said, "for the future."

That oldprop was unconvincing to the fans. Many vowed they would not return to the ballparks even if the strike were ended, and they were to keep their word. Through the first half of the 1995 season, attendance plummeted, reflecting the degeneration of baseball from the national pastime to the national disappointment.

A self-styled "Free Agent Fan" noted lugubriously that businessball had "struck out" with fans. He challenged teams to bid on his loyalty:

> After 30 years of seriously following baseball, the baseball strike has put my future as a baseball fan in considerable doubt. Should I return to the ballpark? Should I watch the games on TV? Should I follow the standings in the newspaper? Most important, does the game really want me back as a fan?[10]

Only a few teams answered, and only one gave away tickets and T-shirts, the Houston Astros. But by World Series time there was joy in Cleveland and Atlanta, and "Nightline" could ask if baseball had been forgiven. Thanks to Griffey and sensational Cy Young winning pitcher Randy Johnson, forgiveness was in Seattle. And there was appreciation also in Baltimore, where Cal Ripken, Jr., the well-mannered, accomplished, and courageous shortstop for the Orioles, broke "Iron Man" Lou Gehrig's record for consecutive games played—a total of 2,132 and still counting.

It was said that in every decade baseball had something to remember: In the 1970s it was Reggie Jackson hitting three home runs on three pitches in one game in the World Series. In the 1980s it was Nolan Ryan pitching no-hitters. It was Cal Ripken in the 1990s. Certainly, no hero was ever more welcomed by baseball than Ripken in his time.[11]

Where It Hurts

Businessball was hit hard in its advertising pocket. Almost $500 million dollars worth of adprop was rescheduled, affecting Anheuser-Busch, Texaco, and Toyota, among others. These companies were forced to spend their advertising millions on football, golf, and sports such as volleyball, surfing, and soccer. There was another indication of disaffection: From a peak of 1.3 billion in 1991, baseball card sales fell to less than 1 billion in 1993 and continued to fall. Young baseball fans had become diverted to video games and other alternatives.[11]

There was another difference. In earlier times, there were baseball cards and sponsorships for only the outstanding players. Babe Ruth got rich doing commercials of all kinds, but only a few other players enjoyed his opportunities. In businessballprop every player is a cog in the promotion. In the NBA college stars are sponsored as they are issued their new uniforms. No player is permitted to look like the unshaven, dustied, and storied Ty Cobb or the equally memorable Pete Rose. They wear designer clothing for their autograph sessions. By the time an autographed $6.50 ball is sold the price has gone up to $79.95, of which the player may receive 25%. Ripken has signed 20,000 baseballs in a year.[13]

IT'S RACEPROP, AS WELL

Sports has been a vehicle for the emancipation of minorities, notably African Americans. There were fears by those who controlled the game that if they opened the door to Black culture it might dominate the sports scene and alienate White fans. That exclusion did not end until 1947, when Jackie Robinson joined the Brooklyn Dodgers; such brilliant players as Satchel Paige, Josh Gibson, and Cool Papa Bell never got their chance.[14]

Black track athletes lagged even behind baseball. Sprinter Jesse Owens had been humbled by Adolf Hitler in Berlin in 1936. But more than two decades later during the international Olympic Games in Mexico City, gold medal-winning sprinters Tommy Smith and John Carlos raised their black-gloved fists above their heads in what became known as the "Black Power" salute. Out of those same Olympics came decathlete Tom Waddell, who as a gay man exploded the myth of nonathleticism of homosexuals. Again, not until the Gay Olympics in the summer of 1994 was there a reprise, this in the coming out of Olympic champion diver Greg Louganis. All these challenges to White and homophobic authority were defining moments, oldprop in their anger, newprop in their desire to gain acceptance in the popular culture.

FALLEN ICON?

A sportsprop drama was acted out through the courts, leading to O. J. Simpson's acquittal on a double-murder charge. College and professional football star, film and television actor, sports broadcaster, and spokesman for corporations, Simpson could not escape public sentiment among non-Blacks that he had gotten away with it. Everyone admired his triumphs, his smile, his cordial demeanor, his matinee-idol looks, and his raw talent. Despite injuries, his body seemed to respond to every demand he put on it.

The contrast between O. J. the sportsprop hero and O. J. the accused murderer was more than some sports fans could reconcile. As friend Al Cowlings drove O. J.'s white Ford Bronco on a prolonged and tortuous course over Los Angeles freeways to Simpson's home, television viewers wondered how O. J. actually could do what he was suspected of doing. O. J. was a gladiator, but was he a murderer? He had not been charged at that time, so many of the bystanders cheered the gladiator on![15]

Sports produced other aberrations in 1994. Olympic ice skater Nancy Kerrigan was attacked by members of rival Tonya Harding's entourage to disable her for competition, and some went off to jail. Golfer John Daly, fighting alcoholism, was suspended after an unexplained playing halt. A number of NBA stars sought reinstatement after drug interludes. Young tennis phenom Jennifer Capriati was charged with marijuana possession.[16]

BASKETBALL BUSINESSPROP

For a decade, NBA President David Stern promised windfall profits to owners and players and delivered them. A decade of promotion and expansion lent basketballprop the sweet smell of success. Stern sent the "Dream Team" to Barcelona for the 1992 Olympics and "Dream Team" became the most often used phrase at the summer games. In late 1995, Stern organized a McDonald's world tournament in London, and the NBA's Houston team (without Hakeem Olajawon) won it.[17]

Big Salaries (and Men) to Feed

When the Los Angeles Lakers NBA basketball team signed 7'1" Shaquille O'Neal to a 7-year, $120 million contract, they had more than 300 pounds of high-priced star to feed. That plunged them further into businessballprop.

Because attendance at professional sports contests usually pays less than half of players' salaries, income must be generated from television and radio rights, marketing, and licensing of merchandise (hats, shirts, shoes, etc.).

Commercial sponsors also buy advertising space, posh suites, and site advertising as well as radio and television time, their synergies producing total sportsprop.[18]

Stern professed that the NBA was an entertainment company and the NBA was a combination TV show, theme park, apparel company, home video producer, and publisher. Vying with the Super Bowl, the NBA spiced up its All-Star Game with slam-dunk contests, three-point-shot competitions, old-timer's games, and all-rookie competitions; that is, total businessballprop.

That was never more clear than in the 1996 NBA finals, which pitted Jordan and the Chicago Bulls against the heavy underdog Seattle Supersonics. A columnist wrote that the NBA wanted an interesting match-up, if possible, but businessball dictated that the Bulls win. Of the $4 billion per year that the NBA sells in T-shirts, jerseys, and jackets, 40% to 45% is Bulls merchandise. It would be good for the NBA if the Bulls remained America's basketball team, just as Dallas once was America's football team. And the longer the series ran, the more opportunities the sports advertisers would have to ply their wares.[19] Seattle coach George Karl complained that there was too much emphasis on the money, but that was businessballprop in the 1990s.

꙳   ꙳   ꙳

In the early 1990s, businessballprop was a downer, disenfranchising the fans through strikes and the moving of professional sports franchises and permitting players to engage in crude and unsportsmanlike behaviors. It took the return from retirement of an old hero, Michael Jordan, to make businessball acceptable. But when NBA President David Stern and the players' union concluded a new contract in June 1995, they met unexpected opposition from the stars such as Jordan and Knicks' star Patrick Ewing, who led a movement to decertify the players' union. Professional sports did have its heroes in the mid-1990s, but it seemed to be reviving them more than creating them judging by the likes of Ken Griffey, Jr., Cal Ripken, Jr., and the return of Michael Jordan and Magic Johnson.

NOTES

1. Those ads have windows and walls . . . (1995, February 27). Kuntz, M., *Business Week*, p. 74.
2. Nike's got Gump-tion. (1994, August 1). Jensen, J., *Advertising Age*, p. 1.
3. Behring: Renovate or we vacate. (1995, November 7). Bruscas, A., *Seattle Post-Intelligencer*, Sec. D, pp. 1/3.
4. Lipsyte, R. (1995, April 2). The emasculation of sports. *New York Times Magazine*, pp. 50–57.
5. The reason they are still calling him Magic. (1996, February 1). Araton, H., *New York Times*, Sec. B, p. 6.

6. Back in play. (1995, May 8). Remmick, D., *New Yorker*, pp. 38–43.
7. Lipsyte, R., ibid.
8. Advertising Duel: Jordan vs. Shaq. (1995, May 7). Wise, M., *New York Times*, pp. 28/52.
9. Halberstam, D. (1994). *October 1964*. New York: Villard Books, pp. 363–365.
10. Letter. (1995, September). Lasday, L., *Hemispheres*, pp. 11–113.
11. The pride of the Orioles. (1995, September 11). *Newsweek*, p. 79.
12. There's always next year—maybe: Baseball advertisers take a hike for '94. (1994, September 5). Jensen, J., *Advertising Age*, p. 1.
13. When the pen is really mighty; autographs by the bushel and money by the barrel. (1995, July 14). Chartrand, S., *New York Times*, Sec. C, p. 1.
14. Conversation with Rick Welts, Vice President, NBA.
15. Real O. J. Simpson: His image masked private complexity. (1995, June 24). *Seattle Times*, Sec. A, p. 1.
16. All the sports world's a stage, and its players are really entertainers. (1994, October 24). Jensen, J. *Advertising Age*, pp. 4–5.
17. British miss point of NBA circus. (1995, October 20). Thomsen, I., *International World Tribune*, Sec. A, p. 23.
18. The real deal on O'Neal. (1996, August 23). Sterngold, J., *New York Times*, Sec. C, p. 1.
19. NBA's banking on Bulls' victory. (1996, June 4). Newnham, B., *Seattle Times*, Sec. E, pp. 1/5.

HUMORPROP
Opiate of the Popular Culture

Perhaps no propaganda acknowledges the individual's grasp of events so re-wardingly as humorprop—the political and social commentaries of late-night television hosts, the streams of consciousness of stand-up comics, the barbs of political cartoonists, the inversions of reality acted out by comic strip charac-ters, and the satire of public figures such as politicians, columnists, and com-mentators, each skewering the other as the situation permits. Each rewards our up-to-dateness by making reality laughable. In its approach to problems, humorprop is predominantly newprop and the opiate of our popular culture.

In sheer volume, variety, and its synergy with politics and the arts, humor-prop contributes to a consciousness of totalprop. Into the 1990s, hosts pack-aged slick humor with glitzy personalities to attract late-night audiences, and stand-up comics and comedy clubs took over cable channels. Every genre of humor was exploited—comedy, wit, irony, parody, and satire, all designed to inform and to entertain. In a nation in which politics was ugly and oldprop, humor made it more human and acceptable. The 1996 campaign saw a flow-ering of satire and wit among political conservatives, modeled by such famil-iar figures as the acute William Buckley, the blustering P. J. O'Rourke, and the acidic Republican presidential candidate, Bob Dole.

Up to Election Day 1996 the late-night hosts were enjoying Dole age jokes. "96?" one asks. "Why Dole *is* 96." David Letterman observed that Dole considered himself an optimist, noting that a lot of people would look at a glass as half empty, but Dole would see it as a great place to put his teeth. Jay Leno asked about Dole's "senior aides" being asked for an opinion. "How old are they, to be senior," he asked, "90 or 100?" [1]

On the Jay Leno and David Letterman comedy shows, the keys to under-standing the psyches of Clinton and Dole are "fat and old." Clinton, of course, is satirized as being fat, and Dole is lampooned because of his age. Clinton likes snacks, and Dole celebrates birthdays.

Polls and focus groups showed that the voters got a lot of information from late-night comedy sketches. Indeed, political humor took on the aura of totalprop as the lines between show business and politics became increasingly blurred. The mimicry of candidates—from the eras of Nixon, Ford, and Carter to Reagan, Bush, and Clinton—became as real as the candidates themselves. Life was imitating art.

If the pun can be forgiven, Dole had a doleful as well as a comedic side, and it provided an appealing panache of newprop. Every incident was grist for his humor mill. He had, of course, telephoned President Clinton on election night to concede his defeat, but 2 days later, responding to Letterman's question as to what it was like to call and admit defeat, Dole said, "I called him collect. My campaign was out of money."

Referring to one of his slogans, "A better man for a better America," he said he now needed to modify it only slightly: "I'm going to Florida and get a better tan for a better America."

His effort to get Ross Perot out of the race didn't turn out too well, Dole wryly conceded. To which Letterman replied, "I can't imagine any visit with Perot turning out too well."

The audience thunderously applauded, marking a moment of political significance where humor served as an opiate for the people.

WHAT IS THIS THING CALLED?

Humor permits us to release in a split-second outburst of appreciation the tensions that trouble and torment us, many brought about by the failures of the most prominent among us. How else to express our doubts about a Dan and a Marilyn Quayle, a Ross Perot, a George Bush, a Bill and a Hillary Clinton, an Al and Tipper Gore, a Newt Gingrich, or a Bob Dole?

Just after the 1992 election, a story was told about the Clintons and the Gores being killed in a crash between Air Force 1 and an alien space vehicle. All ascended to Heaven and were brought before God. After the introductions, God praised Gore for his environmental work and Tipper for her efforts to curb child pornography and seated them to the left. He commended Clinton for his jobs program and NAFTA and seated him to the right. He next asked Hillary about her health program, to which she replied, "I'll tell you about it, God, after you get out of my chair."

Obviously this is a feminist joke; a woman, not a man, is God, and she is first among equals. But we now are entering a period of so-called "post-feminist" humor directed against men that expresses the reality of shifting power relationships. The reversal of the punch lines makes the oldprop humor of male exploitativeness more obvious and the newprop humor of female dominance more appreciated:

Q. Why are all the dumb-blonde jokes one-liners?
A. So men can understand them.

Q. What do you call a man with half a brain?
A. Gifted.

Q. What do you call a man with his hands handcuffed behind his back?
A. Trustworthy.[2]

GENERATIONAL SEGMENTATION

Although politicians can claim some of the territory for satire and wit, the nation's forums are the late-night shows, whose hosts attract more than 10 million viewers nightly. The retirement of Johnny Carson was more than a passing event, it was the changing of the guard. The nation pondered who of those who aspired to his crown would succeed him. One headline read: "Look, everybody! After Carson, A Host of Late-Night Wannabes."[3]

Carson had spanned the generations in his appeal, but the "Carson wannabes" would inherit only fragments of his once diverse audiences. Over a 20-year period, he had suffered an astonishing 50% attrition in viewers from his peak. The inside stories of how the decisions were made by the major networks—Leno to inherit the *Tonight Show*, a disappointed Letterman to shift to the CBS *Late Show*—were told on February 25, 1996 by HBO. However, as described by cerebral host Dick Cavett, they were anything but funny.

The secret was that whatever Carson's legacy might be, it was already in the process of being segmented, not inherited. It would be marketed by each host to its most congenial viewers, whether they were the 20-somethings, the Boomers, the Aarpies, or the new overclasses. Letterman was out in front at the outset, but his ratings went into a slide and by 1995 Leno had moved ahead of him, at which point NBC signed him to a new contract.[4]

The theories about Leno's success vary, but one was that he was more into newprop and doing jokes with "an attitude." He was quicker to exploit the celebrated O. J. Simpson trial, realizing that although they invoked race and politics, substantial issues of ethics and morality waited to be exploited as entertainment.[5]

Impaling Oneself and Others

Audiences reward the comic for inflicting pain on himself, and they do not mind if he takes along his enemies. Letterman and Leno both engage in studied self-deprecation and self-immolation because they recognize that the purpose of humor is not just to enjoy but to reveal, and this aura of intimacy is an essential element of newprop. But when Letterman hosted the Academy Awards, he forgot that the more famous the comic, the less serious the audience wants him to be about his famousness.[6]

Ethnic humorprop learned these lessons early. As oldprop it had demeaned the subject, but as newprop it demeaned the comic as a means of demeaning the audience, transformed into newprop by the added ability to create understanding. As I sat one evening in Caroline's Comedy Club in New York, I was reminded of what Dick Gregory often said: "Look what you done to me that I got to do to you!" Oldprop–newprop understood!

Although Arsenio Hall was a comic by background, humorprop was not his signature. Rather, his "pop icon" approach attracted an MTV-style audience, grooving with such celebrity guests as Madonna, Demi Moore, Magic Johnson, and Bill Clinton (on the sax). Although the 20-something audience was loyal, it was also diminishing, suggesting Hall's impending demise. He could not attract any other generational segment to compensate for his losses.

Called "Obsequio" because of his soft interviewing style (in the pattern of Larry King), Hall nonetheless cultivated a taste for the controversial. Many of his guests were hip African Americans such as rappers and other Black stars who could not otherwise find their way onto late-night TV. It was a harbinger of Hall's passing that he hosted the Nation of Islam leader Louis Farrakhan, but he saw it as an effort to gain community with a diverse audience on the basis of "live and let live," not "kill or be killed."[7]

COMEDY CENTRAL: SEEKING FAME

Comedy Central was launched to provide performers in comedy what MTV afforded for musicians. It ran raunchy and sophisticated sitcoms that other channels would not touch, marathon weekends devoted to old series such as *Soap* or *Monty Python's Flying Circus,* new productions such as "comedy from the heartland," and a talk show with Bill Maher called *Politically Incorrect.* It was newprop because it challenged the imagination, every action rewarded insider knowledge, and every innuendo invited membership.[8]

A soft-spoken exploiter of newprop, Maher carved out the intellectual end of the spectrum, but he did not come up short on outrageousness. In one opening monologue he roamed from Rose Kennedy's death (Oliver Stone saw a conspiracy) to Newt Gingrich: "If poor people need money, let them get their own book deals." He asked George Stephanopoulos, who comes from a family of priests, if he could be a good person in politics. Stephanopoulos ducked an answer.[9]

Maher's guests have included such diverse figures as gangsta rapper Dr. Dre, author Gay Talese, radical talkprop host G. Gordon Liddy, and comic

Jerry Seinfeld. When the cohost of the Howard Stern program assailed helmets and seat belts as regulatory, Seinfeld asked him if he also opposed bumpers, windshields, and safety glass. Thus Comedy Central became humorprop with an attitude, a forum for diversity, and a refuge for the politically incorrect in a popular culture, and ABC will program Maher in 1997, a tribute to newprop.

FALLING ON A DULL SWORD

Humorprop must have a cutting edge, either oldprop or newprop. After becoming the *sine qua non* of those who cultivated outrageousness, *Saturday Night Live* fell on its own dull sword. As it began its 20th season in October 1995, two thirds of its cast and most of the rest of its supporting apparati were new. It used the inevitable O. J. lines: The defense attorney rebuts criticism of his use of the "race card" by insisting that the prosecution first had invoked the "evidence card."

In another skit, hostess Mariel Hemingway affects a role in the soft-porn film *Showgirls* by extending the metaphor of sexual license. In introducing the cast she ignored most of the men but passionately embraced all of the women. Then she sweetly reminded producer Lorne Michaels, "Don't forget to introduce me to your wife tonight!"[10]

Insightfully, the Canadian-inspired humor magazine *Spy* observed that one of the debasing oldprop factors that is indigenous to the popular culture is that it demonizes intelligence and rewards idiocy. Audiences liked to hate Anthony Hopkins in the *Silence of the Lambs*, Tommy Lee Jones in *Blown Away*, and Dennis Hopper in *Cliffhanger* because each portrayed an intellectual villain. People only felt comfortable when someone smart was venal; thus it was comforting that the star cheat of *Quiz Show* was an Ivy League professor who had donned his academic gown to utter the devil's oldprop.

Forrest Gump was a worthy hero because no one in the audience could feel themselves to be less smart. The result was what *Spy* called the "dumbification of America," where it wasn't smart to be really smart anymore. After all, look what happened to Roman Polanski and Woody Allen! Note the constant production of people who are "faux smart;" that is oldprop, for they are only made to seem smart by being granted honorary degrees, authoring (but not writing) books, and getting jobs on network news.[11]

Magazines are producing an erudite humorprop, among them *The National Forum Gallery of Cartoons*, *American Satire*, *Spectator*, and regional tabloids such as the *Northwest Comic News*. Desktop publishing permitted the creation of small political journals. *The Quayle Quarterly* was succeeded by *The Perot Quarterly* and *The Hillary Clinton Quarterly*.

The critics can't leave Hillary alone, and that leads to oldprop excesses for which humor is the only excuse. *New York Times* language pundit William Safire acknowledged that he had been been captured by the vituperative ghost of columnist Westbrook Pegler when he called Hillary Clinton a "congenital liar." Unabashed, Hillary said she hoped this would not embarrass her parents because the implication was that congenital meant hereditary. Then she recalled that Safire had worked for Richard Nixon, and probably still did, with the implication that this was hereditary, too, an exchange of oldprop only made acceptable by wit and by the edification that this implied. But Safire would concede only that the only doubt that lingered in his mind was whether President Clinton, in his widely publicized pique, had intended to punch him "on" the nose, or "in" the nose; ordinary usage seemed to prescribe "in." Thus humor defused a confrontation, celebrating its potential for newprop.[12]

A CONSERVATIVE RENAISSANCE

Safire is only one of numerous conservatives who are bringing about a renaissance in political humor, raising it from the level of an angry oldprop to more intellectualized newprop. Safire suggested that Republicans should use humor to put down the opposition gently and often, thus demonstrating superiority. In an "Age of Right Wit," conservatives would laugh at the Left. In 1996 conservative oracles published five books that made fun of the Democrats, and particularly Bill and Hillary Clinton. Several national magazines also changed their tone from starchy to archy to convey their shift to newprop from the old. O'Rourke wrote in *Spectator* magazine, "Stand warned, 'Boy Clinton,' we're going to laugh you out of office. We did it to the Carters and we'll do it to you." The "merry moralists" even began to poke fun at each other, as when Dole said that Gingrich's aides maintain five cabinets that are full of ideas; the smallest contains Newt's ideas. Dole also compared a Roger Mudd (CBS) interview with the replaying of the film *Jaws:* "75% watched *Jaws* and 25% watched Mudd but only half could tell the difference."

Cartoonists at the Ready

The political cartoonists always have centered on presidents. Gerald Ford was portrayed as a piece of wood; things had to be hammered into his head. Harry Truman was portrayed as a jug of whiskey, Woodrow Wilson as a box of Grape Nuts because they were hard and crackly, and George Washington was portrayed on oatmeal cartons because oatmeal was easy to eat for those who had wooden teeth.[13]

A cartoon asked readers to imagine if the Clinton Administration were an old TV show, what show would it be?

The orginal Star Trek? Perhaps. Al Gore would make a terrific Mr. Spock, but Bill Clinton lacks Captain Kirk's decisiveness.

Batman? Again possible, but who would be Robin? Well, his crime-fighting sidekick, Al Gore. But Hillary is put off by Clinton's slowness to respond, and comments: You wanna sleep on the bat-couch tonight, Batman?

Mod Squad? Of course, it's a scenario where baby boomers speak of change and idealism while working diligently to uphold the status quo![14]

The quarterly *Flush Rush* (Limbaugh) reported that the portly broadcaster became annoyed when late-night host Jay Leno described a 20,000-person turnout for a Limbaugh promotion. "The last time this many conservatives gathered in one place," Leno commented, "was in Berlin in 1935."

After a spate of Limbaugh-authored books capitalized on his first burst of notoriety, the humorists went to work on him in earnest. A former *Saturday Night Live* writer entitled his biography *Rush Limbaugh Is a Big Fat Idiot, and Other Observations*. One satire has Limbaugh not only adopting Newt Gingrich's proposal of putting children in orphanages but shooting the elderly into space. "And think about how many more manned space operations NASA could undertake," he comments, "if they didn't have to worry about getting the astronauts back." This poses the ultimate question of satire as newprop or oldprop; clearly, in defending the right of inclusiveness it was newprop.[15]

One of the most humorous satires in the 1990s was *Primary Colors*, devoted to the presidential ambitions and relentless campaigning of the "extended Clinton Family." The "family" was shown in stark relief—some would say stark naked. What emerged as more amusing was the guessing game that ensued as to the author of the satire, because she or he (or a combination thereof) was published only as Anonymous. (April Fool's Day humor had aficionados obtaining autographed copies!) Clinton was moved to say that in his 3 years in Washington, DC, no secret had been better kept.

When the film rights were purchased by producer Mike Nichols for $1.5 million, the guessing began as to who would play the leading roles. Among those proposed for Hillary were Madonna (she was successful and had played a First Lady as Evita) and Meryl Streep (she had demonstrated that she could negotiate fearsome rapids); Anthony Hopkins would play Clinton (he also had played a President as well as a cannibal); Melanie Griffith would play Gennifer Flowers (no one as beautiful could play dumber better); Michael J. Fox would play Stephanopoulos (he, too, was short). However, disputes arose as to who should play former New York Governor Mario Cuomo (Democrats opted for Al Pacino, Republicans favored Joe Pesci). The subtlety of these jabs was informative and definitely newprop.[16]

Getting Worser and Verser

A Washington columnist produced a roster of "notable rogues" in verse. Inevitably, he lampooned all politicians and celebrities, in this case Newt Gingrich and Larry King:

> On Capitol Hill, he always will pontificate and blast;
> His gray hair thick atop his scalp he talks so slick, so fast;
> If mikes or notebooks are on hand he's always good for quotes;
> If only Newt talked less he'd find a larger stock of votes.
>
> He rasps a lot, he likes to grin, the Brooklyn you can't miss;
> His glasses black, suspenders slack, He cries, "Back after this!"
> The pros mock his squishy style, they claim he ducks the tough (question);
> But if you get on Larry's show, you know that you're hot stuff.[17]

THE COMIC STRIP

The comic strip permits the humorist to invert reality by graphic means. Boomer cartoonist Gary Larson's *The Far Side* put the words of humans into the mouths of animals, plants, and Martians. When Larson said in 1994 that he was going to give up his strip, Jim Borgman of the *Cincinnati Enquirer* caricatured a cone-coiffed matron street person holding a sign that said: "Lost my job in *The Far Side*." What readers lost was a newprop that allowed them to see themselves as others (cows, mostly, but beetles, geese, ducks, sheep, cockroaches, and anteaters) saw them.[18]

When Calvin and Hobbes, the self-centered tyke and his philosophical tiger buddy, departed the comic pages, they left behind a legacy of newprop humor and insight. No longer could readers enjoy wry intellectualizing about good versus evil between mouthfuls of peanut butter, nor would they grit their teeth as sleds plunged into abysses.[19]

Calvin, a mop-haired boy whose only friend was a stuffed tiger, made a living in his cartoon strip life by baiting girls and fighting pretensions with fantasized evil. Despite political incorrectness and a calculated inversion of reality, Calvin's mockery of institutions gained a special moral standing. When Calvin pretended to be God he said his first act would be to destroy the earth, whose puny inhabitants displeased him.

A reviewer (and fan) noted: "The kid is a mess. He's delusional and deceitful. He's a procrastinator and a prevaricator. He's a cynic, a sadist, a sexist. . . . 'I live according to one principle, and I never deviate from it,' Calvin says. 'Look out for No. 1. It's a lot more fun to blame things than to fix them. Every time I've built character I've regretted it.'"[20] The author of the satiric strip, Bill Watterson, "burned out" after 15 years, not long after Larson stopped drawing *The Far Side* and Berke Breathed abandoned his Pulitzer Prize-winning *Bloom County* and then *Outland*.

If any medium of humor could be said to have given prominence to new-prop, it would be the comic strip. Few can eclipse Doonesbury. The satire is caustic and thought invigorating. Our chapter on businessballprop, as an example, should not have left out this dialogue between Garry Trudeau and the management representative:

Panel #4: "I'm vice president of marketing, sir. I wanted to thank you personally for coming out to the park today!" "Well, your 90% discount might have had something to do with it."

Panel #5: "Like it? We wanted to make the ball park experience attractive to families again!" "We also liked the free hot dogs, balls, and parking."

Panel #6: "Well, it's the least management can do, sir!" "Management? What about the players? They have as much to do with the death of baseball as you guys."

Panel #7. "Quite right! Why don't I send up one of our stars to personally apologize to you!" "Which one?"

Panel #8. "Take your pick, sir!" "Um. How about the pitcher? He's not busy!"[21]

HUMOR, O CANADA!

Much more surprising than the impact of humor on U.S. television and films has been the influence of Canadian humorists and other intellectuals. In fact, one must question the capacity of a popular culture to assess itself when its most trenchant humorists are observing it from the vantage point of another culture!

Without Canadians there might have been no *Saturday Night Live*, no *Ghostbusters*, and no *Wayne's World*. Canadian comics include comics Dan Aykroyd, Michael J. Fox, Mike Myers, Phil Hartman, the late John Candy, Rick Moranis, Rich Little, Martin Short, and Jim Carrey. Lorne Michaels wrote jokes for Woody Allen and *Laugh-In* before creating *Saturday Night Live*. Canadian writers and producers were behind such television entertainment as *Monty Python's Flying Circus*, *The Smothers Brothers Comedy Hour*, *Laugh-In*, the *Sonny and Cher Comedy Hour*, *Hee Haw*, and sitcoms such as the *Mary Tyler Moore Show*, *Taxi*, *Home Improvement*, *Seinfeld*, and *The Simpsons*, among others. Canadians felt that U.S. popular culture offered opportunities they could not realize in Canada.[22]

HUMOR AND SOCIAL CHANGE

As the Baby Boomers aged, men were becoming more nurturing, family oriented, and inner directed as women became more aggressive, powerful, and dominant. In terms of humorprop, women initiated more jokes and made men the butts of those jokes. In the low-brow comic strip, *The Lockhorns,* where once Leroy prevailed, Loretta now gives more than she gets.

Women generally were almost as likely to become comedians as were men. Rita Rudner recalled that when she was starting out, clubs would allow only one female on stage a night but now women were put on back-to-back. Rudner now is looking at careers in film and television sitcoms and sitlifes, where women comics are being given a chance to express themselves.[23]

Witty women were not an exclusive phenomena of the 1990s, of course; there are just more of them in the popular culture. "Oldtimers" such as Lucille Ball, Carol Channing, Martha Raye, Joan Rivers, and Jane Meadows introduced a rich and flowing genre of humor to film, literature, television, and the theater. Channing still is doing *Hello, Dolly,* and after a checkered career in film and television, Rivers was cast on Broadway as comedian Lenny Bruce's mother.

TIME FOR SATIREPROP

Political satire has multiplied as our anxieties have intensified. As high-end humorprop, satire appeals to the more educated and informed.

During the 1992 campaign, satire was the mode in *The News in Review* at Del's Down Under in Manhattan:

- Dan Quayle evoked the inevitable adaptation from *The Wizard of Oz,* "If I Only Had a Brain."
- Barbara Walters encouraged the forgetful Ronald Reagan, with help from Nancy, to sing, "I Remember It Well."
- Ross Perot was serenaded with "Billion Dollar Baby."
- Clarence Thomas insisted he "Ain't Misbehavin'."
- Gorbachev did a lounge rendition of "The Party's Over."
- And "Call-my-800 Number" candidate Jerry Brown was pictured in shoulder-length tresses, hairband, and dashiki, singing "The Age of Aquarius."

At the West Gate Cafe in Manhattan, comics observed that Gore won the vice presidential nomination because he was the only man Whiter than Clinton, Pat Buchanan had a secret plan to enter the German elections, and the Christian evangelical tobacco lobby was recruiting new smokers. This was newprop with a twist; enjoyment rested on knowledge but at least a modicum of partisanship.

Saturday Night Live spoke for a generation, but it has shown signs of aging. Star Dana Carvey quickly went on to bigger things in Hollywood. The film

Wayne's World was astonishingly successful. Carvey played the impish Garth, the blond, seemingly left-back and laid-back partner to Wayne, in a television sitcom. For 4 years, Carvey arguably had been a better George Bush than Bush, himself—often more dependably likable and humane in caricature than the real thing. As newprop, he became a treasured presidential asset.[24]

As Beavis in the sitcom put-on, *Beavis and Butt-Head,* Carvey used satire to make life in the popular culture more rewarding. His mimicking of Bush made everyone's day and his own reputation. The truth was that he humanized Bush, and Bush acknowledged it. Bush told Carvey they had been through a lot together; in fact, the Carveys were invited to the White House and spent the night in the Lincoln Room, where it is said that the President gently kissed Mrs. Carvey goodnight.[25]

Magazines were a special forum for parody. *Mad Magazine* parodied Irving Berlin's "A Pretty Girl Is Like a Melody" with "Louella Schwartz Describes Her Malady." And Weird Al Yankovic, a noted parodist, changed Robert Palmer's "Addicted to Love" to "Addicted to Spuds," as follows: "Your greasy hands, your salty lips, / Looks like you found the chips."

As parody is so skilled at doing, The Capitol Steps lifted the Iran–Contra affair from the bitterness of oldprop to a more humorously conceived newprop with "Thank God I'm a Contra Boy," and "I Want a Man With a Slow Mind," presumably sung by Marilyn Quayle. Tonya Harding sang "Breaking Knees Is Hard to Do." President Clinton found expression in a parody called "Both Sides Now."

> I've taken stands on both sides now
> On Pro and Con I've shown them how
> My views I always rearrange,
> That's why I said I stand for change.[27]

A columnist satirized television at the end of 1995 with a poem, "The Maven" (with apologies to Edgar Allan Poe). It described how research determined programming decisions:

> Once upon a broadcast dreary, while reporting market theory; over a quaint and curious pie graph depicting tax-abatement lore. I was wrapping, just recapping, when suddenly there came a tapping, as of someone gently rapping, rapping at my newsroom door. "Tis our pollster," I concluded, "tapping at my newsroom door, only this and nothing more."
>
> Back then to my news desk turning, all my heart within me burning. Soon again I heard a tapping, somewhat louder than before.
>
> "Finally," said I, "an intern is returning with the numbers from the focus group *du jour.* We'll see then where we're trending. As to complex questions ending in subtleties like this week's either/or; And hope the answers vary from last week's quite contrary scientific survey, Framed as 'neither/nor.'"[28]

BREAKING SOCIAL BOUNDARIES

Humorprop has often taken the first step in breaking down social boundaries. Eddie Murphy's brashness and Redd Foxx-type raunchiness had broken down some racial barriers in the 1980s with a hard edge of oldprop, but it was newprop in its definition of morality and the need to free people's minds.

Even earlier, Mort Sahl, known in his youth as "the great moralizer," sought to deflate the pretensions of the mighty. Having read that badcap radio host Howard Stern might run for governor in New York, Sahl asked: "Is Albany (the state capitol) far enough away?"

Capturing the mood of a generation that was disaffected from the goody-two-shoes style of Dwight D. Eisenhower and the meanness of Senator Joseph McCarthy, Republican of Wisconsin, Sahl commented, "Every time the Russians throw someone in jail, we throw someone in, too, just to show them that they can't get away with it."[28]

Sahl became a friend of Oliver Stone, producer of the film, *JFK*, the Jim Garrison story, but he commented about Stone, "I hear (he) is going to film the life of Simon Wiesenthal (the Nazi hunter). That's the good news; the bad news is Kevin Costner is going to play Hitler."[29]

Finding the Limits

But humor can have too much bite; it can be too oldprop in caricaturing marginalized members of the popular culture. Jackie Mason was forced to withdraw from a political campaign because he had commented that although the title for the film *White Men Can't Jump* passed as funny, it was politically incorrect to produce *Schwartzers (Blacks) Can't Fly* or to say "there's never been a Chinese tap dancer; they love to press a shirt." Hip-hop humorist Martin Lawrence said of the film *Driving Miss Daisy* that if it were up to him he'd kick her out of the car.

Perhaps the most contentious of the unacceptable humorprop has been produced by HBO's *Def Comedy Jam*, which attempted to excuse its smuttiness as a reflection of Black hip-hop culture. However, it was condemned as oldprop for exploiting crude language and building walls around its culture rather than making it open to others:

> I've had it up to here with woman-dissing, race-mocking, gay-bashing, crotch-grabbing, toilet-mouthed (blacks). . . . If someone landed here from Mars and watched this show, the visitor would be left with the impression that African-American men are little more than foul-mouthed, sex-crazed animals and African-American women are nothing but sex-for-sale gold-diggers.[30]

The host of the program, Martin Lawrence, went on to become a popular character in his sitcom, *Martin*. But when he used the *Def* technique in a guest hosting of *Saturday Night Live*, he was almost blackballed from the network. Foxx, Buddy Hackett, Richard Pryor, and Dick Gregory proved that sexually exploitative comedians could shift their humor to newprop themes and become successful.

LET'S NOT FORGET OUR COLUMNISTS

Daily newspapers are full of syndicated columnists whose bent is humor, foremost among them Boomers Mike Royko, Dave Barry, and Lynda Barry. Responding to attacks on *infotainment* by William Bennett, former Secretary of Education and "moral whip" of the Republican party, Royko exclaimed humorously that he had not known that Oprah, Jenny Jones, Geraldo, and others were "making us crazy and shredding our national fabric." In his youth moral women stayed at home and watched *Our Gal Sunday* and *Helen Trent*.[31]

Royko devoted a day to Jenny Jones and Geraldo during which he learned about liaisons of 14- and 15-year-old boys with women twice their ages where the boys made the women pregnant and were forced into early parenting and marriage. However, the parents were philosophical; things could be worse. Royko concluded nonetheless that the programming had redeeming social values: No matter how inferior any viewers might feel, they would have to feel better about themselves after viewing the shows.

Dave Barry's syndicated columns appear in hundreds of daily newspapers and he satirizes himself and his Boomer friends as glorified Yuppies. When Barry produced a potpourri of columns about turning 40, the *Seattle Times* characterized him as the Peter Pan of American Letters, and Barry inscribed on his own dust jacket, "Not since the New Testament has this reviewer seen a work of the importance of *Dave Barry Turns 40*. —Dave Barry."

Equally self-deprecating and parodic was Barry's *Guide to Life*, in which he urged his fellow Yuppies to stay fit and healthy until they were dead. First advising his peers how to find a mate, Barry then told them how to divorce them, all in the spirit of the social statistics of the 1990s.[32]

Lynda Barry grew up in the Rainier Valley of Seattle, Washington, and moved to Chicago. She was well-prepared to make fun of the attention that was being focused on Seattle as a nirvana by *Newsweek* magazine. In the comic strip, *Seattle's Siren Song*, two women are talking about life in Seattle. One says that no one can believe "that I've been tempted to move back (to Chicago), except for people who have lived there long enough!" "There's a reason people need so much coffee in Seattle and why computer nerds do so well there. It eventually works its way into everyone who lives there. Even ex-Californians."[33]

There is no more fitting conclusion to a discussion of humorprop than the wisdom of Doctor of Humane Letters Yogi Berra, the irrepressible word mangler who played for and managed the New York Yankees. He left graduates of Montclair State University in virtual stitches with five bits of commencement advice:

First, never give up, because it ain't over 'til it's over.

Second, during the years ahead, when you come to the fork in the road, take it.

Third, don't always follow the crowd, because nobody goes there any more. It's too crowded.

Fourth, stay alert. You can observe a lot by watching.

Fifth, and last, remember that whatever you do in life, 90 percent of it is half mental.

In closing, thank you for making this day necessary.[34]

꜊   ꜊   ꜊

Perhaps no mode of expression best reflects a myriad of values and perspectives as humor. It is a generic newprop that invites a sense of membership and participation in the popular culture.

Writer M. L. Lyke attended "finals night" of a course on stand-up comedy at Skagit Valley College in rural Washington State (if you flunk, you can become a lawyer). The course was dedicated to the proposition that humor was important enough for higher education to produce more of it.

There was no doubt that Republican candidate Bob Dole considered humorprop to be the opiate of the people. In the first of the two presidential debates, he amused the audience with quips and sallies, earning admiration for his quick wit and his ability to use the edge of humor to redefine situations to his advantage.

Now humor on the Internet is vying for attention. Dedicated and relentless as this humor is, not even that may be adequate for a popular culture that is under constant attack and requires opiates of all kinds to assess its present and future.

NOTES

1. The age of right wit: Conservatives find an effective punch: laughing at the left. (1996, March 31). Getlin, J., *Los Angeles Times* (in *Seattle Times*), Sec. A, pp. 1/6/7. See also: Is age-bashing any way to beat Bob Dole? (1996, May 5). Berke, R., *New York Times*, Sec. 4, p. 1.

2. Here's Everybody . . . (1992, August 16). Gerston, J., *New York Times*, Sec. H, p. 1. See also: New Guest on "Letterman": Worry Over a Ratings Drop. (1995, September 25). Bill Carter, *New York Times*, Sec. C, p. 1. See also: Resurgent Leno gets 5-year deal from NBC as Tonight host. (1995, October 26). *Seattle Post-Intelligencer*, Sec. E, p. 1.

3. Look, who's laughing now. (1995, May 3). Freeman, M., *Mediaweek*, p. 1. See also: The late-night-lead turnabout. (1995, November 6). Carter, B., *New York Times*, Sec. B, p. 1.

4. Dave vs. Jay, CBS, Oscar. (1995, July 10). *Newsweek*, pp. 52–53.
5. So long to Johnny, America's sandman. (1992, May 10). Rich, F., *New York Times*, Sec. H, p. 1.
6. The swivel throne. (1993, October 18). Wolcott, J., *The New Yorker*, p. 107.
7. An emptiness in the late night laughter. (1995, May 21). *New York Times*, Sec. H, p. 29.
8. Promotions serious business for Comedy Central. (1993, November 22). *Broadcasting & Cable*, p. 40.
9. Comedy Central romps in uncharted territory. (1995, February 8). *New York Times*, Sec. B, p. 3.
10. Revving up some outrage on "Saturday Night Live," (1995, October 2). O'Connor, J. J., *New York Times*, Sec. B, p. 1.
11. Why it's not so smart to be a savant anymore. (1995, January–February). Barron, J., *Spy*, pp. 37–42.
12. Congenital, liar, punch. (1996, February 4). Safire, W., *New York Times Magazine*, p. 18.
13. A cartoonist feasts on a President. (1994, August 31). *New York Times*, Sec. B, p. 1.
14. *Tom Tomorrow*. (1994, November 10). In *New York Times*, Sec. A., p. 15.
15. Franken, A. (1996). *Rush Limbaugh is a big fat idiot and other observations*. New York: Bantam.
16. Anonymous. (1996). *Primary colors: A novel of politics*. New York: Random House. See also: Let Emma Thompson play everyone. (1996, February 26). Weinraub, B., *New York Times*, *Week in Review*, Sec. 4, p. 3.
17. Washington's notable rogues, in verse. (1995, November 20). Levey, B., *Washington Post*, AmeriCast-Post.
18. Shedding ink over "The Far Side." (1995, January 1). Steinberg, B., *New York Times*, Sec. E, p. 10.
19. Readers lose Calvin and Hobbes as duo sleds off to new possibilities. (1995, December 30). *The Bellingham Herald*, Sec. C, p. 4.
20. What if the world's most endearing megalomaniac actually grew up? (1995, December 29). Rubin, N., Knight-Ridder Newspapers, In *Seattle Times*, Sec. E., p. 1.
21. Readers bid a fond farewell to Calvin and Hobbes. (1995, December 29). Spiegelman, A., Reuters, In *Seattle Times*, Sec. E., p. 1.
22. The most entertaining American Canadians. (1993, June 27). *New York Times*, Sec. H., pp. 1/22.
23. Comic on the go. (1995, February 3). MacDonald, P., *Seattle Times*, Sec. H, p. 3.
24. Saturday Night Live. (1994, October 20). O'Connor, J. J., *New York Times*, Sec. B, p. 3.
25. Danamania. (1993, May 13). Zehme, B., *Rolling Stone*, p. 46.
26. Both sides now. (1995, May 28). *New York Times*, Sec. Y, p. 1.
27. The Maven: (With apologies to Edgar Allen Poe). (1995, December 10). MacGregor, J., *New York Times*, Sec. H, p. 37.
28. The targets have changed but the bite is the same. (1994, March 29). *New York Times*, Sec. C., p. 29.
29. Ibid., *New York Times*, p. 29.
30. The curse of incessant cursing. (1994, July 31). O'Connor, J. J., *New York Times*, Sec. H, pp. 1/28.
31. Oprah, Jenny, Geraldo: Thanks for the eye-opener. (1995, November 3). Royko, M., *Seattle Times*, Sec. B, p. 5.
32. Barry, D. (1991). *Dave Barry's Guide to Life*. New York: Wings Books.
33. Seattle's siren song. (1996, May 20). Barry, L., *Newsweek*, p. 55.
34. A degree of wisdom from Dr. Berra. (1996, May 17). Associated Press, In *New York Times*, Sec. B, p. 15.

PART III

Mediaprop

FROM BROADCASTING TO JOURNALISTIC NIRVANAS

The new mediaprop operates as much at the limits of the popular culture as in its mainstream, and this produces old propaganda as well as new. It can be reasoned that an institution that operates under the protection of the First Amendment should be far more a carrier of the new propaganda than the old, but this would discount diversity and choice.

The most venal oldprop is seen in the angerprop that is vented on talk radio. Hosts such as Don Imus, G. Gordon Liddy, Rush Limbaugh, Michael Reagan, and Howard Stern are talkpropsters of the Apocalypse —purveyors of sarcasm, violence, snideness, bias, and vulgarity; they minimize politicians, parties, and institutions and feed on the alienation of their audiences.

Mainstream journalists continue to seek nirvanas in their adoptions of techniques of objectivity, the new journalism, and public and civic journalism. But journalists who once were anointed as insiders now are once removed, and as such they are caught up in their private searches for nirvanas. They have become alienated from many of their sources and wide sectors of their audiences.

Network television news has also lost much of its mass appeal, devolving into infotainmentprop, simulated reality, and paid news. Certainly there is potential for newprop where new media forms reach out to new audiences, but one must question whether this brings more members into the popular culture or simply creates an oldprop theater of the bizarre.

Meanwhile, mediaprop is under attack as the bearer of messages, and its critics want to shoot the messengers. One example is the researchprop that condemns media for desensitizing children to violence and exploiting the popular culture with lurid sex and pornography. But both violence and pornography are largely in the eyes of the beholders.

Much of the criticism of mediaprop is itself oldprop, a function of old research paradigms and old political bromides. Critics do not look often enough beyond the media for explanations of aberrant cultural behaviors; this is an oldprop of omission, for it fails to address real problems.

14

RADIO TALKPROP
Using Oldprop for Fuel

If there is a milieu in which our popular culture creates oldprop and uses it for fuel, it is *radio talkprop*, a melange of programming that became strident and incessant in the 1990s and was credited in 1994 with helping to elect a conservative Republican Congress. Radio talkprop became a throwback to a mass culture, replete with leader figures and the oldprops of hate and demonization. By 1993, talkprop formats accounted for 10% of the nation's licensed radio broadcasters, double their number over a 5-year period, and quadrupled by 1995.[1]

Market and technological forces coalesced to make talkprop a national force and allow conservative Rush Limbaugh to lead a boom of nationally syndicated radio. Conservative commentator and presidential hopeful Patrick J. Buchanan joined Larry King and Bruce Williams on the Mutual Broadcasting System, giving its syndicate an 18-hour-per-day talk radio format. The controversial former Watergate burglar, G. Gordon Liddy, by mid-1995 was heard on 260 stations nationwide, second only to Limbaugh.[2]

In 1994 Limbaugh attracted 20 million listeners on more than 650 radio stations, and more than 4 million people watched his television show over 224 stations. His first book sold more than 2 million copies in paperback and his television call-in show rivaled the ratings of late-night hosts David Letterman and Jay Leno. But it was a different audience, predominantly made up of conservative, White, politically alienated men.[3]

The trend to talk radio was driven by profit and technologies as well as by personalities and events. A single personality that is featured on 200 stations costs much less than 200 personalities on individual stations. The cellular telephone drove up the ratings of drive-time radio, and lower costs for satellite time and equipment allowed networks to launch nationally syndicated shows.

MASS OR POPULAR CULTURE?

The programs sounded more like a few leaders dominating a mass culture than a diversity of opinions expressed in a popular culture. Self-selected and screened audiences echoed their hosts, which produced more affirmation than interaction. On most of these shows the screening of callers assured monologues that only pretended to be dialogues.

Already a controversial figure, Liddy became more so in the aftermath of the Oklahoma City terrorist bombing that killed 169 people. Prior to the bombing, Liddy had coached listeners on how to respond to armed federal agents if they threatened them: "Shoot to the head rather than to the body, which is shielded by protective vests." Less than a week after the bombing, Liddy replied to a question by a listener as to what to do, "Shoot twice to the body, center of mass, and if that does not work, then shoot to the groin area."[4]

In an astonishing show of support for Liddy, the National Association of Talk Show Hosts voted 16–4 to name Liddy the winner of its annual Freedom of Speech award. Michael Harrison, publisher of *Talkers* magazine, said the award was not given for anything Liddy explicitly had said: "I don't agree with him, and I know he's perceived as a nut, but he is the most prominent talk show host on the edge of public opinion in this country. He was the obvious choice."[5] What Harrison failed to provide, of course, was a pragmatic definition of his concept of freedom in a popular culture: Was it an invitation to participate fairly in any debate or exclusively an oldprop of intimidation and demonization?

The Process of Mobilization

The surge of oldprop on talk radio was brought about by the convergence of long-felt anger about a widespread sense of exclusion and alienation. Ready converts came from the far-flung militias, the Christian Coalition, the pro-life agitators, the antigay believers, disgruntled taxpayers, and antigovernment and anti-Clinton zealots, all attracted to the outspokenness of hosts who encouraged them to express their most troubled thoughts. Downsized out of jobs and discouraged by their prospects, they became angry and cynical. Limbaugh, himself, said his views had been excluded from the mainstream agenda:

> Every day we are inundated by what is supposedly natural, what is supposedly normal, what is supposedly in the majority, by virtue of what the dominant me-

dia culture shows us, and most often it's not us. Most often, what we believe in is made fun of, lampooned, impugned and put down . . . we don't want to feel that way. We want to feel as much a part of the mainstream as anybody else.[6]

Theorizing as to Functions

The late Michael Deaver, a Baby Boomer who conducted free-wheeling, any-thing-goes politicalprop for Ronald Reagan, theorized that radio talkprop had become the people's "new franchise." He saw it simply as an alternative medium to the "elite press":

> Like it or not, talk radio may be fulfilling some of the functions of traditional political institutions—parties, unions, and/or civic groups. It plays the role of a mediating institution that gives people a sense of connection when other institutions do not. They tune into a community of similar attitudes and discontent, and they reinforce one another's views about how bad things are in Washington.[7]

Harry Boyte, senior fellow of the Hubert H. Humphrey Institute of Public Affairs at the University of Minnesota, agreed that although radio talkprop did not have the connective tissue of relationships that existed in party organizations, the callers did identify with hosts: "That's the poignant fact of politics in our age, that people feel they have a relationship with Limbaugh."[8]

But Boyte saw that radio talkprop was divisive and demeaning and cut off debate among differing viewpoints rather than encouraging it. That was a pattern of oldprop; that is, the constituency that it mobilized was sequestered and exclusive rather than reaching out to everyone. The national mood and the 1994 campaign were perfectly suited to the radio talkprop format and approach—angry, and by implication, ugly, unreasoning, demanding, coarse, abusive, antithis and antithat and alienated from the popular culture:

> The problem . . . is that sounding off on talk shows has none of the qualities of public work. You get to vent. You get to whine, basically. When civic life or mediating institutions are replaced by electronic communicationos, people don't get any of the gritty flavor of life, of making a contribution.[9]

As conservative a Republican as John C. Danforth of Missouri, Justice Clarence Thomas' sponsor during his Senate confirmation hearings, agreed that the hard edge of radio talkprop was a problem that threatened the well-being of the popular culture: "The basic problem is the total breakdown of anything that resembles civility, and the fact that the battle is fought not for people's minds but for their emotions."[10]

Exclusivity Enforced

The darkest radio talkprop went beyond a sense of exclusivity to threatening violence. Talking about Jim Brady, for whom the gun control law was named, a radical talk show host in Phoenix, Arizona, Robert Mohan, said that Brady's wife "should be put down . . . a shot at a veterinarian's would be an easy way to do it. Because of her barking and complaining, she . . . needs to be put down." [11]

A Colorado host, Don Baker, encouraged listeners to take guns to Washington to protest bans on assault weapons. Listeners accused him of inspiring a Coloradan, Francisco M. Duran, to fire shots at the White House. By this time, even Baker realized he had gone too far and took himself off the air. [12]

THE HOST WHO TALKS MOST

Limbaugh is the host who talks the most and most glibly. He pretends to be seeking inclusivity, but his point of view and style make him an anathema to discerning audiences. As an entertainer as well as an ideologue, he knows how to hold audiences, combining an artfully contrived indulgence with put-down humor. His puckish capabilities were tested when late-night host David Letterman asked him how he could believe some of the inane things that he says. Limbaugh laughed and mimed and carried the moment.

The ouster of Democrats from governerships and Congress in 1994 was credited in large part to Limbaugh's hammering on three prime political objects: President Clinton, liberal thought, and incumbent Democrats. A preelection analysis observed that just as Larry King served to nominate Ross Perot through television talkprop, Limbaugh was "the surrogate precinct captain" for the Republicans in 1994. For his part, Limbaugh characterized the campaign as "Operation Restore Democracy" and encouraged his followers to get out and vote. [13]

Just 2 years later, his ratings dropping slightly, the emergence of Buchanan in the 1996 Republican primaries cast Limbaugh into a dilemma. Limbaugh, after all, was an entertainer, and the Buchanan campaign had become deadly serious. Ideologically, Buchanan had turned out not to be a true conservative but a populist whose protectionist views on trade would expand the role of government rather than limit it; government would have to build a trade wall around the United States and defend it. [14]

Buchanan followers warned Limbaugh that he had lost touch with regular people and their economic anxieties, and they accused him of caring only about elite economic issues. Why hadn't he joined in the populist demand for inclusivity of a disenfranchised working class? The answer: Limbaugh was not a populist follower, he was a conservative entertainer.

Limbaugh as Scapegoat

Democrats revile in the same coarse terms that Limbaugh himself employs. As comic characters "Mildred and Harold" debated Limbaugh's virtues, Harold pointed to his audience appeal and effectiveness. But Mildred disagreed on three points:

* As to persuasiveness: "He only sells hogwash."
* On leadership: "He couldn't lead ants to a picnic."
* On satisfying his listeners: "He's the current king of the mindless sound bite. He's Ross Perot with a thyroid problem." [15]

What brought on attacks of this kind was the character of the humor that Limbaugh employed; it diminished women, liberal politicians, and environmentalists:

* Women's rights advocates are *feminazis;* so is Hillary Rodham Clinton, and her sexual orientation is doubtful, as well.
* Vice President Al Gore is an environmental fascist.
* The musical theme from the film *Born Free* is puncuated by shots from a hunting rifle.
* Mentions of Senator Ted Kennedy are accompanied by the sound of a car splashing into water.
* President Clinton is a gay lover and a pot-smoking draft dodger.

A full-page advertisement in the *New York Times* in November 1995, quoted from a book about Limbaugh entitled, *The Way Things Ought to Be: Rush Limbaugh's Reign of Error,* cites incidents such as the above and concludes, "His scapegoating and chronic lack of truthfulness have degraded the national discourse, sown seeds of division, and unleashed a flood of misguided anger." [16]

Limbaugh is rivaled by the New York talk show host Howard Stern, who was coarse enough to play a recording by the slain Tejano singer, Selena, in which he punctuated her songs with the sounds of gunfire. [17]

A columnist who is known for her liberal views and her sense of outrage described Limbaugh as only picking on those who can't fight back—the homeless, the poor, women, children, and the defenseless. She described two jokes that Limbaugh told on the air:

> "Everyone knows the Clintons have a cat. Socks is the White House cat. But did you know there is also a White House dog?" He holds up a picture of Chelsea Clinton, aged 13.
>
> Limbaugh says he gets on an elevator. The only other passenger is Hillary Clinton. She tears off all her clothes, throws herself on the floor and begs him, "Rush, make a woman out of me." So Limbaugh tears off all his clothes, throws them at Hillary and says, "Fold those." [18]

Savoring a Political Victory

On the heels of the Republican victory of 1994, Limbaugh's conservative admirers became legion. He was made an honorary member of the freshman class of Republicans and was hailed as the Babe Ruth of talk shows. Surveys showed that among heavy talk radio listeners, three of four voted Republican in 1994.[19] Limbaugh was pleased when Harvard University's John F. Kennedy School of Government canceled its postelection training seminar because so many of those elected were Republicans. The task was taken over by the Heritage Foundation and Empower America, two conservative think tanks who included Limbaugh on their faculty.[20]

Limbaugh declared the vote to be "one of the most massive shifts to the right in any country in any year since the history of civilization, and a repudiation of the most amazing attempt to move this country to the left we've seen in 50 years. The liberal, elitist press lost." Liddy joined him in fulsome oldprop when he characterized the election as the beginning of the end of the "dreadful, disastrous, venal, corrupt, sleazy Clinton presidency. Send 'em back there to the chicken-guts-fouled rivers of Arkansas."[21]

Gingrich lauded Limbaugh and set aside space for radio talkprop hosts in the capitol buildings, promising that he would invite them to Washington regularly "so Congress could talk to those who talk directly to the American people."[22]

Clinton Bashes Back

Obviously irked by the cacophony of attacks by radio talkprop, Clinton engaged in a tirade against television evangelist Jerry Falwell, conservative radio talk hosts in general, and Limbaugh in particular. He denounced radio talkprop as a constant, unremitting drumbeat of (the oldprop of) negativism and cynicism. The violent personal attacks on Clinton and his wife were turning Americans against the political process and the Presidency:

> I don't suppose there's any public figure that's ever been subject to more violent personal attacks than I have, at least in modern history. . . . That's fine. I deal with them. But I don't think that it's the work of God. And I think that's what the issue is.[23]

When Clinton commented that radio talkprop hosts should not be "truth detectors," an ebullient Limbaugh responded: "I am the truth detector!"[24]

A Horsey cartoon pictures two children, one a space cadet, the other a butterfly princess, who beg their mother not to send them trick-or-treating on Halloween:

> "Please, Mom! Don't make us go out there tonight! B-B-Big Bad Bill (Clinton) will take our candy and give it to welfare cheats!"
>
> "An' . . . An' . . . An' horrible Hillary will keep us from seein' our mommies an' daddies and family doctors!"
>
> To which the mother replies:
>
> "I knew it! You kids have been listening to talk radio again!"[25]

The President was especially embarrassed by the comments of a laconic talk show host at a supposedly friendly roasting. Noted for his scathing humor, Don Imus was invited by the Radio and Television Correspondents to host their annual event. Among other put-downs of both Clintons, he at one point referred to the President as a "pot-smoking weasel." Angry because the Clintons expressed surprise at his attacks, he used another occasion to look out at his audience and comment: "I don't see the Clintons here—probably someplace testifying." Imus picked up another 10 stations to add to the 90 he already had syndicated.[26]

For a time angry radio talkprop held Republican presidential nominee Bob Dole at a distance because he was not angry or conservative enough, but they warmed to him after his convention speech. Limbaugh said the speech was so good, so real, and so from-the-heart that it was just right.

But then Dole seemed to have forgotten about radio talkprop, bringing an admonition from an industry editor (*Talker* magazine) and spokesperson, Michael Harrison, that Bill Clinton was poaching on his broadcast territory. That brought a pledge from Dole that he would stay in touch. Even the master oldpropster Limbaugh lamented the loss of contact. That did not prevent him from focusing on Clinton, whom he described as "the Schlickmeister" and "the noted hetero fun seeker." And Imus, another Clinton demonizer, observed that the Republican campaign was being run by morons.[27]

Press 1 for Christian Right

But there are far more extreme views espoused in radio talkprop than one hears from Limbaugh or Imus. The debate in Congress about gays in the military roused Christian Right talkprop host Pat Robertson, erstwhile presidential candidate and host of the *700 Club*. He warned that unless viewers acted promptly, groups like the National Organization for Women (NOW), the National Gay and Lesbian Task Force, the American Civil Liberties Union (ACLU) and other radical groups would gain the upper hand in the popular culture. "So what should a Christian do?" he asked.

The answer: "Call your congressman or woman." By late afternoon more than 400,000 calls had been made, 10 times the daily average. The Reverend Jerry Falwell asked listeners to his *Old-time Gospel Hour* to call a 900 number and sign a petition urging the President to keep gay prohibitions in place. Falwell said more than 31,000 callers signed up.[28]

Host Bob Grant of New York station WABC referred to Blacks as "savages," described former New York Mayor David N. Dinkins as a washroom attendant, and said that if Earvin (Magic) Johnson contracted AIDS and deteriorated, it would be a contribution to society. He characterized President Clinton as "that sleazebag in the White House," and said that the ideal solution to the Haitian immigration problem was drowning. He asked for a mandatory program of sterilization for welfare mothers, and said he would like to put environmentalists against a wall and shoot them. The last straw was a statement that late Secretary of Commerce Ron Brown probably was the only survivor of the fatal plane crash that killed 26 U.S. business leaders and the crew, and that he (Grant) believed that because he was, at heart, a pessimist.[29]

LOCAL RIGHT WINGING

Some local talk radio stations produce more virulent oldprop than national programs. Before he was released by his station, a San Francisco radio host asked if people with AIDS should be quarantined, if bounties should be paid to shoot illegal immigrants, and if President Clinton was controlled by Communist lesbians.[30]

In Seattle, KVI featured Mike Siegel, an unassuming lawyer who as a conservative host appealed to the angry and the disaffected. During the November 1993 local elections, he was criticized for the lack of any pretense of fairness to a popular and presumably liberal African American mayor, Norman Rice. In mid-1996, Siegel came under heavy criticism for publishing rumors about the mayor and his family. The *Seattle Times*, which had put top-notch investigative reporters on the story 2 years earlier, said they had turned up nothing. But Siegel went ahead, anyway, causing Rice to confront him publicly. Within the next few days Siegel apologized, but soon after was suspended from the air by his employers, the Fisher Broadcasting Company, and then fired, only to create a low-wattage statewide network.[31]

When Clinton came to Seattle to raise money for Democratic Senatorial candidate Ron Sims, he asked Siegel why he had conducted such an unremitting campaign against him, the office of the President, and the Democratic party. Siegel demurred politely, but as soon as the President left the air, Siegel again donned his black cape. Nonetheless, Siegel was one of only four board members of the national talk-show hosts' organization to vote against a free speech award to G. Gordon Liddy. He contended that Liddy had done nothing to stand up for the First Amendment; he had just said something extreme.[32]

Another avowed conservative, John Carlson, led a successful fight to curb the spending power of the state government. I was caught up in a local protest movement and was invited by Carlson to appear on his show. It provided insight into the world of call-in shows and other show-biz aspects of the program.

Former Texas conservative politician Jim Hightower leans toward the newprop of humor and insight. He once described George Bush as "having been born on third base, and when he discovered this he decided he must have hit a triple." Hightower asked about NAFTA, "Do we hafta?"[33]

In Denver, Colorado, an African American intellectual was described (unfairly) as the "Black Rush Limbaugh." Ken Hamblin blames African American youth for too readily perceiving themselves as victims and Whites as devils. He fears that the welfare system, multicultural education, and affirmative action stamp Blacks as inferior. Hamblin refers to himself as a Negro and calls liberal Black politicians "dysfunctional demogogues of darktown, dark with misery, hopelessness, and despair." It is a newprop directed at freeing Blacks from their stereotypes, but it has an oldprop edge.[34]

THOUGHT RADIOPROP TO THE RESCUE?

Can "thought radioprop" be successful commercially? Former California governor and perennial presidential hopeful Jerry Brown hosts an urbane late-night show on the Talk America Network, during which he harps on the evils of politics and fat-cat industrialists. He, too, is down on the system, but he insists that he is trying to fix it, thus attaching an insider newprop patina to the old. Add to this his urbanity, intelligence, and dark wit, all of which give him an intriguing cast, and this serves diversity. Ross Perot began his own show in late 1994 by denouncing Clinton as a draft dodger who had created an Iraqi threat to help Democrats win in 1994. But as Sam Howe Verhovek observed:

> If a talk-radio format implies freewheeling conversation between a host and caller, Perot's debut may well have been mislabeled. Typically, callers would ask a brief question that would prompt a homily from Perot, who then concluded by saying that the lines were jammed with callers and he needed to take the next one. Most calls lasted less than a minute.[35]

Perot said he dropped the show because he had too many commitments; the truth was that he had too few listeners. That, of course, is the ultimate test in the popular culture.

🥝   🥝   🥝

Radio talkprop emerged in the 1990s as an oldprop of hate and demonization. Short on knowledge and long on attitude, radio talkprop became argumentative, crude, and exclusionary, more consistent in its manner with the character of a mass culture than a popular culture.

There remains enough anger among special publics to sustain oldprop radio, although not at its highest ratings. A partial antidote is being found in more open talk formats, notably among hosts who combine personal integrity with a talent for entertaining and challenging.

President Clinton continues to feel offended by right wing hateprop. Soon af-

ter his re-election he described it as a venom that was not serving the popular culture.

Another promising alternative to radio oldprop is the Internet and the World Wide Web, which are providing a wide range of knowledge and the ability to interact, both elements of newprop.

NOTES

1. Triumph leaves no targets for conservative talk shows. (1995, January 1). Egan, T., *New York Times*, Sec. A, pp. 1/9.
2. Talk radio explodes in national syndication. (1993, May 17). Viles, P., *Broadcasting & Cable*, p. 34.
3. Limbaugh, R. (1992). *The Way Things Ought to Be*. New York: Pocket Books.
4. Hatred on the airwaves. (1995, May 1). *Seattle Post-Intelligencer*, Sec. A, p. 6.
5. Radio hosts honor Liddy. (1995, May 17). Conklin, E., *Seattle-Post Intelligencer*, Sec. A, p. 1.
6. Talk radio or hate radio; critics assail some hosts. (1995, January 1). Egan, T., *New York Times*, Sec. A, p. 11.
7. In Limbaughland, election jitters. (1994, November 3). Toner, R., *New York Times*, Sec. A, p. 13.
8. *New York Times*, Toner, p. 13.
9. *New York Times*, Toner, p. 13.
10. *New York Times*, Toner, p. 13.
11. *New York Times*, Egan, p. 11.
12. *New York Times*, Egan, p. 11.
13. *New York Times*, Toner, p. 13.
14. Radio talk show host fears for true conservatism's fate. (1996, February 23). Toner, R., *New York Times*, Sec. A, p. 12.
15. Limbaugh is no national security risk. (1994, July 28). Gay, H., *Seattle Post-Intelligencer*, p. 17.
16. They praise Rush Limbaugh. (1995, November 28). *New York Times*, Sec. A, p. 1 (Advertisement).
17. Ugly comments rooted in amazing stupidity of D'Amato, Stern. (1995, April 12). Dexter, P., *Seattle Post-Intelligencer*, Sec. A, p. 15.
18. Limbaugh only picks on those who can't fight back. (1993, October 18). Ivins, M., *Seattle Times*, Sec. B, p. 5.
19. Radio host tells G.O.P. not to trust the press. (1994, November 12). Seelye, K. Q., *New York Times*, p. 11.
20. No Harvard for freshman of Congress. (1994, November 24). *Washington Post*, In *Seattle Times*, Sec. A, p. 2.
21. Election '94: Talk of talk radio. (1994, October 10). *Washington Post*, In *Seattle Times*, Sec. A, p. 11.
22. Gingrich takes capital by storm with eye on history. (1995, January 5). *New York Times*, Sec. A, pp. 1/12.
23. Clinton calls show to assail press, Falwell, and Limbaugh. (1994, June 24), Jehl, D., *New York Times*, pp. 1/10.
24. Host, callers, trash Clinton on talk radio. (1993, July 12). Viles, P., *Broadcasting & Cable*, p. 43.
25. Cartoon. (1994, October 27). Horsey, D. *Seattle Post-Intelligencer*, Sec. A, p. 22.
26. After Imus spoke, more and more radio affiliates started listening. (1996, April 27). Lu, S., *New York Times*, Sec. C, p. 5.

27. Cool to Dole's campaigning, talk radio tries to start fire. (1996, September 25). Clines, F. X., *New York Times*, Sec. A, pp. 1/12.
28. From right, a rain of anti-Clinton salvos. (1994, June 26). Eckholm, E., *New York Times*, p. 1.
29. Bob Grant loses radio job after remarks on commerce secretary. (1996, April 18). Mifflin, L., *New York Times*, Sec. A, p. 14.
30. A San Francisco talk show takes right-wing radio to a new dimension. (1995, February 14), Tierney, J., *New York Times*, p. 6.
31. Rice denounces rumors on radio as 'hate talk'; mayor calls for more civility. (1996, May 13). Matassa, M., *Seattle Times*, Sec. B, pp. 1–2.
32. Clinton coup for KVI. (1994. November 4). Paulson, M., *Seattle Post-Intelligencer*, p. 6.
33. Hey, Rush, Jerry will take what's left. (1994, January 11). *Seattle Post-Intelligencer*, Sec. A, p. 2.
34. In Denver, the surprising new face of right wing talk radio. (1994, January 2). *New York Times*, Sec. D, p. 7.
34. Perot begins radio program with an attack on U.S. foreign policy. (1994, October 9). Verhovek, S. H., *New York Times*, p. 1.

15

TV PROP

From Talk to Infotainment

There is less angry oldprop on television talk shows than on radio. One possible explanation is that too much anger in plain view is a turnoff. That helps to explain the success of Larry King, who in George Bush's words, succeeded in introducing a kinder, gentler news interview that was conducted by the rules of communication rather than the conventions of advocacy journalism. In the King version, the interviewer and the interviewee address problems together rather than define issues separately, substitute accommodation for conflict, and create an environment of inclusion in which the audience feels empowered. As the arbiter of a new medium and a new journalism, King enfranchised a broad spectrum of the popular culture.

Early in the 1992 presidential campaign, the *New York Times* carried a photo of King across the top of a page in his shirt and suspenders leaning across the table toward an intent Ross Perot. The backdrop was a stunning vista of lights that encompassed Los Angeles. The legend in reverse type—white on black —said:

> Larry King, Kingmaker to the Pols: So Larry King, the talk-show host, finally takes a vacation, in May, his first trip to Israel. It's a "Roots" kind of thing for a 58-year-old guy from Brooklyn whose given surname was Zeiger. In Jerusalem, he joins the crowds praying at the Wailing Wall. His heart is full, and he is more than a bit awestruck when suddenly the man next to him, a Hasidic Jew in traditional dress, pauses in his chanting, stares and says:
> "Larry! Is (Ross) Perot for real or what?"[1]

King could have answered "yes," for it was in response to his gentle probing that Perot said he would become a presidential candidate if his followers placed him in nomination. The announcement not only represented a journalistic "scoop" for King but a public affirmation for Perot's followers. In merely chatting with Perot, King had stolen a march on the old media; they would have to keep tabs on the new TV talkprop to keep up with the new news.

When King hosted the decisive debate between Ross Perot and Vice President Al Gore about the North American Free Trade Agreement (NAFTA) in which Gore put Perot to flight, he received a call from President Clinton saying, "I owe you big time." To which the red-suspender-clad King replied to the President, hunching over his telephone: "All I did was ask questions." [2]

Columnist Maureen Dowd conceded that King's questions were not especially taxing ones. "And yet," she concluded, "he wound up in the kingmaking role, pleasing his guests, exasperating journalists, and creating a strong whiff of democracy." This was a new journalism, and it defined newprop, as well as a force for inclusion and participation.[3]

King's new forum permitted the candidates to define their images according to their own lights, and this was newprop. Perot used it to sell his rambunctious style with its freshness and seeming accessibility. King would be criticized for this, but Perot soon revealed his mentoring as a more controlling oldprop. In all, it was good theater: a cornball quip, a riposte, and a sound bite.

JOURNALISTIC AND INTELLECTUAL DISTASTE

Understandably, journalists, politicians, and intellectuals disliked the groupie flavor of King's "electronic town hall." Many feared that Perot might use teledemocracy to bypass the political process and the press. One editor labeled Perot's electronic democracy "a mysterious journey that appeared to take the nation from the splendid individualism observed by DeToqueville (the Frenchman who observed and wrote about early America) to the special isolation and security promised by Perotville":

> Rooted in techno-suburbias where they could enjoy complete personal security, the Perotists each morning would grasp their cellular phones and drive to their nearby glass enclosed high rise office buildings that were crammed with computers and fax machines. These were the new secrets of life. These were the new and eager consumers of the new propaganda.[4]

A Litany of Complaints

Journalists wedded to traditional TV newsprop decried King's willingness to allow a subject to take over the interviewing process. They decried this as neither rigorous nor skeptical questioning; he was serving up journalistic soft-balls. It was no wonder that every self-serving politician from former President Richard Nixon to Clinton, and of course, Perot, would rather interview with King than with them.[5]

But King consciously was pursuing the new news, not the old. In the new news, the viewer got the guest's story, however self-serving; in the old news, the viewer got the journalist's story, however self-serving. The candidates could establish their own agendas, not just respond to journalists' agendas, and they could assert their own truths, not just journalists' truths. Candidates could create synergies with their audiences that the audiences could then call in to validate. An angered King noted that the old media had produced Clinton and Bush rather than Jack Kemp and Elizabeth Dole versus Mario Cuomo and Sam Nunn: "With the old media we're a trillion dollars in debt, we had a cold war for 43 years, and the same dumb questions (have been) asked (by you journalists) at all the White House press conferences."[6]

King's producer, Tamara Haddad, described the sense of intimacy of the new news:

> The cameras stay close to guests' faces. There are no semicircles of chairs (as in PBS's *News in Review*), nor sedate senior journalists in easy chairs, nor the seeming anger expressed by participants on CNN's *Cross-Fire* nor the upright, aloof posture of Ted Koppel on *Nightline*.
>
> The guests want to make Larry's eyes sparkle, so they say things they (do) not intend.[7]

Moments of Old Truths

But there was no complete escape for Perot from the old news and the old journalism. He would be questioned aggressively by the printed press: What were the details about his exit from General Motors? How did he gain his wealth? Had he overcharged clients, including the government? Was the state of Texas going to build him a new (Alliance) tax-free airport?

On *Meet the Press*, the model of the old journalistic television interview format, Perot railed at his interrogators for not allowing him to define his own agenda: "This is an interesting game we're playing today. It would've been nice if you'd told me you wanted to talk about this and I'd had all my facts with me, but you didn't, right?"[8]

Perot's anger and frustration acknowledged that the journalists had exposed gaps in his knowledge and thinking. That was not an unusual outcome for a television interview in which a number of pundits ganged up on a single subject; in their defense it could be said that the style was oldprop but the goal was newprop. Nevertheless Perot became unravelled, and he said he would take a hiatus to reconfigure his positions on the issues. Not long after this came the startling announcement: Perot was dropping out of the race; his tortured explanations seemed improbable even to his staunchest supporters.

Perot was to return, but not all of his followers were to remain faithful to him and his cause. Nonetheless, he had helped to establish a new TV news genre. This was illustrated during the third televised debate among the candidates when the predominantly young studio audience interrupted an exchange of candidate insults to demand that they engage in the new TV talkprop rather than the old.

Clinton Catches On

While Perot auditioned politically on *Larry King Live*, Clinton crashed the *Arsenio Hall* show. There he not only tootled his saxophone to considerable applause, but he gabbed informally with his host. This was an intimate scenario, newprop at its best.

Clinton was one of those who realized that TV and radio talkprop reflected broader trends in the political culture for those who wanted to communicate. A reporter observed his appearance with Bryant Gumbel on *NBC Today*. The time was 7 a.m., Clinton's eyes were puffy, his face red, and his smile weary. Although the program did not show Clinton at his best, it did show him. One writer observed:

> Four years ago the measure of a candidate's media savvy may have been how many times he could get himself on the evening news. . . . This year it . . . is . . . how much exposure he can get interacting with real, live, ordinary Americans (on the talk shows).[9]

Democratic political consultant Ann Lewis said:

> This is a year in which people want to be heard. They have sent a very clear message. We want a candidate who hears what we have to say. With a call-in show, millions of voters can watch (as) you listen and respond courteously to people just like them.[10]

The late Frank Greer, Clinton's media adviser, echoed Larry King's view of the efficacy of the talk show: It gave people a sense that they had a direct role in the political process. This, in turn, cut through the cynicism. "What the public doesn't accept any more is removal," King commented. "That used to work, but now it's passé."[11]

NEW MEDIA, NEW IMAGES

The new media offered the promise of creating new images of Perot, Clinton, and even Bush if he would take advantage of the opportunity. However, Bush felt this was not fitting for a President, and MTV was beneath his personal dignity. He criticized Perot and Clinton for their exploitation of TV talkprop, and he only belatedly entered into it.

When *CBS This Morning*, a venture by the network into talkprop, gave Bush an opportunity to capture a studio constituency, he fumbled it. The producers assembled 125 people in the White House Rose Garden whom they had recruited from the tour line. Bush told the visitors he was grateful for their kindness; their questions were "less controversial" than those asked by reporters.[12]

Bush appeared twice with King, avoiding David Brinkley and Sam Donaldson. Clinton appeared again with King and with Phil Donahue. Perot appeared by himself in time slots that he purchased so he could present the flip charts he had designed. The networks warned him that this was bad theater, but they were wrong: The charts produced a curious fascination in audiences.

By contrast, Clinton saw all the possibilities of cutting through the filter of the old journalism and exploiting the opportunities that were afforded by the new. As a pundit observed:

> Here was a way for this incredibly talented political animal to jump over vicious, crabby people like Lesley (Stahl), Michael Kinsley, and me (Jeff Greenfield) and go directly to the people. . . . On Clinton's first trip to a Washington neighborhood . . . he was going to people on the street . . . who ran barbershops and community action centers, and he made the enormously cutting remark: "You know why I've been ignoring the press? Because I've got Larry King and I can go directly to the people." [13]

On With the Show

Once elected, Clinton returned to the talkprop format and for a brief time he appeared to be in command of the stage and the audience. On one occasion he was framed visually by a background that was bare of all ornamentation: no Presidential seal, no flag, no trappings of power; a bare-bones setting, one-on-one talkprop, provoking this comment:

> Presidents since Andrew Jackson have used whatever means they had to go over the heads of journalists . . . to speak directly to the people.
> Bill Clinton did so to good effect during his campaign last year, and tonight he demonstrated his skills again in an electronic town meeting that owed much to Ross Perot, Larry King, Phil Donahue, and the latest satellite technology.
> Like Franklin D. Roosevelt's fireside chats during the New Deal, and Lyndon B. Johnson's televised appeals during the Vietnam War, President Clinton's question-and-answer sessions are intended to build a constituency in the country at large for programs resisted by entrenched interests or a skeptical press corps in Washington.[14]

Clinton's first electronic town hall meeting was hailed as a forerunner of more of the same. In these formats, Clinton could display his command of issues and his willingness to listen to the people and acknowledge their empowerment. On TV station WXYZ in Detroit, Clinton used satellite technology to link up to studios in other cities, fielding questions from people who seemed to have just stepped off a poster for multicultural unity. This was high drama in the popular culture, bordering on theater.[15]

Thus the Clinton persona became the news. He was no FDR or JFK, but he was remindful of Ronald Reagan, who always conveyed a sense of newness:

> The call-in democracy innovated by King and pursued so ardently by Perot and Clinton reignited the presidential race. A manic-depressive print media found itself swinging like a pendulum from the [old] news that it had invented to public reaction to the call-in shows that were creating a new news.
>
> The news cycle has become a powerful loop; voters see an easy-to-grasp story like Nannygate [the disclosures that two Clinton women nominees for attorney general had hired illegal aliens as household help] or gays in the military; then they call into Washington and their local talk shows, they see all the TV stories about their calling in, and the process begins again.[16]

NEWER-THAN-NEW NEWS

The new news and the new audiences were on the verge of creating new hybrid forms of television news. In the offing there was purchased news, virtual reality news, and brittle psychological renderings called infotainment served up by Phil Donahue, Oprah Winfrey, and a host of acolytes.

Infotainment became the marketing of psychological news about marginalized individuals. By mid-1993 the television spectrum was crowded with a mind-boggling variety of psychological minidramas. By early 1996 there were 21 such shows. In marketing terms, the question became how much of an audience segment could be found for what kinds of "diversity," or was it simply deviance?

What was surprising was how easily performers could be found who could share relevant psychological experiences. Although it could be considered newprop in its intimacy and inventiveness, it devolved into an oldprop of the overproduction of dysfunctional values. Participants had strayed beyond the boundaries of meaningful participation in the popular culture.

Responding to a "pop analysis" of good versus evil values, infotainment host Maury Povich concluded that both actors and audiences on infotainment shows had achieved a functional newprop in that they had refined ideas about evil and its causes. As an example, they no longer accepted "abuse" excuses from those who had perpetrated crimes, but insisted on an independent criterion of personal responsibility; that is, things were right or wrong, and the individual was responsible. A critic concluded that infotainment audiences were bellwethers of the popular culture in many of their judgments about the causes and consequences of antisocial behavior.[17]

Povich himself appealed primarily to prurient interests and to actions that threatened the framework of a popular culture; for example, the Waco cult catastrophe, the murder of a parent, the plight of abducted children, sex scandals, fake genitalia, male complaints about women, and so on. No empowerment was created among participants and viewers, so the clear effect was oldprop. Was there anything more?

Larry King Asks Why

In early December 1993, King sat with several of the leading infotainment hosts—Sally Jesse Raphael, Jerry Springer, and Montel Williams—and asked if they were conducting unlicensed group therapy or if they had a legitimate informing function to perform that would enhance the popular culture.

Entertainment, yes, the hosts conceded, however bizarre, but they also were affording opportunities to communicate information that was beyond the boundaries of mainstream broadcasting media; hence newprop. Infotainment empowered participants and viewers to express their beliefs in public rather than to harbor them in their own minds; they allowed psychological connections to be made, they permitted individuals at the fringe of social boundaries to validate social experiences, and in those ways they supplied what was lacking in the news—opportunities for marginal members of the popular culture to achieve a sense of involvement and interaction with others.

The hosts conceded that infotainment might not always transmit news about complex ideas, distant people, and faraway events. But need their shows do so? They were addressing personal needs and experiences that neither the old nor the new news had encompassed. What was more, they had met a pragmatic test: To attract and to hold an audience social deviance must be translated into entertainment, but to survive in the marketplace, it also must be informative. However, William Bennett, Secretary of Education under George Bush, was not convinced; he pressured advertisers to desert the programs.[18]

A Litany of Intimacy

A skeptical observer watched 9 consecutive hours of infotainment and was appalled by the litany of social, psychological, and physical intimacies that were explored. Yet each of the hosts and hostesses lent a businesslike, plausible, and sympathetic demeanor to the discussions.[19]

Critic Janet Maslin ranked the hosts and hostesses as a royalty of infotainment.

Phil Donahue was crowned as the king of infotainment, most combining the old journalism with the new: He dealt journalistically with the Reginald Denny trial (the beating of a White truck driver during the Los Angeles riots), the anniversary of the CBS program *60 Minutes*, the aging, and landmark lawsuits. His infotainment features centered on crack houses, high school hazing, faking illness, interracial dating, and women who have sex with teenage boys. However, Donahue said he was forced to tilt toward psychological dramas to compete in the ratings. Donahue was the first of the major hosts to voluntarily give up his program—in late 1995. Presumably, he had done it all.

Oprah Winfrey even introduced a book segment linking infotainment to literature. She introduced historic sitcoms, matchmaking for widowers, and family dinners. But she also offered psychological drama, including violence in teen relationships, physical makeovers, romantic swindlers, and male gold-diggers. Winfrey's own triumph over racism, child abuse, and poverty gave these matters a high measure of validity and purpose.

An astonishing incident occurred during the course of a Jenny Jones program; this accented the seriousness with which interaction was addressed. A man who resented being admired by another man on the program later killed him. Jonathan Schmitz killed Scott Amedure because he thought a gesture toward him from Amedure was a gay overture.[20] This was more than enough to set off a new round of criticism of the seaminess of the culture that was presented. Television critic Walter Goodman wondered if the attacks by Bennett denied expression to what might be called an "underclass." The suggestion was made that outreach might be accomplished if opportunities for consultation could be arranged—perhaps through an 800 number—by viewers who wanted to validate messages. It was a social class that was worth saving, even though appearances might be to the contrary.[21]

REALITY PROGRAMMING—NEWER THAN NEW

Infotainment had wider effects, or perhaps it and the old news were responsive to the same societal impulses. It was noted that TV news, itself, was becoming more intimate, more dialogue oriented, and more dramatic. There was an unrelenting emphasis on crime, disaster, and the occult. At its most common level, the unusual story would give rise to contrived chit-chat among the anchors.

At its most exciting level, it would become virtual reality. Programs such as *A Current Affair, Day One, Hard Copy,* and *Inside Edition,* along with the first trial of the Menendez brothers for patricide and matricide, and all-day coverage and nightly recaps of the O. J. Simpson murder trial fed off the coverage of network news. The attack of skater Tonya Harding's minions on rival Nancy Kerrigan was first network news, but within hours it became virtual reality.

The suicide of rock star Kurt Cobain quickly brought the producers of *Hard Copy* to Seattle to purchase the news from the young electrician who discovered Cobain's body. Grocery checkout magazines such as *The Enquirer,*

People, and *The Star* were no longer the only ways that one could achieve a sense of intimacy through lurid news accounts. *Hard Copy* producer Paul Nichols characterized his product as a mix of celebrities, news, and human interest set to music. The national audience each night reached 15 million.

A colloquium of broadcasters and editors concluded that reality programming had become a window to mainstream journalism. Although the networks and even local affiliates felt that they could not produce marginal news, they did feel that they could pursue the story once it had been broken by marginal media. So just as *The Star* and the *National Enquirer* set the stage for the wire services and the national newspapers, they in turn set the stage for network and cable television. Mainstream media were reluctant to go with the Gennifer Flowers or Paula Jones stories until they were broken by marginal media.

Critic Barbara Ehrenreich observed:

> The TV news magazines everybody likes to criticize so much are actually putting on more serious pieces every week than we've ever seen before. Every news magazine has its tabloid piece, but (it) also has its relatively serious piece that relates to something people care about.[22]

The Ultimate O. J.

The O. J. Simpson trial became the apotheosis of virtual reality on television and grocery checkout magazines. *Hard Copy* maintained a 30-person "SWAT team" in Los Angeles to provide daily reports on O. J. One featured *Playboy's* Miss July of 1994, who Simpson had called ostensibly about business, but because it was new—it was news.[23]

After Judge Lance A. Ito, a regular viewer of *Hard Copy,* was profiled, he thanked the program for the "puff piece" and offered comments on its production. One real scoop was to produce the brown garment bag brought back from Chicago by Simpson but carried away from his home by one of his defense attorneys. *Hard Copy* also found the woman who allegedly saw Simpson drive away from the murder scene. She sold her story to the show before she testified to a grand jury.

The National Enquirer became required reading. Their reporters reached Nicole Simpson's Brentwood estate about the same time as the coroner and were the first to report that 5 weeks before the bodies of Mrs. Simpson and her friend Ronald L. Goldman were found, Simpson had bought a 15-inch stiletto knife. They paid $12,500 for an interview with the man who sold it to him. The *National Enquirer* reported that military commandos taught Simpson how to muffle screams while slitting someone's throat during the filming of a show called *Frogmen.*

Cartoonist Horsey pictured a virtual reality oldprop television news crew on a story. The text read:

From the flames of Malibu to the flooding Mississippi; from the brutal streets of L.A. to the bloody sheets of the Bobbitts, these are the stories of TV news, with appearances by Michael Jackson, Joey Buttafuoco, and the Hollywood madam Heidi Fleiss.[24]

Back to Lee Harvey Oswald

One critic traces virtual reality television to the televised shooting of Lee Harvey Oswald, the alleged killer of JFK, by Jack Ruby, a sleazy nightclub operator. Since then, the appetite for televised images of real-life carnage has grown enormously as new video technology has caught up with the appetite for virtual reality:

> If CNN is not bringing us continuous coverage of a war or natural disaster, then Court TV is offering a play-by-play of the behind-closed-doors mayhem practiced by the Menendez brothers. All the world's a Zagruder film that can be endlessly re-examined frame by frame.[25]

A writer found its simplistic plots and counterplots reminiscent of a major function of radio talkprop: "It is confirmation rather than information, beaming back to us over and over again what we think we already know."[26]

The rules of newsgathering that inhibit the old media have not constrained virtual reality. The anchor of *Inside Edition*, newsman Bill O'Reilly, described his most memorable purchased footage as peek-a-boo interviews with Tonya Harding, the Olympic Games ice-skater whose cronies injured competitor Nancy Kerrigan. O'Reilly insisted that paying news sources is little different from paying professional sports stars; both are paid on the basis of the ratings that they are likely to produce.

No Lamentations Here

Walt Crowley, the 1960s radical who edited the newspaper *Helix*, did not lament the "tabloidization" of television news nor did he see it as a passing aberration. Rather, it is part of an irreversible shift toward the democratization of media, which despite its aberrations, he saw whole as newprop; a greater variety of people being served by more varied programming. History is merely repeating itself with different technologies.[27]

Nor does commentary escape that wide brush. A host of participants on supposed high-level commentary programs seem to bark at each other only to add pique to otherwise lusterless and oldprop performances. Such shows are compelled to add a show business quality or they will go off the air. *The McLaughlin Group*, a Canadian-produced show, and *Cross-Fire* both have gained the reputation of being "gong shows." *McLaughlin* manages a five-person, free-speaking, free-swinging, often gleeful exchange that thrives on insider put-downs, sarcasm, and irony. The host spits out metaphors, rates things "zero to 10" and shouts code terms such as "Issue 1" or "Exit Issue." It is intended to be informing as well as entertaining, but it is so bizarre that comedian Dana Carvey parodied it on *Saturday Night Live*.

Cross-Fire is so polarized and mean spirited that the format becomes the message. Pat Buchanan, the conservative political writer and Republican presidential primary candidate in 1992 and 1996, and John Sununu (former top assistant to President Reagan) are the most contentious voices. Michael Kinsley, an editor of some standing, left *Cross-Fire* in late 1995 to become editor of the budding NBC–Microsoft electronic news network. Despite their informative intentions, even *60 Minutes* and *Nightline* depend heavily on shock journalism.

Critic and former *New York Post* editor Jerry Nachman characterized *Cross-Fire* and the *McLaughlin* program as 1990s versions of *All in the Family*, with Meathead and Archie and Edith replaced by Sununu and Buchanan shrieking cultural, political, and ethical clichés at each other.[28]

Critic James Fallows believed that the expansion of cable channels created demands for news programming, and the least expensive news is a panel talk show. That helped to create a political talk industry of dubious quality:

> The differences are thinning fast between John McLaughlin's spawn and Phil Donahue's—that is, between the weekend talk shows about politics and the weekday Jenny Jones–Jerry Springer programs. One features a cast of regulars arguing about Newt Gingrich and Hillary Clinton and the other features a changing cast of nobodies arguing about diets and sex.[29]

The masters of the easy and gentlemanly style such as Walter Cronkite and Paul Duke of PBS (before their retirements)—not to mention a host of other PBS commentators such as Jim Lehrer and old favorites such as David Brinkley and Bill Buckley—exercised intellectual authority from contrasting perspectives that gave substance to newprop. Even Sam Donaldson offered knowledge and gentle instincts to go with his abrasiveness. However, with their high salaries and high-fee speeches, some of the best of them have recast themselves from "muckrakers" to showbiz "buckrakers."

🐾   🐾   🐾

Network television continues to play an enormous role in informing a mainstream audience, but its spin-offs have disappointed those who demand better fare for the members of the popular culture.

In the competition for ratings, television news has pandered to audiences by staging conflict and substituting infotainment and virtual reality for more relevant knowledge. This programming has met audience desires for voyuerism and excitement, but it has not prepared them to participate meaningfully in the pop-

ular culture; much of this peripheral programming possesses only limited utility for a marginal audience, and is more oldprop than new.

NOTES

1. Larry King, kingmaker to the pols. (1992, June 28). Hoffman, J., *New York Times*, Sec. H, p. 27.
2. God in His Kingdom. (1994, April 27). Dowd, M., *New York Times Magazine*, pp. 31–32.
3. *New York Times*, Dowd, p. 32.
4. From DeToqueville to Perotville. (1992, June 28). Mazzorati, G., *New York Times*, Sec. E, p. 17.
5. Hamilton, L. (1995). "Larry King," In *Talking Politics: Choosing the President in the Television Age*. New York: Praeger, pp. 35–47.
6. *New York Times*, Dowd, p. 32.
7. *New York Times*, Dowd, p. 32.
8. Backlash. (1992, July 11). Kurtz, H., *Washington Post*, Sec. W, p. 21.
9. Perot takes issue, while Clinton takes on issues. (1992, June 12). Kolbert, E., *New York Times*, Sec. A, p. 14.
10. *New York Times*, Kolbert, p. 14.
11. *New York Times*, Kolbert, p. 14.
12. Thorns in a rose garden. (1992, July 2). Rosenthal, A., New York Times, Sec. A, p. 1.
13. Talking about the media circus. (1994, June 26). *New York Times Magazine*, pp. 26–62.
14. With a cue from Larry, Phil, and Franklin D. (1993, February 11). Apple, R. W., *New York Times*, Sec. A, p. 1.
15. A prime time for the President. (1993, February 11). Miller, R., Knight-Ridder Newspapers, In *Seattle Times*, Sec. A, p. 3.
16. The manic-depressive media. (1993, February 8). Alter, J., *Newsweek*, p. 29.
17. Staring into the heart of the heart of darkness. (1995, June 4). Rosenbaum, R., *New York Times Magazine*, pp. 36–45/50/58/61/72.
18. Falling ratings threaten all except top talk shows. (1995, December 20). Mifflin, D. *New York Times*, Sec. B., p. 1.
19. Surviving nine hours of talk! On the next Oprah! (1993, October 11). Maslin, J., *New York Times*, Sec. B, p. 1.
20. The aftershock of shock TV. (1995, March 25). Garvey, M., *Washington Post*, Sec. D, p. 1.
21. Daytime TV talk: the issue of class. (1995, November 1). Goodman, W., *New York Times*, Sec. B, p. 1.
22. Ibid., *New York Times Magazine*, pp. 26–62.
23. Simpson case makes for never ending *Hard Copy*. (1994, October 24). Gorov, L., *Boston Globe*, In *Seattle Post-Intelligencer*, Sec. C, p. 1.
24. Cartoon. (1993, November 28). Horsey, D. *Seattle Post-Intelligencer*, Sec. E, p. 1.
25. Infotainment: Hyped up news. (1993, November 28). Rich, F., *New York Times*, Sec. C, p. 1.
26. Diluting the news into soft half truths. (1995, June 4). MacGregor, J., *New York Times*, Sec. H, p. 25.
27. Conversation with the author, January 1, 1995, Lummi Island, WA.
28. Phillips, K. P. (1996, January 28). Breaking the news: How media undermine American democracy. *New York Times Book Review*, p. 8.
29. Fallows, J. (1996). *Breaking the News: How the media undermine American democracy*. New York: Pantheon Books, p. 93.

16

MEDIAPROP
Shooting the TV Messenger

Violence in our popular culture has been reported by *mediaprop* as being of epidemic proportions, and the *critics* want to shoot television as the messenger. Academic researchers, social critics, and politicians have inveighed against TV portrayals of sex and violence. The constancy and the pervasiveness of that criticism already has produced a consciousness of totalprop, and there is little likelihood that the criticisms will be mitigated. What is more, there is little likelihood that television will get the unspoken message: Although it cannnot be proved that it is creating violence in the society, or even mirroring it, it is denying the society the most effective use of the medium and thus limiting the potential of the popular culture.

Television does not create and model violence to the degree that it is charged and with special regard to children. Other far more powerful forces are at the roots of violence. The unwelcome fact is that actual violence has decreased as television violence has remained constant or increased. Television is guilty of a far greater crime—of omission rather than commission— the exploitation of audience time and focus of attention; a far more debilitating oldprop than that with which it is charged.

Fruitlessly, television has defended against these spurious charges with spurious defenses: Its content mirrors life, and violence and sex are understood by its viewers as dramatization or play. However, it is undeniable that the media exploit violence. Television newscasts lead off with crime and violence. Violence as a plot line can be counted on to hold viewers, an oldprop that does little to enhance participation in the popular culture.

Among critics of like mind, Max Frankel described American television as "The Murder Broadcasting System," one that cynically exploits violence to gain attention and rating points so it can sell advertising at the highest price. According to Frankel, the typical half-hour "news" program offers only 12 minutes of news, and more than 40% of this depicts violent crimes or disasters. Commercials consume more than 9 minutes, and sports and weather another 7 minutes, leaving 2 minutes for promotions, banter, and irrelevance.[1] This shortchanging of what might genuinely be useful news—and the implication that television does not think critically about what news might be—has received far less attention from *academicprop* and *governmentprop* than the presumed effects of violence. The real effects—the troubling and dysfunctional effects of a lack of a more balanced diet of news—go virtually unattended.

WHAT'S PLAUSIBLE?

Is it really plausible to believe that violence in television cartoons causes children to direct violence at one another? Do crime and police shows on radio and television, which have occupied radio and television airwaves for almost three quarters of a century, actually produce real-life violence? This is a tired oldprop, yet it does not lack for adherents. There is much less enthusiasm for looking beyond the media to those who have been victimized by race, ethnicity, poverty, drugs, gender, sexual preference, or other aspects of socially impoverished lives. Social statistics that attest to this reality are there for all to see, yet there is a predominance of those who would rather believe in media effects and shoot the messenger.

Academic Researchprop

Academic researchprop that blames violence on the media extends across the social and even biological sciences. Appropriate to his training, an epidemiologist at the University of Washington traced the effects of television on violence as if it were a plague. Dr. Byron J. Centerwall fixed 10,000 deaths a year as the consequence of merely introducing television sets—without respect to content—into industrial nations that previously lacked television.

Appearing with Dr. Centerwall on a television round table, I asked what social factors he had controlled. The reply was, "All I could think of." The question that followed, naturally, was, "Had he thought of everything?" If one looks at the social statistics on drug-related crime, for example, one might have a part of the answer—drug use is more plausibly tied to acts of violence than is television viewing. In fact, members of the drug and gang scenes pooh-pooh the effects of television. They learn violence on the street. For them, television portrayals are faked and have nothing to teach those who live in the real world.

A striking portrait emerged in two major crimes—the mass murder of railroad passengers by a Black man on the Long Island Railroad and the mass slaughter of Arabs by a Jew in a mosque in Hebron in Israel—no effects of television of any kind, direct or indirect, were apparent. In both cases, it was a long accumulation of anger and hate that produced the actions, not a discernible media habituation. That was also the case with the murder of Israeli Prime Minister Yitzak Rabin by right wing zealot Yighail Amir; in fact, no linkages have been found between television viewing and serial murderers.

The most widely accepted finding that comes from such researchprop is that television impacts children by desensitizing them to real violence. It is scarcely plausible that children cannot distinguish between real violence and violence framed by entertainment values. Indeed, researchprop is forced to equivocate as to direct effects.

THE WEIGHT OF THE EVIDENCE

Such mammmoth agencies as the Department of Education, the National Science Foundation, and the National Institutes of Health have funded more than 3,000 studies, and thousands more have been done without federal funding. These suggest that what academic researchprop has lacked in clarity it has made up for in quantity; it has more clouded our understanding of the problem than clarified our thinking about it. This limiting and misdirection of thought has had the effect of oldprop; if the researchprop had stimulated fresh thinking, it would have taken on the character of newprop.

A 1992 study sponsored by the American Psychological Association (APA), *Big World—Small Screen*, correlated the amount of violence on TV with children's behavior. Data generated by "numbers guru" Dr. George Gerbner of the University of Pennsylvania asserted that a typical child would be exposed to 8,000 murders and 100,000 acts of violence before finishing elementary school. (Another such study, commissioned by *TV Guide*, observed that over an 18-hour period more than 2,000 acts of intended violence occurred, the bulk of them in children's programs.)

The APA study followed 875 boys and girls through periods of their development and found that those who were most likely to engage in violence had viewed the most TV violence. A Los Angeles psychiatrist, chair of the 4,000-member Coalition on Television Violence, Dr. Carole Lieberman, asserted that "children's minds were being polluted by the drug of violence on television and demanded that the television industry acknowledge the link between TV and real-life violence."[2] Lieberman might better have said that any content that did not enhance children's minds was "wasting them," but calling for an acknowledgment of links that did not exist was wasting the public mind.

Defending the Messengers

Columnist Henry Gay satirized the tendency to blame TV in "Honey, let's blame the kids!"

Gay pointed out that conservatives who deplored government controls now were urging that society send its children off to tightly policed "boot camps" (similar to the Newt Gingrich proposal for establishing orphanages) to prepare them for a more ordered life, and dedicated liberals who once had argued passionately for civil liberties now saw boot camps as opportunities for youths to work out their frustrations in constructive ways.[3]

Another satirist asked tartly why the television critics did not acknowledge the link between TV and real-life goodness. "No one has been counting the acts of goodness," he commented. "Decades ago the same dire effects were attributed mistakenly to the pulps, comic books, and horror shows on radio." And why hadn't researchprop observed the stimulation to the imagination that was generated by media?

The comic *Cathy* satirized the tendency of *societalprop* to blame the media. Cathy complained to the cashier at her cleaner about damage to her blouse. The cashier refused to take responsibility, blaming everyone but the cleaning establishment for the problem. This prompted Cathy to ask, indignantly:

> "Whose fault is it that you just raised your prices even though you're using cheap chemicals that ruin my clothes?!!"
>
> "Television," the cashier replies. "Too many bad shows have corroded our morals. Dysfunctional families have created bad TV. Inferior education has fostered dysfunctional families. Government corruption has spawned inferior education, and there's no one to sue because the legal system is a joke!"[4]

One writer concluded that TV violence was, if anything, the least influential factor in the incidence of real violence, if a factor at all. Violence on television is no more a factor in creating real violence than rap or rock music, although some of the rappers have criminal records.

Mounting a Defense

As is evident, members of youth gangs who carry guns and engage in shootings are more likely to be acting out the demands of their membership than conforming to portrayals of fictionalized characters on television. And despite the mediaprop that has been directed at rap artists, there is little evidence that violence in music and video has generated violence among their audiences. At most, rapprop exploited the societal violence that had already occurred in Watts and South Central Los Angeles. Television violence is not the best thing for children, but it does not cause children to become violent.[5]

(Dr. Jonathan Freedman, distinguished social psychologist, told a C-Span discussion group in early September 1995 that if all violence were subtracted from all of television, it would have no discernible effect on actual violence in society.)

Indeed, Motion Picture Association of America leader Jack Valenti told a Los Angeles conference of television industry leaders and critics:

> The country was kidding itself if it thought TV violence was the primary reason the society has gone slightly mad. Cure TV, say critics, and the surly streets become tranquil. But wait a minute—the TV shows Americans watch are the same . . . [as those] viewed by Canadians, Japanese and the British. Yet, homicide rates in the U.S. are three and a quarter times higher than those in Canada and Britain and nine times higher than Japan. Why? Is something else out there?

About 2 months later, Valenti said that "the entertainment industry could not take responsibility for real-life violence, and that the great bulk of this human folly occurred when television didn't exist."[6]

A "Doleful" Criticism

In a patent exploitation of political oldprop, Republican Senate Majority Leader Robert Dole, an announced 1996 presidential candidate, lashed out at Hollywood for undermining social values. His acknowledged purpose was to curry the favor of the Christian Coalition and other social critics of Hollywood themes of sex and violence.[7]

Dole asserted apocalyptically that "we have reached the point where the popular culture threatens to undermine the character of the nation." He added to films the words and themes of gangsta rap, which together were producing "nightmares of depravity." Curiously, Dole had not actually seen the films or listened to the gangsta rap; he depended on reviews and summaries as the intellectual bases for his threats.

It was ironic that Dole listed such films as *Natural Born Killers* and *True Lies* as unacceptably violent and *True Romance* as unacceptably sexy, yet avoided criticizing actors Arnold Schwarzenegger, Bruce Willis, and Sylvester Stallone, each of whom starred in those or other violent films. Presumably, it was because they were financial contributors to the Republican party. Instead, Dole aimed his oldprop at filmmakers Oliver Stone and Quentin Tarantino, who were not aligned with the Republicans. Curiously, he did not refer to *Pulp Fiction*, described as a Tarantino metaphor for the constant struggle between the forces of good and evil, the culture war that Dole apparently had taken up.

A 17-year-old and her friends told a journalist: "His (Dole's) speech was really bad. People can make up their own minds. I saw 'Natural Born Killers' seven times. I really liked it. But I didn't go out and shoot someone after seeing it."[8]

Oliver Stone, director of *Natural Born Killers*, accused Dole of modern-day McCarthyism, a reference to the 1950s anti-communist witch hunts that stirred turmoil in Hollywood. Tarantino, author of *True Romance*, said Dole's argument was the oldprop of "whenever there's a problem in society, blame the playwrights." Thus oldprop begat oldprop.[9]

THE ACADEMY REPLIES

A study authorized by the National Academy of Sciences asked academic and scientific disciplines to summarize our knowledge of criminal violence and to make recommendations about it. They offered some surprising findings.

One study reported that although U.S. media were more violent than media in other industrial nations, there was more violence in films and print in the 1930s when there was no television than in the 1990s, when TV was in virtually every home.

The report concluded that an individual's potential for aggressive and violent behavior was influenced by genetics, neurobiological characteristics, and consumption of alcohol and certain drugs; the condition of the mother at pregnancy played an important role, as well. Finally, social disorganization, the concentrations of the poor, and the existence of illegal drug and firearm markets all contributed to the probability of violent behavior.

Even President Clinton suggested that violence was a product of complex social and economic factors. Vacuums in family structure developed first in those who suffered economic deprivation, and it was they who were the most vulnerable to violent images on television and in movies; by contrast, the President said, the lives of middle-class youngsters were organized around work, family, and community institutions. But the President's effort to put a newprop spin on an overwhelming oldprop had little effect.

Probably the worst purveyor of the oldprop of media coercion was Democratic Senator Paul Simon of Illinois. He first asked the broadcasting industry to form an advisory committee to monitor television violence, but then warned that if they did not clean up their act, government and other outside groups were ready to do so: "Either you will initiate the effort . . . or those outside the industry will do it. I started in this effort as a somewhat lonely voice in Congress, but I now find many of my colleagues want to go much further than is healthy for a free society."[10]

Attorney General Janet Reno testified before Democratic Senator Ernest Hollings' Commerce Committee that although she did not believe in direct censorship, she did believe in playing hardball with the industry; that is, exploiting the oldprop of intimidation. Broadcasters could be threatened with the loss of their antitrust exemption if they did not modify their programming, and she opined that TV violence legislation would pass constitutional muster.[11]

Congress demanded an 800 number for parents to register complaints, violence counts, advisory violence warnings, later evening showings of violent programs, control of promotional spots, an advisory commission, and disallowance of tax deductions for violating limitations on commercials in programming for children. Newly named chairman of the FCC, Reed Hundt, who had hailed industry antiviolence plans, now cited the findings of academic researchprop that TV had an innate ability to influence its audiences. This was oldprop recycled for political gain.[12]

It is enough to conclude that *Rolling Stone* magazine noted that television always has been a fat and easy target for ambitious political cowards: "Unable and unwilling to address real violence in America, Washington politicians are boldly determined to stamp out fake violence instead."[13]

Enter Organizationprop

The most aggressive oldprop came from the newly formed Citizens Task Force on TV Violence (CTFTV). Describing the May 1993 "sweeps period" as the "bloodiest in history," spokesperson Senator Kent Conrad (a Democrat from North Dakota) said, "Enough is enough. There's too much violence on television—and it's hurting our kids."[14]

A threat accompanied the message; if the industry did not act itself, public and congressional sentiment would take stronger measures: "Let's use television to send the message that problems need to be understood and dealt with, not 'solved' or 'glorified' with further violence."[15]

As a quid pro quo for promising to make violence less accessible to children, the television industry was given the right to adopt the same standards as film, and it would use prime time to examine drugs, handguns, murder, and rape. The National Cable Television Association conceded:

> We believe that the depiction of violence is a legitimate dramatic and journalistic representation of an unavoidable part of human existence. We also believe that the gratuitous use of violence depicted as an easy and conventional solution to human problems is harmful to our industry and society. We therefore discourage and will strive to reduce the frequency of such exploitative uses of violence while preserving our right to show programs that convey the real meaning and consequences of violent behavior. To these ends we will seek to improve communications with our viewers regarding the violence in our programs.[16]

A CONTEXTUAL APPROACH

There is some hope in the more recent researchprop that has substituted a contextual definition of violence for simply counting acts of violence. If a surgeon on the program *E.R.* cut open an abdomen, the old system would have coded it an act of violence with the potential for creating new acts of violence. By contrast, the new system does not assume that violence will produce violent acts by viewers.

Financed by the television industry (cable has underwritten another study), the purpose of the new researchprop is to permit a debate that is characterized by more intellectual rigor.[17] But within weeks, a far more pretentious study, labeled "the most comprehensive scientific assessment of television violence ever conducted," was released by a group called the National Television Violence Study. This study followed the pattern of earlier research by accumulating data on the number of violent and/or aggressive interactions. The two major findings were that the real consequences of crime and violence were not portrayed, and that perpetrators went largely unpunished. The conclusion that was reached was that this teaches children that crime and violence "pay."[18] But as cartoonist Jeff Stahler in *The Cincinnati Post* pictured it, little George Washington is standing by the cherry tree with a gigantic hatchet in hand. He tells a disapproving father: "Television violence made me do it."[19]

However, the report had a larger political purpose; it would enforce the requirement that V-chips (cutoff chips) be built into new television sets. Putting aside the validity of the study, about which there would be questions, its tone gave it more the aura of a censoring oldprop than an invigorating newprop. In a seamless society in which education, family environments, and social skills are fused into an inseparable network of values, who can say that any one influence is operable for everyone?

                                              ꜰ   ꜰ   ꜰ

Despite the vast number of studies of the effects of the portrayal of crime and violence—notably on television—researchprop has produced an intellectual orthodoxy practiced by generic researchers, most studies being identical in their assumptions, methodologies, and outcomes.

Because of errors of omission, as well as commission, the findings on television violence have failed to produce conclusions that are worthy of policymaking. Notably, they have failed to propose an array of affirmative means of enhancing content and have fostered an environment of censorship rather than a theater of the imagination. This has led to an absorption with oldprop and a neglect of the new, and it does not justify "shooting the messenger."

NOTES

1. The murder broadcasting system. (1995, December 17). Frankel, M., *New York Times Magazine*, pp. 46/48.
2. TV's negative effects prove need for national policy, researchers say. (1992, February 25). Dart, B., *Seattle Post-Intelligencer*, Sec. B, p. 10.
3. '90's Messenger. (1994, April 21). *Seattle Post-Intelligencer*, p. 19.
4. TV causes violence. Says who? (1994, March 6). Cooke, P., *New York Times*, Sec. A., p. 1.
5. Violence debate heats up, shifts from D.C. to L.A. (1993, August 2). *Broadcasting & Cable*, p. 13.
6. Hollywood takes Hill heat on violence. (1993, June 14). Lee, P. C., *Broadcasting & Cable*, p. 68.
7. Dole lashes out at Hollywood for undermining social values. (1995, June l). Weinraub, P., *New York Times*, Sec. A, p. 1.
8. Staring into the heart of the heart. (1995, June 4). Rosenbaum, R., *New York Times Magazine*, p. 44.
9. An angry chorus in Hollywood dismisses Dole's charges. (1995, June 2). Weinraub, B., *New York Times*, p. 1.
10. Senator Simon's message. (1993, August 9). Jessell, H., *Broadcasting & Cable*, p. 18.
11. TV rocked by Reno ultimatum. (1993, October 25). McAvoy, K., *Broadcasting & Cable*, p. 6.
12. Television violence legislation: the handwriting is on the wall. (1993, August 16). McAvoy, K., *Broadcasting & Cable*, p. 31.
13. More Washington show talk: In today's episode, TV ruins everything. (1993, December 9). Wilkinson, F., *Rolling Stone*, p. 38.
14. Task force on TV violence formed. (1993, June 14). Philips, C. L., *Broadcasting & Cable*, p. 69.
15. Reno to head lineup at violence hearing. (1993, October 18). McAvoy, K., *Broadcasting & Cable*, p. 43.
16. Cable promises to curb violence. (1993, February 1). Jessell, H., *Broadcasting*, p. 33.
17. Study of TV's violence points to films. (1995, September 20). Mifflin, L., *New York Times*, Sec. B, pp. 1/4.
18. New report becomes a weapon in the debate over TV violence. (1996, February 7). Carter, B., *New York Times*, Sec. A, p. 1, Sec. B, p. 5.
19. Cartoon. (February 18, 1996). Stahler J., *New York Times*, Sec. E, p. 4.

JOURNALISMPROP
Searching for Nirvanas

Journalists have been searching for nirvanas in the popular culture and have found them to be elusive. Having aided in the emergence of society from a mass culture, the media have become captives of the diversity that they helped to bring about. Ironically, where they sought to discern social problems, they were perceived as mirroring them; and where they pleaded, as in the case of politics and violence, that they only were mirroring problems, they were seen as creating them. It is ironic that the mass media have gained a reputation as purveyors of oldprop when they have produced so much of the new. Even their so-called negativity has brought important problems to light. That has been a relatively selfless task, and despite the criticism, mediaprop has spoken more to newprop than to the old.

One also must acknowledge the sheer volume of information that media have produced, much of it responsive to diversity in the popular culture. In one day's output, the average daily newspaper discourses on local, state, regional, national, and international events—be they business, finance, industry, or trade—and its special sections highlight sports, entertainment, lifestyles, music, social events, and the performing arts. This book could not have been written save for the records of events compiled by the mass media. Yet many Americans fear mediaprop and fail to understand their functioning, as may be the case for the media, themselves.

A one-time investigative reporter summed up the dilemmas faced by media; that is, that it was easier to supply "straight news" to the undifferentiated audiences of a mass culture than to respond to the varied tastes of highly diverse members of a popular culture. Newspapers now are required to produce large amounts of "reader-friendly" news that mirror the extended lives of their readers; a newspaper is no longer a "news shop" but a "news mall," with as many news departments as there are retail outlets. As the newspaper has sought its commercial nirvana, marketing and management systems have created new products that have rivaled and even exceeded the old news as a product:

> The daily newspaper business has undergone a remarkable transformation from when editors in "green eye shades" made seat-of-the-pants news judgments. . . . Today's market savvy newspapers are planned and packaged to "give readers what they want"; content is geared to readership surveys, and newsroom organization has been reshaped by newspaper managers whose commitment to the marketing ethic is hardly distinguishable from their vision of journalism.[1]

SEEKING A NEWS NIRVANA

As the popular culture emerged, the search for a news nirvana continued apace. News, itself, underwent transformations in which it responded to diversity, much of it in the character and goals of journalists themselves. Journalists in the 1990s were less likely to accept blindly the directives of their editors; like the members of the popular culture, they sought more of a sense of participation in decision making and, where appropriate, a forum for the expression of their values and beliefs. Although these often reflected the public mood, as might be expected, some journalistic attitudes were at times distant from the expectations held by sources and audiences. As a result of these gaps in outlook, journalists and mediaprop became perceived as instruments of exclusion rather than inclusion. From this perspective, mediaprop was a harbinger of the oldprop rather than the new. Hence media reached out to new kinds of diversity however they could.

Criticism of mediaprop centered largely on its attitudes toward politics and government. Its usual practice was to trumpet discrepancies of all kinds —whether between word and deed or variations thereof—then go on to another problem. Certainly, in its watchdog role, mediaprop was obliged to report the breakdown of major policies and institutions, but publics could not understand why they were unwilling or unable to observe everyday accomplishments. Orientation to problems but a distancing from solutions contributed to a pervasive sense of oldprop.

Pride and Prejudice

Historically, the media have pursued a number of nirvanas, and some became justifiable sources of pride. The printed press championed Americans who were exploited by giants of industry and agriculture. When Upton Sinclair inveighed against the meat packers, he introduced a nirvana of independence and muckraking. Other eras followed in which more nirvanas were to be found, some of which linked journalists to political leaders.

In the mid-20th century, it was not unusual for journalists to be taken under the wings of Presidents and given the run of the White House; in fact, in earlier eras editors spoke directly for political parties. Insider roles accorded to Walter Lippmann and James (Scotty) Reston gave them access to leaders that contributed to a "mutual mentoring" and were permissive enough to allow them to remain pundits in their own right.[3] The partnership mitigated the likelihood of oldprop and contributed to the promise of the new.

The breakdown of source–journalist mentoring at the national level is attributed to the presidency of Richard M. Nixon. Fueled by anger over his treatment by the press during Watergate, Nixon gave up on mutuality and created elaborate structures of control of information. Reporters were forced to take handouts or to speak to their readers on the basis of their own knowledge. The tactics threatened to reinstitute the oldprop of a mass culture, where only a leader could speak authoritatively to the led.

Some of the lines had been drawn before the Nixon era when journalists, themselves, became employed as "spin doctors" by government. Press secretaries became almost as legendary in the public mind as some of the presidents they served. But from time to time even this system sprung leaks, notably during the Nixon administration, when it brought disclosures of the Pentagon Papers as well as Watergate. Later presidents, from Carter and Reagan to Bush and Clinton, saw their policies, and even their personal histories, tried publicly with respect to Iran, Iraq, and most recently, Whitewater.

Benjamin Bradlee, former managing editor of the *Washington Post*, told in his autobiography how publisher Katharine Graham gave him the go-ahead to print the Pentagon Papers over the protests of the Nixon administration. By that act, Bradlee believed, Graham created the soul of a "new" and autonomous newspaper.[4] However, more recently Graham called for a return to mutual mentoring, suggesting that the government and the press should reestablish their source–journalist relationship by sitting down and listening to what the other says. This would substitute the newprop of accommodation for the oldprop of confrontation.[5]

The Journalistic Overclass

But social critic James Fallows believes that the journalistic overclass—notably elites from the major networks, newspapers, and magazines—is beyond reconciliation. The genie has been let out of the bottle, and it is unlikely that journalists will return to the "gentlemanly" practices of permitting privacy in the lives of public officials. Elite journalists have combined with political elites—candidates and their professional managers—to create networks of influence that often do more to manipulate publics than take their views into account. This approximates a leader principle by which a few journalists and political confreres speak to many publics rather than many publics speaking to those who hold power; the consequence is often oldprop rather than the new.

One critic sees the distancing of the journalist from publics as the "undermining" of democracy (or the popular culture) rather than a step toward sustaining and advancing it. More and more journalists now are graduates of the best universities, and they see themselves as competitive in status to those who hold positions in government or even in business and industry. They want to be consulted by their elite counterparts.

This overclass of journalists has become wealthy as it has marketed its newfound status to the very corporations (and their clients) it once pursued. One measure of the status of the journalistic overclass is that among those who were accustomed to giving lectures about their craft, prices per lecture for network "stars" have skyrocketed to $50,000 and more, and underclass journalists command up to $15,000, once tops for the best known and most sought after.[6] Recognizing the gap that was being created between journalists and their publics, such members of the overclass as Ted Koppel, Dan Rather, Peter Jennings, and Tom Brokaw quit the lecture circuit, but George Will, Mike Wallace, and Cokie Roberts, journalists with varying political views, continue to market their status.[7]

New Source Relationships

With the end of mutual mentoring, investigative reporting was one early answer, but it fell short of a nirvana, because no newspaper could investigate every story. Gaining access to government by freedom-of-information laws helped, a success that led to Nixon's downfall, but it served also to create bizarre sources, as in the supposed persona of Deep Throat. However fabled that legend, it signaled the end of several eras of a political nirvana, and journalists were to be banished from the Presidential hearth.

Journalists' options became limited: accept, reject, drop the story, or construct another reality. The new sources of facts, texts, interviews, and other materials had not yet taken form on the information highway.

Insiders emerged who would talk in confidence, but the journalist could only hint at their importance or worthwhileness. This was scarcely a new tactic but it was the approach taken by one-time Watergate investigator Robert Woodward when he described the problems of the Clinton White House. Had Clinton been a source, a far different picture would have emerged; he and Woodward might have turned to mutual mentoring.[8]

The estrangement of journalists from both sources and publics has led them to turn more to one another for information and emotional support, transforming themselves into sources and validators of sources, as well. Joel

Connelly, a respected national affairs reporter for the *Seattle Post-Intelligencer*, saw this as analogous to procedures required by standards of objectivity that require multiple sources as validation. However, now journalists were relying on one another for validation. Nowhere is that more exemplified than in the sedate PBS show *Week in Review*, where Jim Lehrer and his panel of journalists pose the questions and supply the answers. By closing the circle, journalists become exclusive rather than inclusive, and this smacks more of old-prop than the new.

OBJECTIVITYPROP AS A NIRVANA

Before mutual mentoring came along, "objectivity" promised to become a nirvana that would articulate a criterion for the "unbiased" gathering and presentation of news. This evolved from a form of "new news" that was first introduced when the telegraph was brought to bear on national news dissemination. As a practical matter, the biased political reporting that had dominated one political fiefdom could no longer be tranported to other, often antagonistic settings without being edited sharply. Although the new paradigm minimized bias it did not ensure truth; the technique of citing competing sources constructed a balanced bias that appeared, as well, to be a balanced truth.

As objectivity evolved, its critics learned to describe it as more of a procedure than an outcome; as such, it was a methodology, and like all methodologies, it had finite rather than infinite applications. Its ideological—although not always pragmatic—acceptance by journalists as both procedure and outcome was surprising from the standpoint of professions that made distinctions of this kind. Yet another nirvana was sought to fill the gap.

THE NEW JOURNALISMS

Tom Wolfe and other contemporary journalistic critics recognized that for new times there needed to be new reporting. The so-called *new journalism* that they put forward enfranchised the journalist as a proactive force who would wed the techniques of fiction writing and his or her own presence to give the story more context and hold the interest of readers.[9] Presumably, this would take on the character of newprop, for it would enhance the ability of the journalist to observe and report, and it would contribute to a sense of participation by the reader.

Not surprisingly, both journalists and novelists objected, each contending that Wolfe had blurred distinctions between journalism and the novel genre. But Wolfe replied that the novelists had become arcane, separated from the lives of real people, and that journalists should use the techniques that they had neglected—observing and describing the real world—and renewing a sense of intimacy with the reader. The new journalism piece was useful to the reader because through its intense observational detail the reader was able to visualize the milieux, the dress, and the attitude of the news subjects rather than simply being supplied with an official position and a statement. Wolfe insisted that wordsmithing was as much a fit for the journalist as for the literary figure. Ironically, the journalists objected to the reporting of subjective observations and shied away from more elegant phrase making. These were no substitutes for reporting verifiable events attributed to reliable sources.

The most admired of the new genre was the reporting of the human impacts of *Hiroshima* by John Hersey (which had been published in 1946 but continued to have an influence), and Truman Capote's nonfiction novel *In Cold Blood*. Both took their places as icons of the new journalism movement. Having interviewed several survivors immediately after the bombing, Hersey wrote a novelistic reconstruction of the event as those people experienced it. This foreshadowed Capote's efforts to give reality to the tormented human experience of a killer and his victims, and it characterized Tom Wicker's reporting of the personal impact the JFK assassination had on him and David Halberstam's first-person reporting from Vietnam.

Humanistic Reporting

Proposals similar to those of Wolfe both preceded and followed him. I suggested that journalists could become more humanistic in their news gathering and writing by defining stories from the perspective of those who were affected by events rather than from the perspective of the sources who had imposed the events on them. This approach to newsprop made the reporter empathic as well as proactive.

The emphasis in the story would be placed on steps that were taken to solve problems as readers addressed the "discrepancies" in normative human behavior that had come to light. Rather than resting on these failures in human experience, however, the humanistic reporter would seek out "copers," describing in detail their successes or steps toward solutions and creating, in this way, paths for readers to consider and adopt.

It was important to realize that not every so-called coper reflected a full panoply of success; rather, each contributed its bit to a constructed archetype, the sum of the individual contributions. Nor would any one reader assimilate the entire coping process; each would relate to the most relevant steps that lent themselves to their own use. This, too, was in the lexicon of newprop, for it enhanced the capabilities of publics to deal with problems that were thrust on them.[10]

When the first disputes about the busing of children to achieve racial balance broke out, one of the arguments made by parents was that it was disruptive for the child, and many news reports centered on this assertion. A team of undergraduate humanistic reporters and a journalism professor, the late William Ames, rode buses with the students and observed their behavior. Most of the students said they enjoyed the quiet time on the bus, they got better acquainted with one another, did their homework, and felt they were being given a chance to bridge racial gaps; it was school experiences, rather than the busing, that presented students with their most difficult problems. This ran counter to conventional wisdom.

NEWS GOES PUBLIC

More recently, a movement called *public journalism* has sought to take publics into consideration in defining news and how to pursue it. Not only are public views taken into account in defining the news account, but they also help to determine the news agenda, providing their own answer to the question, "what's news?" This approach acknowledges that newspapers often define news in terms of their own interests, and that the focus they adopt is not necessarily that of the greatest moment to publics.[11] This approach is criticized by traditional journalists, but proponents say that steps must be taken to deal with cynicism about the press and the inadequacies of traditional journalistic approaches.

Both public and civic journalism have sought to address gaps in perceptions between publics and the media. *Civic journalism* addresses how people think as well as what they think and employs research techniques such as polling and focus groups to those ends. The purpose is to identify distinctive public agendas—distinct from governmental and institutional agendas—that will help journalists to formulate more meaningful questions as part of the reporting process. To the extent that it facilitates the talking of many to many, it is essentially newprop.[12]

SOME LIMITS OF OBJECTIVITY

A journalist who covered AIDS for the *San Francisco Chronicle* and who, himself, died of the disease, blamed objective reporting techniques for the inability of the media to see the AIDS story whole. Objectivity not only had its limits, it was designed to observe them.

Randy Shilts concluded that in the case of AIDS, the rules and standards of objectivity were self-serving; they allowed the media to turn away from aspects of the disease that rendered their methodology less relevant; that is, in the case of AIDS, the methodology of objectivity permitted the journalists to play the undemanding role of social stenographers, reporting one set of facts and then the other, one point of view and then the other. This communicating from one to many is the essence of oldprop, characteristic of a mass culture, when a newprop is required that will address the varied perpectives of a popular culture.

Shilts believed that a need for involvement and even passion on the part of the journalist should fuel the reporter's quest, rather than limit it. And if the journalist held professional values—much like attorneys who believe in the innocence of their clients, or engineers who defend the integrity of their vision—the public interest would be advanced rather than endangered by this commitment. Acknowledging the freedom he enjoyed on the *San Francisco Chronicle*, Shilts observed that at the vast majority of newspapers, the practice of objectivity had permitted reporters to distance themselves from problems rather than embrace them; they dealt with intermediaries who were most accessible and with the facts that they brought to hand. Neglected was the bigger story, one that needed to be addressed by other means. His work on *The Chronicle* didn't reach enough of his colleagues, so he wrote the book *And the Band Played On.*[13]

Reporting of the "war on drugs" has been assailed in the same way, resting primarily on what official sources provide in the way of facts, however meaningless they might be. Mindful of daily reports on "body counts" during the war in Vietnam—and how meaningless and even counterproductive that reporting had been—one writer tallied the number of times the phrase "war on drugs" had been used in the media—16 times in 1981, 66 times in 1987, and 511 times in 1989 after then-President Bush used the phrase.[14]

Extending the irony, the war on drugs followed the pattern of reporting of Vietnam; the number of parcels of drugs seized in a given day or month is a statistic similar to how many Viet Cong were killed and reported as body counts. Drug parcel counts could be used as indicators of the progress of the war on drugs just as we had used body counts as an indicator of the progress we had made in the war in Vietnam. The metaphor was damning: "objectivity" deprived the reader of context and meaning.

Whitewater: An Oversupply of Sources

If any story suffered from a multiplicity rather than a dearth of sources, it was Whitewater. Any committee in Congress could produce news that was "objective" on a daily or even hourly basis. Add to that the inquiries by grand juries invited by special prosecutors (as in the case of Hillary Rodham Clinton) and it became a source–reporter game, bound by considerations of making and breaking news. The irony was that the more news of this kind that was produced, the less publics were able to cope with it. As in the case of AIDS, the public was overfed with facts when what was needed was an economy of meaning.

There can be little doubt that mediaprop rafted on Whitewater and continues to do so; it reported the story both in clusters—so-called *pack reporting*—and stretched the coverage out over time, as well. The director for the Center for Media and Public Affairs observed that within a brief period *The Washington Post* ran 12 stories on Whitewater, 6 of them on Page 1; The *New York Times* published 7 stories and 3 editorials; *The Washington Times* ran 16 stories; and the Los Angeles *Times* ran 6.[15]

Clinton's campaign manager, James Carville, insisted that Whitewater was overplayed because the media were intent on pursuing it, *not* because of any extraordinary news value or public interest. A CNN–*USA Today* poll found 71% of their respondents were uncertain as to whether or not Clinton did anything wrong with respect to Whitewater or the investigation of it, yet mediaprop tied Clinton to every Whitewater event—sometimes precedent to saying that he was not associated with it![16]

It was a far more defensible media agenda when Clinton confidant Vincent Foster, a highly visible member of the Clinton team, apparently committed suicide, possibly because he was knowledgeable about Whitewater, and Clinton's aides removed files from his office. Thus a more audience-conscious TV network news, which had given a total of 8 minutes of time to Whitewater in its first 6 months, gave 21 minutes to it in one 2-week period, an increase of more than 3,000%. Tabloids also jumped on spicy and sordid aspects, with sex-mongering and conspiracy theories abounding.[17]

A Vendetta Theory

There was some agreement with Carville that journalists were following their own agenda with respect to Whitewater, whatever the public interest. One believer in "catch-up" theory was President Clinton, who described it angrily to *Rolling Stone* magazine as "a vendetta by the knee-jerk, liberal press." MTV political analyst Jeff Greider said, "the President's anger was an awesome thing to behold, especially when it's in your face."[18] Greider said Clinton backed down on crucial issues to the extent that his own supporters wondered what he was willing to stand up for, but Clinton replied heatedly:

I have fought more damn battles for more things here than any President in 20 years, with the possible exception of Reagan's first budget, and not gotten one damn bit of credit from the knee-jerk liberal press, and I am sick and tired of it, and you can put that in the damn article. . . .

You get no credit around here for fighting and bleeding, and that's why the know-nothings and the do-nothings and the negative people and the right-wingers always win. Because of the way people like you put questions to people like me.[19]

LET THE RECORD SHOW

In fact, all coverage of national politicians has taken on a more unfavorable outlook between the 1960s and the 1990s. At the earlier time, fewer than one third of media references to political leaders were unfavorable, compared to nearly two thirds in the 1980s. Mutual mentoring had given way to adversarial reporting and source resentment in which each side sought hegemony by attacking the other. An oldprop of demonization was holding sway.

The focus by mediaprop on reporting discrepancies has centered often on the failures of our leaders, and it has contributed to a conventional wisdom about them that has not always been faithful to the facts. Not only Clinton, but most politicians do not seem to keep their campaign promises and thus they lack credibility, but research findings suggest that presidents keep most of their promises, and Clinton was no exception. He took steps toward improving the status of homosexuals in the armed services, introduced a tax increase on higher incomes, lifted the ban on abortion counseling in family-planning clinics, produced a health care reform initiative, a family leave program, banking reform, NAFTA, GATT, APEC (an unexpected bonus), a college loan program, the Brady bill, a youth training program, and he sought to preserve the desert wilderness.[20]

Noting President Bush's complaints during the 1992 campaign about the press harping on "what's wrong with George?" a writer concluded that Bush was justified in his complaint. Some 69% of the references to him were unfavorable; about Clinton, 63% and Perot, 54%. Eighty percent of the references to the Democratic party were unfavorable, whereas negative references to Republicans reached 87%. In addition, federal government stories were 90% unfavorable, and Congress had 93% negative reference. No governmental source could be praised.[21]

The Washington-based Center for Media and Public Affairs also found that Bush was correct. Some 51% of the references to the Bush administration, its programs, and his actions were unfavorable. However, the media were even more critical of Clinton; in particular network news, which was 62% negative.[22]

Writer William Glaberson saw the new wave of press criticism as an oldprop that caused publics to doubt the capacity of governing institutions: Mediaprop cast voting for president as a choice between evils rather than candidates of promise. The editor of the *Des Moines Register,* Geneva Overholser, said readers told her that the negativity and cynicism of news coverage left them uncertain as to what was working and what was not. Some concluded that every politician and every action was hopeless.[23]

THE CONSUMMATE NEWPROPSTERS

With the 1996 elections concluded, the consummate newpropster of television pundits, David Brinkley, decided to rest on his laurels. Known as much for his verbal spacing, accenting, and laconic delivery as his skepticism about all those who were engaged in the political process, Brinkley was thought of as fair and notably well mannered. But an open microphone betrayed him on election night and his viewers heard him describe President Clinton as a bore.

Clinton nevertheless kept his interview appointment with Brinkley and graciously excused him for only an occasional lapse in a brilliant career. Clinton was, of course, also acting out the role of consummate newpropster. The man with the most power was being the most generous with it. In return, he received an abject apology, and the duo went on to practice their rhetorical arts.

Brinkley was the headiest of the pair from the *Huntley–Brinkley Reports* for a decade and a half. Laconically, he recalled that Huntley had the big voice and the greater experience as a newsman. For him, style became substance, and because substance already was apparent, newprop luster was added to it. If any television pundit was the forerunner of Paul Duke, Robert MacNeil, and Jim Lehrer of PBS, each possessed of a gentle style, it was Brinkley. Commentary on election night was a nirvana of sorts with Brinkley, Lehrer, and Lehrer's colleagues, historians Doris Kearns Goodwin and Michael Beschloss, and the political insights of liberal and conservative newprop propounded artfully by Haynes Johnson and William Kristol.

A NEW NIRVANA—IT IS FRAMED

A new catchword, *framing*, has entered the lexicon of media criticism. Journalists convey their attitudes to publics by the ways in which they frame stories and what they select as facts to put into them. Framing a story is analagous to a carpenter framing a house.

Writer John Leo saw framing as a nirvana that gives much of the news a more intimate perspective and content; he cited numerous examples of perceptiveness and compassion:

- Homelessness is the core problem of society rather than drugs or mental illness.
- The immigration issue in California is less of a race issue than a distinction between legal and illegal Latinos.

* AIDS has become an "equal opportunity" illness.
* Extreme abortion protestors are more likely to make the evening news than an extreme gay protestor.[24]

But critics are wary of the power that this confers on the journalist. Noam Chomsky, for one, saw this as a passage for journalists to membership in a new class of elites that is able to make important social judgments. Journalists thus would join a social and intellectual class of "new Mandarins" who exercise unwarranted hegemony in the popular culture.[25] That was what the disaffected Perot voters were saying in 1992, the Contract with America voters were saying in 1994, and the Buchanan voters were saying in the Republican primaries in 1996.

The Polls Say It Is Oldprop

The poll results indicate that the media are producing oldprop, leading to the conclusion that the old journalistic paradigms are not working for everyone. About 84% of respondents say the media's own political preferences influence the way media report the news. About two of three persons say mediaprop favors a particular side in presenting political and social news, and more than two of three persons think the press looks out mainly for powerful rather than ordinary people.

Two of three persons say the media emphasize unfavorable news rather than favorable news, and they worry that the media might have too much influence over what happens in the popular culture. Majorities believe that TV has difficulty in differentiating fact from opinion, and reporters are more concerned about getting a good story than hurting people.

About one third of respondents have lost some degree of confidence over the past 5 years, although 23% say they have acquired more. However, those who expressed more confidence in the media did so on the basis of technological breakthroughs in print and television, whereas the critics focused on bias, sensationalism, inaccuracies, intrusiveness, and negativity.[26]

Fortunately, the public gives the media higher marks when they rate them in the abstract—in terms of fairness, impartiality, and accuracy. By almost a two-to-one margin, both television and print media are judged to have a more positive than negative effect on values; hence there is an acknowldgment, in part, of the ascendancy of newprop over the old.

NEW AND NEWER

Journalists are essentially artists, not scientists, so they are not predisposed to give theories much of a chance. However, as dependence for news shifts from traditional broadcasting and newspapers to the resources commanded by the information highway, all media will be required to embrace both new theories and practices, and that will help to bring in the era of newprop that technology always has promised but not always has afforded. Now the prospects appear to be immediate and real.

Although important texts and speeches often are printed in the *New York Times* and the *Washington Post*, new sources will be generated on the elasticized information superhighway. Although C-Span and similar cable outlets broadcast the full texts of speeches, press conferences, congressional resolutions, debates, and other proceedings, in the future those texts, and many others, will be available on request from sites on the Internet for free. What is far more important, and promises profits, is that knowledge sites will process content into new forms of significance. The new media will stimulate an ever newer journalism.[27]

Rather than competing only as sources of facts, the newest news will become sources of insight and contemplation. Rather than devoting most of their efforts to reporting discrepancies, the media will shift their coverage to processes, steps, and proposals and evaluations of possible solutions. It is both challenging and reassuring to know that Congress in early 1996 voted to grant press credentials to reporters on the Internet, on the condition that they provide daily news with significant, original reporting content, and that they either charge a market-rate fee for subscriptions or access or carry paid advertising at a market rate.[28]

Some observers put it more fundamentally. They recognize that the Internet and the Web have become communities that rest on shared tastes and capacities for communicating, and this produces the same effects as the best journalism. Readers of the *New York Times* and other elite newspapers share a sense of community that is based on the extrinsic or value-added nature of the product that permits them to know one another by their journalistic tastes and preferences. This is an extension of the quality of the product, itself; hence it is value-added.

More decisions about news offerings are being made on these bases, and their significance and uniqueness make for the most fundamental sense of newprop. A recent example is the magazine *Slate*, edited by Michael Kinsley, the *Cross-Fire* intellectual, for the Microsoft Network. Kinsley and Microsoft are betting that uniqueness of style and content will attract an audience that will spend time and money to become part of an indentifiable community of readers and thinkers and introduce a new nirvana of journalistic newprop.[29]

ꝑ   ꝑ   ꝑ

Journalists always have sought nirvanas, and they have undergone changes in self-identity in each cultural milieu as they attempted to find their place. Once a political press, then a more independent medium, then a supporting actor in a "mutual-mentoring" era, journalists were forced to seek new ways of defining and validating news.

For some time, journalists relied on the criterion of objectivity to guide their performance, but the limitations of this method forced them to seek other nirvanas. Excluded from mentoring by an angry president, journalists—once again let down by events—depended on one another as not only sources but validators of news. As new elites, they took on the aura of critics of government, and they created publics for this content.

One of the nirvanas was investigative reporting, but not all media could afford it. And when ABC went beyond investigative reporting to "infiltrative" reporting, the courts struck them down. They ruled that it was oldprop to sneak behind the scenes to get a story, and the penalty in damages was something else mediaprop could not afford.

However, some journalists recognized that new ways would be required to define the new news. They would be required to go beyond conflict to problem solving. There were precedents in the humanistic reporting of John Hersey, Truman Capote, Tom Wicker, and David Halberstam, and public journalism became another answer in the 1990s, with similar efforts to bring the reader into the journalistic equation.

The latest search for nirvana coincides with the advent of the new information revolution, in which entirely new techniques of reporting and writing will be required to satisfy the needs of new audiences who are seeking new resonance in the new media.

NOTES

1. Underwood, D. (1993). *When MBAs rule the newsroom.* New York: Columbia University Press.
2. A new press role: solving problems. (1994, October 3). Glaberson, W., *New York Times,* Sec. C, p. 6.
3. The journalism of outrage: investigative reporting and agenda-building in America. (1994, December 12). Gopnik, A., *New Yorker,* pp. 84–88.
4. Bradlee, B. (1995). *A good life: Newspapering and other adventures.* New York: Simon & Schuster.
5. *Post's* Graham addresses the new age of information. (1995, September 20). *Seattle Post-Intelligencer,* p. 1.
6. Fallows, J. (1996). *Breaking the news: How media undermine American democracy.* New York: Pantheon Books.
7. Ibid., Fallows, p. 109.
8. Woodward, R. (1994). *The Agenda: Inside the Clinton White House.* New York: Simon & Schuster.
9. Wolfe, T. (1973). *The New Journalism.* New York: Harper & Row. See also: Johnson, M. L. (1970). *The New Journalism: The underground press, the artists of nonfiction, and changes in the established media.* Lawrence: The University of Kansas Press.

10. Humanistic Newswriting. (1978, June). Edelstein, A., & Ames, W., *Quill*, pp. 28–31. See also, Edelstein, A., Humanistic Writing, *Nieman Reports* (1970, September), pp. 14–16.

11. Public journalism, in Fallows, ibid., p. 10.

12. Civic journalism and the polls. (1996, April/May). Fouhy, E., *The Public Perspective*, pp. 51–53.

13. AIDS and the media: Shifting out of neutral. (1993, May 27). Katz, J., *Rolling Stone*, pp. 31–32. See also: Shilts, R. (1987). *And The Band Played On: Politics, People and the AIDS Epidemic*. New York: St. Martin's Press.

14. The "war" on drugs. (1994, December 18). Frankel, M., *New York Times Magazine*, pp. 28–30.

15. After slow start, network TV grabs Whitewater. (1994, January 14). Kurtz, H., *Washington Post*, Sec. A, p. 18.

16. Carville, J. (1996). *We're Right, They're Wrong*. New York: Random House.

17. (1993, May/June). *The Public Perspective*, pp. 91–93.

18. Bill Clinton, the *Rolling Stone* Interview. (1992, September 17). Grieder, W., *Rolling Stone*, p. 40.

19. Interview with the President. (1994, December 20). Grieder, W., *Rolling Stone*, p. 11.

20. Patterson, T. (1994). *Out of Order*. New York: Vintage Books.

21. Big fog of feeling frames media's coverage of issues. (1994, December 20). Leo, J., *Seattle Times*, Sec. B, p. 5.

22. Candidates run, media run them down. (1993, December 8). Sarasohn, D., *Portland Oregonian*, Sec. C, p. 8.

23. The new press criticism: news as the enemy of hope. (1994, October 8). Glaberson, W., *New York Times*, Sec. IV, p. 1.

24. Ibid., Leo.

25. Choamsky, N. (1969). *American Power and the New Mandarins*. New York: Pantheon Books.

26. Public verdict: The media are obsessed with negative news. (1996, August/September). *The Public Perspective*, p. 60.

27. Conversation with Peter Rinearson, president, Alki Co., Seattle, WA, December 11, 1995.

28. Journalists approve Internet reporters. (1996, March 28). *New York Times*, Sec. C., p. 4.

29. Intellectual popcorn for the net. (1996, April 21). Frankel, M., *New York Times Magazine*, p. 26.

PART IV

Socialprop

ISSUES SEEKING ANSWERS

The swings between oldprop and newprop are marked and dramatic as they articulate social issues in the popular culture and efforts to resolve them.

Gayprop is expressive of the tensions created by the exclusion of a talented sector of the popular culture. As outsiders, members of the homosexual community respond to exclusionary oldprop with a raucously protesting oldprop; as insiders, they engage in a humanistic newprop.

Genderprop exhibits those same tendencies; professional women articulate their achieved status by use of the newprop of equal rights, but when they are constrained by gender-specific problems of sexual harassment and abortion-related issues, they respond to oldprop in like manner.

Race, abortion, and religion present contrasting styles. Race emulates both the oldprops and the newprops of sexuality and gender — witness the studied response by the Black middle class to efforts to end affirmative action and their rejection of radicalness — but abortion and religion, merged in their crusading zeal, sublimate professionalism and class to an unremitting oldprop of hegemony. Much of *lobbyprop*, illustrated by the National Rifle Association (NRA), follows this same oldprop pattern, but environmental issues range across oldprop and newprop as they respond to issue-specific problems (e.g., habitat, water, fish, minerals, timber, etc.).

If any one activity argues the most for the broadest redefinition of popular culture it is *tradeprop*. Such acronyms as NAFTA and GATT — and such organizations as the European Common Market and the Global Council of Seven — have become everyday referents and they are evocative of both the oldprop and the new. Referring to the vote on NAFTA, one columnist asked: "Do we really hafta?" And in an exuberant newprop of hope, President Bush pointed to free global trade as one of his thousand points of light.

18

GAYPROP
One Foot In, One Out

In the 1990s, homosexuals played distinguished roles in the arts and the professions, in business, government, and in the military forces, and with the turn of the century their presence and contributions to the popular culture would be magnified. Despite their contributions, however, they found themselves to be living in two worlds, one the popular culture that was guided by the newprop of equality of status and opportunity, the other a mass culture where homophobes manipulated publics by use of the oldprops of fear, hate, and exclusion.

Sexual identity politics in the 1990s divided the nation along emotional lines. In their anger, zealotry, and breadth of relevance, demands of homosexuals, as well as reactions to them, became throwbacks to oldprop; only in the commitments exerted by many speaking to many did it take on the character of newprop.

CLINTON AND POLITICS

The homosexual movement found itself attached politically to presidential candidate Clinton but at odds with Clinton, the President. Although he was acknowledged to look sympathetically on the problems faced by the homosexual community, he could not fulfill his promises to them that they would be given equal protection and opportunity under the law. They were tired of being invisible, of living in two worlds, one of equal contribution, the other of unequal subjugation. They argued that although the struggle for gender equality had brought results, those same demands from the gay and lesbian communities were rejected as seeking special privileges.

Once again, therefore, gayprop would be forced to defy authority and insist on acknowledgment of their legitimacy. By public debates, demonstrations, political alliances, and performances in the arts, an aggressive gayprop would seek redress for the social, physical, and psychological actions that had excluded them from protection under the laws; it would seek equality in the workplace and in the home and succor from the ravages of AIDS.

High Expectations

The first of the disappointments with Clinton came about because of high expectations—their own, and Clinton's, as well. Clinton had pledged that he would achieve equality for homosexuals in the military. Notably, he would reverse the ban on gays and lesbians. However, after his election he said in more tempered tones:

> We know there have always been gays in the military. The issue is whether they can be in the military without lying about it. . . . I have made no decision on a timetable except that I want to firmly proceed and I want to do it after consulting with military leaders.[1]

Clinton had his own problems. The Christian conservative right attacked his proposals as challenging the central core of their beliefs; they objected to equal rights for gays on moral grounds, and they insisted that homosexuality specifically was forbidden in the Bible.[2] Although there was a supportive tongue-in-cheek protest from author James A. Michener that God was not a homophobe, Ross Perot intimated that he shared the views of the religious front and said, equivocally, that no discrimination would be permitted if he were President.[3]

Reality Takes Over

Democratic Senator Sam Nunn, chairman of the Senate Armed Forces Committee, represented not only power but prestige. When Clinton presented him with the request for protection for homosexuals under the military code, he rejected it out of hand, and others in Congress and the armed forces took the same stance.

The military response invoked an oldprop fear mongering by the armed forces, who insisted that the changes would weaken the moral and social cohesion of troops in the field: It was impractical to create special living quarters for heterosexuals and homosexuals, and even the gradual assimilation of homosexuals and homosexuality in a fighting unit would present insurmountable problems.

Redefining the Problem

Rather than confronting the opposition on the issues, Clinton sought to re-define the problem in terms that permitted a solution. Recruits would not be asked about their sexual orientation; that was a concession by the military. In turn, if recruits acknowledged their sexual orientation they would commit themselves not to engage in homosexual acts, thus satisfying service regulations against homosexual behavior. This was described as the "don't ask, don't tell" policy.[4] Now Clinton could say that he had taken steps to achieve his goals, although admittedly different means had been introduced. He had acted out the axiom of politicalprop that candidates say what they *hope* to do; a sitting President does what he can do. "Should we judge a President by what he says he intends to do or by what he gets done? When is a compromise legitimate, and when is it just another broken promise?"[5]

The logic of the new situation did not satisfy the chairman of the Joint Chiefs of Staff, Colin Powell, a Black man, and he expressed guarded opposition to it. Accordingly, Clinton deferred his announcement until the day after Powell completed his term of office. Nor did the solution satisfy gays and lesbians who had been discharged from the services simply for being homosexuals. They did not want merely to be tolerated, they wanted to be accepted.

FULSOME OLDPROP: THE DC MARCH

When the gays and lesbians marched on Washington, DC, in late April 1993 they invoked both the oldprop of defiance and confrontation—an in-your-face expression of anger. It was fulsome oldprop: dramatic and conflictual, yet festive. The mall from the Washington Monument to the Capitol was packed; a sea of marchers waved rainbow flags, banners, signs, red ribbons, and pink triangles. Chants welled up: "Act Up! Fight Back! Fight AIDS." Gay parents chanted: "Hey, Hey, we're in the PTA." Oklahomans shouted, "Ho ho, hey hey, even farmers can be gay." From North Carolinians came cries of, "Hey, hey, ho, ho, Jesse Helms has got to go." When the Colorado contingent, which fought successfully against restrictive laws in that state, came into view, the crowd roared. And in midafternoon several hundred members of the Gay Men's Health Crisis lay down in front of the White House in a silent prayer for those who had died of AIDS. Not surprisingly, the Christian Action Network labeled the march "a wake-up call to the silent majority whose individual rights are at stake"; many of the signs were abusive and obscene.[7]

Organizers said they had reached their goal of 1 million marchers, but the park police said that although the crowd was larger than that for the Martin Luther King address it was smaller than the abortion rights march and several anti-Vietnam protests. Neither Ted Kennedy nor President Clinton attended

—both were making appearances in other cities—but their messages were read to the assemblage. Other members of Congress did participate and spoke briefly. Thus the marchers associated themselves with a semblance of power.[8]

Newprop Vies With Oldprop

Nonetheless, the marchers were well behaved and conventional in appearance, and that was the image that was conveyed on the evening news. Barney Frank, the openly gay Democratic Congressman from Massachusetts, said the march would encourage the conveying of other, similar messages of newprop. People would become less persuaded that the movement lacked legitimacy, thus countering the misbegotten attitudes reflected in pollprop.

Two marches in Manhattan followed in June, one of them unauthorized and loaded with symbolic oldprop, the other patterned after the mainstream Washington newprop parade. The oldprop march commemorated a raid on a gay tavern in Manhattan, The Stonewall Inn, during which a melee ensued and gays were mauled by the police. The centerpiece was a mile-long, 30-foot-wide, 7,550-pound (almost 4 tons), rainbow-colored flag that symbolized gay and lesbian unity. Thousands of flagbearers paid for the honor of carrying it. Topless lesbians and transexuals populated the marchers, and onlookers held banners that demanded that homosexuals "act up" and uphold "gay power."

The authorized march ran down Fifth Avenue to Central Park and was joined as it entered Central Park. The marchers sought to create a newprop image on television that would appeal more acceptingly to those who tolerated diversity. Marchers included a former FBI agent, a mutiple sclerosis patient, soldiers, sailors, and marines, Green Berets, and Vietnam and Korea veterans.[9]

Local Versus Cosmopolitan

But New York and San Francisco were cosmopolitan scenes where gay and lesbian values could be pursued as both oldprop and the new. The struggles that erupted outside of those capitals were strictly oldprop. Two of the most highly propagandized took place in Oregon and Colorado, one a referendum that would permit Oregon homosexuals no special treatment; the other, in the state of Colorado, rejected legislation that provided special treatment. Both employed the oldprop of reaction and conflict.

The Oregon Citizens Alliance exploited a massive mailing list of more than 250,000 names, 17,000 contributors, and more than $1 million; a Democratic congressman, Peter De Fazio, characterized their efforts as sophisticated and the oldprop as mean-spirited but effective. The leader of the Alliance was Lon Mabon, former state chairman for the Reverend Pat Robertson's Christian Coalition. Mabon advanced the oldprops of morality, hate, and fear by showing films of transvestites marching in San Francisco and New York, and he displayed children's books that offered sympathetic views of gay lifestyles.

In a campaign masterminded by Colorado for Family Values, headquartered in Colorado Springs, state voters passed bills that invalidated ordinances that had been passed in the larger and more sophisticated cities of Denver, Boulder, and Aspen, protecting homosexuals from discrimination in jobs and housing. Also forbidden was the passing in the future of antidiscriminatory measures. The lesbian world-class tennis star Martina Navratilova had backed the original legislation.

The homosexual community fought back: Lambda Legal Defense and Education Fund and Boycott mobilized national gay and lesbian groups to boycott conventions and vacations in all of Colorado's resort spots, including Aspen, costing the state more than $35 million in tourist revenues. Ironically, those areas had voted in favor of retaining gay and lesbian protections and rights but were outvoted by the rural areas.[10]

Gayprop Is Local

In June 1993, a journalist traveled through the small towns of Oregon to test the mood of the citizens. In Junction City, 100 miles from Portland, where gay marches had been held but "a world apart," fears were expressed that homosexuality was threatening the values of that town and others like it. Junction City was itself campaigning for a charter amendment that would prevent the city government from spending any money that would promote or approve homosexuality.

The Alliance denied it was employing the oldprops of hate and divisiveness. Rather, it was reacting to gay insistence on privileged protections:

> "To use government to coerce a majority of citizens to accept and approve their behavior is wrong," said John Leon, district coordinator and a religious evangelist; "that is what creates division. The Alliance doesn't hate anyone; it simply wants to revitalize a standard of morality."[11]

The homosexual commmunity was too diverse to adopt a single tactic of oldprop; it was imperative that they also assert the new. The technique that they adopted was to identify highly respectable individuals who had suffered from the old rules and hold them forth as symbols of deprivation and pain. The purpose was in each case to humanize the individual.

A Perfect Symbol

Navy dischargee Joseph Steffan wrote a book that told about his personal battle as a homosexual in the Navy.[12] As a result of the book, he became a symbol of a need for equity that could challenge armed forces policies. He appeared on network television programs, was interviewed by daily newspapers and news weeklies, made the rounds of talk shows, and toured college campuses and other milieux.

> So great is the burden he carries of being a symbol and so practiced is he at telling his story that he seems more like a walking press release than a man who had his life torn apart. He has become the perfect symbol for his struggle—the well-scrubbed boy next door. No one would label Joseph Steffan "a screaming queen."[13]

The "MacNeil & Son" Hour

A moving story was told about Robin and Ian MacNeil, father and son: Robin is the highly regarded commentator on public television's *MacNeil/Lehrer Newshour*, and Ian a set designer whose homosexual partner was a play director (Stephen Daldry). MacNeil and Daldry were hailed for their ingenuity and vision and won a bevy of British stage Oliver Awards, the equivalent of the American Tonys.[14]

Father and son spoke publicly about the impact on their relationship of Ian's coming out as a homosexual and about the strains that his being gay placed on them. Love and mutual respect permitted them to acknowledge one another's identity and to break through social and psychological barriers that affected their relationships. This was the epiphany of newprop, for it not only enhanced the individuals but it opened doors to others.

A Marine Colonel and Son

The story of Colonel Fred Peck and his 24-year-old homosexual son Scott unfolded during the public debate about gays in the military. Although the colonel and his son differed about the role of homosexuals in the armed forces, they were brought together by a sympathetic understanding of each other's roles and values.

The colonel had returned from service in Somalia to learn that his son was gay, but the initial stormy atmosphere evolved quickly into constructive discussions and the Colonel's statement that he accepted his son's identity with "unconditional love."

Scott, an aspiring journalist, commented, "I had my own stereotypes about Marine Corps colonels, and I assumed because of the life style he chose, he would have certain political views. Knowing what I know now, I wish I had had more faith in my father and talked to him a long time ago."[15]

Bob and Rod Find Mr. Right

Learning to accept oneself and others despite difficulties is consistent with the values of newprop and the popular culture. Bob and Rod were symbolic of those who sought gay self-esteem.

Both handsome and talented, they met in a gymnasium. Bob had won a championship body-builder title, occupied a centerfold in *Playgirl*, and had earned commercial endorsements and contracts. However, when he came out in the body-building magazine *Ironman*, it ended his career. Nonetheless, the two took marriage vows in a Unitarian Church ceremony and chronicled their relationship in a book.

Like Steffan and others, they embarked on a blitz of the talk shows and the college lecture circuit. They joined the Gay March on Washington and set in motion the launching of the nonprofit Be True to Yourself Foundation to promote self-esteem among gay and lesbian teens. They were featured on the February cover of *Out* magazine, the nation's largest circulation gay magazine. Bob and Rod used newprop to change their image from a symbol of a problem to the promise of problem solving.[16]

Soldier of the Year

Jose Zuniga had hidden himself inside a system that forced bonding among men while breeding hatred. He had become decorated and lauded by a famous Desert Storm general as "soldier of the year." He was to become the symbol of the heroic gay soldier who had been abused by the system.

Zuniga recalled the obsession with homosexuality in boot camp. He remembers when the drill instructor screamed at recruits: "I'm going to make men out of you little faggots . . . you little pansies aren't fit to spit-shine my boots! When I'm done with you mama's boys you'll be real soldiers."[17] Zuniga stated his case as a moral imperative:

> We have never asked the military to lead the way in social change; we simply ask that the military catch up with modern society. . . . To ban homosexuals out of fear that acknowledging them would damage morale is a disingenuous attempt to blame the messenger for the message.[18]

DRAMATIZING AIDS

The gay community holds special meaning for the creative and performing arts. Many of their members are artists, writers, directors, and producers as well as members of creative communities in advertising, journalism, and film. What was surprising was not that the creative community intervened, but that it took them so long to do so. Clearly, the arts wanted to be more certain of their ground before they produced theaterprop and filmprop as popular culture.[19]

What better messenger, allegorically, than *Angels in America?* I sat transfixed as *Part I* unfolded before me. *Part II, Perestroika,* would follow. Subtitled *A Gay Fantasia on National Themes,* and winner of the 1993 Pulitzer Prize for drama, the performance literally stunned me. The audiences got the messages. AIDS strikes everyone, the beautiful and the ugly; AIDS is a struggle of life and death; AIDS is reality and surreality; AIDS is denouement and religious revelation; AIDS is a personal catastrophe and a social problem; AIDS strikes the bravest and the weakest; AIDS fosters impossible dreams and the starkest of realities; AIDS tests the fullness of love and the shadows of commitment; AIDS visits angels and devils; AIDS is an obsession and a preoccupation. And because it touches the depths of the human soul, AIDS can be beautiful. All of this is quintessentially newprop.

Playing in major cities, *Part I* mesmerized audiences because of its emotional candor and its startling roles and staging effects. How can one be unemotional at the appearance of an apparition of executed spy Ethel Rosenberg confronting the gaunt and ravaged Roy Cohn, the hated and widely despised colleague of the late Senator Joseph McCarthy, master of the inquisition? The message is that the bell tolls for thee and me. And when the angel tells us that all is done, that one struggle is over and blessed, we are prepared for those that are to come.[20]

Gay Journalists Emerge

In September 1993, the president of the emergent National Lesbian and Gay Journalists Association observed that homosexual journalists were coming out and that they had been welcomed by newspapers as representing another voice and force in the society. The number of homosexuals in attendance almost doubled from 1992 (400 to 750) and major urban newspapers were seeking to interview and recruit gay journalists.

Arthur Ochs Sulzberger, editor of the *New York Times*, had told the first convention that if newspapers were to survive they could no longer be exclusionary bastions of a single view of the world; now David Lawrence, Jr., *Miami Herald* publisher, echoed that the media must have a host of perspectives, including race, gender, and sexual orientation.[21]

A debate broke out at the *Seattle Times*, which prided itself on its diverse staff; yet the editors removed a reporter from a "diversity story" that might be seen to impinge on her objectivity. This brought criticism on the editor for his claims to a pursuit of objectivity. It was better to have someone on a story who understood its implications—in this case, a gay person reporting on a gay march—than someone who had no professed views. But the editor, Michael Fancher, insisted that a reporter could not march and also report, for this would carry the implication of bias, and it was important to avoid perceptions of bias as well as actual bias. There was an implication, however, that those who held majority views were less likely to be biased than those who held minority views.[22]

Literature Emerges

In the 1990s, gay writers were coming out, and they wrote books for straight people. The few books aimed at homosexuals were published quietly by small houses. Soon gay literature had defined itself as a niche market and hundreds of gay writers were gaining their livelihood from it. By the early 1990s, 10 to 15 titles were being published per week. The publishing house of Penguin USA produced a gay-oriented list that featured Martin Duberman's *Stonewall*, Joseph Hansen's *Living Upstairs*, Mary Wing's *Divine Victim*, and Joan Nestle and Naomi Holoch, editors of *Women on Women 2*.[23]

In November 1995, the *New York Times* reviewed Urvashi Vaid's *Virtual Equality*. The reviewer, author of *A Place at the Table: The Gay Individual in American Society*, took issue with the author's opposition to the "mainstreaming" of homosexuality—that is, newprop—as inimical to revolutionary change, but he welcomed her more moderate tone and willingness to expand the basis of the movement. The subculture should be debated honestly and questioned thoroughly; gay people should seek to educate and inform, the essence of newprop, and move toward more integration, education, and conciliation.[24]

TRANSGENDERPROP

Much as gayprop transcended its oldprop beginnings and emerged as a humanistic newprop, transgenderprop is dropping its oldprop patina of drag queen for a newprop of informing and self-legitimizing.

"There's finally a voice saying, enough," said Riki Anne Wilchins, a Wall Street computer consultant and organizer in the movement. "We pay taxes. We vote. We work. When you have people in isolation who are oppressed and victimized and abused, they think it's their own fault, but when you hit that critical mass that allows them to see it happening to other people they realize it's not about them, it's about a system, and the only way to contest a system is with an organized response."[25]

A newprop goal is to represent transgender behavior as simply a homosexual life-style in which participants live ordinary lives and accommodate in dress and behavior the demands of the normative culture. Films produced in the 1990s have portrayed the transgender rebellion, their sense of victimization, and their attempt to achieve a newprop of accommodation. *Stonewall*, for one, commemorates the "Boston Tea Party" that occurred during a police raid on June 28, 1969, at the Stonewall Inn in Greenwich Village during which transvestites fought with police.

Whether or not *Stonewall* represented a sea change event in transgender perceptions is problematic. Other films that more carefully validated incidents of rebellion and repression may be more significant. But even if mythic, *Stonewall* captured the attention of the popular culture. One can point, as well, to the television sitcom *Ellen*, which uses humorprop to advance the newprop of legitimation.[26]

BACK TO POLITICALPROP

As long as the gay movement is proactive, it will generate resistance. When Hawaii became one of a few states that recognized gay marriages, Congress found itself pushed by the Christian Coalition and prepared legislation that would not make it binding on one state to accept the legality of marriages that were adopted by another state. Homosexuals who wanted to marry legally could go to Hawaii to do it, but they could not impose that legality on another state.

President Clinton set off a homosexual oldprop firestorm when he announced that he would sign the bill—and he did. The gay community argued that the President had bought into the right wing oldprop moral position, and had stimulated homophobia; one of his campaign staff resigned in protest. However, a White House aide said that it was more realistic to recognize that same-sex marriage was "way down the road," and that long-term social change would have to occur before most people would accept nontraditional marriages; at the same time, he criticized the White House for insensitivity. As the issue defined itself, the President seemed to the homosexual community to be endorsing a status quo exclusionary policy that was oldprop in its character.[27]

♛   ♛   ♛

Gay pride has demonstrated a capacity to produce both the oldprop and the new—the old in its politics of defiance, the new in its adaptation to the meritocracy and its tendency toward humanism. The newprop about diversity in human sexuality has been enabled by well-educated homosexuals who hold the values of professionals. These homosexuals have pursued their goals by appeals to reason and the newprop of humanism, but angered by social isolation and deprivation, the gay and lesbian community strikes out at their tormentors with a virulent oldprop.

NOTES

1. Changing course: Clinton's statements. (1993, July 20). *Associated Press.* In *Seattle Times*, Sec. A, p. 3.
2. God is not a homophobe. (1993, March 30). *New York Times*, p. 19.

3. Perot vows not to tolerate bias against gays. (1992, July 9). *Los Angeles Times*, Sec. A, p. 1.

4. Modest tack seen on troop ban. (1993, July 13). *New York Times*, p. 1.

5. Clinton's gay policy; cave-in or milestone? (1993, July 25). Friedman, T. L., *New York Times*, Sec. 4, p. 1.

6. Military brass ask Clinton to keep ban on gays. (1993, January 23). *Seattle Post-Intelligencer*, Sec. A, p. 1.

7. Gay Americans throng capital in appeal for rights. (1993, April 26). Schmalz, J., *New York Times*, Sec. A, p. 1.

8. Gays demand rights in 6-hour march. (1993, April 26). *Washington Post*, Sanchez, R., & Wheeler, L., Sec. A, p. 1.

9. Gay march in New York rejoices in history. (1994, June 27). Scott, J., *New York Times*, Sec. A, p. 1.

10. The avalanche that buried Aspen. (1992, December 30). Lichtenstein, G., *Washington Post*, Sec. D, p. 1.

11. Twins divided over gay rights. (1993, June 25). Connelly, J. *Seattle Post-Intelligencer*, Sec. A, p. 1.

12. Steffan, J. (1993). *Honor Bound*. New York: Avon Books.

13. From midshipman to gay rights advocate. (1993, February 4). Schmalz, J., *New York Times*, Sec. B, p. 1.

14. A father and a son; growing up again. (1994, September 4). Dullea, G., *New York Times*, Sec. B, p. 1.

15. Father-son drama over the gay ban. (1993, May 13). Schmitt, E., *New York Times*, Sec. A, p. 9.

16. Bob and Rod. Finding Mr. Right. (1994, February 3). Goodenow, C. *Seattle Post-Intelligencer*, Sec. C, p. 1. See also: Jackson-Paris, Rod. (1995). *Straight From the Heart: A Love Story*. New York: Warner Books.

17. My life in the military closet. (1993, July ll). Zuniga, J., *New York Times Magazine*, pp. 40–41.

18. Zuniga, J. *New York Times Magazine*, ibid., p. 64.

19. Embracing all possibilities in art and life. (1993, May 5). Rich, F., *New York Times*, Sec. B, pp. 1/5.

20. The secrets of angels. (1994, March 27). *New York Times*, Sec. H, p. 5.

21. Gay journalists leading a revolution. (1993, September 10). Glaberson, W., *New York Times*, Sec. A, p. 13.

22. View of journalism as political monkhood is ridiculous. (1996, June 2). *Seattle Times*, Sec. B, p. 7.

23. Love among the ruins: AIDS in our time. (1994, July 18). Kirp, D. C., *Nation*, p. 89.

24. Radically different: Do gay people have a responsibility to be revolutionaries? (1995, November 5). Bawer, B., Book Review Section, *New York Times*, p. 21.

25. Shunning 'he' and 'she,' they fight for respect. (1996, September 8). Goldberg, C., *New York Times*, Sec. Y, p. 10.

26. 'Stonewall' controversy comes to film. (1996, September 1). Hartl, J., *Seattle Times*, Sec. M, p. 4.

27. In gay-marriage storm, weary Clinton aide is buffeted on all sides. (1996, May 29). Clines, F. X., *New York Times*, Sec. A, p. 16.

19

GENDERPROP
Women in Mid-Passage

A great deal of the *genderprop* in the 1990s expressed the needs of women who have professional standing or who were positioned to achieve it. This contributed to a newprop that would work within the mainstream of a meritocracy, but it did not ensure that all of the steps that would be taken on behalf of women's rights would be free of conflict. Many women still turned to oldprop to address discrimination and abuse.

It was not yet an even playing field for gender, as noted by speakers during the International Women's Conference in Beijing in Fall 1995. There First Lady Hillary Rodham Clinton engaged in a propaganda of revelation and protest against the exploitation of women in the Third World. Hers was a fresh voice, because oldprop on behalf of women had not been permitted.

INSIDER GAMES

Even in the United States, professional women have not fully mastered insider games of oldprop. They were shortshrifted in Nannygate, demeaned during Hillgate, and assaulted at Tailgate. Although the professional landscape was changing, many professional women still found themselves blocked by a lack of acceptance and frustrated by the ambivalence of their roles.

Adverse actions by President Clinton on his nomination of women for high office gave rise to the characterization of Nannygate; in each case the President withdrew a highly qualified woman from nomination for cabinet-level office because they violated standards that would not be applied to men. The problem clearly was gender flavored; it revolved around the hiring and payment of social security taxes of alien Hispanic housekeepers as "nannies;" the headline said:

It's Gender, Stupid

Can anyone still doubt that underlying the troubles of President Clinton's first two choices for attorney general was the attitude of a male-dominated society toward women? Can anyone doubt that . . . (it) . . . is steeped in hypocrisy?[1]

The first nominee, highly successful corporation attorney Zoe Baird, had employed an illegal alien to care for her children and had rushed at the last moment to pay the taxes that she had neglected. Baird had done nothing other than what all couples of her professional class had done in Washington, DC; that is, what was expedient, because nonforeign child care was difficult to obtain.

Another nominee, Kimba Wood, a Federal District judge from Manhattan, employed an undocumented alien for child care at a time when it was illegal to do so, but she had paid the taxes. Then it was discovered that as a student in London she had worked as a trainee for 5 days as a Playboy Club bunny. Clinton promptly shelved her appointment, as well. Finally, there was the case of lawyer Lani Guinier, whose imaginative newprop was deemed to be too radical for appointment to a high post in the Department of Justice in civil rights enforcement. Had she been a man, she might have been perceived as courageous, but as a woman she was perceived to be uppity. A year later one of her ideas for achieving proportional voting representation by minorities resurfaced and she was hailed as a visionary, but by that time she was out of the appointment loop.

The Responsibilities of Professionalism

It was difficult at first to discern why women's organizations had not launched a massive propaganda assault on the President in defense of these nominees. The answer was that many were Eastern elitist professional women who eschewed the oldprop of attack and the emotionalism that it evoked. As practitioners of the newprop of accommodation, they preferred insider bureaucratic battles to public appeals. Professional women were expected to look after themselves.

Hillgate: A Matter of Class

Hillgate illustrated the distance that can develop between a revolutionary movement and its propaganda when its members achieve the status of professionals. That explained, in part, why Oklahoma University law professor Anita

Hill, a Black professional woman, could be attacked so openly by Republicans on the Senate Judiciary Committee. In their minds she had deserted class values by publicly charging Supreme Court nominee Clarence Thomas with sexual harassment. Thomas, himself Black, decried not only the racial context but its lack of professionalism.

Professional courtesies had been granted to other women (and men) who appeared before Congressional committees. Ironically, Hill won the battle of public opinion only because the polls transformed the issue from race and professionalism to gender. Thomas adopted oldprop to make political liberals the issue, blurring distinctions of gender and even professionalism.[2]

When a women's group in Oklahoma asked that an Anita Hill chair be established at the University of Oklahoma, where she was a professor in the School of Law, the proposal failed. Hill, herself, was described as receptive but not eager to proceed with what became a highly controversial proposal; indeed, the dean who had favored the proposal found it necessary to resign.

A Watershed Event?

Were the Thomas–Hill hearings a watershed gender event or were there more important factors at work? Certainly, gender began to matter. Pennsylvania Republican Senator Arlen Spector was hard pressed to fend off a woman newcomer, Lynn Yeakal, who exploited Spector's badgering of Hill. Even before he decided to become a presidential candidate in 1996, Spector apologized and said the incident had sensitized him to gender issues; he should have treated Hill as a professional woman, not as a radical feminist who sought to politicize the Senate confirmation process.

There were other gender outcomes. Democratic Senator Brock Adams of Washington state decided not to run for reelection after being accused of sexist acts. In Oregon, Republican Senator Bob Packwood was reelected despite recurring rumors about engaging in sexual harassment; only after his election did the *Washington Post*, some 3,000 miles away, publish the details. The up-to-then-silent Oregon daily newspapers were forced to rationalize publicly their seeming indifference. Women activists harassed Packwood relentlessly, and after a vote of condemnation by the Senate Ethics Committee, Packwood resigned.

THE POLITICAL WOMAN

The political woman prospered in the 1990s. In 1992 the former mayor of San Francisco, Dianne Feinstein, and state legislator Barbara Boxer won their party's nominations and election to the U.S. Senate. Carol Mosely Braun was the first African American woman elected to the Senate from Illinois. Sixteen women won candidacies for the House of Representatives. In the Democratic race for the Senate in New York, the only man running campaigned as a feminist. Janet Reno, a Florida attorney general, was appointed to the cabinet position that Baird and Wood had been so close to achieving, and Dr. Joycelyn Elders, a mince-no-words proponent of family planning, sex education, and abortion rights, was appointed Surgeon General, although she would be unable to stay the course.

Reno achieved status because of personal bravery in the trenches. More than 6 feet tall, she seemed to answer affirmatively the rhetorical question sung in Pygmalion, "Why can't a woman be more like a man?" She tried to defuse the political controversy over her department's actions in the Waco massacre of the David Koresh cult with a resolute defense of her department's seemingly misguided actions.[3]

Exceeding the Limits

Elders, an African American, was criticized constantly by conservative senators because of her open opposition to the Christian right and her views on sex education in the schools. She had labeled some Christian antiabortion leaders as "very religious but non-Christian . . . people who love little babies as long as they're in somebody else's uterus." Elders later was to become a target of the snide humor of talkprop host Rush Limbaugh, who put video excerpts of her speechmaking on camera as a means of ridiculing her speaking style.[4]

Elders espoused a national campaign against unwanted teenage pregnancies, including the distribution of condoms by school clinics. She wanted sex education in the early school years, and she favored providing the contraceptive implant Norplant to drug-addicted prostitutes. She said bluntly, "Poor pregnant teen-agers (many of them Black) (are) like slaves who are breeding another class of slaves at a time when we don't need any more slaves."[5]

This oldprop of confrontation seemed out of keeping with her position and prestige, but it was described by a supporter, Nancy Landon Kassenbaum, a Kansas Republican senator, as empathic, forthright, and appealing to the young; hence in style if not in content an invoking of newprop. However, in early 1995, President Clinton forced Elders to resign after she spoke out frankly on teen sex.

Winning the Establishment

Not all women nominees for high federal posts were to be hazed by mediaprop and the male-dominated Senate. The key was to be perceived as a member of the establishment. That was the case of Jane Alexander, who was appointed chairwoman of the National Endowment of the Arts.

Skilled in newprop, she told the Senate committee that she "had a vision for the arts in America: . . . that each man, woman and child find the song in his or her heart." However, despite her successes, she had a difficult time defending her agency from attack by the Contract With America.[6]

At the time that Margaret Milner Richardson, Washington tax lawyer, was appointed Commissioner of Internal Revenue, it was pointed out that she had been a fund raiser for the Democratic party. However, the Vassar graduate replied, disarmingly, that she simply was going into the biggest fund-raising job in the country—collecting taxes. She said adroitly about tax policies and collections that she "would listen to our customers."[7]

CRACKING GLASS CEILINGS

By the 1990s professional women were poised to exploit the economic opportunities that became accessible to them. A report by female economists in the *New York Times* showed that women in the 1980s had gained in incomes and the value of jobs and positions and that this trend would accelerate in the 1990s. Demand had increased greatly for highly skilled executives, lawyers, engineers, and doctors. Women's salaries still were not equal to those of men, but men's salaries slipped 8% and those for women increased 10%.

More women worked at full-time jobs, and they held 40% of entry-level and middle-management jobs, double their share two decades earlier. Women still were not entering highly paid professions to the same extent as men, but when they did enter those professions, their earnings almost equaled those of men. Although important gaps continued to exist at executive and administrative levels, younger women gained substantially. A more professionally educated, increasingly affluent, and independent woman was making up a constituency that was tuned to newprop.

But in late 1995 a study found that the boardrooms of U.S. corporations were still overwhelmingly male and White. The Glass Ceiling commission said that at a time when more than half of the nation's master's degrees were being awarded to women, 95% of the senior-level managers in the Fortune 1000 industrial and Fortune 500 companies were men, and 98% were White.[8]

Women Talk It Over

Several thousand women in New York for their annual conference on small business management were told by singer Judy Collins that she had broken barriers to become a business success, segueing into a stanza of the Mimi Farina song, "Bread and Roses," a feminist anthem that celebrates the struggle for both art and a living wage. "As women," Collins said, "we were raised to have rescue fantasies. I'm here to tell you that no one's coming (but us)." The tone was newprop, but the message of exclusion was oldprop.[9]

Other speakers included attorney Lani Guinier; Sally Jesse Raphael, talk-show host; Linda Fairstein, Manhattan sex-crimes prosecutor; sexpert Dr. Ruth Westheimer; and Governor Christine Todd Whitman of New Jersey, who told women that they were consensus builders (and thus exponents of newprop) because their life experiences were different.

WHY THE GENDER GAP?

The gap between the political outlooks of men and women has not been growing merely because more women are achieving professional roles. Women remember that government safety net programs helped to support their families and provided opportunities for them to elevate their status.

The successes of women have engendered pessimism in the outlooks of men as more of them are reporting to women in the workplace. That is even more likely to occur because women still are underrepresented in public office—only 11% of the U.S. House of Representatives, 9% of the Senate, and 21% of state legislatures.

It is resentful men rather than women who are joining state militias, and it is angry men more than women who speak out on oldprop radio talk shows.[10]

MEDIA ROLES EMERGE

Three "young" middle-aged women were hailed as contributors to excellence in public broadcasting—early Boomers Cokie Roberts, Nina Totenberg, and Linda Wertheimer. Broadcast journalism in Washington, DC, had been almost as male as football until they came to National Public Radio.

In a Q and A exchange, Totenberg was asked about Senator Packwood's personal diaries. Ms. Dreifus asked, "Do any of you stand a chance of making an unsolicited appearance? . . . [as, for an example] "Today I placed my hand on Nina Totenberg's knee.'" Totenberg replied: "Not unless he's been fantasizing."[10]

It was Wertheimer and Roberts who offended Ross Perot by learning the details of his financial history and asking him about them. Perot became angry on a *Nightline* broadcast and said testily: "He really didn't mind all reporters, just women reporters who were trying to prove their manhood."[11]

It was not only Perot among the conservative politicians who required sensitivity training. Republican candidate Dole announced in early May 1996, that he recognized that there was a gender gap between Democrats and Republicans, and that he needed to do something about it. The Harris poll showed that among women, 53% would vote for Clinton and only 28% for Dole. And a *New York Times*/CBS News Poll found a similar difference—52% to 28% among women would vote for Clinton.

This produced a flood of oldprop from both Dole and Newt Gingrich, with Dole insisting that Republican programs actually worked for women (although he skirted the abortion issue), and Gingrich attributing women's opinions to falsification of claims by Clinton. However, women were conscious of Republicans' positions on social safety nets, abortion, and as book titles began to suggest, "a Republican war on women." Despite the emergence within the Republican party of a women's coalition that was pro-choice, and the promise of a full debate on that issue within the party, Dole was likely to fall victim to women's issues.[12]

STRUGGLE IN HOLLYWOOD

Hollywood—at whom Dole had directed oldprop barbs on "family values" but not for failing to create meaningful managerial or leading acting roles for women—had far to go before professional women would break through glass ceilings that protected men in powerful positions. Women were unable to crack the top tiers of major talent agencies, and they continued to be paid less than their male counterparts.

But women were heartened by the top-level appointments of Lucie Salhany to chair Fox Broadcasting and Sherry Lansing to chair Paramount Motion Pictures. They became the first women to hold top posts at a television network or movie studio. Lansing was at the nexus of critical discussions of women's roles in films.

It was her studio that produced *Indecent Proposal*, where ultrawealthy Robert Redford offered Demi Moore (who was married) $1 million for one night in bed with him. Lansing defended the film, asserting that a woman making a choice is the ultimate feminist statement, however indecent the proposal. "She's deciding whom she wants to sleep with; she's deciding what she wants to do with her body. It was her choice to sleep with Robert Redford."[13]

Feminists insisted that any exploitation of the woman's body—choice or no choice—was oldprop. Women should be three-dimensional characters rather than sexual objects to be pursued or purchased.[13]

A revolution also was occurring on prime-time television, where women became the focus and provided the titles of many of the most popular programs: *Roseanne, Ellen, Cybill, Murphy Brown, Grace Under Fire, Caroline in the City, Sisters,* and *The Nanny.* Among others, *Melrose Place, Central Park West,* and *Beverly Hills 90210* revolved around their female leads. This became alluded to as the "feminization" of prime-time.[14]

Displeasing and Pleasing the Feminists

Felice Schwartz and her firm, Catalyst, consulted with hundreds of corporations to make them more female friendly. Yet she was criticized by feminists for adopting corporate language to advance women, and she was criticized for making concessions, one of them the acknowledgment that women corporate executives were more expensive to sustain than were men, a logic that encouraged a "second-tier" philosophy of placement. Schwartz said she was inspired by Betty Friedan's *The Feminist Mystique*, which had served as a manifesto for millions of alienated middle-class women.[15]

A woman succeeded as editor of *The New Yorker*. Tina Brown had helped *Vanity Fair* become the "hot" magazine of the 1980s and 1990s. Very early in her editorship the verdict was in: She was doing a superb job of balancing the traditional strengths of *The New Yorker* with its potential for being contemporary.[16]

A woman Hollywood producer, Gale Anne Hurd, won her reputation by producing such innovative box office successes as *Aliens, The Terminator, The Abyss, Alien Nation,* and *Terminator 2: Judgment Day*. She went from a Phi Beta Kappa graduation from Stanford University to assistant to Roger Corman, the B-movie king. Of him she said, "The interesting thing . . . was that it was not like the rest of Hollywood; women had an equal chance to do anything. It was complete equal-opportunity exploitation. You had an opportunity to do anything."[17]

The 1993 Academy Awards became the year of the actress. Even so, when Emma Thompson accepted her Oscar for her performance in *Howard's End* she said: "If I have a wish left in the world, it is for the creation of more great female roles," but her tone was an oldprop of protest:

> One of the things we're suffering the consequences of is that the 80's were a fairly repugnant age morally. It was a period of backlash. . . . As you look at the kinds of roles available to women in the late 80's and 90's, they are fantastically curtailed. . . . It is a very complicated issue because it's so tied up with other social advances. As women have taken more power, there's some wish to punish us, and that has become clear in this art form.[18]

RECOGNIZING COMMITMENT

Colonel Marion Berkheimer waited 25 years for recognition of her role and that of other nurses during the Vietnam War. On November 12, 1993, Veterans Day, a memorial was dedicated to the forgotten womens corps of Vietnam veterans. I attended a ceremony honoring Colonel Berkheimer in Seattle. She said, "We were supposed to be the brave ones and not have emotions. Military nurses have repressed so much." And Vice President Al Gore, an Army journalist in Vietnam, said "we never listened to them, and we never properly thanked them."[19]

Tailhook and Oldprop

Tailhook was the characterization given to an annual drinking party held for Naval aviators where decorum was thrown out the portholes. On this occasion, the Las Vegas Hilton hospitality suites were flooded with alcohol, strippers, and pornographic movies. It was here that women Naval officers were attacked by male pilots in a hazing exercise that approached the bizarre.

Several high-ranking officers resigned as a result of the reactions and others endured harsh discipline. Not long afterward, the director of Naval Operations backed full combat roles for women, including that of fighter pilot. Old patterns of behavior were no longer to be tolerated.

An equally staggering demonstration of military insensitivity came after the rape of a 12-year-old Japanese girl on Okinawa by three U.S. servicemen. Admiral Richard C. Macke first said the act was "absolutely stupid," but he clarified this ambiguity by stating that "for the price they paid to rent a car, they could have had a girl," another limitation of thought and public judgment. Missing was a sense of the suffering caused the girl and the uproar the rape had caused. The Admiral resigned and President Clinton, himself, found it necessary to apologize for the nation.[20]

SPOUSAL ABUSE

The revelation that so prominent a public figure as O. J. Simpson had been a spouse abuser set off a media feeding frenzy on spousal abuse. A case worker in Pacheco, California, said that never before had domestic abuse switchboards lighted up as they did after the Simpson reports. Once-shy women came to Battered Women's Alternative offices to pour out tales of beatings by their spouses and fears for their lives. Suddenly there was a new need for training programs. At a Philadelphia agency, Women Against Abuse, calls increased 50%.[21]

Time devoted major attention to the spousal abuse aspects of the Simpson case. It concluded that domestic abuse, once perniciously silent, was being exposed for its brutality in the wake of the murder case. The eight-page essay was complete with photographs of abused women and spiced by intimate accounts of abuse and descriptions of murders. When Simpson was acquitted of the murders, cries raged about the oldprop message that was being sent to women everywhere.[22]

BORROWING FROM IRON JOHN

Iron John is a frankly oldprop book that maintained itself on the *New York Times* best-seller list for 62 weeks by becoming the voice of angry males seeking to regain their sense of power in relation to ascendant females.[23] That resulted in a spate of books of like mind, including Sam Keen's male manifesto, *Fire in the Belly,* and female counterparts such as Gloria Steinem's memoir, *Revolution From Within; Women Who Run With the Wolves,* by Jungian analyst Clarissa Pinkola Estes; and Susan Faludi's *Backlash,* which describes the counterassault on the women's movement. One critic observed that the newest books in defense of the women's movement had stolen author Robert Bly's thunder; they had translated his male imagery into female terms. However, this had been going on for a long time. Women were holding marriages together because they communicated better than men in the home; it was this lack of a male mastery of communication that was testing marriages.[24]

THE HILLARYPROP FACTOR

The *Hillaryprop* factor that caused the First Lady to be muted during the presidential campaign had an even more profound effect. While giving the Republicans a smaller target, it also set off an oldprop stereotyping process by which Barbara Bush became a full-time grandmother, Marilyn Quayle a dedicated housewife, Tipper Gore a plumpish one-time debutante, and a reinvented Hillary a wife and mother.

But Hillary, as well as the others, was something else. As a speaker to a women's international congress she promoted a document that expanded and codified women's rights. Oldprop in its demands, it offered accommodation, as well.[25] What was even more significant was that a global network was born. A newprop would offer ideas about equality that had long been denied. As the Chinese proverb said, women would, in fact, hold up half the sky.[26]

Indeed, the 1990s were being described as the age of the woman icon. Perhaps the apotheosis was reached with the confirmation of former ambassador Madeleine Albright to the position of U.S. Secretary of State, making her the first woman to hold that position. Senator Diane Feinstein of California commented that one more gender door had opened, and it was one more door that never again would be closed.

ɮ   ɮ   ɮ

Women in the 1990s joined a professional class that drew them inexorably from the oldprop to the new. But sexual affronts typified by Tailgate and the actions of Senators Robert Packwood of Oregon and Brock Adams of Washington gave rise to oldprop on the part of offended women.

As professionals, the cracking of glass ceilings required women's mastery of newprop. Women executives, politicians, journalists, and artists reached and exceeded those heights and gave evidence of the likelihood of a continuing ascendancy. As insiders, they mastered the newprop of professionalism and class.

NOTES

1. It's gender, stupid. (1993, February 8). Lewis, A., *New York Times*, Sec. A, p. 15.
2. The burden of Clarence Thomas. (1993, September 27). Toobin, J., *The New Yorker*, pp. 38–51.

3. Janet Reno, hung out to dry? (1993, December 21). Kurtz, H., *Washington Post*, Sec. B, p. 1.

4. Abortive coverage strategy: use the vote. (1993, October 8). *New York Times*, Sec. A, p. 14

5. Ibid., *New York Times*, p. 14.

6. Senate panel gives Alexander its vote, and a rave review. (1993, September 23). *New York Times*, Sec. B, p. 1.

7. A tax lawyer now atop the IRS. (1994, March 30). Hershey, R. D., Jr., *New York Times*, Sec. C, p. 1.

8. Law, education failing to break glass ceiling. (1995, November 25). Swoboda, F., *Washington Post*, Sec. F, p. 1.

9. A few thousand women, networking. (1994, March 27). *New York Times*, Sec. F, p. 4.

10. The gender gap: huge myth; important reality. (1996, August/September). *The Public Perspective*, p. 4.

11. Women take over at PBS. (1994, January 2). Dreifus, C., *New York Times Magazine*, pp. 14–17.

12. Dole says he plans to win the votes of women. (1996, May 8). Seelye, K. Q., *New York Times*, Sec. A, pp. 1/16.

13. Men, women, talk, talk, talk. (1991, June 19). Gamarekian, B., *New York Times*, Sec. B, p. 1.

14. A prime time for women on television. (1995, November 11). Farhi, P., *Washington Post*, Sec. A, p. 1.

15. A feminist and the art of persuasion. (1993, March 28). Noble, B. P., *New York Times*, Sec. F, p. 29.

16. New Yorker's editor sees the future as the past. (1992, September 24). Carmody, D., *New York Times*, Sec. B, p. 1.

17. A woman who knows what men like: action films. (1994, May 3). Weinraub, B., *New York Times*, Sec. B, p. 1.

18. Women's roles in films draw women's fire. (1993, June 2). Weinraub, B., *New York Times*, Sec. B, p. 1.

19. A belated salute to the women who served. (1993, November 12). *New York Times*, Sec. A, p. 1.

20. Remarks in rape case sink officer. (1995, November 18). Graham, B., *Washington Post*, Sec. A, p. 1.

21. When violence hits home. (1994, July 4). Sindowe, J., *Time*, p. 19.

22. Sindow, *Time*, p. 19.

23. Iron John: A book about men. (1993, August 27). Kakutani, M., *Book Review*, *New York Times*, Sec. B, p. 1.

24. Sex, lies and conversation. (1990, June 24). Tannen, D., *Washington Post*, Sec. C, p. 3.

25. U.N. Forum asserts women's sexual liberty; Nations agree to expand human rights definitions. (1995, September 11). Faison, S., *New York Times*, In *Seattle Post-Intelligencer*, Sec. A, p. 2.

26. Beyond gender. (1995, September 4). *Newsweek*, pp. 30–32.

20

TRINITYPROP
Race, Abortion, and Religion

The propagandas about racial bias, abortion, and religion in politics that pervade our society describe an uneasy prevalence of the oldprop over the new. Few other social issues and their propagandas so strain the workings of our popular culture as does *trinityprop*, for they are based on class values that are less subject to change than are attitudes toward other social issues.

Many of the emotional concerns that underlie that trinity of angry propagandas defy knowledge rather than rest on it, create fears rather than confidence, and provoke confrontation rather than accommodation. In their stridency they have given voice to the most pernicious of the oldprops: hate and exclusion. Their propagandas are more appropriate to a mass culture than a popular one.

Of the trinity, racial issues have been both the least and the most amenable to discussion and accommodation. By contrast, the synergy between *abortionprop* and *religionprop* has been the most unyielding to newprop, although the exigencies of the 1996 presidential race pushed some of the religionists away from their most exclusionary rhetoric.

RACEPROP: EMERGENCE AND REVERSION

The amelioration in racial attitudes and rhetoric was brought about by the emergence of middle-class values among a substantial segment of the Black, Asian, and Hispanic populations. For all, it was a question of moving on from the past to the present and the future; they were going ahead with their lives.

For the Black middle class, this was built on accelerated access to major universities, employment by leading law firms, appointments to high offices, and election to others. However, this development was accompanied by a dramatic decline in the relative standing of the Black poor. The new Black elites enjoyed access to the popular culture and adopted newprop as their métier, but the poor remained targets of an angry oldprop that exploited their relegation to poverty and their standing as a marginal social class.[1]

Events have continued to feed those outlooks—the class and racial values that were at the heart of the defense in the O. J. Simpson trial; suspicions and hatreds that were mobilized by the Los Angeles riots and their aftermaths; puzzlement over the mixed newprop and oldprop messages of radical Black Muslim leader Louis Farrakhan and his "million man march" on Washington, DC, and like events.

The Impact of Events

A number of events in the 1990s mirrored the contrasts between the emerging middle-class newprop of racial and cultural multiversity and the regressive lower class oldprop of exclusion and conflict.

+ The O. J. Simpson trial: Football star and actor O. J. Simpson was acquitted in Los Angeles for the murder of his wife and a male friend because of the racism of Los Angeles Police detective Mark Fuhrman, and closing arguments by the defense that heavily played the "race card."

+ Where goest the NAACP? The middle-class National Association for the Advancement of Colored People (NAACP) deposed a leader who proposed radical new directions that called on the oldprop as well as the new.

+ Awakening from a dream? There were indications of malaise in middle-class Black culture with the flagging appreciation of the works of Martin Luther King, Jr., an apostle of newprop to whom the nation had dedicated a national holiday.

+ Affirmative action, yeah or nay? Politics in 1996 raised questions as to the role of affirmative action; the middle class was willing to reconsider it, but lower classes clung to it.

+ Black pride, Farrakhan style: The radical Black Muslim leader organized a "million man march" and assemblage in the Mall in Washington, DC, to affirm Black pride and decry its enemies, invoking both the newprop and the old.

O. J.: Drawing the Color Line, Again

The O. J. Simpson murder trial challenged the myth of colorblindness, the so-called "blind" acceptance of an African American hero into the White middle class. Ironically, the fame of Martin Luther King, Jr. had made him more Black, but Simpson's fame had made him more White. A cartoon satirized the impact of the trial on a typical White male.

> First Cartoon Panel: O. J. is poised, charming, friendly, a likable role model.
> Second Panel: O. J. is a regular guy, warm, smooth, relaxed, self-confident, easy-going, mild-mannered . . .
> Third Panel: The viewer is preoccupied with his thoughts.
> Fourth Panel: The viewer shouts, "LIAR!!"[2]

Thus the viewer had sublimated race for class, but because O. J.'s action hardly befitted his class, the viewer was forced to deal again with the implications of race.

Rage Among the Middle Class.   As the trial proceeded, the question of race was raised more baldly. Fuhrman had conducted taped interviews with a fact–fiction writer in which he used the "N" word more than 40 times and bragged about his prejudicial conduct in the arrests of Blacks. It was a virulent oldprop in which African Americans were denied the most basic protections of the popular culture.

The Simpson defense team at first said that race was not an issue, and it would eschew the oldprop of hate and divisiveness, but Simpson lawyer Johnnie L. Cochran, himself an African American, based his closing argument on righting racial injustice, describing Fuhrman as "genocidal" and likening him to Adolf Hitler. The effect was to recast Simpson from middle-class murder suspect to racial victim. The one-time head of the defense team, Robert Shapiro, of the Jewish faith, said, "Not only had the defense team played the race card but had dealt it from the bottom of the deck," and he told ABC television interviewer Barbara Walters that he was "deeply offended" when Cochran treated Fuhrman's racism in the context of the Nazi Holocaust: "To me the Holocaust stands alone. . . . To compare this in any way to a rogue cop, in my opinion, was wrong."[3]

However, Cochran believed that the place of the Black middle class in the system was "provisional, not permanent," and it was necessary to redefine racial dialog as oldprop or newprop for each class and each generation.[4]

The Polls and the Media.   Polling responses dramatized the differences in views between the diffused Black culture and the mainstream White culture. Prior to the verdict, a poll found that 60% of African American respondents agreed that O. J. was being set up by someone. A Harris poll in February 1995, found that 61% overall thought Simpson was guilty, whereas 68% of Blacks thought he was not guilty. *Newsweek* polls showed a 40% difference between Blacks and non-Blacks.[5] This suggested that only a sense of equal membership in the popular culture permitted individuals to agree on its parameters.

Time made a stunning error in judgment when it darkened and pigmented O. J.'s skin coloration on a cover photo. As a consequence, some people judged him to be more menacing than they otherwise might have concluded. The *Newsweek* cover for the same week portrayed a lighter photograph of O. J. with a white background, but its headline said: "Trail of Blood."[6] *Time* found it necessary to present a full-page apology in its next issue.[7] The process had the effect of removing O. J. from his class and identifying him with his race, a renegade member of the popular culture who no longer deserved its respect and protections.[8]

If the two Simpson verdicts—one of not guilty in the criminal trial, the other of liability for wrongful deaths in the civil trial—established anything, it was the effects of an exclusionary popular culture on perceptions of reality. Where racialprop dominated the criminal trial, retribution underlined the civil trial. Both were exclusionary oldprops that articulated the gaps between social classes.[9]

Where goest the NAACP?

When the newly appointed director of the NAACP, the Reverend Benjamin Chavis, invited the radical, anti-White, anti-Semitic Reverend Louis Farrakhan, leader of the Nation of Islam and proponent of oldprop, to a conference of African American leaders, questions were raised as to where Chavis intended to lead an organization that was bound by its middle-class values to a muted rhetoric of newprop.

Was Chavis advancing an African American version of Mao's cultural revolution, or was he exploring the limits of the popular culture? If the popular culture was boundless, the NAACP should be permitted to conduct any propaganda—old or new. Chavis believed that middle-class values stood in the way of the propaganda that a new NAACP needed to employ.

Chavis was jousting with history. When the NAACP was founded soon after the turn of the 20th century, colored meant negro; it was only after the symbolic revolt against repression that was led by track stars Tommy Smith and John Carlos at the 1968 Olympic Games that it came to mean Black and, ultimately, African American. This was a newprop language of freedom.

The 1977 leader of the NAACP, the Reverend Benjamin L. Hooks, opted for mainstreaming. He sought to bridge gaps by creating a Black middle class that held the same values as Whites. Negro Boomers would ride the waves of economic growth with their White counterparts, establish common interests, and walk through doors that would be thrown open to them. Hooks embraced the newprops of legitimacy, negotiation, and accommodation and eschewed the oldprop of confrontation. Ironically, when its middle class had completed its economic passage, the NAACP lost membership.

The Search for Diversity.   Chavis determined to build a more diverse ethnic and cultural membership that would adopt "color" generically as Black and Brown rather than only Black, much in the pattern of the Reverend Jesse Jackson's Rainbow Coalition. Criss-crossing the nation, he attended youthful street gang conferences, urged gangsta rappers to stop using sexist and violent lyrics, and carried antidrug messages to Chicago's Southside "'hoods." Preaching the newprop of self-enhancement and change, he found converts among young and poor Black and Hispanic prison inmates.[10]

Chavis noted that in the 1960s the racial dialog was among such disparate groups as the conservative Urban League, King's Southern Christian Leadership Conference, the confrontational Congress of Racial Equality (CORE), the Student Nonviolent Coordinating Committee, Malcolm X's Nation of Islam, and the militant Black Panthers. Why exclude diversity now?[11]

But Chavis' thesis would not be tested; he became caught up in administrative and personal problems and was replaced by the widow of civil rights hero Medgar Evers, Myrlie Evers-Williams. The organization had become "a victim of its own successes. Its original, hard-fought goals largely won, it fell along with the rest of the civil rights movement into a morbidly ambivalent state of agenda shock."[12]

Was There a Vision?   Chavis' vision was multiclass, and Hooks had been middle class, but Evers decided to recast the NAACP as upper class. At the first official gathering, she surrounded herself with seven African American federal judges, Black luminaries such as Carl T. Rowan, syndicated columnist; General Colin L. Powell; perennial candidate Reverend Jesse Jackson; Betty Shabazz, widow of Malcolm X; Mayor Marion Barry of Washington, DC; and Vernon E. Jordan, Jr., former head of the National Urban League and a cochairman of President Clinton's transition team. They would not create the same kind of energy that led the organization to protests, lawsuits, and political campaigns that shaped laws on voting rights, desegregation, and affirmative action, but they would present the attractiveness of a new elitism that the middle-class Black would regard favorably. Whatever the agenda, at its annual meeting a participant held a banner that said: "NAACP MUST HAVE A FRESH START."[13]

New Leader, New Propaganda.   The new leader would be prestigious former Congressman Kweisi Mfume. In keeping with the new aspirations, he would shift energies from oldprop oratory and appeals to morality to organizational and strategic goals. He would push equal opportunities and treatment under the law and ask corporations and government to enhance them. Black athletes, businessmen, actors, and others of high status would lend their persons and money to the task. Newprop would be given a chance in a lofty atmosphere.[14]

Awakening from a Dream

By the 1990s African American leader Martin Luther King, Jr., had become a neglected icon. His contributions had been recognized by the dedication of a national holiday. Now apathy had set in, as if America had awakened from

King's dream. Like their counterparts, the African American middle class was treating King's holiday and symbolic anniversary as "a day not at the office."

More than two decades earlier, King had provided the rhetoric that helped to bring about epochal events. His "I Have a Dream" speech was a memorable newprop of hope and dedication that culminated the march of a passionate civil rights movement on Washington, DC. It adopted love and trust as means of bringing an end to segregation laws.

The speech was given on August 28, 1963 on the steps of the Lincoln Memorial to a quarter of a million people. It provided a rhetorical signature that was destined to survive the passage of time. It spoke passionately of suffering, despair, and ultimately, of hope, of White and Black children holding hands in trust and love. It was the best of the oldprop and the new, invoking not only emotion but logic and a sense of joy. Everyone would share in the realization of truths and the attainment of justice. In euphony and rhythm, "I Have a Dream" was an encompassing experience. But King's remembrance came to mean a holiday for the middle class, not a celebration. If King were to have relevance, he would have to be reinvented.[15]

President Clinton understood this mood. In a speech to African American ministers in Memphis, Tennessee, he conducted an apocryphal dialogue with King in which he restated the accomplishments of his civil rights movement and redefined them in the framework of newprop:

• As the ultimate in violence, King's death should be dedicated to the reduction of violence.

• As a fight for freedom, King's death was not intended to permit "the freedom of children to die before they became adults" in gang fights and random violence.

• King's love of children does not permit us to use "the freedom to have children to walk away from them."[16]

The Federal Holiday Commission concluded that a Martin Luther King, Jr., day must become American, not African American. It should become the basis of a newprop of inclusion rather than an oldprop of exclusion, either of class or race. It should be reinvented as a day to perform service for the nation as antidotes to violence.[17]

Affirmative Action, Yeah or Nay?

The Republican Contract With America articulated White anger over the decades-long "affirmative action" policies of promoting less qualified minorities to competitive positions. For many Whites, the terminating of reverse discrimination had been a long-smoldering agenda. There was speculation at the outset about whether any reversals would be framed by the oldprop of conflict or the newprop of accommodation. But when a federal court ruled that quota systems were illegal, steps toward the redefinition of policies began to emerge.

Predictably, middle-class Blacks adopted a newprop of continued commitment to human development while acknowledging the unfairness of exclusionary racial quotas. They reasoned that if Blacks could compete, no reverse discrimination would be required. Successful Blacks, among them Supreme Court Justice Clarence Thomas, saw reverse discrimination as debasing because it made their success dependent on discrimination; the newprop of an earlier era was an oldprop of the present.[18]

Class-Based Affirmative Action. Affirmative action made racial and gender distinctions, but the awards were not distributed always on the condition of need. Sometimes Whites were more in need and more qualified than minorities. It was this exclusionary condition that produced the patina of oldprop. As a consequence, new policies proposed that affirmative action be moved back from points of selection to opportunities for preparation in which race and gender would be implicit rather than explicit factors.

President Clinton's position became "mend it, don't end it," but a then presidential hopeful, Republican Governor Pete Wilson of California, insisted, "End it; you can't mend it."[19] Wilson prevailed on the University of California Board of Regents to abandon its affirmative action policies.[20]

The "Million Man" March

Farrakhan's march was directed at two constituencies: one that was able to respond to the newprops of hope, urgency, and needs for achievement; the other vulnerable enough to be manipulated by oldprop. The hundreds of thousands of young males—females were excluded, and this was hardly newprop—came to pray, to greet, and to share a sense of history. Many held jobs, paid taxes, raised children, and sought a better life, yet felt that membership in the popular culture had been denied to them. Now they sought to reverse this pattern of exclusion. A participant pledged "a fresh resolve, to watch my mouth, treat my brothers and sisters with respect, get my life together, and carry the message back."[21]

Farrakhan's message was that he was proving that he could walk and talk even to Blacks who had dismissed him as a leader of only a marginal group; it was true that a *Newsweek* poll showed that only 14% of Blacks thought he reflected the mainstream of African American thought, but the majority was divided in viewing him favorably or unfavorably, 41% in each case.[22]

This left Farrakhan with a choice: He could shift from the oldprops of bigotry, uncertainty, and exclusion to the newprops of accommodation and inclusion, or he could continue to engage in theater and indulge in ambiguity. That was the course he chose in 1996 when he visited Saddam Hussein in Iraq. It contributed to a Leninist pattern of a single-step-forward newprop (the million man march), followed by a two-steps-backward oldprop.

꙳   ꙳   ꙳

A symposium that tracked Black thought from the 1960s to the 1990s concluded that pragmatism now was in fashion politically and that for the first time there was more receptivity to newprop than to the old. Black pollster Ron Lester, a 42-year-old meritocrat, noted that Clinton's pragmatic choices on social issues meant that he would retain the Black vote, even if Dole persuaded Colin Powell to share the ticket in 1996.[23]

The new Black mayor of San Francisco, inveterate politician Willie Brown, would make no appointments on the basis of race, alone, as had the defeated New York Black Mayor David Dinkins. He would not force the private sector to hire Blacks just to talk to his Blacks; rather, he would create a multiracial meritocracy in which everyone could talk to everyone, the essence of newprop.[24]

Angela Davis, the 1960s agitator, warned that bias expressed itself more in structure and class than in race, and her contemporary, Eldridge Cleaver, noted that the oldprop of racial protest simply got representatives into power who then used that oldprop to remain in power.

James Farmer, a colleague of Malcolm X, observed that the protest problems of the 1960s were simple—a right to the front seat of a bus or a hot dog at any lunch counter—but present-day protestors found it hard to abide by Martin Luther King's demands for individual responsibility because the popular culture had not provided them with a place or a forum for practicing those values. That was an unequal distribution of power and it stood in the way of the functioning of a popular culture.

ABORTIONPROP: INCUBUS OF OLDPROP

Of our trinity, the abortion issue has been most associated with issues of class and maintains a synergy with religious dogmas. It is not surprising, therefore, that each is committed to oldrop. Nonetheless, for a brief time after *Roe v. Wade*—the Supreme Court decision that confirmed abortion as legal—a quiet acceptance settled over the dispute. But in an unexpected redefinition of the conflict, some pro-lifers shifted to an oldprop of demonstrations and violence.

Amid that atmosphere of confrontation, a physician was shot and killed outside an abortion clinic, and in the shadow of the debate over government payments for abortion under the proposed national health care plan, a second physician was killed, along with his bodyguard. In early November 1994, a Canadian pro-choice advocate was shot through the window of his home. This was the oldprop of the deed.

A Record of Violence

Since 1977, 129 bombings and arson attacks have been aimed at abortion clinics, and 200 death threats and nearly 600 acts of vandalism were directed against clinic staffers. An antiabortion propagandist said he would not, himself, kill an abortionist, but others would. About the murderer of Dr. John Britton, he said, "What I don't understand is why he did it publicly."[25]

Roy McMillan flipped through a stack of posters, each of which projects different themes. One shows a cherubic baby and the slogan, "Abortion: Ultimate Child Abuse." McMillan prefers graphic posters such as a decapitated seventh-month fetus. He turned the poster of the headless infant toward passing traffic. As African Americans pulled into the clinic, he switched signs to "Abortion is Black Genocide," an obvious effort to exploit oldprop values of class.[26]

In Gaithersburg, Maryland, a Benedictine monk, Father Matthew Habiger, in an extension of oldprop shock rhetoric, displayed a laminated poster of a bloodied fetal head pinched by forceps and said: "This is one of our most popular items." Antiabortion pamphlets, posters, and plastic fetus dolls surrounded Habiger as he walked through the brick warehouse headquarters of Human Life International. The materials—including a pamphlet that proclaims "Abortion is the greatest war of all time"—are distributed through a national network of radical antiabortionists.[27]

Father Habiger called abortion clinics "death camps," abortion "a holocaust," and homosexuals and radical feminists "protagonists of death." His pamphlets bear titles such as "Infant Homicides Through Contraceptives," an oldprop of hate and fear that inhibits discussion.[28]

Comparing Strategies

The propaganda strategies of the pro-choice movement compare dramatically to those of the pro-lifers. When the pro-choice movement made the legislative and legal gains that resulted in *Roe v. Wade*, they turned from the oldprop of demand making to a newprop of legitimation, and they continued to pursue this tactic. But despite its gains, the ideology of the pro-life movement makes it impossible for them to entertain a similar shift:

◆ Pro-choice ideology focuses on the rights of the individual, whereas pro-lifers place community values and obligations ahead of individual needs.

◆ Pro-choicers have vested themselves in administrative agencies of governments and the decisions of the courts; by contrast, pro-lifers shun any suggestion that government is responsibile, *in loco parentis*, for members of society. Families and even communities should provide for their own care and not rely on governmental safety nets; government is part of the problem, not part of the solution.

- Pro-lifers use pictures and literature to describe the impact of abortions on the fetus; their intent is to frighten viewers so as to limit their abilities to respond.

- Pro-choicers refer to biological effects only in passing; they stress political rights and the consequences of the denial of abortions on the social fabric—more parents who are not fit to raise a child, more children who cannot be cared for, more unskilled parents who are unable to work for an income.

The January 1995 issue of *Harper's* quoted from a book, *The Army of God*, a self-defined "manual" for antiabortion activists that calls for violence. One chapter is devoted to "Ninety-Nine Covert Ways to Stop Abortion":

> You find that you have a very short time to live due to a terminal illness . . .
> Whatever activities are undertaken (torching, bombing, thumb removal, etc.) carry on with reckless abandon!
> Say you are given three months to live. You commit to torching two killing chambers every other day in different cities for 11 weeks. That's 77 destroyed death camps![29]

The radicalness of this oldprop has posed questions as to what is permissible as free speech in a popular culture and what is incitement to violence. Those who run abortion clinics warn that the pro-lifers are "crying fire in a crowded theater" and have exceeded the boundaries of free speech.

Defending an Abortionist

The failed nomination for U.S. Surgeon General of Dr. Henry Foster, Jr., an African American gynecologist who had performed numerous abortions, became a feeding frenzy for oldprop. *U.S. News & World Report* said that abortion raised more peripheral questions than Foster's qualifications.[30]

Caught off guard by questions as to the number and nature of the abortions he had performed, Foster offered disparate statistics, one from memory, the other from records. This set off a credibility debate, but the real agenda was Foster as abortionist.[31]

Foster attempted to shift the agenda from defending against pro-life attacks to redefining himself as a health advocate, as a doctor who had delivered 10,000 babies, and as someone who could attend medical school only because of sacrifices made by his Grandma Hattie. However, this effort failed; the oldprop had preempted the debate.[32]

Enter Buchanan

As Republican candidates battled one another in the 1996 primaries, the battle over abortion raged anew, fanned by Patrick J. Buchanan, who insisted that there be no conditions permitting abortion other than saving the life of the mother—not incest, not rape, not any other condition or necessity—and that as President he would appoint judges to the Supreme Court who would ensure the reversal of *Roe v. Wade.* A supporter in Yuma, Arizona, wore a T-shirt that said, "As a former fetus, I oppose abortion!"[33]

Once Dole had defeated Buchanan for the Republican nomination, the debate shifted to the party platform plank on abortion. Christian conservatives sought to force Dole to make an unequivocal statement that he would preserve the tough antiabortion language in the 1992 platform. The impetus came from Buchanan, whose sister and campaign chairman, Bay Buchanan, had launched a telephone and letter-writing campaign to mobilize anti-abortion activists for an all-out oldprop defense of the platform. Dole yielded but promised to bring a newprop cast to the discussion of the issue.[34]

ßᐱ   ßᐱ   ßᐱ

The sense of special identity and mission that is held by the pro-life forces makes class as well as religious beliefs a focus of their oldprop of exclusion. Pro-lifers will continue to demonize and attempt to exclude from the popular culture those who violate their rules and teachings. For the foreseeable future, abortionprop will continue to exploit the most virulent of oldprops to pursue its goals.

A RELIGIOUS CONTRACT ON AMERICA?

About a month after the new Republican majority in Congress completed its political Contract With America, a 10-point "Contract With the American Family" was presented to the American people by the Christian Coalition (CC). It had been withheld from the Republican political contract on the promise by House Speaker Newt Gingrich that he would lead the religion-based proposals to the "promised land"—in this case to the House floor for a vote.

I watched the Capitol Hill press conference televised by CNN in mid-May 1995, as the boyish-looking CC executive director, Ralph Reed, explained that these were only "10 benign suggestions, not the Ten Commandments." This was an obvious gesture toward newprop: Let's lighten up and discuss this. But the gauntlet had been laid down; the "moral imperativists" would pit the oldprop of hate and exclusivity against "mainstream" religious adherents to seek hegemony over the nations's moral outlook.

Flanking Reed were a dozen Republican members of Congress including Senator Trent Lott, the party whip; Senator Phil Gramm of Texas, briefly a Presidential candidate, and the heads of several House committees. In stating what the presentation was not, Reed elliptically said what it was: "We make no threats, today we issue no ultimatums, and we make no demands of either party. This event today is not about the 1996 Presidential campaign."[35]

The staging of the event in the Capitol and the highly visible support from members of Congress and religionists made their intent clear: Religious politics now was a player at the center of political power, but rather than pursuing the oldprop of exclusion, it would take a *twoprop* approach; it would soften the oldprop of coercion and power for a newprop of accommodation that was more likely to assure the achievement of its goals.

Reed nonetheless asserted that the 1.5-million-member CC would not support a candidate who backed abortion rights, it would continue to pursue the right to prayer in public places, place new restrictions on pornography, and put an end to Federal programs for the arts. Critics said the oldprop nature of this agenda made it a religious contract "on" America.

With the selection of Dole as the Republican candidate, Reed shifted more explicitly to the twoprop approach. He warned the conservative Christians that they risked failure if they attempted to impose a moral agenda on the country through the coercive power of the state. The virulent oldprop must be shunned for a newprop dialogue of charity.

> As a community of faith, we stand at a crossroads. Down one path lies the fate of many other great religiously inspired political movements of the past: irrelevance and obscurity. It is a path defined by its spiritual arrogance and by its faulty assumptions that the most efficacious way to change hearts is through the coercive power of the state. This is the path taken by the prohibitionists, the Social Gospel advocates, the New Dealers, and the architects of the Great Society. It is not the right path for our movement.
>
> Fortunately, there is another way to go, and at the end of it lies not simply wider influence and greater political impact, but a changed society and a thoroughly Judeo-Christian culture. To get there, religious conservatives must shun harsh language on critical issues—chiefly abortion, Clinton-bashing, and homosexuality—and learn to speak of our opponents with charity.[36]

In any case, liberal religious values were out, and conservative values were in, reversing a trend that began in the 1960s and 1970s when intellectual and socially conscious Protestants gained control of seminaries, pulpits, and national agencies of their churches and used this power to address secular ethical values. They created alliances with other churches in a newprop that would advance the civil rights struggle and oppose the war in Vietnam; it was just a short step from there to the support of abortion, gay, and gender rights.

At the time, the newprops of access and freedom signaled that organized religion had helped to strengthen a popular culture. But when the Catholic Church, which has the single greatest church membership in the United States, decided to challenge abortion rights, a shift was motivated in the demeanor of evangelical and fundamentalist churches. It contributed to the emergence of two streams of religious politics—the moral imperativists and the mainstream adherents—a posing of the oldprop against the new.[37]

The Most Extreme

It was not Reed but Randall Terry who carried out the most extreme of the imperativist oldprop rhetoric. He articulated the most fundamental of religious and moral beliefs. Because the Bible commanded them to expose the wicked, he said, they were required to stage demonstrations against President Clinton:

> Bill Clinton is a tyrant, he's a monster. He has violated his marriage vows, promoted baby killing by his support of abortion, and (he has endorsed) sodomy by his support for homosexual rights . . . (And) he has violated the family by his proposals to distribute condoms to teen-agers.[38]

Whereas fundamentalists believed in the perfectability of the Bible, evangelical Christians believed in individual gifts. In 1992 and 1996, Buchanan typified those Republicans who failed to see that religious teachings could conflict.[39] But united in their hatred of Clinton and a paranoia about government, the two religious streams merged in 1994 to elect conservative Republicans. Grass roots campaigners had reclaimed institutions from those who perverted them, namely, Bill Clinton and the Democrats.[40]

Robertson for President

The moral imperativists exploit the potential of television to spread the oldprop political gospel—and make a profit. The richest and most powerful is Pat Robertson, host of the *700 Club* on television and president of the Christian Coalition, which in 1994 emerged as a powerful force in the Republican party.

A one-time candidate for president, Robertson issues massive doses of oldprop religion on television and in the pulpit, and he sells vitamins in the name of God, as well. By 1995, his *700 Club* played to 7 million viewers per week and was full of religious homilies. The Christian coalition includes more than 1.5 million members. But Robertson agreed with Reed that another, more charitable newprop ethic must be pursued if Christians are to gain power.[41]

Robertson attracts moral acolytes, among them Jim Adkisson and his wife, Christie, both members of the Oregon Christian Coalition (OCC), who are motivated in their proselytizing by their need to regain a moral sense of well-being in their commitment to their religious beliefs. They advance the oldprop that abortion and homosexuality are not acceptable family values. Mrs. Adkisson explained:

> The reason I get so emotional is that the things I held dear are just not what they were—our court system, our schools. I don't have the same patriotic allegiance because it's been destroyed by the reality of what those lofty institutions have turned into.[42]

She insisted that her fear of radicals was instilled by unfair anticonservative hateprop. They, themselves, are not radicals and haters. Her husband is a college graduate and president of a computer software company, and she, herself, is a college graduate. She felt herself to be more abused than an abuser of the Gay Alliance:

> (I) . . . watched "Act Up" (the Gay coalition) throw condoms at (me) . . . and my friends' small children. (I've) been shouted at while collecting signatures in malls; people came to protest (against us) in (our) own driveway.
> Homosexuality is unnatural, it is an illness that must be treated, and gays have invaded the curriculum and the classrooms in the schools.[43]

This oldprop of demonization and exclusion meets the needs of those who believe as she does. Among the very religious, many similar to the Adkissons, only 9% would vote for a candidate who did not believe in God, 90% favored prayers in public schools, and 70% would require the schools to teach also the Biblical version of how the world was created. Only 30% saw circumstances under which abortion would be permitted, and one third saw homosexuality as a permissible life-style.

Mainstream Religion

As Reed surmised, the broadly integrated set of religious and secular values held by less conservative Protestants and moderate Catholics has articulated a sense of newprop as well as the old, and offers the best chance for placing majority religious adherents at the nexus of the popular culture.

Reed has recognized, belatedly, that many of those who hold religious faith and perspectives are more accessible to the newprop than the old. They are diffuse in their character: conservative and liberal voters, divided by income, age, and education. Although in 1994 they voted conservative, they were less conservative than the candidates for whom they voted: They were younger, less homophobic, and better educated. Their votes did not mean they had yielded their personal empowerment to a religious infrastructure but were making choices among alternatives.[44]

Organizers of the religiously based Call to Renewal, which met at the same time as the Christian Coalition in late September 1996, had little sympathy for President Clinton but a great deal of it for the poor and dependent children who they said Clinton had spurned. Although it said that is was nonpartisan, the organization demonstrated agreement with liberal views on abortion and safety net programs, as contrasted to the political Christian right.

Its gesture toward newprop was reflected in its desire to become a community of conscience that would practice more political civility and act as a religious counterbalance to the more radical right. A representative of the U.S. Catholic Conference spoke for Christians who worked in neighborhood and poverty and self-help programs rather than in ideological arenas. He condemned political candidates who would rather propose v-chips for television sets than address more complex responses to society's problems.[46]

A Basis for Thought

It is noteworthy that among the mainstream conservative religious majority, Pope John Paul II has become more of a model of the newprop than the old. Despite Church positions, he has communicated an intellectualism, an empathy, and a compassion for those who need a spiritual message. In his tour of the United States in mid-August 1993, Pope John Paul II spoke of the Church's position on abortion as a basis for thought, an appeal to the individual rather than to a social class. The Pope was displeased with President Clinton, but he was disappointed, as well, with the moral breakdown of his own priests within the church, the unwillingness of U.S. Catholics to abide by the teachings of the church, and the reasoning that all was relative and nothing was true and objective, even the beliefs of the church. The reasoning took on the character of newprop, but as one speaking to many it had the character of oldprop.

The Pope suggested that if church teachings and doctrine were followed, society would be better off; the preventative value of the teachings of the Church offered a more promising cure for AIDS than the distribution of condoms. He was worried that American permissiveness had brought about a moral breakdown that could only be remedied by a return to prayer, and he feared that abortion and deaths due to AIDS, coupled with hunger and political terrorism, had ushered in "a culture of death."[46]

But in the Fall 1994, speaking on behalf of the Vatican, the Pope shifted to oldprop: Nations attending the U.N. Population Conference in Cairo, Egypt, must reject abortion as an acceptable means of population control. The Clinton Administration and American feminists did not speak for American thought on abortion; abortion was by no means a "human right," a "gender right," or an acceptable means of bringing about changes in the status of women. The United States was advocating "abortion on demand," and its agenda should be rejected.[47]

In October 1995, once again in the United States, the Pope returned to his newprop of humanism and inclusion. He called on United Nations members to live up to their moral responsibilities and confront the crises of faith:

> It is one of the great paradoxes of our time that man, who began the period we call modernity with a self-confident assertion of his coming of age and autonomy, approaches the end of the 20th Century fearful of himself, fearful of what he might be capable of, fearful of the future.[48]

Writer Gustav Niebuhr thought the Pope was inviting the membership of all to a global popular culture; he would help the poor, assist those suffering from AIDS, provide a haven for immigrants, and assert a global view of peace, justice, and unity. All peoples and societies were to be welcomed to the community of nations, an inclusive newprop.[48]

America's Pastor

Perhaps the apotheosis of mainstream evangelism, if it might be called such, has been the preaching of Billy Graham, called America's pastor. For four decades, without benefit of any church office and despite repeated political errors, Graham has personified American Christianity; widely admired and befriended by the powerful, he is the embodiment of the newprop of inclusion.

Graham is politically ecumenical; he has taken part in every Presidential inauguration—of Republicans and Democrats—over the past quarter-century. He traveled to more countries than any other religious leader, and he maintained balanced views on abortion and homosexuality. Coalition leaders were infuriated by his participation in the Clinton inauguration, but he, like Graham, is a Baptist.[50]

Graham has kept his theology simple and his doors open in the spirit of newprop, emphasizing his professed love for Christ and his belief in God.

ꔹ   ꔹ   ꔹ

Religionprop is variegated; it is social, moral, and political; it is passionate and ideological. At its most ideological, it practices an implacable oldprop; at its most political, it is capable of shifting from oldprop to newprop and back again, fusing one propaganda with the other.

By contrast with fundamentalist religious thought, mainstream religion has a capacity for accommodation because its constituents are better educated, more economically stable, and more variable in their beliefs and practices. This has kept the door open for a fuller participation in the popular culture.

As one reviews the trinity of propaganda—abortion, race, and religion—one is struck by the continued flood of oldprop in the debate over abortion, the variability in religiousprop, and the confounded oldprop and newprop of race and class. Each of these debates is challenging and in many cases expanding the limits of the popular culture.

NOTES

1. The power of pragmatism (The Talk of the Town). (April 29/May 6, 1996). *New Yorker*, p. 47.
2. Cartoon. (1994, July 7). King Features Syndicate, in *Seattle Post-Intelligencer*, Editorial page, Sec. A, p. 11.
3. Acquittal: Joy, Anger. (1995, October 4). *Seattle Post-Intelligencer*, pp. 1/14.

4. Rage from the Black middle class. (1994, January 26). Pols, M. F., *Seattle Times*, Sec. B, p. 3.
5. Black and white and read . . . (1994, August 1). Alter, J., p. 19. (These figures were to climb to 77% 72% respectively as the trial came to an end on September 30.)
6. The Simpson defense: source of black pride. (1995, March 6). *New York Times*, Sec. A, p. 8.
7. To our readers. (1994, July 4). *Time*, p. 4. See also: *Newsweek* (1994, June 27). p. 6.
8. Lessons of Simpson case are reshaping the law. (1995, October 6). Labaton, S., *New York Times*, Sec. A, p. 1.
9. Geography and class in 2 Simpson verdicts. (1997, February 7). Goldberg, C., *New York Times*. Sec. A, p. 8.
10. Chavis embraces the future. (1994, July 16). Gilliam, D., *Washington Post*, Sec. D, p. 1.
11. The Farrakhan sideshow. (1994, July 12). *New York Times*, p. 13.
12. Show me why I should care. (1995, February 23). *Seattle Post-Intelligencer*, p. 15.
13. NAACP faces squabble about its road to the future. (1995, July 12). Terry, D., *New York Times*, Sec. A, p. 9.
14. NAACP, seeking to change fortunes, chooses Mfume. (1995, December 10). Holmes, S. A., *Seattle Times*, Sec. A, pp. 1/4.
15. Results hint at new indifference to race. (1993, November 4). Applebome, P., *New York Times*, Sec. A, p. 11.
16. Clinton makes emotional plea against crime. (1993, November 14). Marcus, R., *Washington Post*, Sec. A, p. 1.
17. King holiday seeks wider acceptance in U.S. (1994, November 4). Applebome, P., *New York Times*, p. 11.
18. Affirmative action dispute embroils the White House. (1995, April 25). *New York Times*, Sec. A, p. 12.
19. President gives fervent support to fighting bias. (1995, July 20). *New York Times*, Sec. A, p. 1.
20. A negative response to affirmative action. (1995, April 18). *Seattle Post-Intelligencer*, p. 11.
21. National Affairs: And now what? (1995, October 30). *Newsweek*, pp. 29–36.
22. An angry "charmer." (1995, October 30). *Newsweek*, p. 32.
23. Ibid., *New Yorker*, p. 47.
24. Black and blue. (1996, April 29/May 6). Anderson, J., *New Yorker*, pp. 62–64.
25. Kill for life. (1994, October 30). Belkin, L., *New York Times Magazine*, pp. 46–54.
26. Debate on role played by anti-abortion talk. (1995, January 15). Cooper, M., *New York Times*, Sec. Y, p. 9.
27. Anti-abortion group disavows new killings. (1995, January 1). Manegold, C. S., *New York Times*, Sec. Y, p. 9.
28. Debate on role played by anti-abortion talk. (1995, January 15). Cooper, M., *New York Times*, Sec. Y, p. 16.
29. Anti-abortion groups continue radical talks. (1995, March 6). Manegold, C. S., *New York Times*, p. 8.
30. See also: The measure of a man. (1995, March 6). Goode, E., et al., *New York Times*, Sec. B, p. 36.
31. Foster faces new questions. (1995, May 3). Hanson, C., *Seattle Post-Intelligencer*, Sec. A, p. 1.
32. Foster maintains dignity, amid political posturing. (1995, May 5). Grady, S., *Seattle Times*, Sec. B, p. 5.
33. At rallies for Buchanan, fervent supporters are part of the show, too. (1996, February 26). *New York Times*, Sec. C, p. 10.
34. Conservatives press Dole on abortion. (1996, May 4). Merida, K., *Washington Post*, Americast-Post.
35. Christian group offers policy "suggestions." (1995, May 18). Berke, R. L. *New York Times*, Sec. B, p. 13.

36. Coalition's Reed: GOP abortion compromise possible. (1996, May 5). Balz, D., *Washington Post*, Americast-Post. See also: "We stand at a crossroads": The religious right must give ground—or risk irrelevance. (1996, May 15). Reed, R., *Newsweek*, pp. 28–29.

37. The denominations: The changing map of religious America. (1993, March/April). Johnson, B., *The Public Perspective*, pp. 3–5.

38. From right . . . (1994, June 26). *New York Times*, pp. 1/12.

39. Christian conservatives counting hundreds of gains in local votes. (1992, November 21). Mydans, S., *New York Times*, Sec. A, p. 17.

40. Religious ties and partisan preference. (1993, March/April). Jelen, T. G., & Wilson, C., *The Public Perspective*, pp. 10–12.

41. God and the grass roots. (1994, October 3). Fineman, H., *Newsweek*, pp. 42–44.

42. An army of the truthful. (1993, April 25). Sullivan, R., *New York Times Magazine*, p. 44.

43. The religious factor in American politics. (1994, September/October). Gavin, G., *The Public Perspective*, pp. 89–99.

44. Christian right defies categories. (1994, July 22). Berke, R. L., *New York Times–CBS Poll*, In *New York Times*, Sec. A, p. 1.

45. A religious tilt toward the Left. (1996, September 16). Clines, F. X., *New York Times*, Sec. A, pp. 1/12.

46. Keeping faith in his time. (1995, October 9). *U.S. News & World Report*, pp. 72–75.

47. The courage to speak bluntly. (1994, September 30). Navarro, V. J., *Wall Street Journal*, Sec. A, p. 12.

48. Confront crises, Pope urges nations. (1995, October 6). Bohlen, C., *New York Times*, Sec. A, p. 1.

49. The Pontiff's positions on many social issues defy political labeling. (1995, October 8). *New York Times*, Sec. Y., p. 15.

50. America's pastor at 74, Bill Graham begins to sum up, regrets and all. (1993, February 3). Steinfels, P., *New York Times*, Sec. A, p. 18.

21

LOBBYPROP
The NRA and the Environment

The popular culture has facilitated the emergence of an increasingly diverse and active *lobbyprop*, but it is straining the bounds of access and equity and has brought about an oldprop that threatens our safety and well-being. Nowhere was this more evident than in the *antiguncontrolprop* of the National Rifle Association (NRA) and the oldprop of the antienvironmental movement.

EVERYONE DOES IT

Lobbyprop is pervasive as a force for good as well as for evil, but it became so pervasive in the federal government that 1992 presidential candidates Bill Clinton and Ross Perot made election promises to prohibit former government officials from becoming instant lobbyists. Perot said former government and White House officials who turned around to serve foreign interests were like generals switching armies in the middle of a war.

However, even the presidential role is, at its best and its worst, that of a lobbyist. President Clinton exploited oldprop on a visit to Seattle to condemn subsidies to Airbus, the European consortium that competes with Boeing, the Northwest aeronautical giant, and he lobbied passionately on behalf of his trade, environmental, health, and gun control policies. Airbus had doubled its share of the market to 30% in a decade, while McDonnell-Douglas had all but lost its commercial market and Boeing was losing big sales to United Airlines and Northwest in head-to-head bidding against Airbus.

As Clinton assured anxious Boeing workers in Everett, Washington, site of the construction of Boeing's new generation of aircraft, that the United States had made a "huge mistake" when it sat by for 10 years and allowed European countries to subsidize their jetliner consortium, British Prime Minister John Major was prepared to tell Clinton that the way to deal with the problem was to discuss it across the table; that is, via newprop, not to engage in megaphone diplomacy (oldprop) with cheering Boeing workers.

A Brian Bassett cartoon in the *Seattle Times* portrayed a bulky Boeing character playing poker with a lean French Airbus worker. Mr. Boeing is smoking a cigar; the Frenchman is drawing on a cigarette in a long holder. Each holds the same number of chips, and each is surrounded by boxes of chips that bear a striking resemblance to ammo containers. The Frenchman says: "Cheating? Moi?? Monsieur, I am outraged! We are playing from the same deck, are we not?"

CREATING A SYNERGY

Although lobbyprop is in many respects indistinguishable from public relations, this was not always the case. It was Robert Keith Gray who persuaded Hill & Knowlton (H & K) public relations founder John Hill to set up a lobbying operation in concert with public relations that would revolutionize the process of influencing government.

Before Gray's suggestion, public relations had influenced public opinion by grass roots methods, similar to the strategy adopted by the environmental movement. Lobbyprop concentrated on a key person, but public relations focused on publics. Gray insisted that his lobbyists be the best informed persons in the network, able to trade on facts as well as on attitudes.

Gray practiced oldprop, as well. Eight days after Kuwait was overrun by the Iraqis, the Department of State contracted with H & K to represent "Citizens for a Free Kuwait;" that is, to lobby for war. Gray contracted pollster Richard Wirthlin to determine which American attitudes lent support to a military intervention. Press coverage was generated by news conferences, Congressional hearings, video releases, a national adprop campaign, and a "National Prayer Day." In this way God became a part of the synergy of totalprop.[1]

LOBBYPROP ABOUT LOBBYPROP

Nothing exceeds the effectiveness of lobbyprop unless it is lobbyprop in defense of lobbyprop. Where once it was thought that both houses of Congress would accede to lobbying reforms that President Clinton had proposed, notably the banning of gifts, a lobbyprop blitz killed the effort. It was said at that time that "even a fruit basket (would) be politically incorrect as a gift to a member of Congress." However, it did not happen. More than a year later, at a curious meeting, Clinton and Newt Gingrich, the House majority leader, agreed in principle on lobbying reform, and the Republican Congress approved it, although many gaps remained to be addressed.[2]

Gingrich helped the Christian Coalition (other than Baptists and Catholics) to defeat Clinton's first effort. A curious coalition of more than 200 groups included such unusual partners as the Free Speech Association (FSA) and otherwise liberal reform groups. All protested restrictions that would "gag" them. Gingrich joined in with a baleful oldprop, warning of White House intentions to suppress all dissent.

FSA sent "talking points" to more than 500 conservative radio talkprop hosts, including Rush Limbaugh, Pat Robertson, and Paul Weyrich, the cofounder of the conservative Heritage Foundation. Limbaugh did not buy into the antireligion argument—that the reforms were an attack on religion—but he stated, elliptically, that there was disagreement as to what the bill meant, and that's what's wrong with Washington.

The massive effort of the Christian Coalition to defeat reforms was described by spokesman Mike Russell:

> We mobilized 250,000 people within a 24-hour period before the Senate vote, with computer bulletin boards, telephone trees, faxes, talk radio outlets to get the word out to both Christian and secular talk stations. We used the high-tech home gadgetry combined with getting on the phone to grassroots members to make the phones ring back in your Senator's office.[3]

GUN CONTROLPROP AND ENVIRONMENTALPROP

Gun controlprop and *environmentalprop* pose two forces and strategies: The NRA exploits the oldprop of anger and its insider access to Congress and to state legislatures, but the environmental movement primarily utilizes participant politics to sound the tocsin.

The oldprop insider approach is best explained by a story: A journalist once asked Marlin Fitzwater, former presidential press secretary, if the $8 million given to then-President Bush at a fundraiser "might have paid for access to the White House?" Fitzwater agreed that it did. When asked if this was not at the expense of those who lacked the ability to buy into the White House, Fitzwater replied: "They have to (and can) demand access in other ways."[4]

Buying access to the White House became a critical issue after the 1996 political campaign, and this oldprop tactic doubtless eroded Clinton's lead over Dole. While during the Republican convention elite donors who gave at least $250,000 were rewarded with a smorgasbord of perks, including special help with their business problems, that paled in contrast to the selling of access to the White House (including representatives of foreign countries) by Democrats for 10 to 20 times those amounts. This included an invitation to sleep overnight in the Lincoln room!

NRA: THE CONSUMMATE INSIDER

In running for election, claiming to be an outsider is a cachet that often contributes to success, but once elected, being an insider is what really counts. The 1994 elections were no exception as numerous insiders claimed to be outsiders. Republican Senator Slade Gorton of Washington state, a longtime state and federal office holder, ran for reelection on an "independent voice" platform, but his contributors were the NRA and a number of anti-environmental "people first" coalitions.

The NRA maintains one of the most active lobbies in federal, state, and local politics. Although 80% of the public supports gun control, the other 20% so emotionally defend it that they will vote those convictions no matter what. No matter who they are, the NRA lobby will take aim at anyone who opposes them.[5]

NRA schools its members to write letters, make telephone calls, and threaten their legislators outright. NRA lists as its most formidable supporters the hunters, farmers, and lovers of weapons who resent any intrusion on their lives, notable among them members of the state militias. Until 1994, because of its superior access to government and the strength of its following, the NRA had become well nigh impregnable. After California Republican Congressman Henry Hyde voted for the ban on assault weapons, he commented: "You don't disappoint or turn your back on people who feel intensely about (gun) issues without considering the consequences."[6]

Guns 'R' Us *Is* Us

Many critics mistakenly think of NRA propaganda as a redneck-inspired activity that speaks only for a hard core of gun owners. In truth, its defenders are more diverse. One book entitles its introduction, "Guns 'R' Us," and points out that the redneck portrayed by cartoonists oversimplifies the appeals of the NRA and its membership.[7]

The NRA clothes itself in the *symbolprop* of the American Rifleman, the hero of the Revolution, and the citizen soldier. Actors such as John Wayne,

Charlton Heston, Roy Rogers, and Kevin Costner are among the Hollywood glitterati who defend the NRA. Heston testified during the Congressional debate on assault weapons that "none of the opponents was telling the truth." But Democratic Representative Nita Lowey of New York replied with sarcasm, referring to one of Heston's biblical roles: "Even Moses can't be right all the time."[8]

The NRA is pragmatic, as well. It recognizes that gun ownership is distributed across social classes and political parties but rises when there are greater perceptions of the prevalence of crime. A series of rapes in one neighborhood in Seattle in early January 1993 brought hundreds of women into gun stores to purchase pistols and to sign up for arms training, and there was a 45% increase in gun sales in the 4 weeks following the Los Angeles riots.[9]

Paranoia Is Us

A festering paranoia led the NRA to misread the significance of the Oklahoma City bombing when it became known that the major suspects had ties to members of militant voluntary militia groups. Instead of seeking an accommodation of views, they opted for an oldprop of denial: "There is no link. This is political speech, and calling people something is not good or bad. It's just the way we do things in this country. We represent a majority who have lost faith in their Government and fear Government abuses."[10]

But even before the bombing, the rhetoric had reached a state of paranoia. *Gun-talk*, an NRA electronic bulletin board on the Internet, described federal forces as "ninja" who are in "full-cry" without fear of any control: "They move mainly at night. They conceal their faces. They use overwhelming firepower and they make almost no effort to identify their targets. They are scarier than the Nazis—who at least never concealed their faces."

The *American Rifleman* continued:

A document secretly delivered . . . reveals frightening evidence that the full-scale war to crush your gun rights has not only begun, but is well underway.

What's more, dozens of Federal gun ban bills suggest this final assault has begun—not just to ban all handguns or all semi automatics, but to eliminate private firearms ownership completely and forever. I firmly belive the N.R.A. has no alternative but to recognize this attack and counter with every resource we can muster.   /s/ Wayne R. LaPierre, Jr.[11]

The NRA oldprop of demonization insisted that "some Federal agents wear Nazi-bucket helmets and black storm trooper uniforms, and harass, intimidate, and even murder law-abiding citizens." The *National Rifleman*, voice of the NRA, reacting to critics who sought to rein in the voluntary militias, asked sarcastically if Congress was going to rein in the Bureau of Alcohol, Tobacco, and Firearms (ATF).[12]

A Public Relations Disaster

The paranoia became transformed into an oldprop catastrophe when the NRA sent out a fund-raising letter that described Federal law enforcement agents as "jackbooted Government thugs." Once aware of it, former President Bush resigned his membership, stating that the broadside against federal agents deeply offended his sense of decency and honor and concept of service to country. The language to which Bush objected came from a documentary film, *It Can Happen Here*, which had been produced by the NRA in 1991. At that time they quoted Democratic Representative John D. Dingell of Michigan about the ATF, "If I were to select a jackbooted group of fascists who are perhaps as large a danger to American society as I could pick today, I would pick A.T.F." [13]

Set back by Bush's action, and soon under attack by President Clinton, the NRA yielded. LaPierre insisted that NRA oldprop was aimed only at the ATF unit that had conducted the Waco operations.

Oldprop as Newprop?

When Clinton insisted that the NRA had given "aid and comfort" to criminals who had profited from their fund-raising letter, he engaged partly in oldprop demonization and partly in newprop refutation. He demanded that the NRA turn over all solicited funds to widows and orphans of the federal officers. He denounced the militias as "false patriots," declaring, "there is nothing patriotic about hating your government or pretending that you can hate your government but love your country." [14]

Oldprop reigned. In a Commencement address at Michigan State University, Clinton derided NRA use of the symbols of patriotism and challenged the NRA to donate the proceeds of their fund drive to all victims of the Oklahoma City disaster:

> How dare you suggest that we in the freest nation on Earth live in tyranny? How dare you call yourselves patriots and heroes? If you appropriate our sacred symbols for paranoid purposes and commit yourselves to colonial militias who fought for democracy, you are wrong. [15]

It was at this point that the NRA decided to shift its tactics to newprop. At its convention in Phoenix, Arizona, LaPierre told CBS's *Face the Nation* that his organization favored an investigation of the paramilitary militias: "We condemn hate groups, terrorist groups. We have never had anything to do with any of these paramilitary-type groups you see on television. That's not the NRA." And he promised that the NRA "would be more careful in its choice of language." [16]

Quoting Clinton, LaPierre defended the rights of militias to freedom of speech and assembly, and the right to own firearms, but the NRA did not advocate violence or the overthrow of the government or encourage illegal activities.

The Brady Bill: A Generic Movement

This bill was named after James Brady, a presidential assistant who had been shot and paralyzed for life in an assassination attempt on President Reagan. For years his wife, Sarah Brady, had advocated gun control as a monument to her husband's sacrifice. Its supporters believed in their positions as passionately as did the gun advocates, and they, too, exploited the oldprops of victimization and demonization. It was the first time since 1968 that the NRA had been beaten on a major measure.[17]

A newly formed coalition outorganized the NRA, linking such generic organizations as Common Cause and issue-oriented groups such as Handgun Control, Inc. (HCI) and the National Coalition to Ban Handguns (NCBH). The HCI was headed by Mrs. Brady. Three other organizations took part: the Washington Ceasefire, the Children's Alliance, and the Stop the Violence Committee. Each group was mobilized by incidents that took members of their families and friends.

A victimization oldprop was carried out in all media. A full-page advertisement in the *New York Times* and other daily newspapers told the story of five random gun slayings:

- A wife watched her husband die while trying to protect her from a random stalking in San Francisco.
- A husband described the pain of losing his wife in the San Francisco high-rise killings.
- A wife mourned the loss of her husband and son in a Long Island train massacre.
- A newlywed wife described how an anonymous man shot randomly into her car, killing her husband of only 3 months.
- The Coalition to Stop Gun Violence arranged for the family of a Japanese exchange student who had been killed by random violence to meet with President Clinton in the Oval Office just a week before the final vote in the Senate. They had spent a year gathering signatures on the petition they presented to the President.[18]

We Shall Return

The NRA blamed its defeat on "lying propaganda": "This shows that if the President weighs in and lies and lies and lies to the public and uses the power of his office, bills can be forced through Congress."[19] Their response came in late 1994 when a parliamentary maneuver prevented the new crime bill from reaching the floor of the House of Representatives. The gun lobby's victory was sweet, but it was short-lived. Clinton again pilloried the NRA and portrayed Republicans as reluctant to act on crime. The Congress caved in, and within a week, a leaner and meaner bill was adopted.[20]

In mid-April 1996 the NRA elected a new president, a woman who was said to be more resistant to gun control than any of her predecessors. She insisted that the oldprop debate had siphoned off the energies of the NRA from conducting safety programs for adults and children. But the NRA spent more than $2 million on oldprop to defeat 30 political incumbents who had supported gun control.[21] There would be no newprop from this "nail-hard" grandmother.

ε   ε   ε

Intensely politicized, gunprop has used its insider position in Congress to get its way, and it will continue to do so. However, in defending the controversial state militias in the aftermath of the Oklahoma City bombing, the NRA found itself caught between old and new constituencies and the oldprop and the new.

Although the old constituencies were happy to have the NRA show the flag of self-protection, freedom, and the citizen soldier as symbolic versions of patriotism, to speak in defense of the militias was offensive. President Clinton exploited the NRA vulnerability with a virulent oldprop, and the pro-Brady Bill forces did the same.

Ironically, when the NRA turned to the newprop of conciliation, it was perceived as out of character. The NRA had become a stereotype, and this image would be difficult to dispel.

THE ANTIENVIRONMENTAL MOVEMENT

To its regret, the environmental movement learned that the new propaganda, however successfully it might function, must be constantly restated and restored if it is to prevail.

The Contract With America of 1994 to 1996 created the impetus for an the demonization of the dormant environmental movement. Bureaucracies were targeted because they had set environmental standards and implemented legislation. Already a party to a campaign against bureaucratic oversizing and higher taxes, mainstream media became an agent of this assault: "Past its prime," *USA Today* said; "Groping for a vision," said the *Los Angeles Times*. *The Nation* rebuked environmentalists as falling into a pattern of "elitism," highly paid, detached from the working class, and a firm ally of big

Government. The Center for the Study of American Business, an economic research group, said it was "time for a shakeout that would not be such a bad thing."[22]

Even the director of the National Audubon Society, Ted Eubanks, conceded that the environmental sector "had lost the imagination of the average guy." Its appeal of inclusiveness had faded into exclusiveness, making it vulnerable not only to attacks by oldprop but leading it to reply in the same way. The one-time newprop of voluntarism had been transformed into an oldprop of pseudovoluntarism. In real terms it became an oldprop of a few to many.

Big environmentalism also was wavering, most of its major actors having lost financial and membership resources. Only The Nature Conservancy, which had held to its mission of buying and conserving wild land, maintained its position. The Sierra Club, the Natural Resources Defense Council, and the Wilderness Society had lost membership and income. By addressing such abstract issues as global warming and protecting obscure animals as endangered species—notably, the spotted owl—they had confused the constituencies that might have supported them. Big environmentalism had also required more money. To raise new funds, it hired larger staffs and pursued media-driven techniques of creating support. They employed the oldprop as readily as the new—some of it highly emotional, misleading, and apocalyptic in tone.

Too Much Power to the Bureaucrats?

As Denis Hayes, director of the first Earth Day in 1970, wrote 25 years later, although the barricades in the 1970s were stormed by energetic environmental groups—a newprop of many to many—their gains were managed by bureaucrats—an oldprop of few to many. Those who created the movement sat back to enjoy its benefits, while those who felt exploited by their actions combined in a counteractivist movement. Their grievances contributed the same kinds of energy to antienvironmentalism once poured into the movement.[23]

Hayes noted that the genius of the original Earth Day had been its newprop of inclusion:

> It enlisted all segments of American society . . . it was not just the Sierra Club talking to the Audubon Society; instead, it reached out to students, teachers, clergy, business, labor, farmers, ethic minorities and civic organizations. Coming on the heels of the polarizing 60's, Earth Day provided a movement in which diverse people could come together to promote their own values. The environmental movement was bipartisan rather than partisan.[24]

Now the antienvironmental movement was set to devour its bureaucratic tormentors. The small property owner, the logger, and the rancher demanded that controls be loosened and that they be compensated for what had been taken from them. Republican Senator Slade Gorton of Washington state led the onslaught on the Endangered Species Act. Arguing that bureaucratic interpretations of the law had almost shut down logging, curtailed mining, and hobbled ranchers, farmers, and other private users of public lands, Gorton and the "people coalitions" that he helped to form worked at the grass roots level; to abet this newprop, corporations provided legal and administrative resources.

Logs Versus People

I watched the televised hearings presided over by Gorton and Republican Congresswoman Jennifer Dunn of Washington in Olympia, the state capitol, where members of the Family Timber Alliance, one of the People Coalitions, described the desolation caused in small timber towns by the Endangered Species Act. To nods of approval from Gorton and Dunn, they described the stifling of "timber-sustaining" and "community-sustaining" logging. Warned that more cutting would lead to the leakage of sludge into salmon-spawning rivers and result in the loss of thousands of salmon-dependent jobs, the message was lost. The timbermen were Gorton's constituency; the fishermen were not.[25]

It Is Access, Again

Intense conflicts soon were generated by the discovery that lobbyists had written Gorton's legislation and were sitting in Congressional committees explaining it. Gorton insisted he had outlined the legislation and the lobby-propsters had simply carried out his intent; he asked them to explain the changes because they had a greater mastery over the details. But with evident sarcasm, Michael Bean, director of the Environmental Defense Fund, noted that the senator required aid from the lobbyists to understand his own bill. Democratic Representative George Miller of California said that Republicans had granted carte blanche access to government.[26]

The utility lobbyists wrote legislation that would make it difficult to regulate large industries such as the Long Island Lighting Company, Southern California Edison, Virginia Power, Pennsylvania Power and Light, Oklahoma Gas and Electric, and the Arkansas Power and Light Company, as well as a coalition of utilities concerned about clean-air regulation.[27]

The law firm of Hunton and Williams helped Senate Republicans to draft the bill in closed-door sessions, and a lawyer who was formerly associated with that firm worked with Senate majority leader Bob Dole. When it was discovered that the law firm also was acting as a spokesperson for the American Bar Association (ABA), the ABA quickly distanced itself, but when the staff of the Senate Judiciary Committee arrived at a briefing they found three lawyers from Hunton and Williams seated to answer their questions. The story noted: "It is not unusual for Congressional aides to consult lobbyists discreetly as they shape legislation; it happens every day. But seldom in the past have they so openly and publicly embraced legislative outsiders with extensive interests in the outcome."[28]

Until the Contract With America, industries and government agencies worked together as an advisory group; that was newprop. Now an adversarial relationship had been introduced by an oldprop that again sought to dump toxic waste into the Great Lakes.[29]

Tears for the Good Old Days

Tears were being shed for the good old days when the environmental movement had its way. Since the celebrated 1970 Earth Day, energy and enthusiasm had found expression in the formation of voluntary organizations, the powerful newprop of the preservation of the ecosystem, and redress for the rape of the environment. Three actions were hailed as "stunning successes" both in the United States and Europe—the Clean Air Act (1970), the Clean Water Act (1972), and the Endangered Species Act (1973). U. S. regulations were less burdensome, cost less than were anticipated, produced strikingly effective results, and strengthened economies rather than endangering them.[30]

However, in the West the fights over old growth timber and the resurrection of the salmon had not been resolved. But a plan was put in place in Portland, Oregon, in April 1993, when President Clinton and Vice President Gore arrived to present it. It turned into a celebration of environmentalprop: The bald eagle was no longer endangered; the Great Lakes were returning to life; air pollution had decreased by more than one third although twice as many cars were being driven; drinking water was far safer; and many lakes, streams, and bays were again safe for swimming. Millions of people were recycling, and conserving. It was a celebration of many speaking to many and formulating actions on the basis of knowledge and reason.[31]

Portland became an exercise in newprop. A compromise was offered that would save two thirds of the timber that was left but would protect streams and nearby flora and fauna. Although it would not continue to protect all of the spotted owls and, by implication, all of the forests, it was a plan to which timber workers, ranchers, farmers, fishermen, utilities, and corporate parties could consent. The plan would govern the logging of big trees in the Pacific Northwest for years to come.[32]

But the compromise carried unanticipated consequences. The courts interpreted it to permit a renewal of old growth logging in the Northwest. In an interview in Seattle in late February 1996, Clinton admitted that the compromise had been subverted, and that the environmental consequences were threatening, but he wrung concessions out of Congress that permitted him to waive some of the most agonizing decisions.

By this time Congress was feeling the reaction to its oldprop environmentalism. The seats of freshmen Republican Congressmen were being threatened; in Washington state, as an example, environmentalists targeted three Republican freshmen—Randy Tate, Rick White, and Jack Metcalf. The director of the Sierra Club said the environment would not be protected as long as they were in office, and it began to air radio adprop that accused the legislators of weakening clean water standards and allowing clear-cutting in national forests. In the participant framework that marked the original movement, volunteers from two conservancy fishing groups hung 40,000 packets on doorknobs of Puget Sound area homes. Despite Senator Gorton's opposition, White introduced a measure in Congress to demolish two dams on the Elwha River to restore salmon runs.[33]

National disapproval of Republican oldprop environmentalism brought House Speaker Newt Gingrich to offer a proposal for a "new environmentalism" that would be committed to strong standards but on a cooperative rather than a confrontational basis. In the spirit of newprop, it would get to confrontation last, not first. The approach would be based on valid science, incentives for compliance rather than punishment for noncompliance, rapid adoption of new technologies, and a search for innovative solutions from communities.[34] Meanwhile, old compromises would be addressed to new problems.

℗   ℗   ℗

Neglectful of environmental gains through newprop, the environmental movement rested on its laurels. Under a reactionary Congress, the environmental agenda of 1994 to 1996 saw the line all but erased between lobbyprop and legislating.

By 1996, however, the assaults on the environment were largely repudiated by public opinion, and a revived strategy of newprop that was undertaken by environmentalists forced Congress to reshape its positions to accommodate the public mood. Speaker Gingrich proposed a "new environmentalism" that stressed accommodation rather than conflict. Environmental newprop again was in, and oldprop was out.

NOTES

1. Trento, S. B. (1992). *The Power House.* New York: St. Martin's Press.
2. Talks in Congress reach an accord to curb lobbyists. (1994, September 23). Seelye, K. Q., *New York Times*, pp. 1/9.
3. Conservatives hobble lobbying bill. (1994, October 7). Seelye, K. Q., *New York Times*, p. 13.
4. Bush earns 8 million for his party and criticism for himself. (1992, April 29). Wines, M., *New York Times*, p. 1.

5. Majority in poll back ban on handguns. (1993, June 4). Baringer, F., *New York Times*, p. 9.

6. In defeating the NRA, gun controllers gain fire power. (1994, May 7). Van Drehle, D., *Washington Post*, Sec. A., p. 1.

7. Sugarmann, J. (1992). *NRA: Money, Firepower, and Fear.* Washington: National Press Books.

8. Bringing out the big guns. (1994, April 20). Hansen, C., *Seattle Post-Intelligencer*, p. 1.

9. Kleck, G. (1991) *Point Blank: Guns and Violence in America.* New York: Aldine de Gruyter.

10. Long before bombing, gun lobby was lashing out at federal agents. (1995, May 8). Butterfield, F., *New York Times*, Sec. C, p. 11.

11. Butterfield, *New York Times*, p. 11.

12. Butterfield, *New York Times*, p. 11.

13. Criticism leveled at the NRA. (1995, April 28). Mintz, J., *Washington Post*, Sec. A., p. 12.

14. Opinion savages militias' ideology of "patriotic hate." (1995, May 6). Richter, P., *Los Angeles Times*, in *Seattle Times*, p. 1.

15. Clinton challenges the NRA to donate letter proceeds. (1995, May 20). Devroy, A., *Washington Post*, Sec. A, p. 12.

16. NRA favors investigation of extremists. (1995, May 22). Ayres, R. D., Jr., *Seattle Times*, Sec. A, p. 1. See also: NRA chief disavows the militias. (1995, May 22). Miller, A. C., *Los Angeles Times*, Sec. A, p. 1.

17. For Bradys, a five year struggle finally pays off as bill passes. (1993, November 21). DeWitt, K., *New York Times*, p. 1.

18. Parents of Japanese students to meet Clinton with anti-gun message. (1993, November 16). Togo, S., *Washington Post*, Sec. A, p. 16.

19. Gun ban still faces long road. (1994, May 6). *Seattle Times*, Sec. A, p. 10.

20. Gun lobby hits bulls eye. (1994, August 19). Solomon, J., Associated Press, in *Seattle Post-Intelligencer*, p. 7.

21. Nail-hard grandmother is taking reins at N.R.A.: New face for theme of right to bear arms. (1996, April 14). Bragg, R., *New York Times*, Sec. Y, p. 10.

22. Big environmentalism hits a recession. (1995, January 1). Schneider, K., *New York Times*, Sec. F, p. 4.

23. Earth Day 25th anniversary. (1995, April 16). *Seattle Post-Intelligencer*, Sec. E, p. 1.

24. Hayes, *Post-Intelligencer*, Sec. E, p. 1.

25. Industry reshapes Endangered Species Act. (1995, April 13). Egan, T., *New York Times*, Sec. A, p. 9.

26. Dispute on Gorton Memo. (1995, April 7). Hanson, C., *Seattle Post-Intelligencer*, p. 1.

27. House passes bill that would limit many regulations. (1995, March 4). Cushman, J. H., Jr., *New York Times*, Sec. A, p. 1.

28. Business leaves the lobby and sits at Congress's table. (1995, March 31). Engelberg, S., *New York Times*, Sec. A, p. 1.

29. Lobbyists helped the GOP in revising Clean Water Act. (1995, March 22). Cushman, J. H., Jr., *New York Times*, Sec. A, p. 1.

30. Here comes the sun. (1995, April 22). Easterbrook, G., *New Yorker*, pp. 48–53.

31. Putting a new spin on Earth Day. (1995, April 16). Pryne, E., *Seattle Times*, Sec. A, p. 1.

32. Timber rider "a mistake." (1996, February 26). Connelly, J., *Seattle Post-Intelligencer*, Sec. A., p. 1.

33. Environmentalists target White, Tate and Metcalf. (1996, April 18). Connelly, J., *Seattle Post-Intelligencer*, Sec. A, pp. 1/4.

34. Gingrich calls for a "new environmentalism." (1996, April 25). Cushman, J. H., Jr., *New York Times*, Sec. A, p. 8.

.

PART V

Tradeprop and Politicalprop
THE PRODUCTION OF LEXICONS

Tradeprop and politicalprop are the major producers of lexicons in the popular culture. The political wars over trade policies exploited the languages of naftoids, fictoids, and visions of GATT. The most re-membered cliché was the "sucking sounds of jobs" going south across the Rio Grande. The most appreciated rejoinder was the observation that only Ross Perot had ears large enough to hear those sounds.

Politicalprop 1992 was lexically the creation of "gridlock" and "credibility." Yet gridlock simply defined was a product of the diversity in the popular culture and the futile efforts of politicians to respond to it. Most of the politicians and the press simply didn't get it.

By contrast, politicalprop 1994 was the apotheosis of angerprop and saw the triumph of talk radio. Its lexicon, the Contract With America, lived a short life. What voters got is not what voters wanted.

Politicalprop 1996 tested the "softprop" of a backtracking Bob Dole against the "sweetprop" of President Bill Clinton. Sooner or later—for Dole sooner than Clinton—hardprop would set in again, and the old-prop would contest with the new.

The polls hinted that softprop and newprop would win the day, and that predicted the reelection of President Clinton, all other things being equal.

22

TRADEPROP
"Naftoids" and a Vision of GATT

The politics of the North American Free Trade Agreement (NAFTA) and the General Agreement on Trades and Tariffs (GATT) began as battles of *factoids* —although few of the facts were completely reliable—and graduated to battles of *fictoids*, where none of the ideas was completely believable.

The debates and their aftermath revealed that the popular culture harbored conflicting and—not surprisingly—self-contradictory theories of international trade.

Advocates adopted a newprop of global trade although conceding that some groups would be excluded from the benefits; paradoxically, protectionists advanced an oldprop of nationalist exclusion but saw it as preserving the membership of everyone at home.

Not since the Marshall Plan, a half-century earlier, had there been so much popular awareness and discussion of *tradeprop*, but at that time the fears of the nation were sublimated to the promise of European and American prosperity. Now, although NAFTA and GATT were global amplifications of the Marshall Plan, the nation was plunged into uncertainty by a staggering rhetoric of factoids and fictoids by all parties to the debate.

FACTOIDS, FICTOIDS, AND NAFTOIDS

The role of factoids first gained prominence during the 1992 Democratic presidential nominating convention—a so-called "politics by numbers." The

275

editors of *Harpers* magazine compiled an index of noncontextual and irrelevant facts—factoids—that had been brought to bear on the convention. By late October—a week before the vote for the Presidency—there was agreement that this had become "the year of the factoid." Someone asked if "stat-slinging" was different from "mud-slinging." It was not: Both demonized, both were obtuse; each was the essence of oldprop.[1]

In the debate over NAFTA, neither side agreed on a factual count of anything, much less whether one could detect the "sucking sound of jobs moving south"—a phrase popularized by Ross Perot—a shift of jobs, factories, or the balance of trade. As disputed factoids proliferated in the media, someone observed that:

> Facts have the same stupefying effect as images of flag factories and furloughed felons. And like these images, facts can manipulate and mislead. Living by the facts and dying by the facts is perilous because it encourages us to ignore questions that may reveal the meanings of those facts.[2]

On November 17, 1993, after a fierce national debate, the House voted by an unexpectedly large margin to approve NAFTA, 234 to 200, and approval by the Senate swiftly followed. Ironically, President Clinton won not because he had produced the greatest array of factoids but because of a mammoth lobbyprop conducted by corporate "big hitters"—including Federated Department Stores, Amana, Whirlpool, G.E., Westinghouse, Caterpillar, Citi-Bank, Fruit of the Loom, and Boeing—that insisted in media adprop campaigns that NAFTA was the key to prosperity.

Déjà Vu (Yet Again)

The debate about NAFTA and GATT may never go away even though it seemingly was resolved by Congress in 1993. During the Republican primaries of 1996, the ultraconservative Patrick J. Buchanan again waved the oldprop bloody shirt of jobs going to Mexico that Ross Perot had raised during the debates in 1992. The result was to place the Republican nominee, Bob Dole, an announced free trader, in a delicate position. To secure Buchanan's publics, Dole had to acknowledge their fears; to maintain his own integrity of thought and policy, Dole had to find another rhetoric.

The consequence was Dolenomics, in which he acknowledged the inevitability of "free trade" but insisted it be "fair trade" and that hard measures be directed toward those nations—notably China and Japan—who did not observe the rules. However, this Doleprop would not be easily served. Dole had too candidly said in New Hampshire that he "didn't realize that jobs and trade and what makes America work would become a big issue," and it was not long before he declared himself unequivocally in favor of most favored nation treatment for China, outpropping Clinton on the conduct of his foreign policy.[3]

Campaign strategists tried to put a better face on Dole's slip but conceded their fears that the awkwardness of his position was bound to be compared to President Clinton's accomplished oratory about "the new economy." However, Republicans hoped to sublimate trade policies by spinning the election as "Clinton versus Not Clinton" rather than "Clinton versus Dole."[4]

In the Beginning

NAFTA first was thrust into the limelight in August 1992 when the leaders of Canada, Mexico, and the United States agreed to create a free trade organization. In its inception it was newprop—a vision of free trade as the instrument of a new world order—and it gained entry into the popular culture as Bush's "vision thing," a larger concept that embraced GATT, as well. But at that time NAFTA was so nebulous a concept that Clinton and Gore had not given it a high priority; GATT was something they would deal with when it happened.

During the 1992 campaign, Bush drove oldprop wedges between Clinton's protectionist-bent labor union supporters, intellectual and environmental constituencies, and free trade economists. If Clinton supported NAFTA, his union and environmental support would be eroded; if he opposed it, intellectuals and his free trade constituency would be offended. An oldprop of divide and conquer, it was practiced artfully. Gleefully, Bush demanded that Clinton "halt his waffling."

Clinton, perforce, reverted to the role of artful dodger. He believed in principle in free trade, but the agreement Bush signed had failed to address important job and environmental concerns. Clinton would insist on further agreements that would better protect U.S. jobs and the environment. But a cartoon in the *Atlanta Constitution* by Mike Lukovich (1995 Pulitzer Prize winner) pictured Clinton and Gore perched atop a tall wire fence on the border between the United States and Mexico. Gore asked: "So Bill—Where are we, exactly, on free trade?"

Coping With an Inheritance

After his election, it was Clinton's obligation to present NAFTA to the Congress. Some counselled that it should be scuttled as too vulnerable to oldprop, but free traders contended it should be taken up as a pillar of a guiding foreign policy of free trade, and it would meet Clinton's promises of a new and dynamic economic agenda.

Just as Bush had anticipated, the unions swiftly adopted a reactive oldprop that portrayed a flow of capital and jobs from the United States to Mexico, and environmentalists pointed to Mexico's failure to curb pollution and its continuing slaughter of the endangered sea turtle. Clinton could only reassure labor and the environmentalists that he would meet their objections through changes to the so-called side agreements, but that was an unlikely outcome.

Setting the Table for Factoids

That set the rhetorical table for the massive production of factoids. There would be no effort to shade facts or conceal them. It would be a textbook example of abundant data, helpful explanation, and acknowledgments of limitations. The first few years of NAFTA would lift U.S. employment, exports, and profits, but later some flight of U.S. jobs would occur. However, Clinton promised that these reductions would not just hit workers; he would "spread the gain and the pain."

The opposition, however, redefined the issues in wider scope and became apocalyptic in their warnings. These were no longer ascertainable factoids with which Clinton could deal but value-oriented fictoids that fed on deprivation and anxieties: Clinton was taking the nation on the road to catastrophe; no developed nation ever had concluded a free trade agreement with an underdeveloped nation. Europeans would not tie it to GATT or blame us if we rejected it—after all, they had insisted that each nation that joined them come up to the mark in worker benefits, pollution control, and political justice.

The head of the AFL-CIO, Lane Kirkland, said Clinton had abdicated his moral role as leader of the Democratic party by taking the unprecedented and near treasonous step of assuring Republicans who voted for NAFTA that he would try to prevent Democrats from using their vote against them when it came to reelection in their districts, a humiliating buyout of the opposition and a sellout of his own party. How was Kirkland to know that not even Democrats would want Clinton's blessing in 1994?[5]

Humpty-Dumpty Again?

There were warnings about the future, as well: Clinton had so divided his winning 1992 coalition that he would never be able to put Humpty Dumpty together again. How could he gain support for health care if he could not count on the Democrats he had ignored on NAFTA? And when the texts of the side agreements were revealed, the AFL-CIO, the environmentalists, and the congressmen from the "Rust States" reacted angrily. Kirkland called it "a poison pill left over from the last administration." Democratic Congressman Richard Gephardt, a protectionist hawk, insisted that the agreements ignored problems of Mexican wages, pollution control, and the lack of sanctions. The Sierra Club, Friends of the Earth, and Greenpeace accused NAFTA's environmental defenders of selling out to Washington. Twenty-five environmental groups in full-page advertisements in national newspapers warned of "8 Fatal Flaws of NAFTA."

From Factoids to Fictoids

Facts, alone, seldom are enough. The pro-NAFTA forces concluded that they had to appeal to the larger contexts that gave meaning to the facts. It was time for a shift to fictoids and a newprop of hope and consideration:

- America was a great nation and could compete with anyone. This was no time to be fearful but to be confident.

- America was the most productive nation in the world, and it would become more so; we must enter confidently into the new world of global competition and win it as we won the great wars.

- We were destined to create a Pax Americana of trade and commerce. If we did not take advantage of the moment, how would the Europeans regard our demands for the opening of GATT markets?

- How could we bargain with Europe after we had failed to secure free trade in our own hemisphere?

These fictoids were substituted for factoids, coupled with oldprop warnings of dire consequences if NAFTA failed.

Mediaprop Is the Message

But the administration was encountering problems with mediaprop. A *New York Times* headline over a picture of disgruntled workers read:

> In Auto-Making Country, Trade Accord is the Enemy
> It is Ross Perot who has captured the nightmare of auto workers—an economy drained of well-paying manufacturing jobs, an economy with no place for people like them, where their jobs simply disappear across the border. Greg Klingler, a skilled tradesman in a General Motors engine plant, quoted Mr. Perot with a smile: "The big sucking sound, right?" (of jobs going to Mexico).[4]

As for network television coverage, the usual scenario had anchors commenting on NAFTA against a backdrop of smoggy Mexico City. There were pictures of companies moving across the Rio Grande, U.S. factories that had been shut down, interviews with displaced U.S. workers, products made by poorly paid Mexican workers, and smoke and sludge pouring from Mexican factories.[7]

A public opinion poll conducted by the *Detroit Free Press* showed that workers agreed with the statement that "Perot was a pretty good watchdog where no one else had recognized and defended their interests." Perot's anti-NAFTA book had a selling price of $6.95, designed to make it accessible to the largest possible number of purchasers. And the most vulgarly appealing line in the book was "that sucking sound you hear is American jobs going south."[8]

At first the White House turned to prestigious figures to counter Perot. Former President Jimmy Carter excoriated Perot for his tactics: "Unfortunately, in our country now we have a demagogue who has unlimited financial resources and who is extremely careless with the truth, who is preying on the fears and the uncertainties of the American public."[9]

That tactic worked. Perot responded angrily to Carter, rather than to the President, saying in a patronizing fashion that if Mr. Carter ever went to Mexico and saw how Mexican employees of U.S. companies lived in one-room shacks with dirt floors, no electricity, and no plumbing, he would be shocked. This was the oldprop of minimization and exclusion, but Carter, himself, did not respond.

Clinton also enlisted other former Presidents—Bush, Ronald Reagan, Gerald Ford, and even Richard M. Nixon. Bush and Ford watched Clinton sign side agreements that his negotiator, Mickey Kantor, insisted were tougher than were first proposed. "When else," Clinton queried, "have all the living Presidents, of different political parties, united in their support for a major policy?"[10]

Putting Down Perot

A means had to be found to put down Perot, and oldprop in a newprop format would be ideal. It was decided that no one could better confront Perot than Vice President Gore, an adroit communicator on television talk shows. Gore's stratgegy would be to demand proof of Perot's positions, place him on the defensive, and fluster him. Perot would be taken off guard by being on his cherished turf, the *Larry King Live* television show. To borrow Perot's metaphor, the "great sucking sound" was Perot being drawn into the debate, and Gore's strategy worked; millions gasped as Gore taunted Perot, interrupted him, loomed over him to demand better answers to his questions, expressed doubt about his responses, and questioned his business ethics:

* What about the special free trade status of the Alliance Airfield near Dallas, Texas, which was owned by Perot's son and in which Perot had a personal financial stake?

* Hadn't that free trade zone been granted to the Perots as a consequence of lobbying with the U.S. Customs Service?

* Didn't Perot want the ordinary American citizen to have the same free trade advantages through NAFTA that his family enjoyed with Alliance Airfield?[11]

The result was an angry Perot who during a commercial break tore off his microphone and threatened to leave the studio.

Confirmed by the Polls

A *New York Times*–CBS poll showed that 72% of the television sets in use were tuned to the debate; 46% watched at least part of it. Some 13.6 million homes watched at some point, the largest rating ever earned by a *Larry King Live* program, and 2.2 million viewers tried to call in with questions.

The polls said that Gore won by a 2–1 margin, and that held equally for proponents and opponents of NAFTA. Where publics had split evenly in ratings of Perot, now about 2 to 1 rated him unfavorably—47% to 24%. Gore climbed to 48% approval, his highest since July 1992 when he was chosen as Clinton's running mate.[12]

The pundits joined in minimizing Perot. William Safire said Perot's veneer of folksiness was shown to be hypocrisy; the hypocrite was "past his pique." Anna Quindlen characterized Perot's efforts as his "last twang," and George Will said the debate moved Perot to the margins (rather than the center) of public discourse, where he belonged.[13]

On the issues, where before the debate a majority believed that more jobs would be lost than would be gained, now a large majority said they favored expanding trade with Mexico and that NAFTA would be mostly good for the United States. Two thirds said free trade agreements were good for the U.S. economy. A cartoon in the *Buffalo News* mocked Perot's fears. A birdlike caricature of Perot said: "I'd like Al Gore . . . to answer just one question: 'Would they be so hot on promoting NAFTA if they knew for a fact that it would disrupt their daughter's wedding?'"

It was a great legislative and propaganda victory—invoking both the old-prop and the new—and a defining moment for the presidency. A Horsey cartoon showed Clinton flying past the Seattle Space Needle dressed as superman. The shield on his chest said simply, "NAFTA!"[14]

ɓ   ɓ   ɓ

The propaganda battle over NAFTA evolved into an interwoven pattern of factoids and fictoids. Because a Democratic president—with business and Republican Congressional support—articulated an unnatural alliance, the outcome was never settled. Both sides began by disputing facts and shifted to promises—from factoids to fictoids. The overall context was one of oldprop, a rhetoric that rested more on the power of the alliances than the understanding and support that each was to generate.

When NAFTA found itself again on the national agenda, it rekindled the same old propagandas and the same emotional freight. Although the President contended that free trade was inescapable, not all were to accept it uncritically, and a Republican nominee was to retreat from a lifelong conviction to a Doleful ambivalence.

WHOSE "VISION THING" WAS IT?

It was surprising that in July 1992 President Bush would introduce GATT as his "vision thing" during the "hoopla" of a Republican nominating convention. Trade seldom was introduced to the glitter of the nominating process. But that is what the President did. He told the convention that a new world order had become possible by the collapse of Soviet communism, a Republican party triumph that should not be shared with Democratic presidents or Congresses. Democrats had ridiculed President Reagan's denouncing of the "evil empire," and Clinton had hung back on Desert Storm.

The President invoked the prestige of revered presidents as if each were his partner in securing America's destiny. He wrapped himself in the flag and in the glory of our first president, George Washington; he recalled such "Republicans" as Abraham Lincoln, Teddy Roosevelt, and Dwight D. Eisenhower. What was more, he linked his vision to Democrats Franklin D. Roosevelt, John F. Kennedy, and Harry S. Truman. His most curious claim was political kinship with Truman, the cussing Missourian who in 1948 ran against a "reactionary Republican Congress" rather than against the GOP standard bearer, New York governor Thomas E. Dewey. However, Bush's reasoning became apparent: As had Truman, he intended to run against the opposition Congress.

It took almost 12 hours for the Democrats to catch up with the President's claims, but they began to ask: "Whose 'vision' was it?" By that time the convention atmosphere had been dissipated. The last of thousands of red, white, and blue balloons had been released, the flag-draped stage was dismantled, and conventioneers had packed their memorabilia and departed.

Now Democratic candidate Clinton insisted that the Cold War victory should not be claimed by one party; resistance to Soviet communism had been launched by the Democrats a half-century earlier, and the instrument of that triumph was the Marshall Plan, a "vision" for its own time and a watershed in foreign policy that would see the creation of the United Nations and international trade organizations.

Tradeprop as Newprop

Bush's "vision" had been etched, in fact, almost a half-century earlier at Harvard University on June 5, 1947, when Secretary of State George Marshall announced a plan for the postwar economic recovery of Western Europe by 1952. The so-called Marshall Plan won support both in the United States and in Western Europe because it promised to strengthen both the United States and Europe.

Its symbol—a red, white, and blue shield—carried a simple and compelling slogan, *For Peace and Economic Recovery*, which although it did not explicitly assert its goal—the containment of communism—nonetheless conveyed that purpose. It was a masterful propaganda: Although it minimized conflict and stressed cooperation, strong undercurrents of parochialism, paternalism, and demonization made oldprop a subtle factor.

The administration recognized that the Marshall Plan could not succeed unless the American people approved of it, so much of the tradeprop was framed in terms of desires for cooperation and an end to conflict. Although this would strike the Soviets, and even the Europeans, as oldprop, it was a strategy that the Truman administration felt it had to follow.

Oldprop Takes Over

American propaganda at home would be guided by a number of oldprop bromides:

- George Washington had warned us about becoming involved in foreign wars. The Marshall Plan would not draw us into European conflicts but would promote cooperation.
- According to the American parable, God helps only those who help themselves. Before the Marshall Plan would help Europe, the Europeans would be required to help themselves.
- The United States would give to Europe as an entity, not to individual countries. The Europeans together would decide who would get what.
- Lending always brought misery. The Marshall Plan would create no new debts.
- Historically, many European countries that had received American aid had not acknowledged nor appreciated that assistance. Now they would do so publicly.

Because they represented demands, they were in the pattern of oldprop, but the process of open discussion and the goals of achieving political consensus met the tests of newprop.

Antecedents to GATT

One can see many antecedents to GATT in the steps that Europe took to modify their economies. They first established an Organization for European Economic Cooperation (OEEC) that required each member country to:

- Transform itself from a single competing nation into a member of an integrated economic community.

- Strike down trade barriers such as subsidies, quotas, and tariffs to promote freer trade.
- Stabilize currency values by becoming a member of a newly created European Payments Union.
- Maximize productivity to others and purchase their products in return; not everyone could produce everything.
- Acknowledge the need for political integration to accompany economic integration.

However, GATT took both the United States and Europe a step further; now the United States itself was required to become a player, not just an adviser, and although the United States dominated international trade through the 1970s, its hegemony had been eroded. Reagan and Bush had writhed in the embrace of free trade standards that were impossible to achieve or to enforce.

Clinton, in turn, insisted that only open and competitive commerce would enrich the United States as a nation. A newprop of global participation, it required a willingness on the part of publics to accept degrees of deprivation, as well. Parts of the economy would prosper, but others would be put at risk. Clinton's trade representative, Mickey Kantor, acknowledged that at any time the President might be required to protect the United States against dumping, call for voluntary limits on exports, insist on the opening of foreign markets, and threaten to retaliate against others. Easy labels such as protectionism and free trade were bound to collide, bringing about climates of oldprop as well as the new.

That made the 1996 anti-free-trade outburst less surprising, this despite that fact that the U.S. trade gap was narrowing because of an export boom and that jobs were being created as well as shipped abroad.[15] That anger in New Hampshire surprised Dole. To his comment that he had not thought the thrust of the debate had shifted to trade policies, Buchanan cried, "Where has Dole been?" Buchanan had succeeded in tying trade policies to an oldprop paranoia in which:

> The nation had "sold out" to New World internationalists and Washington insiders, was under siege from within and without, and was invaded not only by drugs and aliens, but by cheap tomatoes picked by Mexican serfs and underwear sewn by Chinese prisoners.[16]

Campaigning at Mt. Rushmore Memorial Park in South Dakota, Buchanan pointed to the gigantic mountain sculpture of four former presidents—Washington, Jefferson, Teddy Roosevelt, and Lincoln—and cried, "All four of these gentlemen . . . agreed with Pat Buchanan . . . [they] believed that the American economy was designed for the American workers and the American families."[15]

The oldprop debate over NAFTA and GATT would cast its shadow over the 1996 general elections, as well.

🏴   🏴   🏴

GATT was an extension of the Marshall Plan; it had been adopted by the American and European people a half-century before President Bush advanced his "vision" of a new world order. However, the success of the Marshall Plan demonstrated that a great deal of newprop must precede any great proposal, that knowledge must be diffused about it, and policies must be accessible to discussion and debate.

The adoption of NAFTA and GATT demonstrated that although top-down models of gathering votes in Congress produce legislation, lack of public consensus places any legislation at risk. Even when consensus is gained, it must constantly be reinforced. A combination of economic trends—trade imbalances, job losses, and corporate downsizing—led to a new sense of uncertainty about international trade policies, which the 1996 primary campaign could not resolve.

NOTES

1. Politics by the numbers. (1992, July 15). *New York Times*, Sec. A, p. 15.
2. Year of the factoid. (1992, October 29). *New York Times*, Sec. A, p. 19.
3. Buchananizing Bob Dole. (1996, March 11). Talk of the Town, *The New Yorker*, p. 39.
4. Ibid., *The New Yorker*, p. 40.
5. Union chief jabs Clinton on NAFTA. (1993, November 16). Balz, D., & Cooper, K. J., *Washington Post*, Sec. A, p. 1.
6. In auto-making country, trade accord is the enemy. (1993, September 14). Toner, R., *New York Times*, Sec. A, p. 1.
7. TV audiences are victors. (1993, November 3). Goodman, W., *New York Times*, Sec. B, p. 2.
8. Perot, R. (1993). *Save your job, save our country: Why NAFTA must be stopped—now!* New York: Hyperion.
9. Hard Truths from Jimmy Carter. (1993, September 20). *Washington Post*, Sec. A., p. 18.
10. Clinton calls on 3 presidents to promote free-trade pact. (1993, September 15). Ifill, G., *New York Times*, Sec. A, p. 1.
11. TV debate sets a cable record. (1993, November 11). *New York Times*, Sec. A, p. 10.
12. Gore flattens Perot. (1993, November 11). *New York Times*, Sec. A, p. 19.
13. Over and out. (1993, November 11). *New York Times*, Sec. A, p. 23.
14. Cartoon (1993, November 19). Horsey, D., *Seattle Post-Intelligencer*, p. 11.
15. U.S. trade gap narrows again in export boom. (1996, February 8). Drew, C., *New York Times*, Sec. A, p. 1.
16. Buchanan hits home with anxious voters. (1996, February 18). Booth, W., AmeriCast-Post@AmeriCast.com.
17. Exultant Buchanan pushes economic insecurity theme. (1996, February 22). Bennet, J., *New York Times*, Sec. A, p. 1.

23

ASIA-BASHING
A Cultural Oldprop

American diplomacy and propaganda long have been frustrated by Asian cultural barriers. In Japan, the impasses have been brought about by the de facto management of the economy by bureaucracies, the protectionism that shapes trade policies, and uniquely cultural approaches to the negotiation of differences. In China the barriers include an intense trading and political culture that is obsessed with hegemony. Both cultures profess openness, but each practices a political, economic, and cultural hegemony.

JAPAN: A THREE-LEGGED STOOL

Our relationship with Japan has been likened structurally to a three-legged stool—one military, one political, and the other economic—but the legs are held together precariously. Presidents Reagan and Bush stressed the military and political dimensions of the Japan relationship and sought to gain economic concessions by a newprop of accommodation, but Perot and Clinton pursued an oldprop that insisted that this agenda had sold out America.

Clinton vowed to place economic relationships first, and when Japan delayed a long-standing agreement to trade commercial technology for U.S. military technology Clinton retaliated by pushing U.S. commercial efforts in that field. The Japanese cultural shield had evoked a retaliatory oldprop of the deed, and that tendency continued.[1]

Crisis, Not Problem

When I lived in Japan, I noted the Japanese propensity for negotiating and yielding little in the process. I urged the Reagan administration to assert a crisis in trade, not merely a problem, as leverage for the negotiation of concessions. Acknowledgment of a crisis by the Japanese government would permit it to cut through bureaucratic (i.e., cultural) processes. But Reagan yielded to Japanese culturalprop that there was only a problem, not a crisis, and the negotiations foundered. When President Clinton later said the Japanese treated negotiation as a cultural form of saying "no," he was, of course, correct, but the Japanese rejoined that the President was *Japan-bashing*.

Two bizarre incidents in the 1980s and 1990s illustrated how adroitly the Japanese turned alleged Japan-bashing into an effective oldprop.

• One was the discovery in the 1980s that the Japanese firm of Toshiba illegally sold a highly secret submarine propeller system to the Soviet Union. This evasion was carried out in collaboration with a Norwegian firm, but Toshiba took most of the criticism. It was only when U.S. television networks filmed a congressman bashing a Toshiba television set on the steps of the U.S. Capitol that an outraged Japanese mediaprop condemned it as Japan-bashing.

• The second incident occurred soon after President Reagan left office in 1988. Invited to Japan by the Fuji company, which in addition to film includes as part of its conglomerate a daily newspaper and a television channel, the Japanese media largely ignored Reagan; he was merely an actor who had been hired by the competition. But U.S. mediaprop accused the Japanese government of paying off Reagan for his benign treatment of them. Given our ignorance of the facts, it was not surprising that mediaprop condemned it as Japan-bashing. Oldprop begot oldprop.

A Lapse of Newprop

One of the great stages on which worldprop is played out is the summit meeting. The prominence of the actors and the possibility of important decisions command the global communications stage. The summit is so important that it demands success, or at the least, the prospects of success, and a hopeful newprop is its *sine qua non*.

A meeting of the Group of Seven—the major trading nations who accept responsibility for maintaining global financial stability—provided an opening. The United States signaled the opportunity for newprop by saying it would give up its demands for the expansion of "managed trade"—an anathema to the Japanese—if they would yield on tariffs and quotas. The idea was that this might reopen the door to a newprop of accommodation and exchange. The unanticipated effect, however, was to set Japan off on an oldprop that accused the United States of seeking to dominate Asian economies.

Expectations then shifted to the promise of a U.S.–Japan summit, but when a new young prime minister, Morihimo Hosokawa, was unable to deliver as many concessions as had been anticipated, Clinton rejected his offer out of hand, an inexplicable lapse in newprop. The summit had been cast from an exercise in the newprop of accommodation to the generation of conflict.[2]

Redefining Oldprop as Newprop

It was apparent that only a combination of events that operated in the U.S. economic and political interest had the power to reduce Japan-bashing. If we could not solve problems, perhaps we could redefine them to make them manageable. The emergence of positive economic events led to this opportunity.

◆ *Buying and selling America*—The long recession in Japan reduced the motivation and ability to buy—and retain—a good deal of America. Many Japanese investments in Hollywood became losing financial propositions, and they sold them off. In 1995, Mitsubishi divested itself of New York's Rockefeller Center.

◆ *Buying American baseball*—Although viewed with mixed feelings in Japan, American Nintendo purchased a friendly controlling financial interest in the Seattle Mariners, an American League baseball franchise.

◆ *Competition in electronics*—Japan conceded U.S. technological dominance in high-definition TV (HDTV); only a face-saving announcement was made that the Japanese program would be continued in a revised form.

◆ *Plugging technological gaps*—Many Japanese companies made new multi-million dollar investments in U.S. communications industries because they had fallen behind the U.S. technologies.[3]

◆ *Neither lean nor mean*—"Japan, Inc." was less lean and mean. Even Toyota was burdened by white-collar bureaucracy. Offices lacked computers, and time was consumed by endless bureaucratic meetings. Assembly-line precision was being offset by bloated and inefficient staffs.[4]

◆ *Making concessions*—Japan acknowledged the ability of American Motorola to supply the growing Japanese market for cellular telephones. With a Japanese partner, Motorola would soon double its telephone sales and expand its cellular telephone infrastructure.

◆ *A U.S. cartel*—Aided by a government-assisted cartel, the U.S. semiconductor industry regained a substantial share of its market from Japan.

◆ *"Patented" success*—IBM jumped from sixth to first worldwide in 1993 in number of patents awarded, and two other U.S. companies moved into the top five, a step toward reducing Japanese dominance. However, Japan continued to hold 6 of the top 10 spots.

+ *"Drive-by" consortiums*—Boeing was involved with Japan in the manufacture of its aircraft, and computer makers such as Hitachi joined IBM to distribute its products in Japan.

+ *An American keiretsu*—The Lotus Development Corporation, a U.S. leading-edge computer firm, which was taken over by IBM in mid-1995, developed an "electronic keiretsu" that enhanced information-sharing and collaboration among U.S. companies.[5]

+ *An apple a day*—For years, Washington state apple farmers were outraged by the exclusion of their apples from the Japanese market. When the U.S. farmers demonstrated publicly, the Japanese said this was Japan-bashing, but they accepted the apples.

+ *Taking steps*—Japan agreed to open its substantial markets in insurance, glass, medical, and telecommunications equipment.

+ *Reducing trade gaps*—All these steps signaled success and permitted newprop to catch up with the old.

In 1995 the Japanese trade surplus was reduced for the first time in 5 years by 17% and another 18% in 1996. The yen had become too expensive, and the manufacturing and marketing of U.S. products was improving.[6] What was more, Japanese work and lifestyles were changing; less time was being spent at work and more time at leisure, and trade barriers were being circumvented to accommodate this new Japanese lifestyle.

In Spring 1996 the Associated Press reported that U.S. sales of leisure clothing were booming, that U.S. car sales had increased dramatically, that appliance makers such as General Electric and Whirlpool were cracking the Japanese market, and that U.S. cultural food icons such as Snickers bars, Heinz ketchup, Kellogg's Corn Flakes, Campbell's soups, Coca-Cola, and Pringles potato chips now were popular and flooding Japanese shops. Haagen-Däzs had captured 50% of the gourmet ice cream niche. Walt Disney, Kleenex, Xerox, Barbie dolls, Monopoly games, and cartoon picture books were everywhere.[7]

More Oldprop

But the most critical area was automobile and spare parts, the import of which accounted for 80% of the U.S. annual deficit with Japan. As the deadline approached in May 1995, for solving the problem, Clinton launched into an aggressive oldprop; to wit, a failure to lower barriers would bring about a 100% tariff on Japanese luxury cars. In turn, Japan warned that it would take its case to the World Trade Organization.[8]

The newprop solution was to redefine the problem so that it was amenable to solution. The governments no longer would be the principals to the dispute. Negotiations would be conducted directly between the "Big Three" U.S. automakers and the Japanese automakers and dealers. Industrial and corporate hegemony would be substituted for state hegemony.[9]

Cast into the rubric of voluntarism, the trading relationship took on the character of newprop, and when in mid-1996 Japan announced that the yen would continue to lose value to the dollar, and it was disclosed that the current trade deficit had been cut by more than 50%, the newprop that emerged took on a rosy hue.[10]

ᖨ   ᖨ   ᖨ

The oldprop of Japan-bashing was rooted in U.S. frustrations relating to Japanese political, economic, and cultural hegemony. When the United States challenged those precepts, the result was conflict and frustration, the breeding grounds for oldprop. Transitions to newprop were enabled by redefining trade disagreements as nonconflictual and by shifts in trade balances that reduced bases for conflict.

CHINAPROP: AMBIVALENCE INCARNATE

Creating a basis for newprop with respect to China has proved to be far more difficult. For almost three quarters of a century, the United States has been ambivalent about its relationships with China—at times an exploiter, at other times a partisan protector, an outright foe, and a cautious trade collaborator.

Some of the most divisive domestic politics in modern American history came during the 1950s when the radical right wing of the Republican party, led by Senator Joseph McCarthy of Wisconsin, exploited the oldprop of demonization of China and accused the Democrats of harboring spies who "sold out" China to the Communists. This was the apotheosis of oldprop and it ripped the fabric of freedom of speech in the popular culture.

The United States protested the Japanese invasion of China in the 1930s and tried to save the doomed nationalist Chinese government in the 1940s, but the ascendancy of the Communists in 1950 sharply reduced communication with China, and the entry of Chinese troops into the Korean War brought about a U.S. military defeat and the shocking removal by Democratic President Harry S. Truman of conservative hero General Douglas McArthur as commander-in-chief.

The locus of U.S. antagonism to China shifted in the years that followed. American moralists looked askance at the Chinese invasion of Tibet and the raw power of the cultural revolution that was unleashed so savagely on the

Chinese people. But in 1972 President Richard M. Nixon's politically daring Shanghai Communique created a "new opening" and an approach to newprop.

Moral and Political Ambivalence

The U.S. approach has been clouded by moral and political dilemmas. On the one hand, our official line of newprop asserts the importance of human rights and hopes that this goal will become more attainable by engagement of China than by isolating it. By contrast, moralists who are proactive on human rights demonize China and demand trade sanctions. In mid-1995, just before Clinton was to decide on most favored nations (MFN) treatment for China, Amnesty International USA, the Lawyers Committee for Human Rights, and the Robert F. Kennedy Memorial Center for Human Rights opposed it bitterly.

The attack on the students at Tiananmen Square continues to be celebrated each year as an oldprop icon.[11] Ironically, Chinese students continue to debate whether their leadership should have backed away from the confrontation before the onslaught began. Ironically, some of the leaders conceded that they had been caught up in Communist teachings that said that "change must be total or it is nothing," hence they put down dissent in their own front and neglected an opportunity to come to terms with a more pliable Chinese government faction. The result was that the extremists among both students and the government clashed, with an inevitable result. The protestors had failed to seize the opportunity to engage in newprop because they had been schooled in the old.[12]

American mediaprop tracked closely the arrest of all dissidents and their experiences while they were imprisoned. Most notable for their coverage were the saga of Wei Jingsheng, a prominent dissident, and the arrest of Harry Wu, a naturalized Chinese-American citizen, for espionage. Ultimately, Wu was permitted to leave China again, presumably to make it easier for Hillary Rodham Clinton to speak at the International Women's Conference in Beijing.[13]

American mediaprop also closely covers economic issues such as the Chinese invasion of trademarks and copyrights, most notably in intellectual property areas of CDs, films, and video. Even President Bush's autobiography was pirated by four different Chinese publishers. I was startled to find copies of one of my books selling for 20% of its price. But China perceives mediaprop that centers on these reports as *China-bashing*.

Untying Propaganda Knots

To untie some of these propaganda knots, Clinton decided to divest considerations of trade from morality. To give newprop a chance, trade would be governed by economic principles, and moral and ideological positions would be addressed by voluntary and cooperative means. U.S. corporations would establish codes of conduct in their operations abroad that would minimize evils and facilitate problem solving.[14]

China has engaged in all manner of oldprop devices, ranging from overt actions, threats, and co-option to blandishments and mainstream public relations. As an example, just before a decision by Clinton on MFN, a number of Chinese trade delegations shopped ostentatiously across the United States, making billions of dollars in purchases and spending millions on public relations and aggressive lobbying. U.S. corporations objected to human-rights-prop that undermined economic ties to China. In Washington state, a full-page ad in daily newspapers sponsored by Boeing and the Seattle Port echoed the themes first expressed by Presidents Reagan and Bush—that trade itself was newprop because it represented exchanges of ideas and values as well as goods and currencies.

Nonetheless, an emphasis on moral themes was supported by Taiwan lobbyists, American moralists, and mediaprop. But Winston Lord, chief State Department adviser for Asia, cautioned that Asia was becoming antagonized by Washington's belligerence on human rights and its linkage with trade and we ran the risk of being regarded as an "international nanny if not a bully." Thus Clinton asked that standards be set by the entire Group of Seven industrial nations, not just by the United States.[15]

The Politics and Propaganda of Hegemony

If Japan was best symbolized as practicing the politics and propaganda of culture, China is best characterized as practicing the propaganda of political hegemony. When in June 1995 the United States permitted President Lee Teng Hui of Taiwan to visit his alma mater, Cornell University, China viewed it as a repudiation of the Shanghai agreements on political hegemony and a loss of face for China. China informed the Clinton administration that it could not reconcile its relationship with the United States until it had reaffirmed the original agreements on Taiwan and assured China that another such political visit could not recur.[16] President Jiang Zemin himself visited Clinton in late October 1995 to tell him that China would not tolerate actions of that kind.[17]

Because China links its hegemony in politics to trade, it adopted the oldprop of the deed and awarded billion-dollar contracts to Mercedes to build minivans in China and signed another billion-dollar contract with Siemens A.G. to build power stations and airports. Pointedly, the Germans represented themselves as "less bellicose, more tempered trading partners."[18]

The United States again was to challenge China's political hegemony, this time when aircraft carrier task forces were sent to the Taiwanese straits in re-action to Chinese "war games." China expressed its indignation, and again it linked its displeasure to trade, rejecting a Boeing Aircraft bid and signing, in-stead, a multibillion dollar contract with European Airbus.[19]

Newprop for Old?

This created a challenge for Boeing, for China expected Boeing to demon-strate its support by winning concessions from the U.S. government. These include delinking trade issues from political issues, including the defusing of disputes over piracy of intellectual properties (CDs, software, films, etc.), re-ducing its attacks on human rights violations, and in other ways lowering the decibel count of U.S. oldprop. Boeing, in fact, was being tested on its ability to bring this about.

Thus Boeing launched a multifaceted domestic lobbyprop campaign on behalf of trade as newprop, ranging from the recruitment of members of its "American keiretsu"—parts suppliers, subcontractors, and other China-trade-dependent businesses—to entreaties to other corporations who de-pend on China trade. China not only would be granted a 1-year extension of favored nation trade treatment by President Clinton, but Boeing sought to assure China that this was a permanent condition. Boeing also reaffirmed its scheduling of its annual board meeting in Beijing, an innovative newprop.

Boeing also has created a China Normalization Initiative to dispel the mis-understanding and distrust that have taken over U.S.–China relations. It would be aimed at government and publics and take the form of lobbyprop, with videos, brochures, TV ads, and public forums. This effort would be joined by numerous blue-chip corporations: "It's really an overall grass-roots education effort to help Americans understand China relations. We're not trying to apologize for China, but we're trying to help explain what the Chi-nese are all about."[20]

But the oldprop directed at China makes this task difficult. Mediaprop has described the treatment of orphaned children, sales of nuclear technology to Pakistan, crackdowns on political dissidents, new restrictions on religious be-liefs, economic piracy, and threats to Taiwan, all anathema to moral crusades, the intellectual community, and the Taiwan lobby.

Although the Clinton administration again extended MFN status to China, in 1996 it threatened to impose $2,000,000 in customs penalties on imports if China did not curb piracy. Even though China agreed to do so, it called the threat China-bashing, pointing to comparable offenses by Korea, Thailand, and other Asian nations that carried no penalties. The U.S. trade negotiator, Charlene Barshefsky, asserting that she did not seek a trade war, nonetheless insisted that China keep its agreements.

Privatization: A New Newprop

Boeing and the business community believe that the oldprop of conflict and demonization that has characterized U.S.–China trade relations has failed, and they believe that a redefinition of the relationship and a consistent approach to newprop are required. One alternative that Boeing suggested is the privatization of negotiations, much as occurred when U.S. and Japanese automakers agreed to negotiate directly with one another. The popular culture would be extended on a global scale, and the consequence of it would be more reliance on newprop and less dependence on the old.

꙳   ꙳   ꙳

In the 1990s the oldprop of Asia-bashing became more difficult for the United States to sustain and for Asian nations to accept. In most cases, these disputes were marked by cultural dilemmas; that is, the directness of oldprop is as embedded in American culture as passive negotiation is endemic to Japan and political hegemony is first nature to China.

American diplomacy has failed to address successfully the cultural parameters of our relations with Japan and China, and because of cross-currents of moral advocates, intellectuals, business interests, and the old diplomacy, an inconsistency pervades our policies, resulting in a predominantly oldprop rhetoric.

Boeing and other commercial interests are seeking to redefine our relationship through a new propaganda of privatization, a step urged on the automakers by Japan and the United States as a way of solving their problems. Privatization of propaganda in the field of trade would sidestep the imposition of moral values and reliance on oldprop. This, in turn, might free governments to redefine their relationships and shift from the oldprop to the new.

NOTES

1. Japan to help Pentagon acquire technology. (1994, May 10). Pollack, W., *New York Times*, Sec. A, p. 6.
2. Bradley rebukes Clinton on Japan. (1994, February 24). *New York Times*, Sec. C, p. 1.
3. Look who's stuck in the slow lane. (1994, March 28). Armstrong, L., *Business Week*, p. 28.
4. Think Japan, Inc., is lean and mean? Step into this office. (1994, March 20). *New York Times*, Sec. A, p. 11.
5. Computer keiretsu: Japanese idea, U.S. style. (1994, February 6). Manzi, J., *New York Times*, Sec. F, p. 15.
6. Japan trade surplus shrinks for the first time in five years. (1996, January 24). Pollack, J., *New York Times*, Sec. A, p. 1. See also: The yen, down and going lower. (1996, May 26). Norris, F., *New York Times*, Sec. 3, p. 1.

7. Made in America now selling in Japan. (1996, March 21). Kageyama, Y., Associated Press, in *Seattle Post-Intelligencer*, Sec. B, p. 5. See also: Japan is experiencing a retail revolution. (1995, February 19). Dunphy, S., *Seattle Times*, Sec. J, p. 1.

8. White House maintains its hard-line approach to Japan, despite ongoing political turmoil. (1994, April 14). Davis, B., *Wall Street Journal*, Sec. A, p. 16. See also: Kantor vows pressure on Japan will continue. (1994, October 3). Friedman, T., *New York Times*, Sec. C, p. 8.

9. In trade dispute with Japan, both sides see misjudgments. (1995, June 7). Sanger, D., *New York Times*, Sec. A, p. 1.

10. U.S. settles trade dispute, averting billions in tariffs on Japanese luxury autos. (1995, June 29). Sanger, D., *New York Times*, Sec. A, p. 1.

11. Insiders voice hope for deal on China trade. (1994, May 13). Griffiths, L., Reuters, In *Seattle Post-Intelligencer*, p. 1.

12. 6 years after Tiananmen massacre, survivors clash anew on tactics. (1995, April 30). Tyler, P. E., *New York Times*, Sec. Y, p. 8. See also: What eluded the news cameras at Tiananmen Square. (1996, June 4). *New York Times*, Sec. B, pp. 1/4.

13. China detains, interrogates key insurgent. (1994, April 5). Sun, L. H., *Washington Post*, Sec. A, p. 1.

14. Clinton to urge a rights code for businesses dealing abroad. (1995, March 27). Sanger, D., *New York Times*, Sec. C, p. 1.

15. Ibid., Griffiths, p. 1.

16. China outlines its demands for U.S. (1995, July 13). Tyler, P. E., *Seattle Post-Intelligencer*, p. 5.

17. Blunt talk from Deng Ziaoping's likely successor. (1995, October 23). *Newsweek*, p. 42.

18. China gives big van deal to Mercedes. (1995, July 13). Nash, N. C., *New York Times*, Sec. C, pp. 1/5.

19. China trade talks get nastier. (1996, May 16). *Seattle Post-Intelligencer*, Sec. A, pp. 1/10.

20. Boeing's campaign to protect a market. (1996, May 27). Holmes, S., *Seattle Times*, Sec. A, pp. 1/6.

24

POLITICALPROP
1992: Gridlock and Credibility

Political wordprop fuels the popular culture by its manipulation of language, and this was never more true than in the 1990s. Two words—*gridlock* and *credibility*—became the vernacular of mediaprop in the 1992 presidential campaign and framed debates over two major programs advanced by the Clinton administration—the budget deficit and the health care program. Both were exercises in oldprop that reflected an old politics of top-down leadership.

REIFYING GRIDLOCKPROP

The 1993 budget passed Congress by the slimmest of margins, and the health proposal succumbed to a Republican filibuster. At the root of these virtual failures was the misshapen use of political wordprop. The President, the Congress, and the media joined in reifying gridlock as an immovable object and irresistible force, ruling out diversity in the popular culture as the bedrock consideration. And when mediaprop addressed candidate credibility as the overriding consideration in the 1992 presidential race, it encouraged a shortfall of knowledge about substantive issues—the epiphany of oldprop—and it made the popular culture all but irrelevant.

President Bush exploited the gridlock metaphor during the 1992 presidential campaign to explain his failure to push legislation through a reluctant Democratic Congress. As he put it, Republicans were in favor, Democrats were opposed; hence gridlock, or gridlockprop. Adopting the metaphor that had signaled failure on the part of Bush, President Clinton attributed his own failure to win easier adoption of his 1993 budget to gridlock, even though passage was hampered by his own party.

Gridlockprop as Oldprop

Thus gridlockprop in both political camps became a symbol of the triumph of the oldprop over the new, the price paid by politicians and the media for buying into their own metaphors. In their legislating and mediaprop, the politicians and the press had placed legislative processes above public participation, an assault on the popular culture that was not overlooked by its members.

In the case of the budget, the President had positioned himself as a single, powerful voice speaking to many listeners—axiomatic of oldprop—inviting the Congress and the media to do the same. It was only when Clinton realized that his budget plan was in danger that he became more intent on achieving consensus, doing more listening and less talking. Aware by a lack of public response that he could not bask in the Presidency in an aura of infallibility, he reduced expectations to goals that the popular culture would permit and that he could achieve.[1]

The President returned to talk shows and interviews. A Perot-style activist network was built on toll-free telephone numbers, national petition drives, and newsletters. A belated realization had come that the politics of a popular culture must reconcile a diversity of interests, and the last-gasp effort was an attempt to do so. The budget was adopted in the House, but only by two votes, and it was tied in the Senate (broken by Vice President Gore). Diversity was acknowledged too late to play more than a passing role, and it failed, as a consequence, to provide a lesson for the health care plan to follow.

Déjà Vu All Over Again

The President had appointed Hillary Rodham Clinton to direct the *health-prop* campaign. She gathered dozens of experts in a televised gabfest to give it universality, a newprop presumably where many spoke to many; although it was conceded that not everyone could interact with the experts, they could watch them perform. No one, however, asked members of the popular culture if they perceived the invitation to participate in political voyeurism as a genuine newprop or only as a variation on the old (i.e., watching Washington).

To have concluded that attitudes toward health care were measured only by universality of coverage or employer responsibility minimized the vast array of perspectives and constituencies that were to emerge as principal actors. The teach-in had not captured its intended audiences, and the potential for winning approval for a monolithic (single-payer) program faded as a flood of alternative proposals was considered. The defections came slowly, and the erosion of the plan was gradual, but cumulatively they were lethal.[2]

The President was forced to concede that universal coverage would not be realized because it lacked public support.[3] Democratic Senator Edward Kennedy was unable to gain Republican support for even a 50% employer contribution. Rock the Vote, the MTV program to register 20-somethings to vote in 1992, refused to take sides.[4] A belated flurry of proposals trying to capture the new diversity came out of the Democratic caucus in the Senate and House, but it was much too late to be implemented.[5]

A *New York Times*–CBS poll captured this confusion: 80% of the public now was skeptical that a universal health care plan would be passed by the Congress. Although 70% thought it was very important that a plan be adopted, they split on whether employers should pay, almost half in favor but 40% saying employees should contribute.[6]

Lobbyprop as Diversityprop

Even in lobbyprop there was evidence of diversity; the sources of money were not only numerous but varied. The Center for Public Integrity said hundreds of interest groups spent money to influence the health legislation; more than 100 law, lobbying, and public relations firms were engaged, and tens of millions were spent on television, radio, and newspaper advertising, polling, and grass roots campaigns; thus newprop rose in opposition, not in support.

Representatives of a wide assortment of doctors, hospitals, insurance companies, and state officials expressed concern about expanding Medicare to cover the uninsured, and New Yorkers cautioned Governor Cuomo not to support a national reform bill that offered less care than that afforded by New York State laws.[7] IBM, in an unusual gesture, advised its employees to contact their representatives in Congress to express their opposition, pointing out that it would be difficult for IBM to maintain the level of health care support that employees already were enjoying. This was not gridlock, it was process.[8]

Perot Has the Picture

Although with the benefit of hindsight, Perot summed up the failings of the Clinton oldprop. He would have advised them to "start small, build a consensus, and test, test, test." Perhaps if the Clintons had done so they would have recognized the multiverse factors of ethics, religion, philosophies, and even regional preferences that beset their proposals.

Perot suggested that the plan was drafted by well-meaning experts who were out of touch with medical care. Not understanding the relative worth of the product meant not knowing what the American people might wish to have. Nor had the costs been accurately assessed. At the least, the proposals had to be put in plain language. And Perot added disingenuously: "Skip the (old) propaganda."[9]

CREDIBILITY AND CREDIBILITYPROP

Credibility became as misleading a metaphor as gridlock during the 1992 presidential campaign; it, too, was embraced uncritically by mediaprop and pollprop, inducing an irrational "attack campaign" by a once popular George Bush and inviting the opportunism of a Bill Clinton. In 1992, mediaprop continuously assaulted the personalities of candidates, their morals, and their ethics. This was more than simply negative; it was a pervasive oldprop in its persistence, its repetition of themes, and its stridency.

As mediaprop, this was not an unexpected tactic: Attacking candidates was a *sine qua non* of journalistic practice. There was only a belated recognition that much of it was tuned out by publics who perceived it as a surrogate for the discussion of issues. But journalists remembered that by demolishing the credibility of Michael Dukakis in 1988, Bush had, in an instant, transformed the election from a competition into a referendum, and they looked to that same outcome in 1992. After all, Clinton's reputation was sullied and Perot was in virtual flight. Journalists also knew that a preponderance of voters chose more on the basis of personalities and party loyalties than on issues. Because party loyalties had been weakened, they miscalculated, candidate reputations were central.

In a litany of coverage extending from May to November, the practical length of the 1992 campaign, scarcely a day passed that one of the campaigns or the candidates was not belabored by mediaprop for a lack of trustworthiness and character, a demonizing oldprop. According to my calculations, more than 500 newspaper stories, an average of four per day, attacked the candidates, a pattern followed by broadcasters. On many days, six or more stories were in the attack mode. June 29 was one of the biggest days for attacks on Perot. Mediaprop even quoted Bush campaign portrayals of Perot as a threat to liberties, shocking, and frightening.

Mediaprop reported unrelentingly on the corruption that surrounded the Bush administration; he was unable to disassociate himself from the BCCI scandals, the S&L debacle in which one of his sons was a player, the indictments and near indictments of administration figures, and the Iran–Contra hearings in which Oliver North was the most visible symbol. When mediaprop reported that the House had passed the family leave bill and overridden Bush's veto, a vulnerability was hinted at in Bush's previously uninterrupted successes in blocking Congress.

Time's cover story for October 5, 1992 complained that the campaign was erupting into a series of charges and countercharges of dishonesty and deceptions that raised the question, "Is anyone around here telling the truth?"[10] But the question should have been "Is anyone talking about anything but the oldprop of credibility?"

Bush: Search and Destroy

Bush had set the credibility agenda by adopting an oldprop attack mode. He had offended voters in 1988 when he said of the woman vice-presidential candidate, Geraldine Ferraro, that he would "kick (her) butt," and few believed his protestations that he had played no part in the demonizing adprop that defeated 1988 Democratic candidate Dukakis. But Bush lost the ultimate in credibility when he reneged on his exaggerated "Read my lips!" pledge on no new taxes made during the 1988 campaign.

Bush's highest credibility (90% popularity) had come with his creation of the coalition that waged war against Iraqi leader Saddam Hussein. But soon even his foreign policy leadership would be questioned. Desert Storm served as a technoprop and infoprop masterpiece, but the administration concealed the fact that some heralded technology had failed, a deception that turned out to be an epiphany of oldprop. What was more, he had not achieved Hussein's ouster. And further embarrassment came with the public questioning of former U.S. Ambassador to Iraq, April C. Glaspie, whose career was being sacrificed to shield Bush. And when Bush brought the Big Three automakers to Japan to seek concessions, he became ill at a banquet and threw up in the lap of the Japanese prime minister. This produced instant derision on the comedy underground and late-night talk shows.

Mediaprop kept alive doubts about Bush's repeated protests that he had been "out of the loop" with respect to Iran–contra. Four days before the election, special investigator Lawrence Walsh released handwritten notes that described meetings in which Bush had participated, and he was belittled for being unfamiliar with supermarket billing techniques that were everyday experiences to voters.

A Bush attack on Clinton was even more embarrassing, an opaque "McCarthy-like accusation" that Clinton had concealed details of a trip he had taken to Moscow at the height of the Vietnam War. When it was disclosed that the State Department had inquired illegally into the passport status of both Clinton and his mother, Clinton ridiculed Bush, charging that "he's even after my mother." The editor of the once liberal magazine *Commentary* concluded that whereas Reagan was the Teflon President to whom nothing stuck, Bush was the Velcro President to whom everything stuck.[11]

Clinton: Evade and Conquer

Clinton's tactics were to evade, equivocate, and counterattack also more in the pattern of oldprop than the new. Challenged repeatedly about his marriage, honesty, draft record, and patriotism, Clinton attacked the Republicans and equivocated about himself. His oldprop inveighed bitterly against the Republican "attack machine" and Bush's "search-and-destroy" tactics.

Clinton had fought off questions about his reputation as early as the Democratic primary when nightclub singer Gennifer Flowers insisted that they had carried on a long-standing affair. First denying, then equivocating, and finally apologizing for its effect on his marriage, Clinton lost believability and reputation.

On the draft, even after he issued his "final statement," Clinton was forced to answer additional questions. Bush and Vice President Dan Quayle gleefully dubbed him "Slick Willie." He escaped disaster only by persuading Admiral William J. Crowe, Jr., chief of staff under both Reagan and Bush, and other high-ranking generals and admirals to endorse him, a textbook lesson in oldprop; to raise one's own status by employing testimonials from those who enjoy greater prestige.

However, nothing rivaled the ridicule leveled at Clinton as much as his response to a question as to whether or not he had ever smoked marijuana. "Yes," he replied, "but I didn't inhale." Comedy shows milked the punchline. The Clinton campaign quietly offered a confession that although Clinton had been a "bit squirrely" on personal issues, he had not abused the public trust.

Clinton actually suffered less than Bush in mediaprop attacks on his credibility, but they were considerable: On September 29 alone, six Clinton stories spanned the range of credibility issues. One was another attack by Vice President Quayle on Clinton's efforts to avoid the draft. Caught off guard, Clinton explained, unconvincingly, that he not so much used favors to avoid the draft as gathered information about loopholes in the law.

But Clinton was the first to sense that publics were less interested in the oldprop of credibility than in the ability of candidates to define and solve problems. He turned to the needs of the economy and the plights of the generations. He substituted presence for proof, intimacy for suspicion, and youth and energy for reputation. Essentially newprop, they contested with the old, and Clinton survived.

Perot: To Upend or Self-Destruct?

Much like Clinton, Perot possessed few of the trappings of the old credibility. Bush was the President; Clinton at least was a governor. Although Perot both presided over and governed, his fiefdom was business, not government. Perot needed a political party, and he built a surrogate for one, United We Stand. But where Clinton ducked the character issue, Perot rushed to meet it, a formula for self-destruction.

Mediaprop contested Perot claims that he was a reluctant candidate, that his support was legion, that he had the answers to problems, and that he was an organizational genius. Perot was unable to paper over his own statements that he could tolerate gays but would not appoint them to cabinet-level posts; he was insensitive to race when he referred to Blacks as "you people and your people," and he was impervious to gender when he characterized stories by female reporters as "efforts to prove your manhood."[12]

Under the barrage of a negative press and declining poll ratings, Perot withdrew abruptly from the race. Where before his withdrawal he had led in the polls, he never was to approach his previous standing. In the light of the attacks against him, the fact that he achieved so much politically in so short a time was astonishing. Despite the mediaprop, because of the diversity of beliefs in a popular culture, his movement survived him. But when he returned in 1996 he could no longer control the movement. It had fragmented and deserted him.

The Pollsters Join In

Time sponsored a poll jointly with CNN, asking if there was more honesty in government today than 10 years ago. The results: 14% said "more" and 75% said "less." In response to another question, 63% said they had little or no confidence that government leaders "talked straight." Forty percent said Bush usually did not tell the truth, and 36% said the same about Clinton.[13]

Writer Maureen Dowd observed that the candidates had pushed the integrity issue right out of the race; that Bush, Clinton, and Perot had accomplished the impossible: They had made cynical voters even more cynical. Molly Ivins, the acerbic Texas columnist, excoriated Bush for his cynicism; at issue was his reversal on choice.[14]

Although James Carville, the "old boy" Clinton campaign manager, harped on the benefits of attacking Bush, and the President's campaign manager, Mary Matalin, felt likewise with respect to Clinton, Carville concluded that the public was tired of oldprop in the form of attacks on candidates' credibility and reputations. But he realized also that the net effect was to give Clinton a comparative advantage.[15] One *Time* poll showed that 40% of respondents thought Clinton was lying about the draft whereas 37% disagreed; but 63% thought Bush was lying about Iran–Contra, whereas only 22% disagreed.[16]

Nonetheless, Carville concluded that credibilityprop was not the basis on which the voters would make choices. In fact, during the most spirited of the four presidential television debates, young participants objected to oldprop personal attacks and insisted on substantive discussions.

ß   ß   ß

Mediaprop, pollprop, and campaignprop combined to center the 1992 campaign on the credibility and reputations of the candidates. Because all three of the can-

didates were flawed, credibility was a wash. Hence the almost exclusive centering on credibility by media, polls, and candidates left members of the popular culture to determine on their own the bases on which they would make their choices. Perot and Clinton each sought to define other issues but Perot became exasperated by the mediaprop and bowed out of the race for a time, leaving much of the field to Clinton.

Similar questions would arise in the 1996 campaign. Would the media, the polls, and the campaigns again center their rhetoric on oldprop approaches, or would they seek to define new venues that would permit newprop to contest with the old?

NOTES

1. Aura of infallibility. (1993, June 27). *New York Times*, p. 1.
2. First lady speaks out for reform. (1994, July 23). *Seattle Post-Intelligencer*, pp. 1/2.
3. Clinton promises not to surrender on universal care. (1994, June 22). Toner, R., *New York Times*, Sec. A, p. 1.
4. Toner, Ibid., *New York Times*, p. 1.
5. Posturing and principles tactics in the 11th hour. (1994, July 19). *New York Times*, Sec. A, p. 9.
6. Strong support for health plans. (1994, July 20). Dowd, M., *New York Times*, p. 9.
7. Health care developments. (1994, July 20). *New York Times*, p. 8.
8. IBM urges 110,000 workers to help defeat health care bills. (1994, August 19). Rifkin, G., *New York Times*, Sec. A, p. 1.
9. Before we wreck the health system. (1995, August 19). Perot, R. H., *New York Times*, Sec. A, p. 19.
10. Is anyone telling the truth? (1992, October 5). *Time*, p. 10.
11. Podhoretz, J. (1994). *Hell of a Ride: Backstage at the White House Follies, 1989–1993.* New York: Simon & Schuster.
12. On TV, a very public education for Ross Perot. (1992, October 1). Keely, M., *New York Times*, Sec. A, p. 10.
13. When trust is at issue, trustworthy are rare. (1992, September 29). *New York Times*, Sec. A, p. 10.
14. Yes, Mr. President. Character is an important issue. (1992, October 26). Ivins, M., *Seattle Times*, Sec. A, p. 9.
15. Matalin, M., & Carville, J., with Knobler, K. (1994). *All's Fair: Love, War and Running for President.* New York: Random House, p. 371.
16. Ibid., Matalin & Carville, p. 359.

25

POLITICALPROP
1994 and 1995: Restoring Presidentialprop

President Clinton won applause for his rhetoric as he described the state of the nation on January 23, 1996. The address came at a defining moment. The deadlock over the budget and social policies between the two parties had brought on an avalanche of rhetoric. The question was raised as to whether a calculated rhetoric of newprop as contrasted to oldprop would determine which party would prevail.

FIRST STAGES

A Republican oldprop had dominated the first stages of what became the cultural and propaganda wars of 1994 and 1995. But Clinton's state-of-the-nation address suggested that the propaganda field would be leveled by 1996. He would not again feel it necessary to insist on his relevancy, for Republican tactics had transformed him from onlooker to undisputed party leader and titular custodian of the popular culture.

Almost all of the themes in Clinton's address were couched in newprop inclusiveness: He praised the political opposition and asked for their future cooperation; all would work together for change, accept responsibilities for peace and security at home and abroad, enhance education, ensure health and well-being, address the causes of crime, cherish and protect children and families, raise standards of personal conduct, preserve the environment, and ensure the unimpeded workings of government.

As Speaker Newt Gingrich sat behind the President and politely, and quizzically, applauded, Senator Dole readied the Republican response. When he
delivered it over the major networks, it was Dole who was not entirely relevant; his demonization of Clinton and the Democratic party were addressed
more to conservative Republicans in primary states than to the nation as a
whole.

When Oldprop Became "In"

In January 1995, an unusually doctrinaire and assertive entering class of Republicans, their 1994 Contract With America in hand, uncompromisingly
adopted oldprop as their signature. Their ebullient leader, House Speaker
Gingrich, had created a tempestuous propaganda that was newprop in its vision but oldprop in its tone and exclusiveness. *Time* called him "man of the
year."[1]

The Democratic minority leader, Tom Daschle, in noting that exclusiveness, held out little hope for accomplishment in the Congress. House Republicans did not wish to share power but sought to rule; compromise was "a
four-letter word."[2] As if to punctuate this assessment, House Majority Leader
Dick Armey warned that unless Clinton yielded to Republican budget demands, he would cut off the borrowing capacity of the government.[3]

Restoring Presidentialprop

At the outset of the Republican takeover, an intimidated President Clinton
had been forced to rely on—some said hide behind—the pulpit of the Presidency and a minority party. As a President who had been required to insist on
his relevance, whatever he said, or any. action that he took, was dismissed as
nonprop.

It was the defeat of Senator Dole's balanced budget amendment to the
Constitution that restored Clinton to the Presidential "bully pulpit." Democrats averted the passage of the amendment by only one vote, allowing Clinton
to veto it as an overstuffed pork barrel and a soporific to the rich. When his
party sustained the veto, presidentialprop was relevant once more, culminating in a succession of presidential vetoes that affected education, the elderly,
the poor, and the environment.[4]

The President could thank the wise old savant in the Senate, Robert Byrd
of West Virginia, and Ted Kennedy of Massachusetts for that outcome. They
had encouraged the President to stake out an ideological ground that could
command a party consensus. Byrd defended the position with a rhetorical
flourish, condemning the budget amendment as a macabre twisting of the
balance of powers:

> Change is the watchword of the day; change merely for the sake of change is
> suddenly a virtue above all others, a goal to be achieved at all costs. But I will

never, never bow to these messengers of expediency or to the managers of any political party's agenda. The hurricanes may blow, the tides may rise, but there still remain those of us who will never bend.[5]

And Kennedy urged Democrats to stick to their values: "If we become pale carbon copies of the opposition and try to act like Republicans, we will lose— and we will deserve to lose."[6]

Majority leader Armey was as good as his word: He shut down the passport office, national parks and monuments, the distribution of veterans benefits, and laid off federal and state employees whose salaries were drawn from federal grants. But this oldprop of party hegemony foundered as a newprop of broader public inclusion won support. Pollprop framed the Republicans as spoilers and the President as custodian of the popular culture. Clinton argued that the richest Americans should pay the most, not the least. Health care, job training, education, and the reform of lobbying and finance should be expanded, not reduced.

The Protagonists: Clinton and Gingrich

In 1994 and 1995, the protagonists were Clinton and Gingrich, as Dole largely stood aside. In important respects, Gingrich and Clinton were a draw: Both were Baby Boomers, both were intensely ambitious and political, and both were articulate in exploiting the oldprop and the new. But not all Republicans embraced the Contract's agenda, notably the repeals of abortion rights, the softening of environmental controls, the diluting of gay and gender rights, and the shunting aside of the rights of minorities; these issues were expressed in the oldprops of hate and exclusiveness.

In temperament, Gingrich was more the agitator than the propagandist, which pleased his radical freshmen following, but in intellect he sought to persuade more than coerce. He became suspect as a dreamer, because although he offered apocalyptic visions of the future, he succumbed to instant solutions. He had suborned those skills in the service of Reagan and Bush: "It was their job to do the vision and it was my job to be a partisan soldier. That era is over. Now my job is to reshape national policy . . . to renew American civilization and redirect the fate of the human race."[7]

Eclectic Camp Followers

An air of "virtual reality" infected Gingrich's personal entourage and provided insight into a corner of his personality. He acquired a personal retinue that included spiritualists, futurists, self-improvement experts, and cyberspace cartographers—all billing themselves as friends, advisers, and even "gurus." Alvin Toffler talked about the "third wave," Arianna Huffington discussed the "fourth instinct," and Gingrich offered his "Five Newts" as proposals for change. Heidi Toffler and Huffington echoed Third Wave diversity values, talking about "byte cities, brain lords, and cyberpolitics."[8]

A small-college academic, Gingrich savored the role of savant and created his own wordprop of action. He insisted that the transfer of power to the Republicans should not be described as a transition—the term customarily used—but as a transformation. The reason was that *transition* implied movement within the existing structure, whereas *transformation* described the creation of a new and exclusive structure.

Gingrich thus rejected the newprop value of compromise (commonly regarded as a mutuality of steps in giving and getting) as a euphemism for "giving in;" that is, there were no win–win or lose–lose scenarios in which both sides got something or lost something. Someone always won and someone lost. Nonetheless, his looking to the future implied a capacity for newprop despite a predilection for the old: "On everything on which we can find agreement, I will *cooperate;* on those things that are at the core of our philosophy . . . there will be no *compromise.*"[9]

Oldprop C'est Moi

Gingrich's personality was at the heart of his propensity for oldprop. After the 1992 campaign, one-time Democratic Representative Ben Jones of Georgia observed:

> All you have to do is turn on the TV. He accuses his opponents of using "Stalinist" tactics, of being "enemies of normal Americans," and says when he gets control of the House, he will use subpoena power against them. That's the kind of rhetoric we heard in the 1950's from Joe McCarthy, and he's already got more power than McCarthy.[10]

And former Democratic Representative Mike Synar, who considered Gingrich to be a friend, said he was a "control freak": "Newt is dangerous because he's smart, he's articulate, and he's in control of his party. There is no dissension and his principles and philosophy are as flexible as necessary."[11]

Gingrich's standard speech offered the apocalyptic portrait of a "dark and bloody planet" with the warning: "It's impossible to maintain a civilization with 12-year-olds having babies, 15-year-olds killing each other, 17-year-olds dying of AIDS, and 18-year-olds getting diplomas they can't read."[12]

Gingrich used taunting phrases to demonize "McGovernites, liberal elitists, elitist media, and the counterculture." He pledged that he would restore middle-class order and values from a time when society was far more emphatic about right and wrong. The instruments would be compulsory prayer in schools, the banning of abortions, and adopting an acceptable version of history. He promised that during the first 100 days of Congress the Contract would be read every day at the start of business:

It is impossible to take the Great Society structure of bureaucracy, the redistributionist model of how wealth is acquired, and the counterculture values that now permeate how we deal with the poor, and have any hope of fixing things. They are a disaster. They have ruined the poor. They recreate a culture of poverty and a culture of violence. And they have to be replaced thoroughly. We have to say to the counterculture; "Nice try. You failed. You're wrong." And we have to simply, calmly, methodically reassert American civilization.[13]

Gingrich later was to concede that he had said too many things that were inappropriate to his role, and he acknowledged that he had underestimated the resiliency of Clinton and his core beliefs. When he dared Clinton to veto the Republican budget and debt package, and Clinton did so, "our strategy failed," Gingrich conceded. "The President and his aides were tougher than I thought."[14] And Democrats were to assert that the extremism of the Republican Congress had united them. Representative Barney Frank observed that "Republicans had freed Clinton to make a sensible defense of Democratic principles without having to worry about the Democratic Left."[15]

Exploiting Oldprop

One of the most profound consequences of the rehabilitation of Clinton and the bully pulpit was a shift by the Democrats from the defense to the attack, and at the outset it invoked far more of the oldprop than the new. It exploited Gingrich's off-handed suggestions that orphanages for displaced children might be preferable to the welfare system, school lunch programs should be turned over to the states, and food-stamp allocations should be reviewed or shifted to the states.

"The White House tries to make it look as if I'm Charles Dickens and they are Norman Rockwell," Gingrich complained. Clinton rejoined by condemning Gingrich's assertion that a quarter of the White House staff were recent drug users. Gingrich could only complain that his shoot-from-the-hip political style was preferable to the "old-style, smoke-filled room" oldprop of concealment and deviousness practiced by old-time politicians.[16]

Setting Off a Culture War

Elites reacted angrily to Gingrich's caustic criticisms of public broadcasting and his threats to terminate continued federal support. That oldprop of demonization of PBS was intended by the Republicans to foreshadow a day of reckoning for its tormenting coverage of the Army–McCarthy hearings, the impeachment hearings of President Nixon, the embarrassment of Supreme Court Justice nominee Robert Bork, the Clarence Thomas–Anita Hill confrontation, liberal positions on social issues, and prime-time programming that was intellectualized and elitist.

The oldprop of confrontation with PBS boomeranged, however, arousing a defense on its behalf that was reminiscent of the NAFTA battle of factoids. It devolved into a flurry of "Newtoids" in which Gingrich was the target. Funds were reduced, but not eliminated, as Republicans themselves came to PBS', support.[17]

A Capacity for Newprop

But Gingrich also had a capacity for newprop, according to Representative Congressman Sherwood Boehlert, in his ability to listen and to respond to all points of view. Because Gingrich and Clinton both came off poorly in confrontations, making Dole appear to be the more mature statesman, Clinton and Gingrich had something to gain by sitting down together.[18]

Thus came the somewhat surprising announcement in January 1995, that Gingrich and Dole would meet with Clinton in the White House to discuss welfare overhaul, tax cuts, a balanced budget, and an attempt at a sincere search for compromise, the word that Gingrich had discredited.[19]

The opportunity came when an off-handed comment by Clinton opened the door to their participation in a Town Hall meeting in New Hampshire that produced a polite debate over Medicare, foreign policy, budget problems, and a promise to launch a bipartisan search for lobbying and political reforms. The Associated Press wrote:

> Far from the rancorous discord of Washington, the Democratic president and Republican speaker held court outdoors for an hour with an audience of elderly voters, using their five questions as a springboard for a calm but candid outline of their myriad differences.
>
> "Never before," Gingrich said, "had a president and speaker appeared together at a town hall—never mind the elected leaders of different parties. This is a historic moment."[20]

But this aura of newprop was not to last. Gingrich became caught up in violations of rules governing tax-exempt funds for campaign purposes. Conceding his mistakes, he was reprimanded publicly by the House and fined $300,000. That, too, was an historic moment of oldprop that left Gingrich in disgrace.

      ⌐   ⌐   ⌐

The contest for hegemony between the Republican Congress and the White House unleashed a propaganda that was essentially oldprop, but that sometimes invoked the new. As such, it produced unanticipated outcomes.

For one, the Gingrich-inspired oldprop forced the Democrats to regroup around President Clinton, reestablishing the power of the White House bully pulpit. Ironically, it was the vetoes Clinton exercised and the newprop he was able to affect that enabled him to regain the aura of the presidency and restate his claim as titular custodian of the popular culture.

NOTES

1. Man of the Year. (1995, December 25). *Time*, pp. 48–99. See also: Gingrich, N. (1995). *To Restore America.* New York: HarperCollins.
2. G.O.P. Revolution is stalled by forces it cannot control. (1996, January 21). Clymer, A., *New York Times*, Sec. A, p. 10.
3. A default threat is hinted as way to settle budget. (1996, January 22). Sanger, D. E., *New York Times*, Sec. A, p. 1. See also: Armey, D. (1995). *The Freedom Revolution.* Washington: Regnery.
4. Despite GOP vow, pork barrel keeps on rolling. (1996, January 1). Goldstein, S., Knight-Ridder Newspapers, in *Seattle Times*, Sec. A, p. 3.
5. Excerpts from Byrd and Dole remarks on balanced budget amendment. (1995, March 1). *New York Times*, Sec. A, p. 12.
6. Kennedy implores Democrats to stick to their party's values. (1995, January 12). Clymer, A., *New York Times*, Sec. A, p. 11.
7. With fiery words, Gingrich builds his kingdom. (1994, October 27). Seely, K. P., *New York Times*, Sec. A, p. 1.
8. King Newt and his court explore virtual America. (1995, January 11). Dowd, M., *New York Times*, Sec. A, p. 1.
9. Newtonian linguistics. (1994, December 4). Safire, W., *New York Times Magazine*, pp. 36/38.
10. Gingrich's life: the complications and the ideals. (1993, October 26). Seely, K. O., *New York Times*, Sec. A, p. 1.
12. Newt Gingrich, authoritarian. (1994, November 13). *New York Times*, Sec. E, p. 14.
13. Anger and reality. (1994, November 11). Lewis, A., *New York Times*, Sec. A, p. 19.
14. Firebrand who got singed says being speaker suffices. (1996, January 22). Clymer, A., *New York Times*, Sec. A, pp. 1/13.
15. Democrats credit GOP "Extremism" for their newfound bonding. (1996, June 2). *Washington Post*, Americast-Post@Americast.com.
16. Gingrich offers defense of plan on orphanages. (1994, December 6). *New York Times*, p. 13.
17. Public Broadcasting System. (1995). *Setting the Record Straight: The Facts About Public Television.*
18. The brink of the Clinton-Gingrich wars. (1995, January 11). Phillips, K., *Los Angeles Times*, In *Seattle Times*, Sec. B, p. 5.
19. Moderate Republicans seek an identity for Gingrich era. (1994, December 26). Wines, M., *New York Times*, p. 1.
20. Clinton and Gingrich stage polite debate on questions. (1995, June 12). King, J., Associated Press, In *Seattle Post-Intelligencer*, p. 1. See also: Two genteel giants stage polite debate on questions. (1995, June 12). Mitchell, A., *New York Times*, Sec. A, p. 1.

26

THE 1966 CAMPAIGN
Softprop and Hardprop

The 1996 campaign devolved into a more subtle battle than in 1992 when Clinton succeeded in voiding the character issue and substituting newprop issues for the old. The question looming in 1996 was if Dole could soften his approach so that he could be regarded as an acceptable alternative to an incumbent President who by position and inclination already was feasting on a political diet of newprop.

Dole could continue to embarrass the President with a steady barrage of oldprop—the character issue, broken promises, shifting positions, marginal moral conduct of the Presidency, and so on—but to define himself as an acceptable custodian of the popular culture, he needed to soften his positions on such issues as pro-life, Medicare, Medicaid, gun control, and the environment.

Dole started with a personal handicap: He had not mastered newprop, and it was doubtful that he could; at best he could be successful with softprop—the projection of tolerance across those and other issues—but he would have to limit his dependence on a litany of oldprop to succeed. It was not enough for him to say that Clinton had promised a welfare reform program but vetoed one, that he wanted tax cuts but vetoed them, and that he wanted a balanced budget but vetoed one. This was deceptively oldprop because they were Republican bills.

The polls bore witness to the emergence of these contrasting positions. Only 22% opposed Republican programs in January 1995, but by November opposition had reached 45%, and positive support eroded from 49% to 35%.

With federal workers being furloughed throughout the country, more people thought Clinton was, in fact, defending the popular culture. A *New York Times*–CBS poll gave Clinton a 51% favorable rating, his highest in 2 years. Some 61% thought Clinton was trying to find solutions to problems, compared to 43% who gave the Republicans credit, and as Clinton continued to veto Republican bills that affected the viability of Social Security, Medicare, safety nets for the poor, and the environment, more people thought he was being presidential, the ultimate vantage point for dispensing newprop.[1]

A poll conducted in the bellwether state of Michigan in mid-November 1995 found that a majority had shifted to Clinton, accompanied by a corresponding loss of popularity of Gingrich, bringing a request from his colleagues that he adopt a softer rhetoric or "shut up." Indeed, that gave rise to a book title.[2]

Where a year earlier 61% said they trusted the Republicans more to balance the budget, that fell to 41% and Clinton improved from 28% to 41%. An NBC/*Wall Street Journal* poll showed that the public more blamed the Republicans than President Clinton and the Democrats for the impasse.[3] A *Washington Post* poll reported in October 1995 that Clinton had become less disliked than Gingrich, his most constant adversary. Gingrich's favorable rating was 29%, compared with Clinton's 54%, and his unfavorable rating was 45% compared to Clinton's 41%.[4]

ENTER "CITIZEN DOLE"

By resigning his cherished Senate seat, Dole hoped to transform himself into another persona, one with a much softer image. He would become Citizen Dole, a member in good standing in the popular culture. Even the name of his airplane was changed, from "Leader's Ship"—a reference to his Senate role—to "Citizen's Ship," a reflection of his new role. He set out to listen to "the heartland" of America—the smaller cities and towns of the Midwest and the conservative South. Presently unemployed, he jested, he shared a bond with Americans who had lost their jobs or were fearful of losing them.[5]

Softer Means Inclusive

Early on, Dole's best opportunity to shift to softprop centered on a widely debated "tolerance clause" regarding the party platform on abortion. More than any other issue, the hardprop position taken by pro-lifers had made it difficult for Dole to be perceived as inclusive and accommodating of diversity, no matter his inclination. Indeed, the hard-edged pro-life rhetoric had created a gender gap that threatened to fragment the Republican party. Women had put aside Clinton's lack of personal morality to opt for a public policy morality that defended their rights to abortion, protected safety-net programs for unmarried mothers, and attacked unfairness toward women in jobs and professions.

To address the gender gap, Dole now would urge on his party a tolerance of all views on abortion, a softprop that promised inclusiveness. Why emulate the Democrats, who had in fact been exclusive, banning a pro-life statement from their platform? Dole would say that different views on abortion were held among Americans in general, and that was no less the case in the Republican party.[6] That exploitation of softprop could take on the character of newprop if its inclusiveness could be demonstrated.

Writer Kevin Phillips encouraged Citizen Dole to return to his roots and point to his own family experiences in profiting from safety-net programs. His grandparents were on welfare in depression-era Kansas, he profited from governmental medical care when he was wounded in the Army during World War II, and he served for almost a lifetime as a public servant. A softer Citizen Dole should relive these truths as shared experiences, and where there was something to give, sharing was newprop.[7]

TOO LITTLE, TOO LATE?

Pollprop suggested that Dole's shift to a softened "citizen" status might have come too late to win over many voters, particularly when he returned so often to oldprop denunciations of Clinton on the character issue. Actually, women who intended to vote for Clinton believed that Clinton was more within the boundaries of the popular culture than was Dole in defense of women's issues.[8] Even a succession of seemingly revealing books about Clinton failed to bring about defections, and the scandal surrounding the subornation of FBI files showed only temporary effects.[9]

The Democrats, in turn, were unwilling to permit Dole to soften his image; in fact, they would seek to harden it. *Newsweek* magazine said the Democrats would link Dole with Gingrich, the unpopular architect of the Contract With America; to cigarette manufacturers and the problems of teenage smoking; and to "lunatic fringe" characters such as Patrick Buchanan. One of Dole's more persuasive themes, intended to marginalize Clinton as a leader, was that he had appropriated Republican issues and platforms. Yet a large proportion of voters (79%) continued to see important differences in what Clinton and Dole stood for. In fact, Clinton seemed to be wounding Dole more with attacks on the cigarette issue, linkages to Gingrich and Buchanan, and gun control than additional disclosures about Clinton affected him.

THE SHOOTOUT AT COURIC CORRAL

The headline in the *New York Times* was telling. It said:

Despite Dole's best effort, softer side loses ground.

For a week when he and his wife were supposed to show their softer side and gain headlines for a book about love, marriage, and Midwestern values, Bob Dole is getting into some surprising political scrapes."[10]

First Dole had appeared on *Live With Regis and Kathie Lee*, a daytime show that deals with softer subjects than abortion, and he acquitted himself well. He showed an inclusive, softer, and gently assertive persona when he agreed with a suggestion that he should take New Jersey Governor Christine Todd Whitman as his running mate. Her pro-choice position would not bother him, he said, for it would demonstrate that the Republican party was inclusive and that he, the nominee, intended to illustrate that by his choice. This exceeded softprop, it was newprop.[11]

However, the next morning Dole became combative with Katie Couric, coanchor of NBC's *Today* show, engaging in a bitter exchange with her about tobacco money, the addictiveness of nicotine, and media bias. He accused Dr. C. Everett Koop, the former Surgeon General, ironically a Dole supporter, of being brainwashed by the "liberal media" as to the dangers of tobacco. He warned Couric that she might be violating federal regulations by always sticking up for the Democrats and "advertising their line on your show."[12]

He returned inexplicably to a defense of his linkages to the tobacco lobby, this despite the efforts of his wife, Elizabeth, to change the agenda. Dole not only sublimated his softer side, but he had set up Clinton as a defender of children and families who had become addicted to tobacco.[13] Dole not only had failed at his efforts to project softprop, he had confirmed Clinton's position as the progenitor of newprop.[14]

The consequence was that many Republicans expressed doubts about Dole's ability to hold to a softprop or newprop line in unscripted situations, not just talk shows but the debates to come. Dole had lapsed into the oldprop that had damaged his 1988 campaign for the Republican presidential nomination when he growled that "George Bush should stop lying about my record." That earned him a reputation for nastiness, and he remained fearful of a repeat.[15]

The "Snowe" Job

Olympia J. Snowe, the pro-choice Republican Senator from Maine, had been quoted widely and had appeared on a number of television talk shows on which she had expressed the importance of a clear-cut "tolerance" policy of diversity within the Republican party and in the convention platform. For several weeks Dole had been echoing that softprop line. Not only would Dole welcome a pro-choice woman running mate, but the plank on pro-choice would be rewritten to contain tolerance language. It would not please others, but he was the nominee. However, that turned out to be a "Snowe job."[16]

Senator Snowe did not learn of Dole's hardened new position until she saw press reports of it. The tolerance phrase was to be introduced elsewhere in the platform, not added to the pro-life plank. Dole had yielded to the threats and the promises of the Christian Coalition in the personas of Pat Robertson and Ralph Reed. Nor was Snowe mollified by the news that a Republican Congresswoman with a pro-choice background would give the keynote speech at the convention. This was not softprop, it was *sopprop*.

The Christian Coalition had built a high-tech communication system to keep in contact, enabling them to wage instant totalprop against any threat to the platform they had fashioned. This was made up of a war room, infantry whips, and a new wireless digital paging system instrumented by hand-held comppters with specially designed software that used a frequency that had just been approved by the Federal Communications Commission.[17]

CONVENTIONPROP I: PROMISES OF NEWPROP

Vice presidential nominee Jack Kemp made preconvention promises of newprop; he and Dole would advance their economic plan and leave the oldprops of demonization and deviousness to others. Their acceptance speeches invoked God, freedom, honor to oneself, and service to country, subjective as they were in their promises of self-enhancement and fulfillment.

But how much of the convention totalprop was oldprop or newprop in its character? As might be expected, an amalgam of both: It was newprop in its promises of racial, sexual, gender, and political inclusiveness, but it was oldprop in the selectivity of the cameras as they focused on the audiences, exaggerating the number of minorities, children, and women, and speakers exaggerated the extent to which they would reduce the role of government, build expensive missile defense systems, cut off illegal immigration, wage a successful war on drugs, and reestablish the intact family. But these claims were not entirely oldprop; they were within the bounds of political discourse.

The same could be said of the promise for a 15% tax cut; in one respect it was a liberating newprop, but a considerable question remained as to its its impact on a balanced budget, interest rates, and the safety net programs that nominee Dole promised to defend: for the poor, Social Security, Medicare, and veterans. But here again the promises fell within the bounds of political discourse.

But contrary to the preconvention pledge. a variety of speakers did engage in demonization, impugning Clinton's honor, ethics, truthfulness, and loyalty. Dole, himself, placed Clinton and his administration outside the pale of the popular culture by describing them as feckless elites:

> It is demeaning to the nation that within the Clinton administration a corps of the elite who never grew up, never did anything real, never sacrificed, never suffered, and never learned, should have the power to fund with your earnings their dubious and self-serving schemes.

Finally, there was an oldprop of omission. Once a party that was distinguished by an overclass of highly educated and socially conscious suffragettes who had created the League of Women Voters and Planned Parenthood and struggled for the Equal Rights Amendment, the Republican pro-life platform had been written by an underclass Christian Right.[18]

When three modern suffragettes—Congresswomen Susan Molinari and Kay Bailey Hutchison, and New Jersey Governor Christine Todd Whitman—addressed the convention, they avoided any direct references to their pro-choice positions. Instead, they turned to put-down humor and litanies. Molinari observed that "a President Clinton promise lasted no longer than a Big Mac on Air Force One." And Hutchison delivered an acerbic demonization of Clinton as:

> high taxing, free-spending, promise-breaking, Social Security-taxing, health care-socializing, drug-coddling, power-grabbing, business-busting, lawsuit-loving, U.N. following, FBI-abusing, I.R.S.-increasing, $200 hair-cutting, gas-taxing, over-regulating, bureaucracy-trusting, class-baiting, privacy-violating, values-crushing, truth-dodging, Medicare-forsaking, property-rights taking, and job destroying . . .

Soon after the convention a "bump" in the polls reported a shift to Dole, but it seemed to reflect more the effect of total conventionprop than the inclusiveness that had been promised by newprop.

CONVENTIONPROP II: TARGETING AUDIENCES

Where the Republicans adopted abroad inclusiveness as their strategy, the Democrats targeted narrowly defined audiences, combining it with an inclusive newprop of opportunity, commitment, and community.[14]

College students would be given loans; working parents would be permitted to take their children to school and meet with their teachers; new mothers would be permitted to stay longer in hospitals in defiance of cost-conscious managed care; guns would be kept out of the hands of convicted spouse abusers; tobacco sales to miners would be cut off; volunteers would help children to read by the third grade; and education would become the *sine qua non* of opportunity that would provide a bridge to the new century. Government's newprop role was helping everyone, as individuals, to do their own thing. These were family values. And although they were promises that were yet to be kept, they fell within the bounds of political discourse.

The embracing theme was the newprop of inclusiveness. Paralyzed actor Christopher Reeve, one-time Superman of films, said he had come to the realization that everyone in the nation was family and every member of this family should be valued, the ultimate in inclusiveness. Congress should allocate research funds that would get people out of their wheelchairs and into productive roles. Rejecting criticism of Hillary Rodham Clinton's "it takes a village," Reeve pleaded that it took a village and more for everyone to reach out to everyone, a quintessential newprop.

Sarah Brady, wife of James Brady—President Reagan's press secretary who was shot during his attempted assassination—pleaded that guns threatened a sense of community. She echoed President Clinton's demand that any spouse found guilty of assault should be denied a gun. Replying to Dole's criticism of teachers' unions, school superintendent John Stanford, a former Army general, urged everyone to reach out and hug a teacher.

But backstopped by flashed images of despised Republican senators Al D'Amato of New York and Jesse Helms of North Carolina, Democratic Senator Robert Kerrey of Nebraska denounced Republicans for appealing to the hurtful side of human nature. Vice President Gore accused Dole and Gingrich of trying "to slice and to dice Medicare, education, and the environment"; the chairman of the Democratic Congressional Campaign Committee called the Republican Contract With America the scariest legislative nightmare he had ever encountered, and Democratic consultant James Carville, who headed the Clinton 1992 campaign, mocked Dole's condemnation of teacher's unions. "Yeah," he said, "the teachers are for the Democrats and the cigarette companies are for the Republicans. When your kid grows up, would you like to see him teach or smoke cigarettes?"

Thus, again, the oldprop of demonization was invoked. Although the President had insisted that contrasts could be drawn only on issues, he, himself, demanded pointedly that Dole stop attacking his wife.

THE DEBATES AND THEIR AFTERMATH

As Dole prepped for the televised debates, he adopted a subtle oldprop of minimization by seeking to inoculate viewers against Clinton's presumed advantages as a debater. But as the first debate proceeded, Dole turned to humor as a means of minimizing Clinton. When the President said that the country was better off than it had been 4 years ago, Dole quipped that Clinton was better off, too, and so was Saddam Hussein!

It was in the aftermath of the first debate that Dole shifted to a strategy of demonization. Guided by the knowledge that more voters "trusted" him than Clinton, Dole said that his word was good, Clinton's was not. He picked up on a comment that Clinton and Gore were "bozos," and he promised that he would return to such ethical issues as misuse of FBI files, abuse of White House travel officers, and Whitewater.

But Dole made a distinction in the final debate between the candidates on "public ethics" and "private ethics," and despite the protestations of the Clinton campaign that the distinction was dubiously drawn, Dole pursued his course. After all, discussion of public ethics should fall within the broad mandate of open and competitive voices in a popular culture. It could be argued fairly that the lack of public ethics constrained opportunities for citizens to gain access to public policy; at the same time, however, attacks on private ethics took on the aura of demonization, a fine line that easily could be crossed.

Clinton refused to join in the debate about public ethics, an oldprop tactic on his part, but he objected to the oldprop character of Dole's attacks on his private ethics. He insisted that ad hominen attacks did not solve problems (unless, it might be said, it was established that they were clearly, as Dole contended, a public problem). Ambiguous a conclusion as they might be, several polls showed by almost identical 2–1 margins that Clinton was perceived to have won the debate. Although he had ducked and parried Dole's attacks on both public and private ethics, this was perceived by many viewers as preserving the integrity of the debate.

It was in the debate between the vice presidential candidates that the major economic and social issues were most thoroughly explored, giving rise to speculation that Kemp and Gore would be returning in the year 2000 as heads of the two major party tickets.

Oldprop themes ultimately became the bookends of the 1996 political campaign, initiating and concluding presidential politics in flurries of demonization and exclusiveness.

The Democrats effectively demonized the Republicans before the two major political party conventions were held, labeling the Republican Congress as extremists who were intent on excluding women, the young, minorities, the poor, and the elderly from the protections and opportunities of the popular culture.

Having effectively exploited oldprop, Clinton turned to a targeted newprop and affected a presidential aplomb that promised that benefits would continue to flow from a fiscally responsible popular culture to those who required them rather risk an ill-fated Republican tax "scheme" that could destroy the economy.

For most of the campaign period, Dole pleaded his tax cut case, only occasionally raising the trust and character issues. However, once having concluded that his centerpiece 15% tax cut plan had been undermined, Dole shifted to a full-throated demonization of Clinton. A cacophony of oldprop painted the President as liberal, unethical, and as someone who could not be trusted. "Where is the public sense of outrage?" Dole cried. But this oldprop did not cut into Clinton's lead over Dole; in fact, some of Dole's tacticians wondered if it did not undermine his description of himself as someone who was steady and reliable.

The Dole campaign probed insistently for oldprop resonance on the "character issue," but with 2 weeks to go, it let up somewhat. The tactic had boomeranged. Polls revealed that Dole actually had lost ground to Clinton because of those tactics. But because other themes were not working, either, Dole returned to the character issue, this time posing it as a meaningful comparison: "positive Dole—negative Clinton." In this way, the newprop could be tied to the old.

This allowed Perot to get into the oldprop act. He likened Clinton to someone with a criminal record who no sane voter would allow into his home, a McDonalds' employee who would steal from the till, and someone who had been accused of crimes but would not respond directly to the charges. The heightened demonization had its consequences; some voters who were put off both by Clinton and Dole shifted to Perot, increasing his support from 5% to 9%.

Exclusiveness became a major factor in Dole's campaign in California. Here and in nearby states, the Hispanic American minorities turned out strongly to express their hostility to changes in immigration laws that Dole had embraced. Clinton also carried by large margins the Black voting centers of such major cities as Oakland, San Francisco, San Jose, Sacramento, and Los Angeles, many of whose voters were angered by Republican efforts to roll back affirmative action, again oldprop policies that Dole had endorsed.

If any one theme sounded the newprop tocsin for the Clinton campaign, it was the promise to use education to open the doors of the popular culture to everyone. All children would be literate by the age of 8, all teenagers could look forward to 2 free years of junior college education after high school, and parents would receive a variety of tax credits for educational expenditures. By these and other steps, Clinton was widening the newprop circle of inclusion in the popular culture.

Clinton's victory led both parties to conclude that the public wished the oldprop rhetoric of campaigning to be subordinated to the newprop of governing. Clinton saw this as a new opportunity for inclusiveness and broached the idea of a multiparty cabinet. But the Republican majority leader, Senator Trent Lott of Mississippi, made it clear that oldprop would be kept in play. Citing Medicare, he accused the President of sleight of hand and demagogery. The 1996 campaign was over, but the 1998 campaign had begun.

🏳   🏳   🏳

Campaign 1996 would not replay the 1992 agenda on credibility and morality but would turn on Dole's ability to create a softprop that would promise inclusivity based on tolerance of diversity in the popular culture. But women, the poor, minorities, and intellectuals continued to see Clinton as the fountainhead of newprop and the surer custodian of mainstream values.

NOTES

1. Clinton rating over 50 per cent in polls as G.O.P. declines. (1995, December 14). Berke, R. L., *New York Times*, Sec. A, p. 1.
2. *Tell Newt to Shut Up!* (1996). Maraniss, D., & Weiskopf, M. New York: Touchstone/Simon & Schuster. See also: Focus on issues of character marks rally. (1996, June 8). Merida, K., *Washington Post*, AmeriCast.
3. Clinton showing strength among Michigan's voters. (1995, December 4). Berke, R. L., *New York Times*, Sec. A, pp. 1/13.
4. Clinton's "morning in America." (1995, November 12). Williams, J., *Washington Post*, Sec. 1, p. 1. See also: For Clinton, the battle is about image. (1995, November 11). Devroy, A., *Washington Post*, Sec. 1, p. 1; Big Risk for G.O.P.: In confrontation with White House, Congress may project a rigid image. (1995, November 11). Clymer, A., *New York Times*, Sec. A, p. 8.
5. Dole begins drive to cut capital ties; travels to "heartland" for "real campaign" (1996, June 13). Nagourney, A., *New York Times*, Sec. A, p. 12.
6. Dole seeks words to broaden plank on abortion issue. (1996, June 7). Seelye, K. Q., *New York Times*, Sec. A, p. 1.
7. Gender gap puts Dole, GOP on defensive. (1996, June 10). Phillips, K., *Seattle Times*, Sec. B, p. 5.
8. Voter ratings for President change little. (1996, June 5). Berke, R. L., *New York Times*, Sec. A, p. 1.
9. The search for a silver bullet. (1996, May 20). *Newsweek*, p. 27.
10. Despite Dole's best effort, softer side loses ground. (1996, July 3). Bennet, J., *New York Times*, Sec. C, p. 18.
11. Dole shows openness on running mate. (1996, July 2). Nagourney, A., *New York Times*, Sec. A, p. 1.
12. Ibid, Nagourney.
13. Dole, on TV, criticizes media as biased on tobacco issue. (1996, July 3). *New York Times*, Sec. A, p. 1/Sec. C, p. 18.
14. Clinton stresses what he didn't do or allow. (1996, July 3). Purdum, T. S., *New York Times*, Sec. C, p. 19.
15. Ibid., Purdom, p. 1.
16. Dole's Snowe job. (1996, July 17). Rich, F., *New York Times*, Sec. A, p. 15.
17. In abortion war, high-tech arms. (1996, August 9). Goldberg, C., *New York Times*, Sec. A, p. 10.
18. A Doll's House: Not too long ago, the G.O.P. still had room for suffragettes. (1996, August 19). Blumenthal, S., *The New Yorker*, pp. 30–33.
19. Where real people live: Those "small issues" Morris fashioned for Clinton aren't so small to the voters. (1996, September 9). Alter, J., *Newsweek*, p. 38.

27

POLLPROP
Court of Last Resort

Overwhelmed by mediaprop, and perplexed by the multiversity around them, publics often look to the polls to inform them about what others are thinking. When *pollprop* is intrusive and creates agendas that are responsive only to exclusive interests, it is producing oldprop. However, when it responds to diversity and is sensitive to nuances in values and perspectives, it enables the popular culture to communicate its problems clearly, and this is newprop.

The growing variety of special interest groups spawned by a popular culture has generated needs on the part of everyone for information about how others think. Environmentalists, feminists, and homosexuals — as examples — increasingly have been told by surveys how publics regard them. And in response to changing market and social forces, demographers are redefining the import of age, income, education, and other longtime predictors of attitudes and behaviors.[1]

Conscious of misgivings and fears about social change, pollprop has given us insight into the persistence of values across generations. As an important example, it has assured us that youthful generations share more values with older generations than we believe. For example, 60% of first-year college students over the decades continue to believe that helping others is the most important value; youths still say there is too much materialism but they continue to believe in making money; and although outlooks on sex, divorce, drugs, and education have changed, values centered in religion and family life have persisted. Access to these data has made it easier for the popular culture to communicate about itself.[2]

Most recently, pollprop warned us about the fears that exist about media-prop in the popular culture. Focusing on television, films, and contemporary music, a *New York Times* poll found that a cross-section of the population objected to excessive sex and violence, but they conceded that the essential context for childrearing and family integration was in the home and the neighborhood. In many families both parents held jobs, leaving much of the rearing of children to peers, schools, churches, neighborhoods, and to some extent, to media.[3]

MOSTLY NEWPROP

As pollprop became a more compelling informant in our popular culture, it became all the more necessary to utilize its scientific approach and its knowledge-based attitudes to mirror emerging beliefs and attitudes. Rather than forcing a priori conclusions, the new pollprop generated knowledge that could be used as individuals saw fit; that is, believe it or doubt it, a counterpoint to mass cultures where leaders shaped public attitudes and behaviors. The late George Gallup once told me that he preferred the polls to politics as an arbiter of public thought because they were more timely and pertinent and produced more wisdom. Another pollster suggested that just as economic signals described the behavior of the markets, public opinion polls mirrored the vicissitudes of the popular culture: "Like traders who 'free-ride' on better-informed traders by watching stock prices, some citizens may 'free-ride' on those more politically informed by relying on reports of the opinions and experiences of others."[4]

Attacking the Polls

Pollprop often is condemned by purveyors of oldprop who wish to dominate national consciousness. As the late 1995 debate about Medicare warmed up between the political parties, Republican House Majority Leader Newt Gingrich attacked a *New York Times*–CBS poll because it ostensibly asked questions calculated to prompt unfavorable public reactions to Republican proposals: "This poll is a disgraceful example of disinformation. What we get are deliberately rigged questions that are totally phony that come out the morning of the vote (on the House's tax and spending bill)."[5] And at a later time, when the polling results on the Republican Contract were challenged, Gingrich attacked pollsters for asking "totally dishonest questions."[6]

However, editors said the questions were balanced and the methodology was sound. The results were similar to other findings that showed skepticism about Republican plans to balance the budget. But there were specific questions that Gingrich could contest, and one was the use of the word "cut" in reference to Medicare; it misstated the fact that the Republican program only would "slow down projected growth," not "cut it."[7]

Ironically, soon after the 1994 sweep, Republican pollpropster Frank Luntz, a Gingrich protege, admitted that he had not, as he had intimated, directly measured the popularity of elements of the Contract With America before asserting that 6 of 10 Americans supported each of the 10 provisions of it. He only had tested approval of adprop slogans and inferred their relevance to the Contract.

A subsequent NBC/*Wall Street Journal* poll found that a majority actually disapproved most of the Contract. (The irony was that Luntz's deceptive old-prop had been believed; unknowingly, his critics had criticized the tactic of "driving issues" with presumably valid poll results.) Actually, there was a sharp decrease in favorability from January 1995 to July 1995 in support of Contract "issues," and older individuals were unfavorable by a dramatic 2–1 margin.[8]

Luntz had attracted attention for exploiting another biasing technique; that was to "push" a respondent away from a particular candidate by using questions that tested the extent to which the respondent could hold to his or her position. One of his most successful uses of "push" techniques was to employ focus groups to help Ross Perot discover the frightened and disappointed voter and to exploit those fears.[9] At their May 1996 national meeting the American Association for Public Opinion Research condemned "push–pull" polls such as these as deceptive and unprofessional.

Pollsters as Spin Doctors

It has increasingly become the case that many pollsters are spin doctors or work on behalf of them. As an example, Luntz extracted words and phrases that should be exploited or avoided in the battle over Medicare. As examples, if Republicans talked about "cutting" Medicare they would lose, but if they described their position as "increasing spending at a slower rate" they would prevail. As the debate intensified in September 1995, Gingrich and other Republicans followed Luntz's advice, but the poll data indicated that the old-prop tactic of putting the best face on an actual reduction in services was not working.

At the time that President Clinton proposed his crime bill, Luntz attacked it with the phrase, "the midnight basketball bill" (the bill contained funding to keep gymnasiums open at night to keep at-risk kids off the streets), an old-prop technique of diminishing the proposal that brought Luntz to Gingrich's attention and thence to the selling of the Contract With America.[10]

At a time when criticism of government was rife, pollprop cautioned us that this expressed the views of only a small percentage of the public. What was more, pollprop told us that distrust of government actually decreased following the terrorist bombing of the Oklahoma City federal building. These data reassured people as to the effectiveness of government in a popular culture and conveyed the essence of newprop.

As examples, most people said they basically trusted the government and that Americans were too quick to criticize. A residue of distrust remained, but where it was a choice as to whom the publics most trusted, the government or the militias, the response in favor of the government was overwhelming. Up to that time one could not come to this judgment from reading newspapers, watching television news, or listening to talk radioprop. In fact, many people said that the alternative to government would be crazies running the country.[11]

COMPLEXITY COMPOUNDED

The numerous perceptions of government are not easily explained, and that requires more polling than normally is expended on a single issue. As an example, much of the resistance to government was based on a sense that government, particularly the more remote federal government, was not able to solve all problems. What was at issue was not so much a hatred or distrust of government but a reaffirmation by a diversity of publics of their growing sense of self-reliance and an accompanying ethic of self-sufficiency. This is the epiphany of participation in a popular culture.[12]

Whereas considerable sentiment is expressed in polling data in favor of downsizing government, pollprop also reports that government is appreciated for the tasks that it best performs, as in Social Security, national security, and protecting people's rights. Within this, publics want individuals to assume more personal responsibility.

In keeping with this growing sense of looking inward, a Gallup poll found in early 1996 that 58% of respondents believed the federal government is doing too many things, and not doing those well, contrasted to 35% who said the government should be doing more. Part of this is explained by the fact that the younger generations, and even some of the Boomers, no longer believe that Social Security will be their best insurance for the future. Those among them who are the most successful are advancing a credo of self-sufficiency that, in some cases, depicts a willingess to reduce, or "downshift," one's needs and expectations, thus producing less of a need to depend on government, business, or other institutions. This, too, is a newprop of self-actualization, and contrasts with the oldprop nihilism that is linked to paranoia about government.[13]

One poll noted a dramatic shift in response to the question of being able to "trust the government to do what's right." But it was pointed out that the diversity in a popular culture makes it more difficult to do things right for everyone. That is particularly true for environmental regulations. Pollprop becomes oldprop where it communicates data it does not explain.[14]

Health Care: Saying Versus Meaning

The health care issue became a challenge to pollsters to distinguish between what people said or simply agreed with as statements about the complex issues. One pollster noted that if one aggregated the responses in support of the universal health care provision across 17 polls, an average of 71% would be affirmative, but many qualifications should have been entered:

• Yes, universal care would be great if the nation could afford it.

• Yes, if it did not limit the choice of doctors.

• Yes, if it did not raise taxes significantly.

• Yes, if it did not cause employers to cut jobs.

• Yes, health care should not be taken away, or denied because of considerations of money, but in no case should it be a free ride.[15]

Because that complexity was not indicated, pollprop became dysfunctional for the popular culture. As a consequence, leaders concluded that they should not be guided by the polls but decide health issues based on their own perceptions of complex attitudes.

How Do We Ask?

Given the need to observe as a surrogate for others, pollprop becomes old-prop when it adopts the agendas of others, usually those of mediaprop and politicalprop. Pollsters often borrow questions from other polls, and there is a related tendency to adopt media and political party agendas by asking their questions rather than formulating original observations. As a consequence, pollprop becomes a purveyor of oldprop rather than the new.

A Washington state poll sponsored by media was part of a larger "public journalism" forum that was devoted to listening to publics, but instead of creating its own questions it borrowed questions that mirrored the attitudes and phraseologies of hard-core government critics and proponents of religious and "family values."

One question asked for agreement or disagreement with the statement: "The federal government controls too much of our lives." This assertion eschews the complex role of government as reflected in other data.

Another question asked if families "in this country" were threatened more today by the economic climate than the moral climate. Other than calling for information that it would be unrealistic to expect, the question called for an acontextual comparison; that is, economics and morality do not come from the same universe of thought.

Finally, in response to a question, most respondents agreed that "America was getting too far away from God." But we do not know if the respondents treated the question as anything other than a metaphor, because no unequivocal evidence exists as to our distance from God. Clearly, those who originally asked the question were addressing exclusiveness rather than inclusiveness, and this takes on the character of oldprop.[16]

Addressing the Unknowns

There are near-mythic things about human thought and behavior that pollprop never will know and others it will never know exactly. The reason is that no matter how sensitive the poll, it will be unable to describe the most complex of thoughts and experiences that center on considerations of sexuality, race, and religion. It is difficult, obviously, to determine how much individuals overstate or understate their thoughts and behaviors in these areas.

With respect to sexual behavior, of those who are willing to discuss it, the National Opinion Research Center reported that 21% of men and 13% of women admit to having cheated on a spouse, but an ABC News–*Washington Post* national telephone poll in 1987 said only 11% of respondents said they had an affair while married.[17] The disparities are obvious.

By contrast, a survey by idiosyncratic methodologist Shere Hite said that 75% of women who were married for more than 5 years reported having affairs; Dr. Joyce Brothers said 50% of wives had affairs; and the Kinsey Institute of Sex Research at Indiana University estimated 37% of married men and 29% of married women as unfaithful to one another. But writer M. L. Lyke described a picture of sexual activity if not commitment on the part of married couples; that is, they are more sexually active than nonmarrieds. The study was based on interviews with more than 3,400 respondents 18 to 59 years of age.[18]

Each of these studies used different methodologies, making them largely noncomparable except in the abstract. Most recently, Hite reported data from an international study that said that there was no crisis of the family; the so-called crisis actually represented a birth of freedom of the individual to bring destructive personal relationships to an end, and an element in that was the loss of marital fidelity. Pollprop on sexual mores and behaviors thus views it as newprop as well as oldprop, an expression of diversity in the popular culture.

As for racial perspectives, the trial and acquittal of football legend O. J. Simpson, an African American, for the murder of his wife and a male friend provoked countless polls, many of them reflecting a crisis in diversity in the popular culture. Some 20% of Blacks said they believed Simpson was set up by police, and another 12% saw racism as the motive for the set up. A broader question showed that 60% of African Americans compared to only 23% of other Americans believed that Simpson was set up, and that was before the disclosure of the racist remarks of detective Mark Fuhrman.[19]

From the perspective of this book, this did not reflect diversity but divisiveness. The races were not bringing a common core of knowledge to bear on a decision that would affect them both; rather, they were remote from each other contextually and politically. Each relied on a repository of knowledge that was rooted in their exclusive experiences and produced, in each case, a quintessential oldprop. A Black minister, Rev. Wanda Henry-Jenkins, characterized it in that way: "When a black man gets to a place where he has power, manifested through money, prestige, and popularity . . . there's definitely a hidden invisible society that goes looking into that man's life to destroy him."[20]

In many other pollprop situations, minorities feel at risk and are uncomfortable with the racial and ethnic stereotypes that are used to characterize them. The Asian stereotype that some polls produce is craftiness, unscrupulousness, and deviousness in business; the Muslim religion condones and supports terrorism; and Whites are insensitive, bigoted, and dominate others. Such findings, a consequence of built-in assumptions, perpetuate oldprop.

Characterizing Religious Values

In the face of the debate and attention given to the religious right, pollprop has produced more newprop than oldprop. Some polls have enlightened the public by reporting that the Christian Coalition does not typify the variety of religious values that are brought to politics, and fears as to the hegemony of the religious right are unfounded.

Although 95% of all citizens say they believe in God, and 79% say that prayer is an important part of their lives, only 35% say it is appropriate for religious leaders to mix politics with religion, and 64% say religious leaders should not influence voting.

Thus pollprop has revealed that religion in the abstract does not always translate into religious values governing the political process. As examples, only 6% said they had voted for a candidate because of religious beliefs. If conservative Christian leaders endorsed a candidate, only 14% said they would be more likely to vote that way, whereas 18% said it would be less likely; 64% said it would not affect their vote.[21]

WHAT PRICE SYNERGY?

At a time when the popular culture requires more diversity in pollprop, alliances have been forged by major pollsters with major newspapers (e.g., the CBS and ABC networks, the *New York Times* and the *Washington Post,* and other leading newspapers), and this trend is continuing. Certainly, the pollsters benefit by having greater resources and heightened in-house reporting of the results. But one may also view this as overemphasizing in-house pollprop at the expense of competing voices.

Nonetheless, joint polls have earned respect. They were the first to question media acceptance of the popularity of the Republicans' 1994 "Contract With America," and they suggested that the public knew less about the Contract before the election than they afterward learned through the media. They suggested that the Contract was exploited as postelectionprop to consolidate the political victory. A combined media-pollster survey found that most Americans were dubious about Contract provisions on Medicare, welfare, crime, military spending, and the budget deficit.[22]

Curiously, the Republicans repeated the mistake that the Clintons had made on health policy. Oblivious to signals that the public did not demand a complete overhaul of the political system but simply wanted correctives to be applied, the Republicans were not "getting it" on aspects of public reaction to the Contract that they pushed so aggressively.[23]

Potential Pollmania

Is the growth of "pollmania" a threat to the diversity of views that might express themselves in other ways and, in that sense, a problem for the popular culture?

Yes, and no, it is argued. During the 1992 campaign, Clinton's polling was said to have attained a state of pollmania. About $20,000 a night went into a national sample to question constituencies. This polling frenzy exceeded even that conducted for Ronald Reagan, the great communicator, who gained a step on his constituencies by knowing what they thought before he spoke to them.

Clinton's staff used a half-dozen focus groups where two or three groups normally would suffice. They agreed that paying taxes was a patriotic duty, so Clinton pressed that button in his nationally televised address. However, that was not quite the phrase, so it was removed from his State of the Nation address. Terms such as *change, sacrifice,* and *investment* were substituted. Then those themes were tested by a *New York Times*–CBS Poll carried out in early February 1993.[24] Cartoonist Mike Luckovich captured that with Clinton reading an opinion poll and announcing: "I'm 67% against same-sex marriages and 83% for balancing the budget!"[25]

However cynical that oldprop use of polling data might be, there are underlying implications in it for achieving an understanding of the public mood; this would not be limited to the answering of questions but to the asking of them, and this would not be limited merely to those questions and answers but to the interests and intellectual processes that produce the foci of opinions and how they are formed by the individual. If the polls were to achieve this level of insight and performance, the nirvana of the popular culture would be more realized than merely dreamed about.

One of the most thoughtful pollsters in the Pacific Northwest has held electronic town hall meetings to pursue the premise that citizens, not so much the experts, should take the lead in framing and providing answers to thorny public policy questions. Dr. Stuart Elway defines his nirvana as a gathering that could be compared to the deliberative citizen forums of ancient Athens.

The discussion is grounded in the quest for knowledge, the sharing of it, and civility as a process. One participant said she watched television's versions of town halls but seldom thought that others spoke for her. "I have all these things I want to say," she said, "but I never get a chance." Elway's goal was to incorporate the often thought but seldom said into questions that would be more an expression of the diversity of the popular culture, and less a reflection of pollsters' more exclusive domains. This is enlightening for individuals; some said that before they heard the discussion they thought no one agreed with them, and they were wrong; others said they thought that everyone agreed with them, and they, too, were wrong.[26]

On this ground, pundit George Will, who speaks for an intellectual conservative opinion, rejects the criticism leveled at Clinton—and other Presidents—for excessive use of polls, arguing that if Clinton actually had read more polls, more carefully, he would have avoided the backing and filling that became so politically damaging to his office. Would Abe Lincoln have used pollprop if he had the chance? Most certainly, Will concluded, and it would have been newprop rather than oldprop and accelerated the emergence of the popular culture.[27]

ERRORS SPELL OLDPROP

Despite the extent of the polling on the Presidency, few polling organizations got the presidential forecast right in 1996. Almost all reported that Clinton held a substantial double-digit lead over Dole, but the margin turned out to be only 8 points (49% to 41%), with Perot (8%) and other candidates making up the remainder.

The Dole supporters said this was oldprop, the result a discouraging forecast that came from intellectual bias and consequent polling bias.

Granting that their first assessments were accurate, polls failed to capture the erosion in Clinton's support. Was it a last-minute realization that the money connections meant that outsiders, notably foreigners, were gaining more access to their President than were the voters? Was it a sense of being "taken for granted" that spurred the beginnings of a voter revolt? Whatever the logic of the situation, when the polls cannot measure what needs to be measured—but only what they are able, or wish to measure—oldprop takes over. That happened in 1996.

☟   ☟   ☟

Pollprop has become a constant communicator in the popular culture. The polls have transcended their roles as providers of knowledge and attitudes to communicating about a broad array of social issues.

Pollprop has the capacity for oldprop as well as newprop. It has contributed to oldprop by reproducing itself rather than reflecting a diversity of opinions. And it has been guilty of "pushing" and "pulling" respondents into responses that serve to manipulate rather than permit them the degrees of freedom that a popular culture requires among its members.

Pollprop as totalprop became self evident across a range of 1996 political campaigns. Prestige media-pollster operations reported constantly on the national races, and state and regional polls monitored sectional issues. Every variety of survey, focus group, Web site, and tracking operation was consumed by political junkies, and even the most ordinary members of the popular culture could monitor the beliefs and intentions of every other member and talk about them, as well. In this way pollprop generated its own version of totalprop.

Despite the criticisms and failures of the polls, they must be assessed as quintessentially newprop. They have informed citizens about one another's values and beliefs in a timely fashion, creating a new stream of consciousness in the society and a sense of inclusion in the popular culture.

NOTES

1. Political Generations and Shifts in Public Opinion. (1992, July/August). Mayer, W. G., *The Public Perspective*, pp. 11–13.
2. What's happened to youth attitudes since Woodstock? (1994, May/June). Wardets, S., *The Public Perspective*, pp. 19–24.
3. Americans despair of popular culture. (1995, August 20). Kolbert, E., *New York Times*, Sec. H, pp. 1/3.
4. Impersonal Influence in American Politics. (1992, November/December). Mutz, D., *The Public Perspective*, pp. 19–21.
5. Gingrich attacks *Times*–CBS poll on G.O.P. Plans. (1995, October 27). Fisher, I., *New York Times*, Sec. A, p. 1.
6. Ibid., Gingrich, October 27, 1995.
7. Ibid., Gingrich, October 27, 1995.
8. Pollster may have misled GOP on contract. (1995, September 12), *Seattle Times*, Sec. A, p. 23.
9. Perot wins! The election that could have been. (1993, January/February). Black, G. S., & Black, B. D., *The Public Perspective*, pp. 15–16. See also: Is it "pushing" or "polling"? Loaded questions draw fire. (1995, June 3). Mokrzycki, M., *Seattle Times*, p. 3. See also: The vocabulary of votes: Frank Luntz. (1995, March 26). Kolbert, E., *New York Times Magazine*, pp. 46–49.

10. Public opinion polls swerve with the turn of a phrase. (1995, June 5). *New York Times*, Sec A, pp. 1/10.

11. Poll shows support for government has grown, but about 11 million consider it the enemy. (1995, May 18). *Seattle Times*, Sec. A, pp. 1/17.

12. A reaffirmation of self-reliance? A new ethic of self-sufficiency? (1996, February/March). Bowman, K. H., *The Public Perspective*, p. 5.

13. Measuring American Society. (1995, June/July). Ladd, E. C., *The Public Perspective*, pp. 1–3.

14. Pollsters see a silent storm that swept away Democrats. (1994, November 16). *New York Times*, Sec. A, p. 4.

15. Yankelovich, D. (1991). *Coming to public judgment: Making democracy work in a complex world.* Syracuse, NY: Syracuse University Press.

16. Readers climb on the porch, have their say. (1996, May 9). *Seattle Times*, Sec. A, pp. 1/18.

17. Sex, Lies, and Social Science. (1995, June/July). Lewontin, R. C., *The Public Perspective*, pp. 4–6. See also: Michael, R., et al. (1994). *Sex in America*. Chicago: University of Chicago Press.

18. Fool School. (1993, June 16). Lyke, M. L. *Seattle Post-Intelligencer*, Sec. C, p. 1. See also Michael, R., et al. (1994), *Sex in America*. See also: No family crisis, says Shere Hite. (1995, May 20), *Seattle Post-Intelligencer*, Sec. A, p. 6.

19. Black and white and read all over. (1994, August 1). Alter, J., *Newsweek*, pp. 18–22.

20. Poll reveals prejudices among all races. (1994, March 3). Goldberg, H., Associated Press, in *Seattle Post-Intelligencer*, Sec. A, p. 3.

21. The religious factor in American politics. (1994, September/October). Roper Center for Public Opinion Research, *The Public Perspective*, p. 17.

22. GOP gets mixed reviews from public wary on taxes. (1995, April 6). Toner, R., *New York Times*, Sec. A, p. 1. See also: Poll finds public doubts key parts of G.O.P.s agenda. (1995, February 28). Berke, R. L., *New York Times*, Sec. A, p. 1.

23. The anger ever deeper; why is the public so frustrated by politics? (1994, October 16). *New York Times Magazine*, p. 37.

24. Public ready to make some sacrifices, poll finds. (1993, February 16). Dowd, M., *New York Times*, Sec A., pp. 1/8/9.

25. Cartoon. (1996, May 28). Luckovich, M., *Seattle Times*, Sec. B, p. 7.

26. Conversation with the author, June 19, 1996. See: Bradley strikes chord at 'electronic' forum. (1996, June 10). Pryne, E., *Seattle Times*, pp. B1–3.

27. Read polls, heed America. (1994, May 6). *New York Times*, pp. 48–49.

28

ENDPROP
The Road Ahead

This book was easier to begin than it was to end. And to borrow a phrase from software guru Bill Gates, there's a long road ahead.

The foremost question is whether forces in the popular culture impel it toward the oldprop or the new. The diversity in the popular culture makes it certain that it is not headed in a single direction, either all oldprop or all new. What is more, the boundaries of the popular culture are being pushed outward rather than receding inward, a promise of change rather than stasis. We can be certain that the synergies that the popular culture reflects, and the energies that it brings, will contribute to a growing consciousness of total propaganda.

On the downside, oldprop has dominated entire arenas of public discourse. Militia posturing has threatened nearby communities, angry talk-radio has minimized and dehumanized its enemies, church burnings have denied human and religious rights, and the shrillness of moral and religious zealots on abortion have given rise to an oldprop that shows few signs of abatement.

These and other currents continue to raise troubling questions as to the perceived efficacy of the popular culture. It has been questioned by those who are convinced—albeit mistakenly—that national elections no longer produce candidates who can be admired. A cacophony of media criticism has held that voting choices have deteriorated from choices among quality candidates to settling for the "least worst" candidate. Voters are judging candidates on the basis of who might be the least frightening or harmful to them, not from among those who might be most helpful. A popular culture, it would seem, should promise more choice, not less.

The fear of a loss of choice extends across the personal and social spectrum. In the dispute about assisted suicide, some of the terminally ill fear a loss of personal choice about life and death; many women fear the loss of choice when it comes to abortion; others fear the efforts of institutional religion to blur the lines of separation between the church and state; and there are fears among the aged, the ill, and the poor about the loss of social safety nets of various kinds; television, film, and cyberspace fear the erosion of First Amendment guarantees and constraints on what they can produce and distribute. If producers are constrained, there is a loss of choice among the audiences for news and entertainment. All these fears contribute to an atmosphere of oldprop and inhibit the emergence of the new.

Rockprop, rapprop, and MTVprop were roundly criticized for their sexual and aggressive content, yet music typically has spoken for more members of each generation than it has excluded.

Are the "character" themes being pursued by contemporary political rhetoric only aberrations brought on by situational factors (i.e., by candidates whose behavior demands a treatment of "character") or has the now institutionalized oldprop of demonization by media and political actors taken on a life of its own? As mediaprop seeks its nirvanas, will it continue to drive potential candidates out of the political arena save for those who somehow can endure it?

What has become remarkable in our popular culture are the synergies that have evolved among such seemingly disassociated issues as adprop, businessballprop, lobbyprop, sitlifeprop, and humorprop. Add to these the environment, international trade, and Asia-bashing, each of which is as likely to become subjects for popularprop and late-night comics as have been the celebrities of yesteryear.

Yet there are other areas where newprop is competing subtly with the old. These are found in unlikely places—in sitcoms, which this book describes as sitlifes, in the institutionalized practice of humorprop through the late-night shows, humor magazines, cartoons, comic strips, and a host of other sources; and even in adprop, in which the theme is not exclusively that everyone must be perfect but that everyone can be cool.

There are other areas where the contest between the oldprop and the new are fully joined—gender, race, and sexual rights. Although the institutional fight over campaign finances, and lobbyprop has nibbled only at the fringes of oldprop, newprop codes of conduct are emerging.

The structure of the popular culture also is changing dramatically, Its members no longer are thought of only as generations—however useful this has been in the past—but as spin-offs of generations. The new overclasses of

cybercrats, the quickly rich, and the media and political elites have set themselves apart from the popular culture even as they have sought to manipulate
it. Some observers fear that the popular culture will spin off as satellites of
corporate culture, cyberprop culture, and the emerging culture of wealth.

After reading this book you may conclude that oldprop always will be ascendant or that the popular culture will create an unassailable bulwark of the
new. Whether your glass is half full or half empty, this book warns us that the
popular culture requires a wide-ranging and continuing surveillance of its
propaganda!

NAME INDEX

SUBJECT INDEX